T0228653

RESISTING
THE RIGHT

RESISTING THE RIGHT

HOW TO SURVIVE THE GATHERING STORM

ROBERT EDWARDS

FOREWORD BY JAMES CARROLL

OR Books
New York · London

© 2024 Robert Edwards

Published by OR Books, New York and London

Visit our website at www.orbooks.com

All rights information: rights@orbooks.com

All rights reserved. No part of this book may be reproduced or transmitted in any form or by any means, electronic or mechanical, including photocopy, recording, or any infor-mation storage retrieval system, without permission in writing from the publisher, except brief passages for review purposes.

First printing 2024

Cataloging-in-Publication data is available from the Library of Congress.

A catalog record for this book is available from the British Library.

Typeset by Lapiz Digital Services.

paperback ISBN 978-1-68219-602-1 • ebook ISBN 978-1-68219-603-8

They say "America First," but they mean "America next."

—Woody Guthrie

Contents

Foreword

James Carroll

The ideal of "political nonpartisanship" holds not only in journalism, but also in other areas of interaction, such as between classroom teachers and students, physicians and patients, librarians and patrons, preachers and congregations, research scientists and the broader public. Government employees are restricted in their political activity, and, most consequentially, so are many foundations and advocacy nonprofits whose tax exemptions can be at stake. *Leave politics out of it!*

But there's a problem. The principle of "nonpartisanship" depends on the firm adherence of political parties to the basic order of the common good. If one party abandons such a commitment—devoting itself to the destruction of essential democratic norms—then the "nonpartisanship" that forbids explicit denunciation of that activity—or support for its opposition—effectively becomes complicity in the destruction of democracy itself.

That is where we are in America today—as the clear-eyed Robert Edwards shows with this meticulous diagnosis of the nation's political condition. Edwards makes the case with two eyes—one cast back on the history of the Republican Party's being taken over by what once seemed a lunatic fringe, and the other eye squarely focused on the present political emergency, with that fringe—including not only blatant white supremacists but also what he calls "would-be theocrats"—having occupied the Party's dead center.

No: political nonpartisanship will not do when classroom teachers are required to falsify history, librarians forced to censor books, physicians forbidden to offer medical care, preachers left with a hollowed-out faith, science denigrated, government workers expected to break the law, and nonprofits threatened with tax penalties for doing what's right. Welcome to the Republican Party's America.

The GOP has become an efficiently functioning machine devoted to the demolition not just of democratic structures, but of the very procedures necessary for governance itself. Indeed, the destruction of the democratic commonwealth has become the Republican Party's very raison d'être. This is seen perhaps most clearly in an overt and well-coordinated assault on voting rights and the voting process itself. Years in the making, this campaign reached its apogee and climax in the crimes for which Donald Trump has been charged and brought to court—crimes that boil down to a brutal mugging of the ballot itself.

But the Republican attack on voting has been carried out at every level of governance in states across the nation. That is especially so in the twenty-three states where what Edwards tags as "trifectas" control the two legislative bodies and the governor's office. Gerrymandering; onerous registration requirements; improvised eligibility obstacles; polling place intimidation; manipulation of archaic constitutional ambiguities; state office holders abusing the public trust: in all of this, the voting booth has become democracy's barricade, and a legion of wannabe Trumps have been storming it. The Republicans have abandoned the political party's traditional goal of merely winning elections in favor of a blatant corruption of elections altogether. Edwards shows all this to us—and more.

A commitment to the resolution of policy disputes through compromise is as much a pillar of democracy as free and fair elections, but this commitment too has been abandoned by the Republican Party. On matters as varied as the nation's debt limit and timely budgeting, to the routine confirmation of military officials and diplomats, to the process of selecting and vetting judges, to the undermining of public health systems (even as pandemics rage), to the very meaning of the words "fact" and "truth," so-called "moderate" Republicans have yielded so completely to the extremist fringe that these nihilists have *become* the Republican Party. And this is to say nothing about the way in which the Republican Party's corruption was brought to its climax by Donald Trump, whose appearance has caused something new to happen to our politics. Something horrifying and dangerous.

Leaving behind the impotent hand-wringing of most punditry, Robert Edwards sounds the alarm loud and clear, warning that

American structures of order have failed to adjust to this emergency. And here the ideal of nonpartisanship looms as a primary case in point. "Balanced" journalism; "neutral" nonprofits; politically detached public servants; classroom teachers forced to withhold their opinions; courts upholding manipulated laws; military officials confronted with illegal orders; universities and corporations pushed back into the "color blindness" that undergirds white supremacy; "religious freedom" redefined to enshrine bigotry; sex education weaponized by Roundheads: one political party has betrayed the etymologically constitutive idea that it is only "part" of the broader commonwealth and has instead imposed itself on everyone in the nation.* The part has become the total—as in totalitarian.

The marvel of this book is that Edwards finds it possible to denounce the abuses and deceits of Republican reactionaries without abandoning the commitment—essential to the ideal of liberal democracy—to let other people be other people, even when he stoutly disagrees with them. That willingness to tolerate difference is what we mean by pluralism, and it defines the difference between Left and Right in America now, with the Right firmly devoted to the cult of the shout-down, the rule of force, the ready recourse to banishment, and the politics of intimidation. Why else do right-wingers need all those guns? And why else is there no such thing, as Edwards notes, as left-wing talk radio? What Edwards wants is not the deportation of radical nutcases, but their exclusion from any position close to the levers of power.

So naturally Robert Edwards's clear-eyed political analysis yields in this book to a passionate call to action. He reminds us of the ways in which ordinary citizens have risen to such challenges in the past—not just in the storied instances of the Civil Rights Movement, say, or the heroic Polish trade union that sparked the Soviet downfall, but in the most mundane of citizen-responses that have become pointed acts of political transformation. Comedy (The Smothers Brothers on Vietnam; Tina Fey on Sarah Palin), religion (break-ins by anti-war Catholic priests and nuns at draft boards and nuclear

---

* The political theorist Nancy Rosenblum drew my attention to "part" as the root meaning of "party."

weapons facilities), Trump-era public servants simply doing their duty (election workers, governors, prosecutors), educators (whom Edwards calls "essential partners in a pro-democracy pushback"), journalists (the solitary voice of I. F. Stone; the empowered pen of Margaret Sullivan daring to call out her colleagues)—such are the front lines of the culture war, and all citizens are being summoned to action.

Edwards gives us an invaluable "survey of pro-democracy measures," and the effect of his supremely well-organized and deeply researched account is energizing and edifying. Every reader of this dark book will see fresh flashes of light illuminating a way forward in the most consequential American contest since the US Civil War.

James Carroll is the author of many novels and works of history, including An American Requiem: God, My Father, and the War That Came Between Us, *which won the National Book Award, and* House of War: The Pentagon and the Disastrous Rise of American Power, *which won the PEN-Galbraith Award.*

PART ONE
THE CURRENT CRISIS

CHAPTER 1

How to Tell When Your House Is On Fucking Fire

Historians have it easy compared to fortune tellers. With the luxury of time and hindsight, it's relatively simple to connect the dots of what is past; why do we even hand out academic degrees for the people who do that? It's harder to grasp the contours of events while they are unfolding—the task of journalists—and even harder to predict what will happen next—the task of prophets. But sometimes one finds oneself in such a state of eyepopping emergency that only the somnolent or willfully blind, or the gleeful perpetrators of that very emergency, can deny it.

We Americans are in such a moment right now.

The two-party system under which the United States has operated since roughly 1854 has its shortcomings, but for almost 170 years it has at least provided political stability, if not the best possible public service to the full spectrum of our citizenry. Its most glaring flaw—and inherent danger—becomes apparent, however, when one of those two parties openly rejects representative democracy. Over the past fifty-five years, and rapidly accelerating in the last seven, the Republican Party has abandoned any pretense of belief in democracy, representative or otherwise, engaging instead in an overt assault on the fundamental principles of the American experiment. This assault is unprecedented in this country by a major political party, and one aimed at permanent control of these United States. Not two years ago, the undisputed leader of the erstwhile Grand Old Party fomented a violent self-coup in an attempt to overturn the results of a free and fair election. Far from repudiating that attack, the party has since embraced it, defending it as "legitimate political discourse," lionizing its perpetrators, and alternately downplaying its violence or insisting it was a false flag operation—sometimes both at once.[1] More importantly, the party has also shielded the senior leaders of that *autogolpe* and used every available lever to thwart efforts at accountability, including aggressive manipulation of the courts and of Congress. When that has failed, it has turned to brazen defiance.

Even before Trump, the GOP was already engaged in a methodical, decades-long, and highly successful campaign to game the mechanisms of the electoral system to its advantage, through gerrymandering, voter suppression, obstructionist abuse of parliamentary procedure, and a flood of money, among other methods. But now that campaign has reached a chilling new level, as the party has successfully convinced a majority of its members, about 70 percent—about 30 percent of the electorate—that the last presidential election was stolen from its candidate.[2] In the process, it has deliberately undermined public faith in the integrity of the election system, with terrifying implications for future votes.

To justify all this, the Republican Party has mounted a propaganda campaign that has swept up tens of millions of Americans who believe that all these measures are necessary, even heroic, in order to "take our country back." Many of them have stated that they are unwilling to stop there, and would support violence to achieve their ends, if necessary.[3]

The platform that the Republican Party would institute should it regain power is retrograde, plutocratic, and fundamentally revanchist. That is not new for the GOP, and Americans can debate whether we wish to embrace it or not. What *is* new is the contemporary Republican rejection of the fundamentals of representative democracy and its eagerness to seize and hold power antidemocratically, irrespective of policy. As I write these words, the GOP is bluntly announcing that it will not accept the results of future elections unless it wins. Having failed at overturning an election in 2020, it has set about taking control of the electoral process upstream so that no such drama will be necessary in the future, a kind of preemptive putsch of an even more insidious order, enabling it to deliver victories to its candidates regardless of the will of the people. Under the Orwellian pretext of preserving "electoral integrity," it is instituting restrictive new rules for voting and intimidating election officials in order to replace them with Republican loyalists empowered to reject ballots, turn away voters, and otherwise skew the results. It is full of officials at all levels who refuse to acknowledge that Joe Biden is the rightful president and who refuse to commit in advance to respecting the results of their own elections. To that end, the party is very deliberately focusing on offices that control the vote itself—governors and secretaries of state in particular—as well as members of Congress who might have the final say in any disputes, and the judges who would adjudicate those disputes, including a Supreme Court where it already holds a 6-3 supermajority.

None of this is being done in secret. As a matter of sheer principle, even mainstream Republicans and other true conservatives should object. Few have done so.

The Republican willingness to go to such extremes is driven by its own existential dilemma, which is a kind of terminal diagnosis. Even as the number of our fellow Americans who are comfortable with right-wing radicalism remains alarming, demographics are trending heavily against them. The researcher David Atkins, who runs the qualitative research firm The Pollux Group, reports that "the country is becoming more diverse and more urban every day. Americans under 40 are overwhelmingly progressive. This is the present and future of America."[4] Unable to win the popular vote in a presidential election (Republicans have done so only once in the last eight elections), and with these trends moving inexorably against them, the GOP has only two options:

1) Change its platform to attract more voters, or
2) Cheat.

No one who has observed the GOP's wanton lack of principle over the past decades ought to be surprised that it has chosen Door Number 2.*

---

* There is actually a third option, which is that the GOP might go the way of the Whigs or the Know-Nothings, or splinter into factions that spin off into new parties. But hoping for that does not constitute what is commonly known as "a plan."

In short, we are facing an unprecedented domestic threat to the American republic, one that demands immediate attention and action. The modern Republican Party has embarked on a concerted effort to subvert the will of the people, to eviscerate the foundational principles of our representative democracy, and to install itself in permanent power. It is doing everything within its considerable might to ensure that Democratic voters cannot make their voices heard in numbers that accurately reflect the polis, to enable its own right-wing minions to control the electoral process, and even to give itself the unilateral power to overturn elections that do not go its way.

In a free society, reasonable people can disagree and advocate for their positions in the marketplace of ideas using legitimate political discourse that does not involve bear spray. But once free elections have been compromised, and the citizenry no longer has recourse to the vote in a credible way, that society is in a state of dire emergency. "A democracy can survive intense policy disagreements over taxes, government benefits, abortion, affirmative action and more," as *The New York Times*'s David Leonhardt writes. "But if the true winner of a major election is prevented from taking office, a country is not really a democracy anymore."[5]

BULLET-DODGING AS A WAY OF LIFE

Is it really that bad, you ask? After all, the 2022 midterms were widely seen as a repudiation of Trump and Trumpism, an announcement that Americans were tired of the circus, tired of the politics of grievance and divisiveness and incivility, tired of waking up every morning asking, "What fresh hell?"

It is true that the electorate turned back Big Lie candidates up and down the ballot in almost every major race. Even Doug Heye, a veteran Republican strategist, told Fox News that "the MyPillow-ization of the GOP has been a disaster."[6] One might think such a result might even spur self-reflection within the Republican Party itself. But it did not.

Just as the GOP failed to heed the lessons of its own self-commissioned "autopsy" after Romney's defeat ten years before, a third straight losing election cycle—2018, 2020, and 2022—failed to prompt any significant reforms in its strategy.[7] Having been presented yet again with still more evidence that it cannot win national elections with policies it champions, the GOP did not react by excommunicating the election deniers and other extremists, but instead rewarded them with even more power in the Republicans' narrow House majority. Yes, a modicum of sanity was cited in America, like a rare bird thought to be extinct, as a slim majority of Americans made it clear that it didn't want election deniers and insurrectionists and hatemongers running the government. Still, it was alarming how close it was and how many of our fellow citizens remain fully committed to budding right-wing autocracy, or at least are not sufficiently bothered by it to run the Republican Party out of business for good.

Did anyone really believe that the epic thumping that the GOP took would cause it to come to its senses? As Tom Hall of the political blog *The Back Row Manifesto* asked, would Republicans really be "chastened into good governance and policies and tack to the center"?[8] On the contrary: even as it was made abundantly clear that the American public by and large does not want Trumpist candidates, the seditionist faction of the GOP will exert even more power going forward, because the so-called "normie" branch of the party made a Faustian bargain with them from which it cannot extricate itself.

In a strange way, it may be tempting to find this pattern cheering, in that the Republican Party seems hell-bent on self-destructing as an electable entity. Except that the GOP is openly pursuing a path in which electability is irrelevant. Even if we were assured that the Republican Party was doomed to self-immolation, it is deeply alarming to watch one of our two major parties barrel further and further into neofascist extremism. Moreover, we can by no means rest assured that it will in fact fail.

'Our two-party system has only one party left that is willing to lose an election," the journalist Barton Gellman wrote in a widely heralded 2020 piece for *The Atlantic*. "The other is willing to win at the cost of breaking things that a democracy cannot live without. Democracies have fallen before under stresses like these, when the people who might have defended them were transfixed by disbelief. If ours is to stand, its defenders have to rouse themselves."[9]

In a nation that clearly yearns for small "d" democratic rule, a party that has thrown its lot in with the global autocratic movement represents a clear and present danger. Electoral defeats render such a party more dangerous, not less, because it knows it will continue to be defeated at the polls and must pursue an alternative strategy.

The much-welcome victory of democracy in the midterms, therefore, is far from the end of this threat. All those election deniers, white nationalists, and would-be theocrats are still out there, along with a great many kindred spirits. Next time, they may not leave their fate to the will of the American people. The Republicans are like a gang of bank robbers who have brazenly boasted of their plans to knock over the local savings and loan. It does us no good to relax because they have not done it yet.

Even if they are somehow prevented from cheating or from gaming the system, the Republicans will almost certainly regain power sooner or later by simple law of averages.

David Atkins has written of what he calls "thermostatic behavior," meaning the reliable urge among the American electorate to "throw the bums out." In an elegant December 2021 piece for *Washington Monthly*, Atkins laid out in clinical prose how, in "layman's terms, the electorate grows cranky and dissatisfied for reasons often out of government's direct control (gas prices, a pandemic, economic fluctuations, and so on), and the party out of power gains an advantage accordingly. Voters of the dominant party become complacent even as the opposition grows angrier and more determined."[10]

In short, even in a fair system, history suggests that one way or another the Party of the Big Lie will eventually win sufficient power to take control of American governance—if not in 2024, then in 2028, or 2032. That they are willing to rig the system in order to do so, or even openly defy it, only increases their odds of success. What makes that eventuality so terrifying is that the Republican Party has made it clear that, if it does succeed in regaining power, it does not intend to surrender it ever again.

As Atkins writes: "Democrats would need to win every single election from here to prevent the destruction of democracy, while Republicans only need to win one. And the American system is set up so that Republicans *will* win sooner or later, whether fairly or by cheating . . . Blue America needs to start thinking about and planning for what 'Break glass in case of emergency' measures look like—because it's more likely a matter of when, not if. It not only *can* happen here; it probably *will* happen here."[11]

In 2024, we may well see the GOP regain control of the White House and both houses of Congress. It already has control of the House, and appreciable command of the judiciary at all levels, including the US Supreme Court, with its supermajority of archconservative justices and their lifetime appointments—three of whom are only in their fifties. It also already controls a majority of governorships and state legislatures (including twenty-three "trifectas," or full control of both chambers and the governorship), and in many cases, the crucial position of secretary of state as well.[12] Even as it is losing the demographic battle, its structural advantages in the electoral system allow it to maintain this edge and give it a real possibility of extending it. Perhaps that will occur legitimately, through the thermostatic effect and general American dumbfuckery, or perhaps through electoral suppression, chicanery, or sheer brute force. But when it does, barring internal reforms for which not even the most starry-eyed optimist could hold out hope, the GOP will do its damnedest to install permanent, unvarnished, white nationalist, Christian supremacist authoritarianism in America.

We will not be able to stop that eventuality from within the system, one in which we play by the rules and they do not. Yes, we should try to pass the John Lewis Voting Rights Act, and turbo-charge our get-out-the-vote efforts. Yes, we should call out and mount legal challenges to extreme gerrymandering and obviously partisan congressional redistricting. Yes, we should push back against anti-democratic legislation to take the electoral process out of the hands of neutral administrators. "But those things alone cannot stem the tide against a determined fascist party in a thermostatic two-party system," Atkins writes. "Conservatives are guaranteed to make every attempt to turn America into the next Russia or Hungary. It will take coordinated, overlapping solidarity among both regular people and elites across various institutions to stop it."[13]

In 2016 some Americans could claim that they did not really know Donald Trump's true character when they voted for him. That is no longer the case, with prosecutors delivering new and shocking evidence of his criminality almost daily. (That we can still be shocked at this stage is itself shocking.) And yet there remains a strong possibility that this man will again be President of the United States.

Should he win in 2024, Trump has made no secret of his plans to institute what can, without exaggeration, be called a dictatorship, and to rule in an unconstrained, vindictive manner that will make his first term look like a garden party. In fact, he is campaigning on it, playing to the deep-seated right-wing attraction to the so-called strongman, for whom such plans are a feature, not a bug. Should he lose, he is sure to insist the election was fraudulent, further inflame his followers, and do still more damage to our democratic system.[14]

Jelani Cobb reminds us that Trump was no more the creator of the rancid stew of racism, xenophobia, misogyny, kleptomania, and general sadism that animates the contemporary GOP than he was the developer of the real estate properties, frozen steaks, Chinese-made neckties, and vodka on which he slapped his name as a private businessman. All were rife within American conservatism long before his arrival, and as Cobb writes, "there is no reason to believe that his absence would cause them to evaporate."[15] When Trump launched his political career, he latched onto that toxic strain in American culture and it embraced him in return: not just a preexisting menagerie of right-wing radicals who have long been at war with the US government—Second Amendment nuts, sovereign citizen adherents, and neo-Nazis among them—but also garden-variety suburban reactionaries who moved comfortably in polite society. Trump "promised to return his constituents to an imaginary past in which their jobs and daughters were safe from brown-skinned immigrants," Masha Gessen has written, one "in which the threat of what Trump called 'radical Islamic extremism' was vanquished or had never existed, in which white people did not have to treat African Americans as equals, women didn't meddle in politics, gay people didn't advertise their sexual orientation, and transgender people didn't exist."[16]

That promise was a fantasy and a lie, of course. As Cobb observes, "it has always been apparent that everything Trump offered the public came slathered in snake oil," but "fixating on the salesman misses the point. The problem is, and always has been, the size of the audience rushing to buy what he's been selling."[17]

Trump, as has been noted ad nauseam, was never the cause of the Republican descent into madness, only a symptom and accelerant. Did Donald Trump make us worse as a nation? Undoubtedly. But then again, he was never *sui generis*: we are the soil from which he sprang, and the ones who hoisted him to the heights which he attained. His racism, misogyny, apathy, sloth, and hubris reflected the worst of a country that liked to see only its best. A nation that put this man in power was not a nation that could remotely claim to be in good health. One that is considering putting him in that position again is even more unwell.

Of course, there remains the possibility that Donald Trump may not be the Republican nominee in 2024. His legal jeopardy may do him in (though I wouldn't count on it), or his lifelong diet of cheeseburgers and Diet Cokes may do so. But the dark future of a Republican autocracy is not predicated on Donald Trump being the GOP nominee in 2024, or even remaining among the living at all.

Trump has so fundamentally altered the GOP that all its future presidential nominees promise to be demagogues in his mold, differing only in the ratio of carnival barkerness to cold-eyed efficiency. There is almost no prospect for the GOP to reform itself without an epic internal reckoning that it has shown neither the ability nor the willingness to conduct. Even the Republicans who have inched away from Trump, like Bill Barr[18] and Mitch McConnell,[19] have stated that they will vote for Trump again in 2024 if he is the GOP nominee. Mere partisanship is not sufficient to explain it: this is blind tribalism at its worst, and it speaks to the deeper disease within the GOP. These "conventional" Republicans embraced the scorched-earth politics that had come to define the GOP over the preceding decades; they allowed it to happen—facilitated it, in fact—and even now are complicit. As there is no reasoning with Trump's true believers, at least not unless or until their spell is broken, our focus then ought to be not only on destroying his morally bankrupt cult, but also discrediting this "mainstream" that abetted his rise and continues to lend him crucial support.

Trumpism has undeniably conquered the GOP and that sickness will carry on with or without him. Ten percent of Americans in favor of right-wing autocracy is not heartwarming, but it is manageable.

Thirty percent, which is roughly where we currently stand, is considerably more worrying.

It gives me no pleasure to report on this hopelessly diseased state of the GOP. I came from a Republican family, of the old school Eisenhower variety, and a military one at that. I was weaned on conventional conservatism, and even voted for Reagan my first time at the polls, in 1984. My own process of disillusionment and separation from the party was complete long before Trump, the final nail driven in by the pointless, disastrous, deceit-ridden 2003 invasion of Iraq. But I take no solace in seeing what has become of the GOP since then, nor in having the United States stripped of a sane conservative political party, and worse, of watching that party turn into a wrecking ball aimed at the very foundations of democracy.

SLEEPER CELL

Over our nearly 250 years as a sovereign state, Americans have come to take long-term political stability in this country for granted. We are lucky in that regard, and spoiled.

In 1980, Tom Wolfe opined that "The real lesson of Watergate was, what a stable country! Here you've got the president forced out of office, and yet the tanks don't roll, the junta is never formed."[20] True enough. But an unfortunate by-product of that stability is a complacency that makes it hard for many among us to register when a clear and present domestic danger has arisen. Talk of an authoritarian takeover, the rise of a police state, and similar alarms are often greeted with scoffing and eye rolls, dismissed as a vast overreaction, fever dreams better suited to bad dystopian fiction, or worse, the dishonest fearmongering of those with a political agenda of their own. "It can't happen here," as the saying goes. But it can and it is.

In their 2018 book *How Democracies Die*, the Harvard political scientists Steven Levitsky and Daniel Ziblatt write: "If, twenty-five years ago, someone had described to you a country in which candidates threatened to lock up their rivals, political opponents accused the government of stealing the election or establishing a dictatorship, and parties used their legislative majorities to impeach presidents and steal supreme court seats, you might have thought of Ecuador or Romania. You probably would not have thought of the United States."[21] Levitsky and Ziblatt report that on Freedom House's Global Freedom Index, where the US had for years routinely ranked among the most democratic countries in the world, it has now sunk "lower than every established democracy in Western Europe" . . . lower even "than new or historically troubled democracies such as Argentina, the Czech Republic, Lithuania, and Taiwan."

But in fact, there have been autocratic elements in play in the US since the very founding of this country, varying from region to region and in prevalence and measure, largely aimed at vulnerable minority populations and women (not a minority), usually defined by race, religion, gender, sexual orientation, economic status, political belief, and place of origin.

In an October 2022 piece for *The New York Times*, Jamelle Bouie writes that "for most of this country's history, America's democratic institutions and procedures and ideals existed alongside forms of exclusion, domination and authoritarianism."[22] Dating back to the 1890s, "close to three generations of American elites lived with and largely accepted the existence of a political system that made a mockery of American ideals of self-government and the rule of law." Black Americans who suffered under slavery and Jim Crow, and then under various other forms of bigotry, discrimination, and oppression—including horrifically violent terrorism perpetrated both by state and non-state actors—have been waging a resistance movement in this nation for more than four centuries. Women, who got the right to vote barely a hundred years ago, were long barred from full participation in the work force, in the military, in athletics, and in numerous other aspects of American life. To this day, they earn only seventy cents on average for every dollar that men do. Gay people, trans people, Jews, Muslims, adherents of other faiths, atheists, immigrants . . . the list of marginalized and openly oppressed communities goes on.

In short, the American promise of "liberty and justice for all" has long been only aspirational . . . or less charitably, a hoax perpetrated by the privileged classes who had access to those things and did not much care that others did not. What is new in our current moment is the expansion of that autocracy to the broader culture, and to populations that heretofore have escaped its impact.

Apropos of the public response to Watergate, the second part of Tom Wolfe's comment from that 1980 *Rolling Stone* interview is also worth recalling.

"I don't think there was even a drunk Republican who went out and threw a brick through a saloon window!" Wolfe said. "Everyone enjoyed it. That was the greatest show on earth. Everyone sat back and watched it on television and enjoyed it when Jerry Ford, who had been handpicked by the man they just threw out, stumbled from one side of the country to the other."[23]

Allowing for hyperbole for comic effect, Wolfe may have been right at the time. But the zeitgeist has changed considerably in the intervening forty-three years. In retrospect, it feels almost quaint that a president with demonstrable disregard for the rule of law, imperial in his view of his office, who committed wanton war crimes and showed himself more than willing to employ the full power of the federal government in order to protect his grip on power, nonetheless had enough respect for American democracy to abdicate, rather than putting the fundamental stability of our governmental system at risk. A subsequent Republican president, forty-seven years later, would do no such thing, nor would any senators from his party ask him to, as the Republicans of Nixon's time had done. On the contrary, all but seven of them voted to acquit him of crimes that virtually all of them knew he had committed.

A country that allows a powerful group of would-be autocrats to try to overthrow the government—and get away with it—is a country whose days as a democracy are numbered. As the saying goes, a failed coup that meets with no consequences is just a dry run.

There has hardly been an existential emergency of this magnitude for the United States since the Second World War, and in some ways, this one is worse.[24] It's one thing to be conquered by an authoritarian foreign power, which the US did not come close to in the '40s. It's another thing to willingly tear down your own 240-year-old democracy and institute a homegrown autocracy.

Alarmism, you say? Chicken Little-like howling concerning the sky's imminent collapse? Perhaps. But over the past several years we have been repeatedly told that the "system" is stable and that various frightening actors pose no real threat. And yet at nearly every turn, things have taken a darker and more pernicious turn than even the most nervous observer predicted. If there's one thing the election of Donald Trump should have taught us, it is that nothing in American politics is too far-fetched.

Ironically, pollsters tell us that a great many Americans of all political persuasions do recognize that our democracy is under unprecedented threat and are deeply worried about it. But what Democrats and Republicans see as the nature of that threat varies diametrically. That itself is part of the crisis.[25]

The threat to the very heart of representative democracy in America could hardly be more dire. We are in the political equivalent of a housefire, and there can be no ignoring the flames licking up the walls and beams and rafters all around us. Perhaps we will get lucky and the fire will die out, but the laws of physics tell us that that is not likely . . . particularly when there are enthusiastic arsonists pouring gasoline on the blaze.

HANDBOOK FOR RESISTANCE

The corollary to the long history of autocracy within the American experiment is that resistance to it is not a wheel in need of reinvention. We can draw on the experience and efforts of generations of brave and determined Americans who have fought oppression and injustice throughout our country's history, and similar movements across the globe.

This is not to say that we should give up on trying to prevent an autocratic takeover; not by any means. But while we are working to stop that outcome, it would be foolhardy not to prepare contingency plans for the worst-case scenario. Even if the United States manages to avoid the ascent of autocracy in the near term, we will almost certainly have to confront it sooner or later, so long as the Republican Party remains committed to its autocratic experiment and a fanatical minority of tens of millions of Americans support it.

But let us be clear and precise in our terms.

In the Trump years, "the resistance" became a commonplace rubric for everyone opposed to that administration, from inveterate left-wingers to anti-Trump Republicans who, for decades prior, had been part of the GOP mainstream. But in September 2018, during the dark heart of the Trump era, Michelle Alexander, author of *The New Jim Crow*, published a landmark *New York Times* opinion piece called "We Are Not the Resistance" in which she argued that resistance is a "reactive state of mind," one that can cause us to "set our sights too low and to restrict our field of vision to the next election cycle," rather than keeping focused on the broader goal. "(T)he mind-set of 'the resistance' is slippery and dangerous," she wrote. "There's a reason marchers in the black freedom struggle sang 'We Shall Overcome' rather than chanting 'We Shall Resist.'"[26]

More broadly, then, and notwithstanding the title of this book, Alexander argues that the entire view of the pro-democracy movement as "resistance" is backward. Her argument is for a much more far-reaching and sweeping kind of change, rather than the mere eviction of Trump and the reversion to a status quo ante that, while preferable, remains deeply flawed and similarly susceptible to the rise of similar threats in the future. "Merely tinkering with our political and economic systems will not end poverty or avert climate disaster, nor will mere resistance to the status quo. As the saying goes, 'What you resist persists.' Another world is possible, but we can't achieve it through resistance alone."[27]

That warning is echoed in Slavoj Žižek's maxim that "resistance is surrender," suggesting that the very mindset of resistance plays into the hands of the powers that be.[28] Even in the most repressive police states, tolerance for a certain amount of dissent is usually built in to prevent real opposition from coalescing—a mechanism that also allows the authorities to deflect charges of oppression.

You can't win a fight if you fundamentally misunderstand its nature and the disposition and strength (or weakness) of your opponent, and especially if you foolishly cede them the psychological advantage by accepting that they are in a position of power when, in fact, they are not.

"A new nation is struggling to be born," Alexander writes of the United States in the present moment, "a multiracial, multiethnic, multifaith, egalitarian democracy in which every life and every voice truly matters."[29] The fight against autocracy, therefore, is not a defensive one, but a proactive one, to create a better world for all, and in it we have the numbers and human nature on our side, no matter how much our foes would like to convince us otherwise. As Rebecca Solnit wrote in December 2021, quoting Alexander (who was herself using the civil rights hero Vincent Harding's metaphor), we are not the resistance at all, but rather "the mighty river they are trying to dam."[30]

For more than two centuries the citizens of the United States have been outrageously fortunate in the political security and relative liberty we enjoy—some of us much more so than others. That we are now in a moment when those privileges are under extraordinary threat is sobering. But if we refuse to face the threat, we stand no chance of preventing it from overtaking us.

This handbook will examine the state of the current crisis, the events that brought us to this precarious point, the likely scenarios we can expect, and what can be done to forestall such a grim turn of events. It will contemplate possible permutations of Republican autocracy and offer a range of contingencies in response across a broad spectrum of arenas: protest and civil disobedience, economics, the media, education, organized religion, medicine and public health, governmental institutions, the arts, and interpersonal relations. It will also consider the systemic long-term measures that can be taken to reclaim the republic and inoculate it against autocratic assault in the future.

In other words, we aim not just to "survive" the gathering right-wing storm, but to emerge from it stronger, and in its aftermath, redress some of the wrongs that led us to this state of affairs in the first place.

In that endeavor, I will use the term "autocracy" to refer to the state of affairs in question—what the journalist Anne Applebaum calls an "illiberal one-party state," which is "not a philosophy" per se, but merely "a mechanism for holding power."[31] In the United

States, it is one in which a conservative, plutocratic elite has allied with so-called "populist" elements to institute an authoritarian right-wing regime. (Populist is itself a misnomer, as it more frequently refers to mob-mobilizing demagoguery rather than a genuine grassroots movement on behalf of the people.) "Conservative," of course, is also a howlingly incorrect description of the current GOP, which has inarguably been taken over by a faction that, far from holding fast to the status quo, is aggressively seeking radical change in an even more retrograde direction. "Right-wingers" is therefore a more accurate depiction of the driving forces in the twenty-first century Republican Party.[*]

Lastly, I am reluctant to use in this tome words like "fight," even metaphorically, nor frame this struggle in military terms—speaking of "tactics" and "strategy" and "battleground states." Still, you may have already noted an undercurrent of anger in this book. Fair warning: it's not going to abate, all the way through to the index. It's a righteous and justified anger, in my view, and laced with sorrow. The danger is that it will fuel self-righteousness and blind us to our own limitations, flaws, and failures. Let us therefore approach the task of stopping autocracy with a sense of humility, empathy for even our most fanatic foes, and recognition that we are just as fallible.

We are a nation that, perhaps to a fault, prides itself on its fortitude. Now is the time to prove it. Most Americans—white ones, anyway—have long had the luxury of relying on the mechanisms of official power to protect us from the sinister forces that would do us harm and undermine our free and open society. That is not the norm in most of the world, nor for large chunks of our less fortunate countrymen. As a nation, we now find ourselves in that harsher, more bare-knuckles realm.

We better begin acting like it.

---

[*]   Similarly, one often hears conservatives insist that the US is not a "democracy" at all, but a "constitutional republic," an argument that only betrays the bad faith of those who make it. We are indeed a constitutional republic, and also a representative democracy. What conservatives are really after is an intellectual rationalization for subverting that public will in favor of rule by an autocratic minority. Theirs, to be specific.

CHAPTER 2

The Plot Against America

Is it smart to start a book by saying that historians have it easy, with their dot-connecting of what is past? Maybe not, if the second chapter relies on that dot-connecting to make sense of the current crisis. For in order to understand the origins of what we are now facing in America, it's helpful to understand how the Republican Party came to be in this diseased state. Tomes have been already written on the subject and will surely continue to arrive for years to come. For our purposes, a brief review will suffice.

THE SOUTHERN TRAVESTY

Contemporary Republicans are ostentatious in identifying themselves as "the party of Lincoln," and quick to declare that Democrats are the real racists, citing the agrarian, pro-slavery party of Jefferson's time. But political parties are protean. In the 158 years since Lincoln's assassination, America's two major parties have transformed radically, completely swapping ideologies, such that today the former Confederate states are uniformly ruby red Republican strongholds, and not because they suddenly saw the wisdom of Honest Abe's way of thinking.[1]

By the eve of World War II, the Republican Party had evolved into the home of the "America First" isolationist movement, whose sympathies for the Third Reich were thinly masked behind a façade of neutrality. In the postwar period, in order to assuage Republicans who found him "soft on communism," Eisenhower was compelled to choose a young California congressman as his running mate who had made his reputation as an attack dog on the House Un-American Activities Committee. Richard Nixon was his name.[2]

I'll repeat that: American conservatives of the 1950s were insufficiently convinced of the patriotic bona fides of *Dwight D. Eisenhower* that they wanted Nixon by his side to reassure them.

In 1964, despite that purported purge of the party's far right wing, Barry Goldwater was the GOP's presidential nominee, running on a platform that "extremism in the defense of liberty is no vice." Four years after Goldwater was trounced in a landslide, the party chose as its nominee that same Richard Nixon. Nixon's ascent, almost precisely a hundred years on from Lincoln's assassination, marked the first of four key inflection points in the journey of the contemporary GOP to where it stands today, with the development of the so-called Southern Strategy.

When Johnson succeeded in shepherding the Voting Rights Act of 1965 into law, he reportedly said to aides that the Democrats "had lost the South for a generation."[3] What followed in the 1968 presidential campaign is almost always described as "dog whistling": an allegedly subtle signaling by the GOP to racist voters, in the South and elsewhere, that it shared their antipathy toward Black people and would do everything it could to oppress them. We can quibble over how subtle that signaling really was. What is undeniable is that it worked. In the 1968 election, the South split between Nixon and the openly racist independent candidate George Wallace, formerly the segregationist governor of Alabama. In 1972, in a two-man race against McGovern, the incumbent Nixon won the South handily. The Democrats' last stand there was native son Jimmy Carter four years later, but by 1980, Ronald Reagan swept the region (apart from Georgia) *despite* Jimmy Carter's homefield advantage. Thus was the Republican conquest of the former Confederacy complete, as was the polar reversal of the Reconstruction-era alignment of the two parties.

But the Grand Old Party was only beginning its fuller transformation.

A MORAL MAJORITY THAT WAS NEITHER

The second key inflection point in the descent of the Republican Party came in the late '70s, leading into that 1980 contest between Carter and Reagan.

Forgotten in the rosy, amnesiac afterglow of his eight years as president and misplaced nostalgia for the avuncular "Great Communicator," the Ronald Reagan of 1980 was better known for having called for a bloodbath on college campuses in response to protests against the Vietnam War.[4] But with his actorly skills, Reagan was an indisputably strong candidate, a far cry from the awkward coldness of Nixon, and presaging an even more pervasive age of celebrity candidates to come. And it was no coincidence that his ascent coincided with another crucial strategic move by the GOP, which was its alliance with fundamentalist Christians.

Religiosity had quietly undergirded much of the conservative movement from the very founding of the country.[5] But until the 1980s it was considered untoward for churches to mix openly in politics, both in terms of Biblical admonitions against such behavior, and traditional separation of church and state under the US Constitution. The rise of the Moral Majority and the Christian Coalition changed all that. The terms referred respectively to organizations founded by the Baptist televangelists Jerry Falwell and Pat Robertson, but came to refer more broadly to the entire swath of right-wing Christian political activism, sometimes lumped together as the more generic but equally alliterative "religious right." Fundamentalist leaders such as Ralph Reed, Falwell, and Robertson—who in 1988 would become a presidential candidate himself—enthusiastically led a movement to mobilize the demographic power of their followers on behalf of the conservative causes they favored, prominent among them opposition to the gains of the Civil Rights Movement.[6] Republican leaders were more than happy to welcome them into the fold.

The so-called "Reagan Revolution" marked the triumph of hardcore Movement conservatives and their conquest of the Republican Party at the expense of more moderate voices.[7] But those Movement conservatives were defined by policy: a massive military buildup and aggressively interventionist foreign policy; deep cuts to social programs; the slashing of taxes on the wealthy as part of the grift that was supply-side economics; and a general effort to return the country to a Darwinian, pre-FDR state of every-man-for-himself governance. These were not policies that had any religious component to them, and in fact stood in direct opposition to Christian ideals of service to the poor, of humility, and of nonviolence. But once they were married to a commitment to advancing the cause of Christian quasi-theocracy, America was faced with a potent and dangerous brew that came at us with messianic fervor.

Over the next four decades, American conservativism would largely conform to lockstep submission to the theocratic dictates of Christian fundamentalism. That its "fundamentals" bore little resemblance to the actual teachings of the historical Jesus of Nazareth was irrelevant. It was wanton hypocrisy, a phenomenon familiar in the world of tent revival evangelists and televangelists, and one that would grow exponentially in the years to come until Republicans eventually no longer even felt compelled to hide it.

By definition, religious fundamentalism is characterized by an impervious-to-reason faith in the correctness of one's beliefs, the moral imperative to impose them on others, and the depiction of those who will not submit as literally evil. The transference of that mentality to politics—a realm defined by compromise and "the art of the possible"—was a recipe for crisis.

EYE OF NEWT, TEETH OF FOX

With its unholy stew of regressive economics, belligerent foreign pol-icy, and Christian supremacism, the GOP of the post-Reagan era was already plenty dangerous, but undeniably formidable: by the time Bill Clinton won the presidency in 1992, the Republican Party had held the White House for twenty of the preceding twenty-four years. The turn that it would take in response to Clinton's victory would prove earth-shaking.

As a gravedigger of democracy, Newt Gingrich has been some-what overshadowed by the likes of Mitch McConnell and Donald Trump, but his rise as Speaker of the House after the 1994 mid-terms—ending forty consecutive years of Democratic control of that body—is a seminal moment in the decline of American politics into the cesspool where it now dwells.[8] I am loath to give a figure like Gingrich a place of any prominence in American history, but what we are discussing here is blame, not credit.

Gingrich rejected the mutual tolerance between political parties that is essential to democracy in favor of a vision of the other side as demons from hell deserving of extermination. In 1990 his political action committee sent a memo to Republican candidates advising them to describe their Democratic opponents with words like "sick," "corrupt," "bizarre," "pathetic," "destroy," "decay," "traitors," "radical," and "anti-flag."[9] Kim Phillips-Fein writes that Gingrich himself incessantly described "Democratic politicians as the 'enemy of normal Americans' and calling for a 'war' against the left to be fought with 'a scale and a duration and a savagery that is only true of civil wars.'"[10] Moreover, Gingrich's rise corresponded almost exactly with the founding of Fox News, which went on the air in 1996, signaling a new era of aggressive right-wing propaganda masquerading as broadcast journalism.

Pundits predicted a backlash from voters. Instead, the GOP was rewarded. "Even some Republicans were surprised by what they were getting away with," *The Atlantic*'s McKay Coppins wrote in a 2018 profile of Gingrich,[11] including an "up-and-coming senator named Mitch McConnell (who) was quoted crowing that opposing the Democrats' agenda 'gives gridlock a good name.'"[12]

Gingrich eventually overstepped, undone by his overweening self-importance, his inflated estimation of his own smarts, and above all, his petulance in shutting down the US government over his bruised ego. His grandstanding impeachment of Clinton had similar Wile E. Coyote-like results. Coppins reminds us that Gingrich's final vote as a congressman was to impeach Bill Clinton for lying under oath about an extramarital affair with an intern, following months of relentlessly attacking Clinton for his immorality and his unfitness to lead.[13] We now know that at that exact same time Gingrich himself was engaged in an extramarital affair with a congressional aide.*

Less than four years after becoming Speaker of the House, Newt Gingrich's career as an elected official was over. But the damage he did in his brief tenure would reverberate for decades, as the template he established would become the norm in Republican politics, wantonly debasing the entire US political system in the process.

Here we must stop and address the obvious retort from the right. It goes like this:

---

* That aide became his third wife, Calista, who went on to be the US ambassador to the Vatican under Trump.

"When you progressives attack Republicans and other right-wingers as a threat to America as we know it, when you portray them not merely as political foes with a differing point of view but as dangerous radicals who would destroy the very republic itself, are you not engaging in the same hysteria and toxic demonization of which you accuse conservatives?"

It's a predictable counterattack, but one that withers under even casual scrutiny. It was way back in 2000 that *New York Times* columnist and Nobel Prize-winning economist Paul Krugman famously quipped, "If a presidential candidate were to declare that the earth is flat, you would be sure to see a news analysis under the headline 'Shape of the Planet: Both Sides Have a Point.'"[14] But neither the sincerity of their beliefs nor the volume of their shouting will make the flat-earthers correct, nor justify treating their view as equally credible. Only one party is engaged in an open campaign to undermine the electoral system, only one party defends political violence, only one party openly advocates autocratic rule over a democratic one, only one party embraces racism and its tropes to advance itself, only one party seeks to impose religious strictures on secular life, only one party has made the refusal to respect the results of fair elections its norm, and only one party has abandoned anything resembling principle in its pursuit of raw power.[15]

The GOP would like us to believe that what it is doing is just politics as usual, in which both major US parties engage, and that is very much part of what makes its march toward autocracy so insidious. When Republicans claim that their jeremiads about the evils of the Democratic Party and the precipice on which American democracy is teetering are no different than the rhetoric of the other side, they are engaged in yet another example of the gaslighting that has become their stock in trade.

For that, we have Newt Gingrich to thank.

WITHER DEMOCRACY

It's impossible to imagine the rise of Donald Trump had New Gingrich not normalized blood sport in American politics. Newt himself, un-surprisingly, is a huge fan, seeing Trump as the fulfillment of his own vision. For once he's not wrong—except it's not a compliment.

It was, and remains, a popular trope to talk of Trump's "takeover" of the GOP. But it was no such thing. He was the natural result of a morally bankrupt party that had embraced racism as a political strategy, that had mobilized an army of religious fanatics to advance its cause, that had grown accustomed to speaking of its foes in apocalyptic terms, and had boldly announced that it would respect no boundary and forgo no tactic in its pursuit of raw power.

Trump could command public fascination in a way that the nakedly unlikable Newt never could. Ironically for a party that claimed to champion religious piety, Donald was a living embodiment of all seven deadly sins, as well as a buffoon, a braggart, a coward, a cheater, and a functional sub-literate. But like many a disreputable preacher before him, he undeniably had a con man's skill for galvanizing an audience, which worked not only on those who bought his act, but also on those who did not, who actively hated him, yet could not look away.

If Nixon had dog whistled to racists, Trump used a bullhorn, which worked even better. Gaffes and scandals that would have sunk any previous candidate of either party—from scoffing that John McCain was no war hero, to being caught on tape bragging about grabbing women by their genitals—buoyed him. Soon the entire party adopted his crude, insult comic-style political persona, or tried to.

"I could stand in the middle of Fifth Avenue and shoot somebody, and I wouldn't lose any voters, OK?" Trump famously told rallygoers in Sioux Center, Iowa. "It's, like, incredible."[16]

Yes, it was, like, incredible. And a portent of worse to come.

The sour and nihilistic mood of the country in 2016 was ready-made for this man, a perfect vessel for the anger and grievance of a segment of the American population that was so apoplectic at the very idea of a Black president that it had whipped up a racist fantasy by which it could not be so. Trump, of course, was one of the foremost proponents of the birther movement, and in fact had jump-started his political career off it.[17] That white voters should rally instead to a thrice married, serial bankruptcy-filing, inveterate con man and third-rate TV game show host spoke volumes. Indeed, white rage over Obama was so central to Trump's rise that, as Ta-Nehisi Coates wrote, "It is as if the white tribe united in demonstration to say, 'If a black man can be president, then any white man—no matter how fallen—can be president.'"[18]

The press had no idea how to respond to a media terrorist like Trump, who turned every norm inside out and weaponized the Fourth Estate's own protocols against it. Worse, the press showed little *interest* in finding an adequate response, unable to resist the ratings bonanza of hanging on his every contemptible word. It also didn't hurt Trump that the Democrats were running a candidate who was at once perhaps the most qualified would-be president ever, yet widely unpopular, having had the poor judgment to be born with a vagina.

In the aftermath of the election, we were subjected to chin-stroking dispatches from practically every major newspaper and magazine in the country, seemingly all of which deployed intrepid reporters to the hinterlands like so many Napoleon Chagnons in the Amazon in an attempt to understand and explain the phenomenon of the Trump voter as observed in his or her natural habitat. Ironically, the process itself smacked of the exact dynamic it sought to condemn: a kind of condescending, anthropological view of the denizens of the "flyover states" as reported by journalists who parachuted into Red Hat Nation for but a brief stay, seeking to explain this exotic but provincial species for the chattering classes.

The even more galling part was that there was never any reciprocity. Blue America was relentlessly implored—commanded, in fact—to open its collective mind and "understand" Trump voters, to empathize with whatever had driven them to support this monstrous cretin, and to reach across the heartland to begin the healing. Rarely—in fact, never, to my knowledge—were Trump voters asked to think about their 66 million fellow Americans who voted for Hillary and the 81 million plus who voted for Biden four years later—a majority, I hasten to note, in both those elections. As Rebecca Solnit writes, "When only half the divide is being tasked with making the peace, there is no peace to be made, but there is a unilateral surrender on offer."[19]

It is hard to grasp the scope of the destruction wreaked by such an otherwise negligible and unsubstantial figure as Trump. Almost daily for four years we asked ourselves if the republic would wither and die under this ignorant, would-be despot, if he would destroy

240 years of democratic traditions and lead us into some obscene form of postmodern fascism. That was an extreme scenario—hysterical and histrionic, conservatives assured us. But those same people assured us that Trump would never even stay in the 2016 primary race, would never win the nomination, would never win the general election . . . and when he did, that he would bow to the norms of American politics, would moderate himself and his positions, that he would "pivot" and become "presidential."[20] They also assured us that if defeated in his re-election bid, he would leave the White House gracefully.[21]

LISTENING TO YOU, I GET OPINION

The contemporary Republican Party is at once the logical result of the downward trajectory marked by these four milestones, and yet unrecognizable from the GOP of only a few decades ago. Both Nixon[22] and Reagan[23] would be ostracized from the Republican Party of today. On taxes, on the environment, on foreign policy, on nuclear arms control, on wage and price controls—across a range of issues, they championed ideas that would cause the contemporary GOP to scream liberalism, or even socialism. More likely, if I may speculate, those men, operating in today's climate, would have quickly changed their tune, as so many other contemporary Republican politicians have done, keenly aware of the melody that the right-wing piper is calling.

All political parties look for wedge issues to peel voters away from their opponents, but the GOP has made an art form of it. In his 2012 book *The Party Is Over: How Republicans Went Crazy, Democrats Became Useless, and the Middle Class Got Shafted*, Mike Lofgren, a longtime GOP congressional staffer, pulled back the curtain on this kayfabe, declaring in an interview with Truthout that same year: "The primary purpose of the GOP these days is to provide tax breaks and other financial advantages—such as not regulating pollution and other socially costly externalities—to their wealthy donor base. All the rest of their platform, all the culture wars stuff, is simply rube bait."[24]

That "rube bait" included guns, abortion, homosexuality, trans rights, immigration, and a whole slate of other social issues that the plutocratic wing of the party did not really care about. Trump himself—who had been a registered Democrat for almost a decade before running against Clinton—was very much on record as being pro-choice, moved comfortably in circles with gay people, and was generally live-and-let-live . . . appropriate for someone who was himself so libertine.[25] But he was also happy to reverse course like a stunt car driver doing a screeching, rubber-burning one-eighty when it served his ends. Prior to that, Trump's low-information liberalism was largely a function of the well-to-do Manhattan milieu in which he moved. It was not a world where Confederate flag decals and gun racks were often seen on Lincoln Town Cars. But as a natural-born shitbag with a long history of ignorant, incendiary, unsolicited commentary (see: the Central Park jogger case), Trump had no problem whatsoever feeding the most disgusting instincts of the GOP's aptly named base.[26] But like all demagogues, he also took his cues from his audience, and tailored his act to suit it. In that regard, he was simultaneously leading the mob and following it.

For example, the Republican Party of the twentieth century had always had a nativist bent, but the euphemistic "family separation policy"—better described as a deliberate and openly sadistic campaign of kidnapping small children and caging them in inhuman conditions—represented a new low of almost incomprehensible depths. As Caitlin Dickerson concluded in her Pulitzer Prize-winning reportage for *The Atlantic*, "family separation" wasn't an unfortunate by-product of Trump's border policy: it was the goal, aimed purely at punishing migrants and thrilling the base.[27] Or Adam Serwer wrote, in what might be the single most memorable comment ever made about the Trump administration, "The cruelty is the point."[28]

This willingness of both casual conservatives and diehard denizens of MAGA Nation to get onboard with Trump's worst atrocities was a worrying sign—a chilling homegrown demonstration of Arendt's banality of evil, and the crucial complicity of the great swath of nonchalant citizenry in abetting the monstrous actions of authoritarian regimes. And it would only accelerate throughout his time in office.

This hold Trump had on his followers—and still has, for many of them—has led many observers to refer to Trumpism as a "cult-like" phenomenon. But other experts argue that the modifier is unnecessary.

In a 2018 piece for *Truthdig* called "The Cult of Trump," the journalist and author Chris Hedges outlines the ways in which Trump's followers meet the dictionary definition of a cult, and not just metaphorically, noting that the "more outrageous the cult leaders become, the more they flout law and social conventions, the more they gain in popularity."[29] Hedges goes on at length: about the use of the language of hate and violence; of fearmongering and divisiveness; of the denial of objective reality and the malleability of facts and truth, even when it comes to the leader's own past statements; of the leader's bombast and grandiosity, emotional abusiveness, and insecurity; and of the fawning obedience they demand, and the psychology of their followers' willingness to submit.

Sound familiar?

Of course, not all Republicans can be said to be in the grip of the Trumpist cult of personality the way that its most Kool-Aid-drunk adherents are. In some ways, however, the Republicans who are not Trump cultists but merely making a cynical, utilitarian calculation are worse, in that they cannot be excused by reason of mental incapacitation. They are quislings and collaborators who will one day face history's harshest verdict.

As *New York* magazine's Jonathan Chait writes: "Would-be dictators gain crucial support from allies in the political system who may not be committed authoritarians themselves but side with a factional leader who will advance their policy goals at the expense of democracy," a segment the Spanish political scientist Juan Linz calls "semi-loyal actors."[30] In *The Breakdown of Democratic Regimes* (1978), Linz, who was born in Germany on the eve of the Nazi era, writes that in order to stop a political party that is showing autocratic tendencies, reasonable political parties that are otherwise in opposition to each other must join together—in other words, put country before party.[31] It happened in Belgium and Finland in the early 1930s, successfully stopping the rise of homegrown authoritarian parties even as kindred spirits rose to power elsewhere in Europe. As recently as 2016 it happened in Austria, despite that nation's chilling history of susceptibility to fascism. In the United States, it would have meant key leaders of the Republican Party breaking ranks to join with Democrats in opposing Trump, publicly announcing the threat he posed to the nation, and perhaps even declaring their support for Hillary Clinton. Precious few did, and those were all excommunicated, or left the GOP willingly before that sentence was pronounced upon them.[32]

The question of whether or not Trumpism is a literal cult, then, is ultimately moot. Even absent Trump himself, right-wing fanaticism in the United States remains extraordinarily dangerous, such that—as Hedges points out—the mere demise of the man and the breaking of the fever of his followers will not solve our long-term problem. We must salt the ground from which it sprung.

THE DEATH OF NORMALCY

The enduring notion that Trump was an aberration in US politics, or that the GOP would return to some sort of "normalcy" if and when he is ejected from a position of power, flies in the face of history.

Trump represents the logical end state of the process that had begun with the Southern Strategy. The GOP's alliance with segregationist dead-enders, and then with Christian fundamentalists, and finally with outright white nationalist semi-fascists comprising both of those strains, was a deal with the devil that had finally come due. The plutocrats had imagined that they could use these allies as shock troops, and for a time they did. But now the center of gravity in the party has shifted to its openly seditionist, neo-Confederate faction. We should therefore postpone any mourning parties for the "Rockefeller wing" of the GOP, which after all, brought this fate on itself, and continues to be a willing—now junior—partner in this antidemocratic axis. The irony of its sorcerer's apprentice-like plight in no way mitigates the danger to the entire nation, and world, that it unleashed.

It's true that the tension between MAGA Nation and those Republicans who merely grit their teeth as they bend the knee to Trump may help keep the party paralyzed, a case of malevolence tempered by squabbling. But as the anti-Trump conservative Jennifer Rubin notes in *The Washington Post*, the media rarely holds the GOP "moderates" to account and does "a disservice to the voters by characterizing them as somehow more sensible than the Freedom Caucus crazies."[33] Team Normal, as it likes to style itself, has thus far not shown enough courage to power a nightlight, belying its own self-flattering moniker.

The fact is, there is little evidence that the policies that the moderates wish to pursue are much different from that of the party's far-right wing. As Rubin writes, "it would take only a few of them to defeat radical measures. Yet time and again, they cave"—because the ends they seek are largely the same even if their methods are less aggressive.[34] Caving, then, is almost too generous. The pattern of centrist submission suggests either cowardice or dishonesty, with these alleged moderates using the seditionists as cover to advance far-right policies with which they privately agree.

Rubin's fellow conservative Robert Kagan goes further, arguing that these ostensibly anti-Trump Republicans, consciously or not, are actually aiding the Trumpist cause by insisting on business as usual "even though they know that Trump's lieutenants in their party are working to subvert the next presidential election."[35]

> Revolutionary movements usually operate outside a society's power structures. But the Trump movement also enjoys unprecedented influence within those structures. It dominates the coverage on several cable news networks, numerous conservative magazines, hundreds of talk radio stations and all kinds of online platforms. It has access to financing from rich individuals and the Republican National Committee's donor pool. And, not least, it controls one of the country's two national parties. All that is reason enough to expect another challenge, for what movement would fail to take advantage of such favorable circumstances to make a play for power?[36]

Personally, I am astonished that any American gives the Republican Party even passing consideration as a viable political organization, or that any candidate can run under its banner without crippling shame. But apparently you can kidnap and cage children as a matter of deliberate policy, preside over the deaths of half a million Americans through sheer malevolence, and try to overthrow the government on your way out, and *still* demand to be treated like legitimate public servants.

Why do people continue to support this openly neofascist, would-be theocratic party that is openly rife with corruption, brazenly antagonistic to the basic ideals of this nation, eager to suppress your vote, and dedicated to a long-discredited brand of reverse Robin Hood economics that hurts the very people it claims to champion? I know that just asking the question invites withering criticism for being a snotty and condescending "coastal elite." But the Republican Party did so much damage to this country in so many different ways during the Trump years (we can go back further if need be, but that period will suffice) that no sentient American ought to give it the time of day unless and until it undergoes a radical reformation of a kind it seems unlikely to undertake.

In a 2022 interview with Al Jazeera, Noam Chomsky noted that, in the past, he had typically described the Republican and Democratic Parties as merely two wings of the same "Business Party." But that characterization no longer obtained. The GOP, he argued, had ceased to be "a political party in the traditional sense," but was now "a radical insurgency that has abandoned any interest in participation in parliamentary politics."[37] The Party itself gleefully announces it.

Once again: When we say that, are we guilty of the very charge I levelled at the likes of Gingrich? No and yes. The GOP empirically *is* no longer a proper political party, but only by virtue of its own refusal to engage in fair elections, respect the right of its foes to exist, and participate in legitimate democracy. Were it to do those things— even if it continued to pursue retrograde policies—it would be welcomed back into the fold. But rejecting the very basis of democracy is an automatic disqualifier.

So let's be clear. The Grand Old Party has no business presenting itself as any kind of reliable steward of the public trust, and its efforts to do so ought to be dismissed out of hand. I am not astounded that Republicans are brazen enough to say and do the things they are currently saying and doing: their shamelessness is well-established. But I am astounded that we are letting them get away with it.

CHAPTER 3

Alarm Will Sound

Just two days after Trump's 2016 victory, Masha Gessen wrote an influential piece in the *New York Review of Books* titled "Autocracy: Rules for Survival" that drew on their experience of growing up in the USSR and as an adult in post-Soviet Russia. As a progressive, a journalist, and a queer person of Jewish descent, Gessen could hardly have been a more tailor-made opponent of Putin-style authoritarianism if they had been created in a lab for that very purpose. And it showed, because their piece was both prescient then and prescriptive now.

Gessen began by imagining a concession speech from Hillary Clinton that directly called out the threat to democracy that Trump represented.[1] Of course, no one really expected her to give such a speech, and we can imagine the spittle-flying furor from the right wing if she had. (As it was, there was spittle aplenty from that crew over anything Hillary said, even if it was "Puppies are cute.") But as it turns out, that kind of warning would have been precisely on target, at a time when most observers were still assuring us that Trump wouldn't be as bad as we thought, or that he deserved the benefit of the doubt, or that fears of authoritarianism were overblown. Few Americans in the fall of 2016 imagined that our country could so quickly and dramatically slide into neofascism, except the ones who had long wished for it.

Gessen then proceeded to lay out six rules "for surviving in an autocracy and salvaging your sanity and self-respect." The first and most important of these was to "believe the autocrat" and resist the urge to rationalize that he's exaggerating or bluffing. The other rules warned us not to be taken in by small signs of normality, to abandon expectations that institutions will save us, to maintain outrage, and to reject compromise, even though democracy is defined by it.[2] In a 2017 follow-up to the original article, Gessen wrote grimly of the failure of the "outrage" rule to find purchase, in that none of Trump's heinous acts, nor all of them collectively, had generated enough outrage to cause him to be removed from office, nor even hurt his chances for reelection. "Not Charlottesville. Not the revelation of a Trump Tower meeting with a Russian lawyer who promised to deliver dirt on Hillary Clinton. Not the regular revelations of past acts of corruption and of current lies. Not the continued spectacle of a government of haters and incompetents."[3]

Three years later, they could have added to that list: "Not even the summoning of a mob in a violent attempt to overturn an election and lynch his own vice president."

THE SOREST LOSER

Rejecting the peaceful transfer of power is the most fundamental sin against democracy. But as far back as 2016 Trump had declined to say whether he would accept the results of that election if he lost, making him the first US presidential candidate to refuse to do so.[4] He did not add that he would also question the results even if he won. That itself was a kind of norm-breaking that would have elicited a hair-on-fire reaction from Republicans had Hillary said it. (For her part, Mrs. Clinton wryly noted her opponent's history of crying foul when he lost any contest, even when his TV show, *The Apprentice*, failed to win an Emmy.[5]) But the crickets of 2016 would be even more deafening four years later when Trump, hedging his bets, mounted a months-long campaign to undermine public confidence in the vote ahead of Election Day.

The widespread expectation, even among Republicans, was that Trump would sulk and pout for a while before submitting to the inevitable. "What's the downside for humoring him for this little bit of time?" one senior Republican infamously—and anonymously—told *The Washington Post* in the immediate aftermath of Biden's victory. "No one seriously thinks the results will change. He went golfing this weekend. It's not like he's plotting how to prevent Joe Biden from taking power on January 20."[6]

Ever since his rise in the 2016 primaries, we had been asking when the GOP would finally break with Trump. With each successive outrage and scandal, we wondered: Was this the moment at last? But it was the wrong question from top to bottom. Republicans don't *want* to break with Trump. Why should they? He has delivered to them almost everything they ever wanted. All they had to do was surrender every last shred of decency they had, a stockpile that was already running dangerously low. Not even a violent attempt to overthrow the government was enough to make the party change course.

It was a grim and sobering moment when it became clear that January 6 would not be the end of Trumpism at all, but only the beginning of a new and even more disturbing phase. Incredibly, defense of the Insurrection and fealty to the Big Lie would instead become dogma in the GOP, a nonnegotiable prerequisite for any candidate running under its banner.[7] Professor Ruth Ben-Ghiat of New York University, an expert on authoritarianism and the author of *Strongmen: Mussolini to the Present*, noted that the "genius of the Big Lie" was not only the physical attempt to keep Trump in the White House, but also that "it prevented his propagandized followers from having to reckon with the fact that he lost. And it maintains him as their hero, as their winner, as the invincible Trump, but also as the wronged Trump, the victim."[8]

Even as he slunk out of office in disgrace—still fulminating with recriminations and self-pity and insisting he had been robbed, with the blood of hundreds of thousands on his hands and boxes of top secret documents in his possession—Trump managed to convince between 30 and 40 percent of all Americans that the new administration was illegitimate, and encouraged them to crippling obstruction, if not armed uprising.[9] The insurrectionists who were prosecuted for their actions are presented in right-wing media as political prisoners.[10] The lone rioter who was shot and killed as she broke through a glass barrier and tried to breach the Capitol's inner sanctum where members of Congress were sheltering is held up as a martyr, and the police officer who shot her as a "thug."[11] Trump has announced that, if reelected, he would pardon or consider pardoning most of those convicted in the uprising (possibly himself included).[12] In that regard, it was not the attack on the Capitol but the aftermath that truly marked the nadir of Republican degradation, venality, and cowardice.

Prior to November 2020, an American politician who refused to yield power would have been radioactive. Trump has made it OK—attractive, even—for Republican officials to openly reject the legitimacy of the electoral process, often in advance of a given election itself.

According to reliable polls, the vast majority of Republicans— some 70 percent, as measured in the summer of 2022—continue to believe that Biden's victory was illegitimate.[13] (Forty-seven percent of Republicans don't even believe Trump lost the popular vote to Clinton in 2016.*[14]) When a significant percentage of the American public has come to believe that our elections are no longer legitimate, the most foundational element of our system of government has been fatally damaged. And once a political organization makes that wholesale rejection of the integrity of the vote a matter of party dogma, that party is no longer engaged in participatory democracy.

When Trump ultimately failed in his legal, extralegal, and flat-out seditious attempts to hang onto power, there were self-congratulatory op-eds aplenty crowing that "the system had worked." But it had not. Trump's coup failed only because of his ineptitude in carrying it out, and the integrity of a few stalwart officials in key positions at the federal, state, and local levels, not because of impenetrable barriers in our constitutional framework. In the end, it may well have come down to just a handful of Capitol Police officers who prevented a bloodthirsty mob from lynching Mike Pence and seizing the Electoral College ballots.

Off the Big Lie, the GOP has embraced the notion of widespread election fraud as a pretext for undermining American democracy full stop, such that it will never have to face the nuisance of a free election ever again. Trump and his allies—Giuliani, Flynn, Eastman, Graham, Stone, and the rest—had tried something truly difficult:

---

* Other polls show 52 percent of Republican respondents blaming Biden, not Trump, for the attack on the Capitol, according to *The Hill*, while *The Washington Post* reported that a quarter of all Americans believe it was a false flag operation by the FBI.

to reverse the results of an election after the fact. What the GOP is now seeking is to ensure future victories by obtaining a chokehold upstream from the certification of the electoral votes, such that it can control the outcome of elections well before the results are tabulated: no Capitol-storming, Pence-lynching, or bear spray necessary.

The primacy of the vote in a democratic society can hardly be overstated. Every other nightmare, no matter how horrible—whether it's a policy of forced birth, or of kidnapping immigrant children, or of accelerating an environmental catastrophe that threatens the very future of human life—can be addressed so long as we have recourse to free and fair elections as a means to eject elected officials with whom we are unhappy. But once that is gone, democracy is gone with it.

The GOP has long ridden the hobbyhorse of alleged electoral fraud as justification for manipulating the vote to its advantage.[15] But this new crusade is an order of magnitude more extreme. It is a path to power for Republicans at a time when they face a losing demographic battle in the United States and grim electoral prospects going forward.[16] It is also the specious premise under which Republicans have given themselves permission to do anything and everything to seize that power. Because the Democrats are, allegedly, engaged in a criminal conspiracy to steal elections, nothing is off-limits in the GOP campaign to fight back.

Ironically, there *is* an American political party that is actively trying to rig our elections, but it's not the Democrats. But as we have seen, projection is now the guiding principle and go-to modus operandi for the American right wing on pretty much everything. It's page one of the fascist handbook: accuse your enemies of your own crimes.

Therefore, a new, mind-bogglingly cruel irony now looms. Should the Republican Party manage to win the presidency through skullduggery, voter suppression, or even more nefarious means, the reasonable majority of American citizens may *also* lose faith in the legitimacy of our democracy, and with good reason. In that scenario, right-wingers will surely rediscover their belief in the integrity of the electoral system, even as they make their own lie come true. That is a conundrum worthy of Kafka. For Democrats to say the precise thing that Trump and his followers said last time—"The election was fixed!"—even if fully justified in this case, will invite charges of howling hypocrisy, with the victorious right wing sure to deny us the very means of legal recourse that it embraced in 2020.

In short, the GOP intends to make sure that it will never again need to overturn an election, because it intends never again to lose an election, and it is remaking American politics to that end. It wants to make sure that its supporters vote in numbers that overwhelm the opposition, and it will not rely only on a passionate turnout but also a skewed system. It wants to make sure Democrats face obstacles in casting their votes, or better yet, are cowed into not voting at all, and that it controls the counting of those votes once cast. It wants districts drawn such that the results give Republicans representation in Congress disproportionate to the actual will of the people, and with it a disproportionate share of electoral votes. Through that same redistricting, it aims to obtain supermajorities in state legislatures and give those legislatures the ability to appoint only Republican electors to the Electoral College. If challenged in the courts, it intends to have a judiciary packed with archconservative judges groomed and installed for the express purpose of ruling in favor of the right-wing regime. And this entire system will be supported and enforced not only by the usual mechanisms of state power, but also by the ever-present threat—and occasional application—of politically motivated violence carried out by right-wing militias, vigilantes, and other goons.

As the Yale historian Timothy Snyder notes in his book *On Tyranny*, when free elections disappear, few citizens realize they are voting in the last one.[17] That paradigm, of course, is common in many nations that succumb to autocracy. In the modern era, the demise of a democracy via an extralegal takeover, violent or otherwise, is much rarer than one that begins at the ballot box, with an authoritarian party ascending to power through legitimate or quasi-legitimate means, then slowly choking off the very mechanisms it used to gain that power and installing itself in permanent control.

In *How Democracies Die*, Levitsky and Ziblatt offer voluminous historical examples, including Mussolini and Hitler of course, but also Fujimori, Chávez, Orbán, Erdoğan, and to some extent even Putin.[18]

Almost all follow the same pattern, which involves capturing the courts, controlling the media, neutering (or co-opting) the legislature, and installing loyalists in every relevant arm of the bureaucracy. Surprisingly, control of the military and law enforcement—the chief tools of old-school autocracies—are less important, and typically fall into place once the other goals are achieved. Also omnipresent in these scenarios: vicious demonization of the regime's critics and opponents that justifies their subjugation.

For America to go down that dark path, all that remains is for the GOP to obtain control of the US government, which it very much aims to do in 2024. When it does, it is unlikely ever to give it up.

VOTER SUPPRESSION

The Republican attack on democracy is multipronged, but it begins with the simplest step of all: suppressing the vote itself.

Making it hard for people to vote—especially constituencies that tend to vote Democratic—has been the oldest and most basic part of the Republicans' antidemocratic project, and one that has dramatically increased in scope and intensity since 2020. Some methods of suppression are cloaked in highfalutin rhetoric and legislative means, like stymying voter registration, or restricting early voting and voting by mail. Others are more nakedly brutal. But regardless of technique, it would seem patently obvious that a party that doesn't want you to vote is fundamentally untrustworthy and un-American.

The forces of white nationalism in America, whether under the banner of the Republican Party or others, have been engaged in this suppression for centuries.[19] One can trace it all the way back to the Constitution itself, which enfranchised only white male property owners, continuing in opposition to the Fifteenth Amendment of 1869, which established the right of Black men to vote following a bitterly contested congressional fight, and in opposition to the suffrage movement, by which American women got the vote barely a hundred years ago. Voter suppression carried on well into the mid-twentieth century, with Jim Crow and its literacy tests and poll taxes and outright terrorist violence.

The numbers tell us why these white nationalists were so worried. In the two years between 1866 and 1868, Black voter registration rates exceeded 90 percent in many states. In response, Levitsky and Ziblatt write, "all eleven post-Confederate states reformed their constitutions and electoral laws to disenfranchise African Americans." As a result, "Black turnout in the South fell from 61 percent in 1880 to just 2 percent in 1912."[20] It was a state of affairs that would last half a century until the Voting Rights Act of 1965. Even today, rates of registration and voting in communities of color remain depressed, and not accidentally.[21] As we have seen, the former Confederacy has become a Republican stronghold, one that is threatened only by the Democratic-leaning Black vote—hence the GOP's urgency in trying to suppress that vote there to maintain its regional dominance.

Another Republican ploy to deny the American people a voice in the governance of their country is simply to question who they are and whether they have a right to vote at all.

Using the canard of electoral fraud, for many years the GOP has actively lobbied for voter ID laws and against mechanisms that made it easier both to register and actually to cast a vote, such as the 1993 Motor Voter Law (formally, the National Voter Registration Act), which allows Americans to register when applying for or renewing a driver's license or when applying for public assistance.[22] According to every credible study, in-person voter fraud is virtually nonexistent.[23] Yet such legislation was introduced in thirty-eight states between 2008 and 2012, and passed in twelve of them—all states where Republicans controlled the legislature.[24]

Republicans argue, correctly for once, that many advanced democracies do require identification at the polls.[25] What they neglect to note is that most of those countries have universally issued national ID cards. For the poor, the elderly, the handicapped, and many others, accessing the necessary paperwork and traveling to the proper facility in order to obtain even a simple state-issued identification card is no trivial task.[26] According to one study, 37 percent of Blacks and 27 percent of Latinx people did not hold a valid driver's license, while for whites the figure was just 6 percent.[27] (As many as 11 percent of all Americans lack government-issued ID of any kind, according to the Brennan Center. Among Black Americans the figure was more than double that, 25 percent.[28])

Republican strategists know this very well, which is why they are also highly selective about what forms of ID, tailored to their right-leaning constituencies, are suitable. In Texas, for example, a gun license counts but a student ID does not.[29] Poll workers have also been known to demand ID even though it is not required by law.

Since many Americans instinctively think having to show an ID to vote is common sense, and insisting otherwise only reinforces the stereotype of progressives as wild-eyed radicals, some strategists have argued that it might be wiser to concentrate on getting every citizen a national identification card of some kind, if a passport or driver's license is out of reach.[30] But naturally, the same Republicans who insist you ought to be required to present identification in order to vote are dead set against any such national ID, which they howl is a step on the road to totalitarianism.[31]

But the voter ID movement is only the most benign edge of Republican efforts to scare away voters.

In 2012, the national elections coordinator for True the Vote, a right-wing group dedicated to voter suppression, was quoted as saying he wanted voters to feel like they were "driving and seeing the police following you."[32] In August 2022, Florida's newly formed Office of Election Crimes and Security arrested nineteen people for voter fraud even after they had been assured by state officials that they could vote.[33] In Georgia, Republicans are challenging Democratic voters en masse, swamping the ability of state election offices to respond.[34] Georgia's GOP-controlled state legislature has also limited voting by mail, reduced the number and availability of ballot drop-off boxes, and made it a crime to send out pre–filled-out absentee ballot request forms or even to give water to people standing in line to vote. (Those deliberately long lines, of course, are also a form of voter suppression.[35]) This is hardly "securing the vote," even by the fake standards of the GOP's own rationalizations. It is solving a problem that doesn't exist . . . unless the problem isn't "voter fraud" at all but the fact that your party can't win a fair fight.

The GOP effort also includes intimidating the officials who administer elections, down to the humblest volunteer poll worker.[36] One in four elections officials report having been threatened with violence, including death threats, according to a 2022 survey by the nonpartisan Democracy Fund.[37] In perhaps the most famous and appalling example, Donald Trump personally turned the full power of the US presidency—and his cult—onto two innocent election volunteers in Georgia: Wandrea "Shaye" Moss and her mother Ruby Freeman, who were later proven to have done everything by the book.[38] Nationwide, a great many election workers have left their jobs as a result of harassment, creating vacancies for Republican partisans eager to oversee the vote.[39] Volunteer "voter fraud hunters" are similarly being recruited from the ranks of hardline Republicans,[40] as in Georgia, where six right-wing activists have been allowed to challenge the voting rights of almost 100,000 of their fellow citizens.[41] Meanwhile, vigilantes—sometimes masked, armed, outfitted in tactical gear better suited to the streets of Fallujah—have taken up positions at polling places and ballot drop boxes in states like Arizona.[42]

However, as *The New Yorker*'s Jeffrey Toobin has observed, "One of the ironies of the Republicans' obsession with fraud is that theirs is the party with the more significant recent history of misconduct at the polls."[43]

Since 1981 the GOP had been operating under a court-ordered consent decree that has limited its ability to harass voters on Election Day. The decree arose from the New Jersey gubernatorial election of that year, when the Republican National Committee created what it called the National Ballot Security Task Force, consisting mostly of off-duty police officers, some of them armed and wearing "NBST" armbands, who harassed and intimidated voters in largely Black and Hispanic neighborhoods. In 2018, after years of GOP efforts to have the consent decree lifted, a federal judge finally agreed. The RNC promptly recruited some 50,000 volunteers across fifteen states to monitor polling places and challenge any would-be voters they deemed suspicious. In late 2019, a senior lieutenant in the Trump reelection campaign, speaking to an audience of Republican lawyers, was caught on tape talking about the importance of "EDO"—Election Day operations—gleeful that "the consent decree's gone," which he went on to describe as a "huge, huge, huge, huge deal." (He was subsequently promoted to deputy campaign manager.) During the 2020 Democratic convention, Trump himself boasted to Fox's Sean Hannity that "We're going to have sheriffs and we're going to have law enforcement and we're going to have, hopefully, US attorneys" monitoring the polls.[44]

Other methods of voter suppression include three-card monte with polling places; leaflets and robocalls with the wrong information about election dates and rules; purging of voter rolls; and "voter caging"— sending mail to voters in hopes that it will be undelivered, which then opens the door to a challenge at the polls.[45] Republicans have even floated a plan to raise the voting age to twenty-one or even higher.[46]

Laws disenfranchising felons also serve to skew the vote in Republicans' favor, a method of voter suppression that likewise goes back to Reconstruction. Those laws become particularly significant when we consider that the US notoriously incarcerates more of its citizens than another other nation—more than Russia, more than Iran, more than North Korea.[47] Even if one takes the uncharitable view that the loss of the right to vote is a penalty for criminal behavior, a disproportionate percentage of that sky-high incarcerated population are people of color. As of October 2020, an estimated 5.1 million US citizens—a jaw-dropping one in every forty-four—were disenfranchised for the upcoming presidential election because of a felony conviction; 1.1 million of those in Florida alone.[48] For Black citizens, that rate rose to about one in every sixteen. Some states lifted these restrictions prior to 2010—including Florida, Virginia, and Iowa—but Republican governors have since put the restrictions back in place.[49]

Ironically, if Trump—a Florida resident—wins in 2024, we might have a president who is himself not eligible to vote.

Finally, in addition to concrete barriers to voting, another of the GOP's favorite tools is the simple cultivation of apathy. The Republican Party wants you to believe that your vote is meaningless, the same way it wants you to believe that government itself is inherently dysfunctional (which is why it serves the GOP's purpose to beclown the very practice of governance and then make it so). But as a great many wise observers have noted, if you think your vote is worthless, ask yourself why these people work so hard to keep you from casting it.[50]

COURTING DISASTER

Suppressing and skewing the vote is reprehensible enough. But the Republican Party has shown that the game of politics is much easier to win when you own the referees. Indeed, the modern GOP intends to own not only the refs, but also the commissioner, the stadium, the scoreboard, the concessions stand, and the parking lot, too.

Infamously, the American right has long been engaged in a determined campaign to gain control of the courts at every level, from the lowliest local magistrate on up. The most powerful force in this campaign has been the Federalist Society, under founder and CEO Leonard Leo, which for four decades has diligently identified arch-conservative jurists as early as law school, groomed them for judgeships, and shepherded them onto the bench (as well as into other key positions like state solicitor general).[51] In terms of the public spotlight, most attention is focused on the US Supreme Court, where the confirmation process has become a partisan shitshow, but the same principle is in effect up and down the chain.

In the words of Jason Stanley, a philosophy professor at Yale and the author of *How Fascism Works*: "Once you have the courts you can pretty much do whatever you want."[52] Mitch McConnell certainly agrees, having publicly stated that he believes that confirming conservative judges is the most important thing the GOP could do to have "a long, lasting positive impact on the country."[53] I would quibble with the adjective "positive." But there is no doubt that the GOP has prioritized that goal, and very successfully.

Shame on the Democrats for not being similarly strategic, especially once they realized what the Republicans were doing. In fact, "judges" is a reason cited with tedious regularity by conservatives who claim to dislike Trump when asked why they held their nose and voted for him.[54] Twice.

In his lone four-year term, Trump was able appoint 28 percent of all 816 judges on the federal bench.[55] The numbers are even more galling when we recall the Republican obstructionism that hindered Obama's judicial appointees. *The Guardian* further notes that "the vast majority of (Trump's) appointments were white males—not one of his 54 appellate judges is Black," and that the average age of the appellate judges was 47, five years younger than Obama's nominees, meaning "that Trump judges will serve 270 more years than Obama's judges, and they will decide thousands more cases," according to the Federal Judicial Center. "Trump's judicial appointments will shape American jurisprudence for decades to come."

Similar efforts are underway in the individual states. In Florida, Ron DeSantis was able to put three new justices on the state Supreme Court in a span of just three weeks in January 2019, all of them archconservatives vetted by Leo, replacing three liberal justices who—with godawful timing—were retiring.[56] The result was a court that has acted as a reliable rubber stamp to the full range of autocratic actions the governor has been keen to take, putting the people of Florida—a swing state not very long ago—under one of the most radically right-wing regimes in the country.

Control of the courts is a crucial step in controlling the electoral process, as it removes the primary form of recourse available to the opposition party and the public at large when an antidemocratic movement attempts to seize control. When, instead, an archconservative judiciary defends, endorses, and codifies injustice and even neofascism, the loop on the autocratic project is definitively closed.

Writing in 2021, the Harvard law professor Nikolas Bowie called the Supreme Court "the ultimate source of antidemocracy in the United States"—and Bowie was writing before the Court's flurry of extremist decisions the following year.[57] That same year the GOP managed to get before the Supreme Court a case called *Moore v. Harper*, involving state legislatures' authority to oversee the federal vote. The argument of the Republican plaintiffs hinged on something called the "independent state legislature theory," which, in its most extreme version, would have allowed those legislatures to throw out the results of the popular vote in a presidential election and allot that state's electoral votes to whatever candidate it wished.

What could possibly be more un-American? Even as the Supreme Court gutted the Voting Rights Act, *Roe*, environmental protections, gun laws, and even the once-inviolable separation of church and state—a run that Naomi Klein called "a shock-and-awe judicial coup"—few people thought that the very concept of one-person-one-vote would be next on the chopping block.[58] Senator Sheldon Whitehouse (D-R.I.) observed that "The fact that the Court is even considering a case involving such an extreme idea shows how beholden it is to the right-wing donors who got so many of the justices their jobs."[59] (No surprise: a chief advocate of the ISLT was the Honest Elections Project, a front for the 85 Fund, a deep-pocketed conservative nonprofit linked to Leonard Leo.[60])

Miraculously, the Court ruled against the Republican position in a 6–3 decision, defying the expectations of those like Klein, who had written that "There is no reason to believe that a group of people whose very presence on the bench required grotesque abuses of democracy would somehow draw the line at thwarting it."[61] But the mere fact that this cockamamie theory gained enough credence to be taken up by the Court in the first place remains deeply alarming. It also suggests that, even though Republicans lost that round, they are sure to return with a new legal challenge to basic tenets of democracy.

And sooner or later, they are sure to win.

CHAPTER 4

Oxygen and Cordite

As worrying as the Republicans' antidemocratic efforts are, they are not the source of the crisis threatening our country, only its manifestation. The problem is not that a right-wing cabal is trying to blow up the United States as we know it—the problem is that tens of millions of Americans are totally fine with it.

Rare is the autocracy that needs to maintain power through total repression of a seething, resentful populace, or can. More often a Stockholm syndrome takes effect, an invitation to conspire in one's own bondage. "The truth about many in the GOP base (is) they prefer authoritarianism to democracy," writes Jennifer Rubin, noting that about 26 percent of the US population qualify "as highly right-wing authoritarian," according to a recent study—twice the number of the runners-up, Canada and Australia.[1] In order to keep the American experiment alive, we will have to reckon with this demographic, the one that facilitates and gives oxygen to the Republican Party's campaign for countermajoritarian power and is energized by it in return.

POGO WAS RIGHT

A huge part of the postmortem of the 2016 election was endless handwringing about how globalism had left enormous numbers of working-class Rust Belt dwellers high and dry and susceptible to Trump-brand snake oil. But this analysis ignored the vast numbers of middle-class and upper-class Americans who suffered no such economic hardship but nevertheless supported Trump.[2] It also obscured the racism that animated so many Trump voters, in much the same way that anti-tax sentiment was a flimsy pretext for the founding of the Tea Party at the very moment that a Black president raised his right hand and was sworn into office.[3]

Beyond the economic kabuki lies a very real and undeniable panic among a lot of white conservatives: hence the vile battle cry "Take Our Country Back!" in all its not-so-crypto-racist glory. A 2018 study by the political scientist Diana C. Mutz of the University of Pennsylvania determined that among the greatest predictors of support for Trump was not economics at all but racial anxiety and a sense of threat to status among white Americans.[4] The previous year Ta-Nehisi Coates had already demolished the economic argument in his essay "The First White President" (excerpted from his book *We Were Eight Years in Power*) citing the statistical evidence of Trump's resounding support among whites at all income levels.[5]

Do conservative Americans really believe they are a besieged tribe in a society where the levers of power are unavailable to them? Under Trump, the Republican Party controlled the White House, the upper chamber of Congress (and for his first two years in office, the lower one as well), secured a 6–3 majority on the Supreme Court, and controlled an increasingly large chunk of the federal judiciary in addition to a majority of state legislatures and governorships. And that doesn't take into account all the other advantages, tangible and intangible, that the dominant race, class, and religious group holds in this society.

It's true that, in the long term, that segment of society is holding the short end of the demographic wishbone. Nativism therefore remains a particularly potent rallying point for the GOP. The percentage of immigrants in the American population—now approaching 14 percent—has nearly tripled since 1970, amplifying longstanding racial and ethnic fears among white Americans, as elucidated in the "Great Replacement Theory."[6] But that hardly makes white Christians an oppressed caste.

Yet if you dive into the online conversation among a great many rank-and-file Trump supporters, you will find what seems to be a genuine, deeply aggrieved sense that they are under constant—and even literally physical—attack. They see themselves viscerally menaced by antifa, which in the right-wing world is a force as numerous, ubiquitous, and powerful as the Cold War–era Red Army.[7] They bemoan the hatred that they say is spewed from the left, the attacks on the former president (often identified as "our" president), and the way that—in their view—liberals sow division in our country.

"Victim" used to be a pejorative for conservatives. For years they sneered at the word, especially when deployed by folks whom they had a hand in victimizing, seeing it as emblematic of the "taker" class and instead valorizing rugged individualism and pioneer-style self-sufficiency by contrast. (Top pioneer skills: selling smallpox-laced blankets, pretending corporate welfare isn't a thing, and not noticing public services like police, firefighters, and roads.) But once the right wing realized how powerful victimhood was as a weapon, it didn't take long to embrace it. Now the word "victim" is a badge of honor.[8] And with Trump, that phenomenon reached its apotheosis.

In truth, of course, the fiction of white people as a valiant breed beleaguered by sinister forces—mostly darker-skinned—is as old as Western civilization, and rich when measured against the violence that people of color actually face in the United States, often at the hands of the authorities themselves.[9] But it is a worldview that sits perfectly within the Orwellian perversion of truth that is the sea in which Trump swims, and where we are all drowning

What we are dealing with, then, is the last gasp of white nationalism, the racist, quasi-theocratic strain that has been a poison in the American bloodstream since the first pilgrim set foot on Plymouth Rock. It had a good run—over four hundred years. But with modernity trending against it, a desperate sector of Americans sees its unjust, centuries-long grip on power slowly slipping away. But white nationalism has made it clear that it will not go quietly. Enraged that Brown and Black people, people who don't necessarily speak English, women and gay people, and anyone who does not bow down to their god are being given a share of power, its adherents will go to the mattresses to hold onto power, even if it means destroying American democracy in the process. Frankly, they never much liked it anyway.

During the 2016 presidential campaign, the conservative writer Michael Anton captured the imagination of many Republicans when he wrote that the Trump/Clinton contest was "the Flight 93 election: charge the cockpit or you die."[10] That's a metaphor that, to say the least, plays directly to right-wingers' arrogant vision of themselves as underdogs and martyrs and heroes while casting Democrats and progressives as America-hating terrorists bent on mass murder. But as Levitsky and Ziblatt write, "One of the great ironies of how democracies die is that the very defense of democracy is often used as a pretext for its subversion."[11] It's also worth noting that even in that self-chosen metaphor the Republican Party ends up suicidally crashing the aircraft that represents the USA, killing everyone onboard.

"All effective actions require the passport of morality," Saul Alinsky wrote in *Rules for Radicals*.[12] Ruth Ben-Ghiat notes that authoritarians have always tried to label democratic systems as tyrannical.[13] In our present moment, it is an endless mantra of the American right that Joe Biden, perhaps the most avuncular and jovial US politician since Hubert Humphrey, is a horrific dictator who is forcing us to wear masks, announce our pronouns, and surrender our hamburgers, pickup trucks, and guns. Like all rebels, American reactionaries must feel that they are on side of freedom and justice when they go to such extremes.

Perhaps the strangest manifestation of the moral high ground on which the right wing imagines itself perched—and the most galling—is what Ibram X. Kendi calls "the second assassination of Martin Luther King, Jr."[14] After four hundred years in which white people used race as the single defining marker of privilege, those same people—clutching their pearls—now argue that we must be color-blind and "race-neutral" in all matters, and point to Dr. King's words to justify their argument. For reactionaries, be they tiki-torch carrying white nationalists, or much-esteemed jurists in black robes, it is a stance as brazen as it is deceitful, and—conveniently—achieves the net effect of maintaining their own dominance.

A neat trick, fellas. But we will not let you get away with it.

CIVIL WAR REENACTORS

Just as the Republican push for autocracy depends upon the support of a mass of ordinary Americans, it also operates on two fronts: in the legitimate political realm, to include the media space, which is the purview of the organized GOP and its associated entities, and in decentralized political violence that undergirds those formal politics.

If the number of committed insurgents who are willing to go to war against their own country is reduced to a very small number, that threat can be handled at the law enforcement level with ordinary policing and detective work, even if the legal consequences the perpetrators face rise above ordinary street crime and into the realm of national security matters. However, if that insurrectionist faction metastasizes, we will have a much bigger problem. Then we begin to drift into the realm of what the US military calls "low-intensity conflict."[15]

The best and most famous definition of war has always belonged to the nineteenth-century Prussian general and strategist Carl von Clausewitz, whose "continuation of politics by other means" is a formulation that every military officer in the Western world is taught. To that end, low-intensity conflict refers to political struggle at the light end of the spectrum, from simple agitation and propaganda to terrorism and counterinsurgency.

As I say, I hesitate to use martial terms. But political violence is already upon us, even if it does not remotely approach civil war by any reasonable definition of the term. We do not want to define fellow Americans as enemy combatants, or blur the distinction between law enforcement and military operations in confronting political actors who use violence for ideological ends. Those actors, by contrast, deliberately want to blur that distinction, and invite draconian suppression, so that they can claim the aforementioned mantle of martyrdom, accuse the ruling government of tyranny, and justify their own acts of violence ex post facto as blows against the empire. That is Guerrilla Warfare 101.

Here we enter into worrisome terrain with the militarization of everyday life, even if it is in the interest of preserving democracy. That is very much what the pro-Trump terrorists—like all terrorists—want, because it creates a self-fulfilling prophecy in which they are the victims. In other words, their own violent behavior prompts a violent reaction from the state, which they then point to as evidence of the monstrousness of the state, which justifies their initial violence in the first place.

It is also a conflict in which soft, civilian centers of gravity—schools, workplaces, airports, public transit stations, power grids, restaurants and clubs, concerts, and other public places—tend to be the most common targets, and one in which the foe is highly amorphous.

"There is no single principle that unites these Americans in their violence against their fellow citizens," writes *The Atlantic's* Tom Nichols. "They will tell you that they are for 'liberty' and 'freedom,' but these are merely code words for personal grudges, racial and class resentments, and a generalized paranoia that dark forces are manipulating their lives. These are not people who are going to take up the flag of a state or of a deeper cause; they have already taken up the flag of a failed president, and their causes are a farrago of conspiracy theories and pulpy science-fiction plots."*,16

The US would not be the first Western democracy to wrestle with a homegrown terrorist movement: the majority of major European countries have done so going back to the 1970s. But in this struggle, we will face an additional complication that we have not faced in any of our foreign counterinsurgencies. Al Qaeda was plenty dangerous, but one thing it never had was the support of one of the two major American political parties.

It's beyond ironic that radical Islamist extremism may ultimately prove to be far less of a threat to the United States than far-right white nationalist terrorism made in the USA. In fact, statistically, that is already true.[17]

THE WAY OF THE GUN

Since 2015, the Reverend Dr. Norvel Goff, Sr. had been a presiding elder in the African Methodist Episcopal Church, overseeing thirty-three congregations in South Carolina. One of them was Emanuel AME in Charleston, commonly known as Mother Emanuel, the oldest African Methodist Episcopal church in the South and a house of worship with a long history of civil rights organizing.

---

*   In fact, *The Turner Diaries*—a dystopian novel written in the 1970s and popular with today's right-wing fanatics—lays out precisely such a plan as part of its fantasy of a right-wing uprising against a tyrannical US government controlled by Blacks and Jews.

On June 17 of that year, Rev. Goff and his wife, Ann-Marie, left a Bible study in the church. Twenty minutes later, a white supremacist gunman entered and joined in the discussion. Soon after, he produced a .45 caliber Glock pistol and opened fire on the thirteen others present, all of whom were Black, including senior citizens and a five-year-old child, shouting racial epithets as he murdered nine of them.[18] (The child survived by playing dead.[19]) Asked mid-massacre about what motivated him, the killer replied, "You rape our women and you're taking over our country. And you have to go."[20]

The past decade has seen a deeply disturbing rise in the number of politically motivated hate crimes.[21] The targets are typically members of minority communities whom the grievance-obsessed American right despises—Black people, Jews, Muslims, and the LGBTQ+ community especially—from Mother Emanuel to the Tree of Life synagogue in Pittsburgh to the Pulse nightclub in Orlando. Of late, that target list has been expanded to include political leaders of both parties whom the right similarly perceives as traitorous.[22] Off the record, members of Congress from both parties admit to fearing for their lives, and their families, and with good reason.[23]

The right consistently downplays these acts of violence, usually insisting that they are isolated incidents, disconnected from any political motive, and carried out by mentally ill "lone wolves."[24] (The GOP's actual interest in improving mental health care in the United States is not commensurate.[25]) Republicans are also keen to convince us that "both sides do it," in hopes that we will believe that day is night, up is down, and urine is rainwater if they say it long and loud enough.

The fact is, over the past decade, right-wingers have been responsible for about 75 percent of the 450 murders committed by political extremists in America, with nearly half of that number tied to white supremacists, according to a study by the Anti-Defamation League. Left-wing extremists were responsible for a paltry 4 percent. Political violence is not a "both sides" problem, and Republican efforts to insist otherwise are pure misdirection. The data is clear: only one party engages in this sort of thing in any appreciable way.[26]

Unlike the right, there is simply no left-wing mediasphere filled with relentless hatemongering available to incubate the rare left-wing shooter, such as the one who shot House Majority Whip Steve Scalise and several others at a softball game in 2017.[27] Moreover, there is no one in the leadership of the Democratic Party who regularly encourages and incites such behavior. No Democratic politicians have been posting "comic" videos of themselves murdering their political opponents,[28] or running campaign commercials in which they demonstrate their alleged skill with firearms[29] (sometimes even using talismans of the opposing party as targets[30]), or mailing out Christmas cards where they pose with their spouses and children smiling and cradling assault rifles.[31] Georgia's Marjorie Taylor Greene has even endorsed the idea that Nancy Pelosi, Hillary Clinton, and Barack Obama should be executed.[32]

It's time to begin viewing much of the stochastic gun violence that rocks American life with sorrowful regularity as part of this right-wing insurgency. The idea that these are radicalized loners acting on their own initiative, and not directed by a unified command structure, shapes the specifics of the threat, but does not alter its fundamental nature. The killers need not be overtly controlled by the Republican leadership to function as an arm of that insurgency, especially given the continuing winking incitement of political violence by many of those leaders, and the utilitarian benefits the GOP gains from such violence.[33]

Al Qaeda—"the base," in Arabic, in a bitter parallel—was a highly decentralized movement in the post 9/11 era, not a hierarchical organization on the Western military model.[34] A not insignificant number of suicide bombings and other terrorist attacks by radical Islamist fundamentalists over decades of what the US called "the Global War on Terror" were planned and carried out by individuals acting on their own, inspired by the likes of Bin Laden, Khalid Sheikh Mohammed, or Ayman al-Zawahiri, but not directed by them or anyone else in the Al Qaeda leadership.[35]

How do we describe what went on at Mother Emanuel that June day as anything other than terrorism, part of a centuries-long campaign of violence toward Black Americans committed by racist whites?

"To this day I don't say the name of the person who committed that heinous act, that terrorist act, that racist act," Rev. Goff told me.

"I refuse to give his name power in my mind and thought. I know what it is, but I don't speak it."[36]

After the mass murder, Rev. Goff took over as interim pastor of Mother Emanuel and steered the community through the traumatic aftermath. "There's still people out here who talk about how Dad saved the city of Charleston," Norvel Goff Jr. says in the documentary film *After Sherman*, directed by his brother, Jon-Sesrie Goff. "Black folk, they'll talk to me, like, 'We were gonna burn this place down. Your father saved this city.'"[37]

I asked Rev. Goff if we can do in the whole country what he did in Charleston.

"I believe we can. How do we deal with voter suppression and gerrymandering and other unfair practices that don't reflect the will of the people? Through vigilance and hard work. And it's mundane. We've got to go to the meetings and the public hearings where there may only be twenty people there; we've got to push the legislators, and not just in Washington DC, but at the city and county level and the state level. It's not glamorous, but everything is local, and then it becomes regional, and national. We have to hold not only the Republicans accountable, but the Democrats and the independents too. No one gets a pass on this."

OLD TIMES THERE ARE NOT FORGOTTEN

Barbara Walter, professor of political science at the University of California at San Diego and the author of *How Civil Wars Start: And How to Stop Them*, notes the three-stage pattern that typically precedes a civil war, using methodology developed by the CIA.[38] First is a pre-insurgency, in which groups of militants organize around a given grievance or set of grievances. In the second "incipient conflict" stage, isolated acts of violence begin to occur that the government and general public fail to see as part of a broader pattern. The nascent insurgent groups also begin to develop an armed component, recruiting from military and law enforcement groups (very easy in a country like the United States that has been at constant war for the past two decades), as well as infiltrating members into the military to obtain experience and training and to conduct intelligence gathering and reconnaissance. Lastly there comes open war.

We have already seen the first two of these steps take place in the contemporary United States.

Right-wing radicalism within the military has been widely documented.[39] About one in ten of those who stormed the Capitol on January 6 had served in the military, including some who were still on active duty.[40] Of those charged with crimes, the number was nearly one in five.[41] (Only 7 percent of the general American population are veterans.) At its most basic, martial training and experience within the right-wing insurgency is a practical problem. The scenario of Trump insisting that an election was rigged and calling on the military to disobey the rightful winner is even worse.

Perhaps the highest profile example of a military professional who has gone through the looking glass into Trump World is retired Lieutenant General Michael Flynn, former head of the Defense Intelligence Agency, who infamously lasted all of twenty-two days as Trump's first National Security Advisor before being forced to resign for failing to register as a lobbyist for a foreign power (Turkey) and for lying to the FBI about his contacts with Russian ambassador Sergei Kislyak (a crime for which he was eventually pardoned by Trump). Once a highly respected military intelligence officer, Flynn has morphed into a rabid Islamophobe and COVID-19 conspiracy theorist, leading "lock her up" chants in 2016 and suggesting that Trump seize voting machines and declare martial law after his loss to Biden.[42]

Pro-MAGA sentiment runs similarly high in the law enforcement community, from local sheriffs (some of whom subscribe to the fringe theory of the "constitutional sheriff," whose power supersedes that of the federal government) all the way up to the FBI.[43] A former FBI supervising agent was revealed to have been among the Insurrectionists on January 6, caught on bodycam video calling DC police officers "disgusting," "Nazis," and "the Gestapo."[44] Rudy Giuliani bragged of inside information he received from friendly FBI agents during that 2016 campaign.[45] The arrest of the FBI's top counterintelligence official as a Russian double agent in 2022 also suggested the ways that the Bureau helped Trump get elected.[46] Most recently, the FBI was reported to have been resistant to searching Trump's Mar-a-Lago home for stolen classified documents, or even opening an investigation into his role in the Insurrection.[47]

Other law enforcement agencies have also shown bias that contributes to the complications of combatting violent right-wing extremism. Witness the genteel reaction of the police when met with AR-15–toting, tactical gear–clad anti-COVID radicals standing nose to nose with them, spittle flying as they screamed in their faces on the steps of the Michigan state capital. (Please don't call these people "demonstrators" or "protestors." Demonstrators and protestors carry signs and placards, not assault rifles and zip ties.) Such restraint is in direct contrast to the militarized reaction of law enforcement to the George Floyd demonstrations later that summer. It hardly bears repeating that the latter protests were set off not by anti-science paranoia and *Call of Duty*-style cosplay, but by a legitimate grievance—the brutal but shockingly casual murder of yet another unarmed Black citizen by a white police officer while his subordinates watched.

This kind of kid gloves treatment that right-wingers have consistently received from law enforcement, from Lansing to Kenosha to the Capitol, has surely emboldened these vigilantes.

"Candidly, implicit bias and race is a huge part of the problem," Tim Heaphy, a former US Attorney and assistant attorney general for the state of Virginia, told me. "Law enforcement does not take threats posed by middle-aged white guys as seriously as it does threats from people of color."[48] Heaphy led the investigation into the August 2017 white supremacist rally in Charlottesville, in which counter-protestor Heather Heyer was murdered and which prompted Trump's infamous "very fine people on both sides" remark. More recently he was the lead investigator for the House Select Committee on the January 6 attack, memorable to TV viewers as the attorney who questioned Bill Barr and others during their taped depositions. He notes that that same blinkered mindset was at work in the failure of authorities in the District of Columbia to prepare for possible violence on that day, even when chatter online and other intelligence indicators made it abundantly clear that such violence was coming.[49]

Maybe the violent strain of pro-Trump domestic terrorism will peter out in favor of mere grumbling and low-boiling white grievance at Kid Rock shows. If not, we will have to face the fact of an enduring right-wing guerrilla war within the US, waged by committed, well-armed

American terrorists happy to kill their fellow citizens.[50] The ostensibly respectable leadership of the Republican Party is well aware of this groundswell of seditionist belligerence and is privately happy to exploit it. That represents a bitter turn for the Party of Lincoln.

Thus has the Confederate battle flag ceased to be a regional symbol, or an emblem of some long-ago nineteenth-century war, and become an ideological one: the banner of middle-finger reactionaryism nationwide, flown from the backs of pickup trucks in Ohio and stuck on the bumpers of Dodge Chargers on the New Jersey Turnpike and in front of houses in Oregon, which wasn't even a state during the Civil War. It's no fluke that it was paraded through the US Capitol on January 6, a military achievement that even Robert E. Lee did not accomplish. Also weirdly prominent that day was the yellow-and-red flag of South Vietnam, as if the Insurrection were a Burning Man for devotees of all manner of lost causes.

The Republicans' autocratic endeavor therefore cannot be neatly blamed on a small cabal of archconservative politicians: it would not exist without the support of millions, or their own alarming comfort level with authoritarianism (so long as it benefits them). But the juvenile flirtation of what these adherents imagine to be 1776-style political violence, and their vision of themselves as armed patriots—fed by irresponsible demagoguery by Republican leaders from Trump on down—is among the most dangerous and alarming aspects of the current threat.

Let us now turn to the question of what kind of country they seem bent on turning us into.

CHAPTER 5

Autocracy for Amateurs

What would an American autocracy under far-right Republican rule look like?

Drawing on decades of experience in counterterrorism/antiterrorism and emergency management in the national security community, Glen Woodbury, formerly director of the Center for Homeland Defense and Security at the Naval Postgraduate School, told me that it's a mistake to fixate only on the worst-case scenario. "That kind of narrow focus can keep you from envisioning alternatives and variations that are just as likely to emerge. In other words, it's essential to consider not just a single vision but a spectrum."[1] When it comes to the state of American democracy, these range from the all-but-unthinkable—a true authoritarian state, on the order of Russia, Iran, or China—to the merely awful—an oxymoronic "illiberal democracy," akin to Hungary, Turkey, or the Philippines. Probably the best we can hope for is a functional constitutional republic with its antidemocratic elements sufficiently suppressed but requiring eternal vigilance to keep them that way. Frankly, that would be a step up from where we are now, where those forces cannot reasonably be described as "suppressed" at all. Beyond that, dare we dream of a society that might emerge from this crucible better than the one we have now, or ever had before?

RIGHTS AND WRONGS

No one is happy in a police state, except the police. But the jackbooted authoritarian regimes of the '30s and '40s are passé these days. In the postwar period, much more sophisticated forms of "soft" autocracy have arisen, carefully cultivated pantomimes of democracy that are no less brutal in many cases, and more treacherous for their veneer of legitimacy: what Moisés Naím, the longtime editor of *Foreign Policy* magazine, calls "stealthocracy."[2] These Potemkin republics feature the trappings of legitimacy—fair elections, a free press, commitment to civil rights, limits on the power of the head of state—but in truth employ them only as camouflage while the state maintains tight control of all the mechanisms that would otherwise serve as checks on its power.

Sham democracies are nothing new. Throughout history tyrants have found it useful to put on a show of benevolence and liberty, both for the sake of their subjects and foreign powers. But the modern incarnation tends to do it with more sophistication, and therefore more successfully. Putinist Russia was once the best example, though it has lately devolved into something more like old-fashioned totalitarianism—what *The New Yorker*'s Joshua Yaffa, who has reported from Russia for many years, describes as a "state that didn't bother hiding its claws."[3]

In its absence, Viktor Orbán's Hungary is the model most enthusiastically cited by the American right: an authoritarian kleptocracy with a strongman prime minister and tight controls on the press, the judiciary, and academia, in addition to suppression of opposition parties and ostentatious xenophobia. Affection for the Hungarian model has gripped Tucker Carlson and Ron DeSantis, and has even led CPAC to hold its annual conference in Budapest the last two years running. On the economy, on taxes, on the environment, on health care, on criminal justice, on foreign policy, on abortion, on guns, on immigration, on education, on religion, on civil rights and LGBTQ+ protections, and so much more: the agenda that Republicans would foist on America if given unified control of the government is uniformly horrid, and will be exponentially worse if they are able to institute and manage it with Hungarian rigor.

Furthermore, that Orbán-style America would not be one that the individual states would be free to deviate from.

In yet another embrace of Confederate ideals, over the past six decades the GOP has also become a vocal proponent of "states' rights," a philosophy almost always invoked to defend the worst policies imaginable. That argument was disingenuous from the jump, of course: a self-serving attempt to preserve their fiefdoms of revanchism rather than any commitment to real ideological principle. But even that has proved to be a farce.

Conservatives have insisted for decades that, even if federal law on such matters were swept away, blue states could still allow abortion, gun control, or single-payer health care, just as red ones could chose otherwise.[4] But no sooner was the metaphorical ink dry on *Dobbs v. Jackson Women's Health Organization* than emboldened Republicans in both the House and Senate introduced legislation for a federal ban on abortion in all fifty states.[5] That is a bellwether and then some. In his concurring opinion on *Dobbs*, Clarence Thomas explicitly suggested that not only marriage equality, but also contraception and even certain sex acts between consenting adults in the privacy of their own homes ought all to be reconsidered. *Loving v. West Virginia*, which established the legality of interracial marriage, would surely be on this list as well, though Thomas pointedly omitted it.

David Pepper, author of *Laboratories of Autocracy*, argues that many US states are already no longer functioning democracies, which is tragic enough.[6] (Were they ever?) But it is clear that if the GOP were to obtain sufficient power, New York, Massachusetts, or California would not be allowed to decide their own positions on gun control, tax policy, or health care: Texas and Arizona and Idaho would decide for them. In that regard, the battle over abortion *is* the battle over democracy.

However, the Republican affection for states' rights would not vanish altogether, as it remains a useful arrow in their quiver. Rather, it would be applied selectively: yes in the case of discrimination against LGBTQ+ citizens, no in the case of protections for reproductive rights or common-sense firearms restrictions. The autocracy would allow any GOP-controlled state to abrogate constitutional rights as it sees fit, while preserving the federal government's authority to declare null and void any legislation by a Democratic-controlled state that it did not like.

As one progressive activist told me, "When Republicans say 'states' rights,' what they mean is 'my state.'"[7]

In contemplating a second Trump administration, many observers—Barack Obama among them—have opined that it would mean the end of the republic, suggesting that the United States was sturdy enough to survive one Trump term, but probably not a second.[8] Trump himself has openly boasted that he will be a dictator—on Day One at least—and suggested he would invoke the Insurrection Act on the very day of his second Inauguration. As *The Bulwark*'s Jonathan V. Last notes, "Most aspiring dictators try to hide their intentions. Trump doesn't."[9]

One thing of which we can be certain is that he would be even more dangerous than before, thanks to four years of experience and the freedom of never having to face the voters ever again. Having bristled against the political professionals, institutionalists, and other grown-ups during his first administration, Trump has clearly learned the importance of seeding any future administration with myrmidons who can be trusted to follow orders and are not at risk of defying him. We can expect hardcore loyalists and slavish yes-men in every corner and crevice of the federal government. In fact, shortly before the 2020 election, Trump issued a sweeping executive order that radically remade the entire civil service system.[10]

For his senior deputies, Trump would likely rely on acting appointees and skip the pesky business of Senate confirmation—legally or not—especially if Congress did not force him to follow the rules.[11] Michael Flynn or someone like him would be made National Security Advisor or Secretary of Defense, with similar MAGA lackeys installed at the FEC, the EPA, and the Federal Reserve, not to mention the CDC. Imagine Rudy Giuliani as Attorney General, Matt Gaetz as Secretary of State, or Marjorie Taylor Greene as Secretary of the Treasury.

The politicization of the Intelligence Community and the Department of Justice would be particularly worrisome. The placement of Trump loyalists atop the CIA, NSA, and other intelligence organizations would likely trigger a mass exodus of career professionals, even as our allies abroad would be understandably reluctant to share intelligence with us, wondering if those secrets will be waved around Mar-a-Lago or Bedminster on weekends.[12]

In that effort he is aided by a group called Project 2025, a coalition of more than sixty-five right-wing organizations under the aegis of the far-right Heritage Foundation, that has been openly crafting this authoritarian playbook for America.[13]

As a first order of business, he would surely use every institution at his disposal to try to quash the prosecutions pending against him, which would plunge the US into all manner of unprecedented and unforeseeable constitutional crises.[14] Indeed, the entire apparatus of government would be weaponized in the service of the Party and its leader, from the FBI to the IRS to the Secret Service and beyond. Trump repeatedly made it clear that he viewed those organizations as "his," much the same way he spoke of "his" generals at the Pentagon, or saw the Attorney General as his personal lawyer, and was furious when the individuals who held that post did not, in his view, do enough to protect him from the law.[15] He would then turn that power outward, appointing special prosecutors to attack his enemies in baseless, spitefully motivated investigations, audits, and—ideally—criminal indictments against people like Chris Wray, Merrick Garland, Liz Cheney, Adam Schiff, Jamie Raskin, Letitia James, Alvin Bragg, Jack Smith, Fani Willis, and, yes, Hillary Clinton, Joe Biden, and Barack Obama.[16]

Internationally, Trump's return would likely mean US withdrawal from NATO and the UN and a general retreat from international security commitments full stop.[17] This would not be the sort of prudent pullback from military misadventurism that would cheer progressives, but rather, a catastrophic earthquake for global peace driven by the shortsighted, delusional belief that the US can become a kind of Fortress Atlantica disconnected from the cause of democracy worldwide. The one surefire winner would be Vladimir Putin. US aid to Ukraine would evaporate, leading to almost certain defeat for Kyiv, and ultimately, an end to Ukraine's very existence as a country.[18]

Among the other initiatives Trump has already proposed for a second term are disbanding the Department of Education,[19] executing drug dealers a la Philippine President Rodrigo Duterte,[20] and rounding up the unhoused and putting them in tent cities ("camps," some might call them).[21] He has also suggested that he would reinstitute the policy of taking migrant children away from their parents.[22] May Day-style military parades would be back on the Pentagon's to-do list. In the likely event of widespread demonstrations against the Trump regime, those marching soldiers might

be deployed for purposes more than ceremonial, setting up potential American Tiananmens.

Trump's admiration for tyrants is well-known. The kind of
America over which he would rule in a second term would be a
nightmarish manifestation of that desire. In fact, it practically begs
labels that go far beyond mere illiberalism.

THE "F" WORD

Despite the prideful belief in American exceptionalism, the fact that
authoritarianism has never taken hold in the US is more likely a
lucky accident than a testament to anything uniquely resistant in the
national soul. The enthusiasm with which millions of Americans
thrill to Trump's hatemongering, eagerly accept his mendacity, and
stubbornly refuse to acknowledge his manifold hypocrisies, failures,
and criminal behavior give the lie to this self-flattery. Indeed, there
are many ways in which the United States is particularly at risk for
authoritarianism: through our parochialism, monolingualism, geographic isolation, Puritanism, and the pervasiveness of repressive
and oppressive religiosity. But we have never flirted with it so openly
as we have with Trump.

Of course, when it comes to the myth that "it can't happen here,"
the go-to maxim is that when fascism comes to America, it will arrive
wrapped in the flag and carrying a cross. The cliché is worn out by
now, but that is only because it is so blazingly correct. The form of
rising authoritarianism that we now face has been uniquely tailored
for the American circumstances, heavily weighted with mawkish
appeals to reactionary values. In the US, that means God, guns, and
fanatic white nationalism. Donald Trump, never one for nuance, has
on multiple occasions helpfully provided a living embodiment of
this maxim, like a live-action Nativity scene, by ostentatiously hug-
ging the American flag in photo ops, a display of faux patriotism to
match his equally ostentatious and fake displays of religious faith.[23]

In May 2016, before Trump had even secured the GOP nomination, Robert Kagan rejected the conventional wisdom that Trump's
appeal had to do with so-called "populism," writing in *The Washington
Post* that what Trump really offered was "an attitude, an aura of

crude strength and machismo, a boasting disrespect for the niceties of the democratic culture that he claims, and his followers believe, has produced national weakness and incompetence. His incoherent and contradictory utterances have one thing in common: they provoke and play on feelings of resentment and disdain, intermingled with bits of fear, hatred and anger." Helpfully, Kagan explained: "This phenomenon has arisen in other democratic and quasi-democratic countries over the past century, and it has generally been called 'fascism.'"[24]

In fact, Kagan's piece was boldly titled "This Is How Fascism Comes to America."

The use of the "F" word in relation to Trumpism inevitably invites paroxysms from conservatives. In August 2022, President Biden gave a much-noticed speech in which he called the direction of the GOP "semi-fascist." While many cheered a candor that felt long overdue, there was much rending of garments and gnashing of teeth on the right, and even the center, as numerous pundits accused the president of hyperbole, slander, and undue alarmism.[25] (If the alarmism is due, is it alarmism at all?) But the real critique should have been the appendage of the qualifier "semi."

The following month Biden gave a speech in Philadelphia—not a randomly chosen location—in which he used the term again, and again many on the right developed the vapors, among them Donald Trump, who at a subsequent rally of his own called it "the most vicious, hateful and divisive speech ever delivered by an American president."[26] Trump accused Biden of "vilifying 75 million citizens . . . as threats to democracy and as enemies of the state," while, again, embracing Stalinist verbiage himself in referring to Biden: "He's an enemy of the state, you want to know the truth," Trump told his crowd. "We are the ones trying to save our democracy."[27]

But right-wing displeasure at the label does not mean that it is incorrect, or unfairly applied. And Trump did not help his case when he later took to describing his enemies in the explicit verbiage of 1940s fascism, calling them "vermin" who deserve to be "crushed."[28]

It is undeniable that, as a slur, the term "fascist" has been devalued through overuse and exaggeration almost to the point of meaninglessness. As *New York* magazine's Jonathan Chait writes, "To most Americans, *fascist* simply means 'bad,' and nobody self-identifies as 'bad.'" In an October 2022 piece, Chait noted that fascism is almost too complimentary in terms of giving Trump credit for an ideology when he really has none, calling his authoritarianism "sub-ideological." Pointing out that democracy and fascism are not "a simple binary," Chait observes that "the middle ground between Reagan and Mussolini is where the Republican Party's most influential ideologists and power brokers are consciously heading."[29] In that regard, Biden's semi-fascist neologism, flip as it sounds, quite accurately describes the state of play.

In his 1995 essay "Ur-Fascism," Umberto Eco, who grew up in Mussolini's Italy, discussed that devaluation of the term, laying out fourteen signs of the genuine thing, which included anti-modernism; thinking as a form of emasculation; intolerance for questioning and dissent (including hatred of science); fear and hatred of the Other; portrayal of the enemy as both contemptibly weak and terrifyingly strong; pacifism as treason; extreme machismo; and manipulation of language.[30] In her book *Fascism: A Warning*, former US Secretary of State Madeleine Albright offered a much simpler definition of a fascist: anyone who claims to speak for an entire nation, is unconcerned with the rights of others, and is willing to use any means, including violence, to achieve his or her goals.[31]

In the end, the debate over whether the modern Republican Party is a fascist movement may help us name and reckon with what we are facing: "not to defame—but to diagnose," as David Frum writes.[32] But if it diverts our energy and gives ammunition to the foe, it ceases to be of help. If you've been shot with a crossbow, and have an arrow sticking out of your chest, you don't need to know the manufacturer of the arrow, the factory it came from, or the birthday of the archer who fired it.

You just need a doctor.

PART TWO
THE CLOSEST CROCODILES

CHAPTER 6

Systemic Reforms (One)

Ahead of January 2025, while those committed to democracy still control certain key institutions like the White House and the Senate, there are a great many policy choices that would help shore up (or move toward) a fair, functional system that provides equal justice and human rights for all. None of the suggestions that follow are new, and many already have book-length dissertations all their own, but they have never been more urgent. As in all emergencies, it only makes sense to deal with the most pressing threats first—to attend, as the saying goes, to the crocodiles closest to our canoe.

But before proceeding into details, it's incumbent on us to anticipate a frequent objection to many of these changes, which is the cry that they would violate the intentions of the Founding Fathers. That may be so—and we should welcome it.

This argument by the right wing rests upon a near-religious reverence for the Founders, a reverence so great that merely evoking their intents (or what some insist were their intents) is presumed to obviate all critique. The implication is that the centuries-old wisdom of these men and the Constitution they drafted is sacrosanct, and that we are somehow foolish or disloyal for daring to tinker with it. A better question would be why any of us feel biblically bound to a verbatim reading of a 234-year-old document drawn up at a time when women were chattel, child labor was routine, and leeches figured heavily in medicine.

The Founding Fathers did not intend to create a true representative democracy as we now conceive of it. Among those modern expectations are a commitment to the principle of "one-person-one-vote," a head of state chosen by a majority of the people, and a parliament that reflects a proportionate representation of the population.

We have none of those things. What the Founders envisioned, and established, was a patrimonial oligarchy ruled by white, male, Christian, property-owning elites—many of them counting human beings among the property they owned—the legacy of which remains with us to this day. It's no wonder contemporary right-wingers deify them without qualification.

The fact that these men deliberately bequeathed to us several fundamentally antidemocratic institutions as part of the revolutionary system of government that they devised does not make those institutions any less antidemocratic. It would be self-destructive to cling to them just because a bunch of slaveowners in powdered wigs and knee socks said so two centuries ago.

The best scholarship suggests that the Founders were well aware of the contradictions between the quasi-democratic society they aimed to create and the seminal dilemma that the institution of slavery posed to it.[1] Observers of the American experiment going back to Tocqueville recognized this inherent conflict, which came to a head in the Civil War and has continued to define American society to the present day and into the foreseeable future.

Even the Founders themselves did not claim godlike powers of omniscience or accord themselves the infallible, deity-like status that modern conservatives do. Understanding that any viable political system has to be flexible with the capacity to adapt over time, the Founders built in methods for so doing, principally in the provision for amendments to the Constitution. They certainly did not intend to create a permanent system, calcified in the year 1789, like Moses descending from the mount, tablets in hand, no matter how much conservatives would like those tablets displayed in public school classrooms.

We must recognize that this clear-eyed, historically accurate view of the Founders, and of the founding of our country, is disturbing to many Americans. It flies in the face of deeply ingrained, comforting myths with which we were all raised—comforting above all to the privileged class of economically well-off, putatively Christian white people. But we need not demonize the Founders any more than previous generations lionized them. They were complex and flawed figures who bequeathed us a complex and flawed country. It's up to us to make it better.

Let's honor them, if that's our goal, by doing that.

PROTECT VOTING RIGHTS

If the right to vote is the cornerstone of representative democracy, and attacks on that right and on free elections are the heart of the Republican threat, then it follows that protecting the sanctity of the franchise is the top priority and first line of defense.

Congressional Democrats attempted to put some of the most basic reforms in place with the For the People Act, first introduced in 2019 and again in early 2021 after Joe Biden took office. That legislation would have provided for a vast array of voting rights protections, including same-day registration at the polls, online registration, automatic "motor voter" registration, and pre-registration of those about to turn eighteen. It would have expanded voting by mail and mandated early voting; provided penalties for voter intimidation, caging, roll purging, and the spread of disinformation; facilitated voting for the disabled and for US military members voting by absentee ballot when deployed overseas or otherwise away from their home of record; required the use of paper ballots to preempt hacking and facilitate recounts; instituted changes to the composition of the FEC to reduce gridlock; halted felony disenfranchisement; stopped partisan gerrymandering by mandating independent commissions to draw congressional districts; tightened campaign finance laws in order to stanch the flood of money into American politics; established new rules of ethics for federal officials, including the Supreme Court; and made disclosure of tax returns mandatory for presidential and vice presidential candidates.

In other words, it was a comprehensive and ambitious attempt to address weaknesses and injustices in our electoral system and fortify free and fair voting in America.

Senate Republicans killed it with a filibuster.[2]

Those Republicans also blocked passage of the John Lewis Voting Rights Act, which was designed to reverse the Supreme Court's 2013 ruling in *Shelby County v. Holder* that stripped key provisions of the Voting Rights Act of 1965 and helped protect extreme gerrymandering by the GOP. Like For the People, that act also passed the House with widespread public support but was twice filibustered by the GOP-controlled Senate.[3] The Democrats could have overcome those filibusters, but were stymied by two of their own, Joe Manchin of West Virginia and Kyrsten Sinema of Arizona, who refused to carve out an exception even though they had been willing to do so in order to raise the debt ceiling that same month. (They were later seen in Davos, high-fiving over it.[4]) Manchin subsequently proposed an even narrower voting rights bill, the Freedom to Vote Act, which dropped numerous aspects of For the People while adding a voter ID requirement as a sop to Republicans. That bill had the support of an eyepopping 72 percent of the American people.[5] It too was killed by the GOP, twice, with Manchin again declining to carve out an exemption, even to his own legislation.

A number of Republicans objected to all these bills as "federal overreach" that infringes on states' rights.[6] But the truth is that there is nothing in the area of protecting voting rights that Republicans find acceptable: their entire goal is to disenfranchise a huge swath of the electorate for their own partisan gain.[7]

Which is more infuriating: Republicans' willingness to block an ambulance from coming to the aid of our grievously wounded democracy, with no apparent concern that Americans will hold them accountable, or a pair of nominal Democrats who were willing to help them? In the meantime, democracy lies bleeding. If we do not act to save it, and to ensure and protect its good health going forward, we may look back on those legislative failures as among the most tragic milestones in the ultimate demise of the republic.

The John Lewis Act and Freedom to Vote Act, while not perfect, remain on the Senate's plate. Efforts to pass them, or some similar legislation, should be an urgent Democratic priority.

DISBAND THE ELECTORAL COLLEGE

One of the most obvious ways to rescue our democracy is to put an end to the antiquated and inherently antidemocratic institution of the Electoral College. The Electoral College was antidemocratic even in 1789, when the most populous state at the time, Virginia, had only thirteen times as many residents as the least populous, Delaware, according to the first US Census, taken the following year.[8] Today, the biggest, California, has *sixty-seven times* as many as the smallest, Wyoming.[9] How does that translate into voting power?

Nancy Gibbs, director of the Shorenstein Center on Media, Politics, and Public Policy at Harvard, cites another small state, South Dakota, where a vote counts approximately twice as much as a Texan's vote in presidential races, and a whopping twenty-eight times as much when it comes to the Senate.[10]

Such a system would not pass muster in any junior high school civics class. If a nascent democracy in the developing world were to propose this plan as the centerpiece of its electoral process, UN election observers would howl bloody murder.

Not coincidentally, these sparsely populated Western states tend to vote Republican by enormous margins and are overwhelmingly white (Idaho at 88.4 percent according to the latest available figures, North Dakota at 85.7 percent, South Dakota at 83.8 percent, Montana at 87.9 percent, and Wyoming at a head-snapping 90.5 percent).[11] As a result, the far right starts out with a huge structural advantage in American elections. Of course, whiteness is not an ideology per se, and white people certainly don't all vote the same. But a place like Wyoming that savagely turned on a scion of the arch-conservative Cheney dynasty, calling her a "traitor" for opposing Donald Trump, has little wiggle room to hide its politics.[12]

Twice in the past six presidential elections the results of the Electoral College have contradicted the popular vote, both times benefitting Republicans: the first time narrowly, by about half a million votes, the second by a whopping three million. Not surprisingly, the GOP is very keen on maintaining this patently antidemocratic system.*

On that front, the right stands sanctimoniously on the fact that, despite the obvious simplicity and inherent fairness of choosing the head of state by popular vote, the way other countries with presidential systems do, the Founders specifically chose the current system for a reason. That is true . . . but the reason is damning. Let us recall again that those Founding Fathers, for all their undeniable vision, were not small "d" democrats. They were all white aristocratic men very much of the century in which they were born, leery of the hoi

---

* Prior to that, it had happened only three times: John Quincy Adams in 1824, Rutherford B. Hayes in 1876, and Grover Cleveland in 1888.

polloi, and fearful both of mob rule and of a homegrown tyrant. They did not want the president elected by a majority of the people, whom they felt were unfit to make such decisions, or worse, would make decisions that the privileged class wouldn't like.[13] The franchise itself was extended only to white landowning males, but even that gave the Founders agita. The Electoral College was therefore deliberately conceived as a way to minimize the power of the people and maintain the power of the economic elite.

Ironically, those Founders created the EC out of fear of public susceptibility to a demagogue.[14] What we have now is a system where that institution facilitates this very threat. Like many aspects of the structure of the new United States, it was also a compromise over slavery.[15] A system that shared power among states, rather than among the citizenry as a whole, helped protect the power and independence of those slave states, some of which were already rightly worried that an essential element of their infrastructure and economic might—human bondage—would come under attack.

But the Republican appeal to the wisdom of the Founders is dishonest in any event. As *The Bulwark*'s Jonathan V. Last writes, "the right would never tolerate the reverse scenario—namely, the system repeatedly rewarding political power to their less popular opponents."[16] One suspects that if the twisted arithmetic of the Electoral College somehow favored Democrats, any right-wing devotion to the Founders would rapidly evaporate, and Republicans would long ago have been out in the streets with torches and pitchforks demanding its abolition.

As it is unlikely that any of the small, right-leaning states will ever voluntarily surrender their unfair advantage, or that the Republican Party would let them, another solution will have to be found.

The National Popular Vote Interstate Compact is a plan by which the states would agree to assign their electoral votes to the winner of the popular vote nationwide. Since its introduction in 2006, sixteen states and the District of Columbia have adopted it, comprising 195 of the 540 total electoral votes, which is roughly 72 percent of the 270 needed to win.[17] By design, the compact would not go into effect until enough states comprising that majority is reached.

Though legal questions remain about the constitutionality of such a plan, an end to the Electoral College would radically improve presidential politics, and not just for Democrats. Candidates of both parties could no longer ignore "safe" states, nor take for granted massive hauls like California's fifty-five electoral votes, Texas's thirty-eight, or New York's twenty-nine. A Republican voter in rural, solidly red Susanville, CA, to take one example, currently powerless in a winner-take-all system where its votes are inevitably swamped by bright blue Los Angeles and San Francisco, would suddenly be of equal value to a presidential candidate. Similarly, the two parties could no longer surgically target isolated swing counties and pour tens of millions of dollars into them as if from a cement mixer. Western states with populations smaller than Brooklyn (there are fifteen of them) would no longer wield outsized voting power, and a handful of "battleground states"—Michigan, Georgia, Wisconsin, Pennsylvania, Arizona—would no longer decide presidential races. Hence a fairer system for all, one that can't be gamed, and one that is truly representative of the will of the people. Do we want that or not?

If the Electoral College can never be dislodged, then at least critical reforms are necessary for the Electoral Count Act of 1887, the arcane law that governs how presidential electors are counted and certified in Congress, which proved central to the attempted coup of January 6. Miraculously, Congress did pass important changes to the ECA in December 2022, clarifying that the vice president's role is purely ceremonial, raising the bar for objections, and instituting important safeguards for the appointment of electors at the state level. It would not be cynical to believe that the willingness of some Republicans to support these reforms was not due to a sudden outbreak of principle, but because they recognized that the system might break against them at some point. In passing these reforms, Congress also proved that it can in fact accomplish the simplest of tasks in a bipartisan manner, on occasion.

END GERRYMANDERING

If the most basic principle of representative democracy is one-person-one-vote, an essential corollary is a fair and accurate representation of that vote in the elected bodies it creates. The very concept of gerrymandering, then, is contrary to democracy at the most fundamental level. Even more so than the Electoral College, and rivaled only by the toxic influence of money, it might therefore be the single most destructive element plaguing our political system.

David Daley, author of *Ratf**ked: The True Story Behind the Secret Plan to Steal America's Democracy* (2016), notes that the US is "the only democracy in the world that allows the politicians to draw their own lines and essentially choose their own voters."[18] Given the option of handing that power to a nonpartisan commission, American voters in state after state consistently choose to do so.[19] But politicians predictably cling to that power whenever possible, and when it is taken away, do all they can to infiltrate and take over those ostensibly neutral bodies.

From the postwar era into the 1990s, Democrats had become accustomed to controlling a majority of state legislatures by a factor of two to one.[20] Ahead of the 2010 midterms, the party still controlled more than 60 percent of state legislatures. But in that year the GOP created what it called the Redistricting Majority Project (REDMAP), charged with maximizing Republican domination of state legislatures so that it would control the nationwide redistricting that would follow the upcoming census. With eighteen state legislative chambers in the country where the majority hinged on just four votes or fewer, the GOP was able to pour money into those races and flip enough of those seats to win those chambers, giving themselves an outrageous electoral advantage for the next decade. For a minimal financial investment—"less than the price of a losing Senate race in a small state," as Daley writes—the GOP made it effectively impossible for Democrats to gain majorities in numerous state legislatures, even when they win a majority of the popular vote statewide.[21]

In other words, rather than retooling its policies to win the support of a majority of the American people, the GOP simply changed the rules so that the majority didn't matter.

As *Mother Jones'* Ari Berman writes, Republicans ended up with "control of nearly every important swing state and the power to draw four times as many state legislative and House districts as Democrats. Nearly a decade later, Republicans still control every legislative chamber in heavily gerrymandered states like Michigan, North Carolina, Ohio, Pennsylvania, and Wisconsin."[22] Thus, from the ruins of defeat in 2008 when Barack Obama foretold demographic disaster for the GOP, the Republican Party miraculously found a way to game the system such that it not only staved off that fate, but actually managed to get a chokehold on American governance for the foreseeable future.[23] It was morally reprehensible and in stark opposition to the spirit of democracy, but it was altogether legal. And the Democratic failure to see it coming, let alone counter it before it was too late, was a form of political malpractice.

As a matter of simple arithmetic, extreme gerrymandering in Republican-controlled states also creates some safe seats for Democrats. However, that very process ghettoizes Democratic voters such that reliably blue districts are far fewer than red ones, effectively rendering their representatives powerless, and functioning as another part of a deceptive veneer. Of course, ever-changing demographics mean that the makeup of voters in any given district can shift over time. But if the Republicans have a lock on the legislature, and on the courts, they can always redraw the maps as needed.

Of late, some states have thrown out gerrymandered electoral maps, which would be a welcome development if were being applied evenly across the national board. It is not. In New York, Maryland, California, Colorado, New Jersey, Virginia, and Washington, maps favored by Democrats have been rejected by the courts or by bipartisan commissions, while in Wisconsin, Tennessee, Florida, Georgia, Kansas, Ohio, Texas, and Louisiana, maps that had been heavily gerrymandered to favor Republicans have been allowed to stand.[24] In four states—Alabama, Georgia, Louisiana, and Ohio—the GOP simply ignored court decisions and used rejected maps anyway.[25]

You can't win when you are made to play fair and the other side isn't.*

Before 2019, gerrymandered maps could be challenged in federal court. But that year, the US Supreme Court, with its 5-4 conservative majority, ruled that they could not. That decision, in conjunction with its gutting of the Voting Rights Act in Shelby six years prior, has rendered the traditional methods of fighting

---

* A 2022 study by *The New York Times* downplayed the impact of gerrymandering in the US House of Representatives, while admitting that it remains a problem in state legislatures. Which is like saying that you shouldn't worry about your brain tumor because you don't also have lung cancer.

gerrymandering obsolete.* Groups like Eric Holder's National Democratic Redistricting Committee are pursuing legal challenges to redistricting, backing independent commissions to conduct that process going forward, and trying to seed state legislatures with principled Democratic legislators who can resist Republican efforts to create hyperpartisan maps and restrictive voting laws.[26] But even this process depends on fair elections.

Ultimately then, as in all things, it is only the voice of the people demanding fair representation, and the ensuing pressure it creates, that will force change.

KILL THE FILIBUSTER

In the same way that no other country lets legislators draw their own districts, there is no other advanced democracy where a tiny sliver of radical legislators is allowed to hold the entire nation hostage the way that the filibuster allows US Senators to do.

The recent Republican use of the filibuster to kill protections for voting rights is only the latest in a long, disgraceful tradition attached to that device. The filibuster was used by segregationist senators in the 1930s to stop anti-lynching legislation, and later to block civil rights bills, including a 1957 solo filibuster by Strom Thurmond of South Carolina that lasted a full twenty-four hours, and a sixty-day filibuster by Thurmond, Richard Russell, Robert Byrd, William Fulbright, and Sam Ervin to block the Civil Rights Act of 1964 (though it ultimately failed).[27] Still, the political scientists Sarah Binder and Steven Smith note that there were only twenty-three manifest filibusters in all of the nineteenth century, and only thirty between 1880 and 1917. From 1917 to 1970, the first fifty-three years after the cloture rule was established, the Senate found it necessary to invoke it on only eight occasions. But the use of the filibuster grew almost exponentially over the next four decades. By 1993–94 that number had climbed to eighty,[28] and with the ascent

---

** In November 2023, the Republican-dominated US Eighth Circuit Court of Appeals removed another key provision of the Voting Rights Act, ruling that only the US government, not private groups or citizens, could challenge violations of the act, in a decision authored by a Trump appointee.

of Barack Obama in 2009, Mitch McConnell and the GOP made the filibuster standard operating procedure.[29] Though absolutes are hard to pin down given the imprecision over the term itself, it is fair to say that Republicans blocked as many judicial nominees under Obama as all Congresses had blocked for all other presidents prior to that time.[30] This Republican obstructionism of Obama's judges was not merely a matter of sticking it to the Black guy, designed to thrill the GOP's neo-Confederate base. It was also a deliberate attempt to preserve its long-sought dominance of the courts by keeping Democratic nominees off the federal bench. For Republicans the technique also has the added advantage of allowing it to create chaos that feeds its preferred narrative that government is inherently dysfunctional and "bad."

"As a political strategy, McConnell's tactics were vindicated by the 2010 midterms," *Vox*'s Matthew Yglesias wrote in 2015.[31] But the cost was congressional credibility. In 2013, Public Policy Polling found that as a result of such antics, "Congress was less popular than Genghis Khan, traffic jams, cockroaches, or Nickelback. In a less joking spirit, Gallup found that the voters have less confidence in Congress than any other American institution, including big business, organized labor, banks, or television news."[32]

As Minority Leader during the George H.W. Bush administration, Harry Reid adamantly defended the filibuster, predicting in apocalyptic terms that its removal would be "the end of the Senate" as we know it.[33] But by 2013, faced with that GOP obstructionism toward Obama's nominees, he reversed himself, exercising the so-called nuclear option and dispensing with the supermajority threshold for executive appointments and judicial confirmations, except for the Supreme Court. Four years later, as Majority Leader under Trump, and facing a Democratic minority livid over his outrageous blockage of Merrick Garland's nomination, McConnell shitcanned that provision as well. Without that maneuver, Neil Gorsuch would not be on the Supreme Court today, nor would Kavanaugh nor Barrett.[34]

Though the popular image of a filibuster is of a Jimmy Stewart-like senator standing on the floor of the Capitol holding forth for hours on end, in the modern era what we casually call a filibuster is more accurately described as the mere threat of one, with nary a word spoken. The so-called "silent filibuster" was birthed with the 1972 introduction of a two-track system that allowed the Senate to conduct its regular business separate from the consideration of a filibuster, and a 1975 rule change that reduced the number of senators needed to invoke cloture to sixty from the previous requirement of two-thirds of those present and voting.[35] Ironically, that rule change was instituted to neutralize the power of a filibuster to stop Senate business. But in contemporary politics it has only served to make it a painless tactic disproportionate to its punch.

But the filibuster is not a core aspect of American democracy—in fact, there is some evidence it arose accidentally[36]—and the diehard loyalty to it so ostentatiously displayed by Manchin and Sinema or any number of Republicans is contemptible, particularly as they have been plenty willing to make exceptions when they feel like it.[37] At a bare minimum, an end to the two-track system and a return to the old-fashioned "talking filibuster" would be a step in the right direction. Let's see how keen our aged, infirm Republican senators are to use the filibuster when they have to stand for hours on end, like Gitmo detainees, to spout their blather.

But ending it altogether would be even better. The Voting Rights Act of 1965 remains in tatters, with the federal government unable to enforce the law on states that seek to disenfranchise Black voters and indeed anyone who might vote Democratic. It is the filibuster—and the pry-it-from-my-cold-dead-hands defense of it, valued above democracy itself—that stands in the way of protecting those rights.

It has to go.

ABOLISH THE SENATE?

The Nation's legal correspondent Elie Mystal calls the filibuster "a rule invented by senators to make their institution even less democratic than the Constitution requires it to be." But he doesn't believe that reforming it will address what he calls "the rot at the heart of the Senate."[38] An even more blunt solution would be the simple abolition of the venue where it is used.

With its status as a coequal half of the legislative branch, its power to confirm or reject presidential appointments including Supreme

Court nominees, and—as we have painfully seen—its authority to convict or acquit an impeached president and bar that individual from public office (or not), the Senate's role in American governance is enormous. So when it becomes a bastion of obstructionism and an instrument of countermajoritarian sabotage, the damage is vast and the stakes are high.

An upper house of the legislature where each state is equally represented irrespective of its population represents another inherently undemocratic mechanism, more reflective of a confederacy than a federal union. Like the Electoral College, this arrangement too was a compromise, again designed to strengthen the power of the slave states.[39]

By definition then, the smaller, less populated states—again, typically in the West, and again, typically Republican—have an unfair advantage in the Senate, and it is only going to get worse. "[B]y 2040, about 70% of Americans are expected to live in the 15 largest states," said David Birdsell, dean of the school of public and international affairs at Baruch College, in 2017. "They will have only 30 senators representing them, while the remaining 30% of Americans will have 70 senators representing them."[40]

If abolishing it is off the table, introducing a small measure of proportional representation—allocating states two, three, or four senators, based on population—might help make the Senate marginally more just. A similar proposal is to give each state a baseline of one senator, with additional senators apportioned by population. Under numbers compiled in 2017, this system would give twenty-six states a single senator apiece and twelve other states two each. Eight more states would have three or four, while Florida and New York would have six, Texas nine, and California twelve.[41]

But advocates of abolishing the Senate altogether, like Mystal, make a fiery case that an "institution that is so profoundly antithetical to democracy cannot be 'reformed' . . . simply by changing the method of picking its antidemocratic leaders."[42]

At the same time, there are strong arguments against disbanding the Senate that don't rely on a sclerotic or sentimental attachment to such an old and established institution. Unlike congressional seats, senators are chosen in statewide races impervious to gerrymandering, which is how states under the heel of Republican control, like Arizona or Georgia, are still able to send two Democratic senators apiece to Washington. Similarly, though the US Senate these days hardly resembles its claim to be the "world's greatest deliberative body," it does retain some semblance of its role as a legislative "cooling saucer," as George Washington once imagined it. Even amid the endless filibusters, the obstructionism on confirming judges, the shameless impeachment acquittals, and the grandstanding, the Senate often manages to rise above the tawdry antics that so frequently occupy the House, if only through sheer patrician arrogance. The thought of a unicameral legislature consisting only of the Ringling Brothers–like House of Representatives is not enticing.

Still, that does not redress the inherent racial inequity that the Senate represents. Mystal makes what he calls "a pretty educated guess that the overwhelming majority of senators will continue to be white, even as the country browns." Of the almost two thousand people who have served as US Senators over the past 234 years, a grand total of twelve have been Black, and only three of those were women. "You can't reform a system that is committed to whiteness," he concludes, or "overcome the structural geographic advantages the Senate gives to white voters."[43]

EXPAND THE HOUSE

Unlike the Senate, reform of the House calls for just the opposite: expansion.

As Harvard Professor Danielle Allen, a political theorist and director of the Edmond and Lily Safra Center for Ethics, explains, until 1929, the size of the US House of Representatives was adjusted with each decennial census, a system provided for by the Founders themselves. However, that year it was capped at 435, meaning that representation in that body has grown increasingly disproportionate with each passing year. As a result, the slight edge that the Constitution originally gave less populous states has turned into a significant one, and the chances of a disconnect between the popular vote and the Electoral College have risen.[44] It's no coincidence that of the five times that this has happened, two have been in the past twenty years. And that imbalance will only worsen going forward.

Allen actually opposes abolishing the Electoral College, believing that there is value in giving less populous states some additional protection in a federal system, but not nearly as much as the current system does. An expansion of the House would address both issues. The new number of House seats she proposes is actually quite modest—585—with future expansions pegged to the cube root of the national population.[45] To blunt gerrymandering would require a simple tripling of the current number of seats, to 1,305. Each party would also have representatives from every state, which is not the case now, making for healthier and fairer deliberation.[46]

Almost all other advanced democracies adjust the size of their parliaments periodically, and many of them have larger legislative bodies than we do, even though they have smaller populations.[47] The Founders' original design for the House aimed for a ratio of one representative for every 30,000 constituents.[48] Today that average is about one per 762,000, heading towards one per million by 2050.[49] Expanding the House would address all three issues in one elegant swoop.

REFORM THE SUPREME COURT

Not too long ago, the Supreme Court was the governmental institution that Americans held in the highest esteem, as a body both impartial and above politics.[50] No more. In September 2022 Gallup reported that public faith in the Court had fallen to its lowest point in the history of that poll, with just 40 percent approving of its performance, and only 47 percent expressing trust in the judicial branch at large.[51]

In particular, the nomination and confirmation processes, once admirably nonpartisan and dedicated to putting the best possible jurists on the bench, have turned into something more like professional wrestling, rocking faith in the integrity of the Court, and by extension, the moral force of its decisions. Mitch McConnell's outrageous refusal even to meet with Merrick Garland in 2016, let alone hold confirmation hearings for him, was among the most egregious examples of Republican perversion of that system. Joe Biden was able to put Justice Ketanji Brown-Jackson on the Court in 2022 thanks to a slim Democratic majority in the US Senate, but in the context of current Republican obstructionism, where no wins are ever conceded to the other side, it seems unlikely that a GOP-controlled Senate will ever again confirm the Supreme Court nominee of a Democratic president under any conditions.

It is especially enraging that three—count 'em, *three*—of the six justices that comprise the archconservative supermajority on the US Supreme Court—fully a third of the entire Court—were put there by Donald Trump, the most openly criminal president in US history.[52] That supermajority has wasted no time in flexing its muscles in a series of decisions that fly in the face of the prevailing desires of the American people—on abortion, on guns, on religious freedom, on the environment, on affirmative action—clearly announcing that the Court intends to take the US back to a nineteenth-century vision of the republic. The party that once decried what it called "judicial activism" (when practiced by Democrats) sure has turned out to be keen on engaging in it itself.[53]

To be clear: the Court bucking public opinion is not necessarily, in and of itself, wrong. In 1954, when the Court ruled in *Brown v. Board of Education* that segregation was unconstitutional, it was rejecting the view of millions of racist Americans. Throughout the tenure of the Warren Court, SCOTUS was consistently ahead of public opinion on matters of civil rights. What I am arguing for is not an end to judicial activism, only reforms to the Supreme Court that would give progressive ideas a fighting chance, rather than have them strangled in the cradle by an archconservative supermajority that cheated its way there in the first place, and now feels gleefully unconstrained in its power to remake America along the retrograde lines that it favors.

Expanding the Court—"packing it," in the pejorative, New Deal-era term—is an obvious solution. The Constitution does not mandate the number of justices, which has varied from as few as five to as many as ten over the course of American history. The right shrieks in outrage at the very thought.[54] But, as with the Electoral College, no thinking person can doubt that, were the situation reversed, and if a Republican administration were faced with a 6-3 progressive supermajority enacting policies that it abhors, a Republican president would not hesitate for a moment to add four (or more) new justices to the Court—public outcry, opposition, and optics be damned.

Yes, expanding the Court risks an arms race, as some conservatives have warned.[55] (In this case, they are not wrong, merely announcing their own plans). But not taking aggressive steps to reform the Court simply because we fear the Republican countermeasures is a self-destructive kind of timidity. The GOP has already destroyed the Supreme Court as we once knew it. Efforts we now take to reform and salvage the Court will not make it worse.

However, there are other measures short of court-packing that are also advisable.

One proposal is to rotate the nine seats by lottery from the pool of roughly 170 federal appeals judges who have already been confirmed by the Senate for that lower court.[56] Another would be to give the justices themselves a say, although letting six right-wing ideologues decide which other right-wing ideologues should join their club is not particularly appealing. During the 2020 primaries, Pete Buttigieg—like the former McKinsey consultant he is—proposed a fifteen-member Court, with ten justices equally divided between the two parties and five more chosen by that ten.[57] Yet another proposal is to eliminate the Senate's role in the process altogether, and simply let the president place his or her nominees on the Court by fiat.[58] That would make a Supreme Court justice subject to less scrutiny and checks and balances than a US Marshal or an undersecretary of transportation. But then again, so is a US President.

All those solutions, convoluted as they are, seem preferable to the current, calcified, hyperpartisan arrangement and the toxic environment in which it operates.

The terms of an appointment are also in play. The US is the only advanced democracy whose Supreme Court justices are subject to neither term limits nor a mandatory retirement age.[59] Both parties have therefore taken to choosing the youngest nominees possible, tending to pass over some of our nation's most distinguished jurists in favor of more youthful but less accomplished ones. Today a justice appointed to the Supreme Court at age fifty-three, like Brett Kavanaugh, or fifty-one, like Ketanji-Brown Jackson, or forty-nine, like Neil Gorsuch, or forty-five, like Amy Coney Barrett, can expect to spend four decades there. The notion of term limits—say, ten or even twenty years—therefore seems reasonable.

A less dramatic but still important reform is the establishment of a binding code of ethics, something lower courts operate under—as do employees of almost every other federal agency—but which the Supreme Court never had or needed. The justices had always policed themselves under a fungible honor system, deciding on their own, for example, whether to recuse themselves from cases or not. But that changed in 2023, after ProPublica reported on Samuel Alito's undisclosed fishing vacations and trips on the private jet of a billionaire Republican donor,[60] and Clarence Thomas's similarly undisclosed ties to another billionaire Republican benefactor who paid his grandnephew's tuition and bought his mother's house.[61] In an earlier era, those revelations would likely have prompted bipartisan demands for their immediate resignation. So might Mrs. Thomas's role in trying to overturn the 2020 election even as her husband ruled on cases related to it.[62] The two scandal-ridden justices might even—perish the thought—have voluntarily stepped down, out of what used to be called "shame." But in the current climate, it was only ProPublica's reporting, and the resulting pressure from Congress, that prompted John Roberts to announce that the Supreme Court would henceforth adopt a binding code of ethics—a proper response, but also an embarrassing admission of how corrupt the Court had become. Just how binding it proves to be remains an open question, but initial indicators are not good.

Of course, the state of the Supreme Court is not the only judicial crisis we face: the broader right-wing domination of the American judiciary must also be countered, a project that will require the same decades-long diligence, patience, and determination that the right showed in securing that domination in the first place. In the long term, despite the Federalist Society's vast head start, seeding the judiciary with progressive judges will both improve the court system at all levels and create a broader pool of potential high court nominees.[63]

The Court will surely resist all these measures, as will its patrons in the GOP—indeed, it is already doing so. No matter. As Naomi Klein writes: "The first rule of an emergency is that you do what it takes to end the emergency and get to safety. You don't throw up your hands because the task is too hard. You certainly don't let a gang of unelected, lifetime appointed political operatives—several of whom only have their seats because of trickery and lies—get in your way."[64]

AMERICAN EXCEPTIONALISM: THE BAD KIND

In their 2023 book *Tyranny of the Minority*, Levitsky and Ziblatt note that over the past century, almost every other advanced democracy has instituted the exact kinds of reforms we have just listed: proportional representation in parliament, dissolution of the upper chamber, an end to the filibuster, judicial term limits, abolition of an electoral college.[65]

Part of the problem, they note, is that the US Constitution, the first of its kind, served as a model for the rest of the world, but is also one of the hardest to amend. "With the Republican Party's transformation into an extremist and antidemocratic force under Donald Trump, the Constitution now protects and empowers an authoritarian minority."[66]

"All liberal democracies have *some* countermajoritarian institutions to stop popular passions from running roughshod over minority rights," *The New York Times*'s Michelle Goldberg writes. "But as *Tyranny of the Minority* shows, our system is unique in the way it empowers a minority ideological faction at the expense of everyone else. And while conservatives like to pretend that their structural advantages arise from the judicious wisdom of the founders, Levitsky and Ziblatt demonstrate how many of the least democratic aspects of American governance are the result of accident, contingency and, not least, capitulation to the slaveholding South."[67]

All the more reason to fix them.

CHAPTER 7

Systemic Reforms (Two)

There are numerous other actions we could take before the autocracy descends upon us, in hopes of forestalling that fate. Congressional Republicans have been adept at exploiting the tools available to the minority and monkeywrenching from within, for vile ends; Democrats may need to do the same for the sake of the common good. The pushback will no doubt be immediate. Republicans who brazenly defied subpoenas by the House Select Committee on January 6, for example, will no doubt rediscover their belief in the sanctity of such mechanisms and scream bloody murder if Democrats mimic their behavior. Get ready to hear lots of drivel about lawlessness and disrespect for the Constitution from people who themselves treated that Constitution like Charmin.

Would a descent to the Republicans' tactics render us just as bad as they are, and destroy the village we are trying to save? It's a risk. But the huts are already ablaze; the greater risk is doing nothing and letting the GOP burn it all down while we watch.

MAKE NEW STATES

If the Electoral College and Senate are not going to be eliminated, statehood for the District of Columbia and Puerto Rico are only logical in order to give proper representation to almost four million American citizens who currently have no voice in Congress. There have also been proposals for populous blue states to split, like a blackjack hand. If a reliably Democratic state like California were to break in two, it would double its number of senators, and gain two electoral votes in the process. (And if California, Oregon, and Washington were all to split, they would have twelve senators among them rather than six, and their collective seventy-four electoral votes would become eighty.[1]) Of course, red states could also split and increase their representation in the same way. Before long an arms race would likely ensue, resulting in a country of hundreds of states, some with smaller populations than a Taylor Swift concert.

However, statehood for the District of Columbia and Puerto Rico remains viable and would help address the imbalance in the Senate. This would also offer a more accurate representation of the American population and provide agency for millions of citizens who currently have none. In the Electoral College, it would help balance the scales by adding Puerto Rico's likely seven electoral votes and DC's three. If someday Puerto Rico and the District of Columbia were to turn red and tilt the Senate and EC to the GOP, so be it: that is how democracy is supposed to work.

CHANGE THE DEMOGAPHICS

If making new states is too extreme, another idea is to alter the make-up of the current fifty.

Let us return to the bright red state of Wyoming, with its tiny population of only about 576,851 residents, according to the 2020 census—less than the city of Memphis, Tennessee.[2] In the 2020 presidential election, about 267,000 of those Wyomingites voted, going for Trump by roughly 70 percent to Biden's 26.6 percent.[3] It would therefore take the migration of only about 130,000 registered Democrats to turn that state blue.

Suppose a progressive-minded tech company—a Google, an Amazon, a Microsoft—were to set up a major facility in Cheyenne and move 50,000 employees and their families there. Of course, we could not assume that all of those people would be Democrats, but a fair number would be. And they would attract more of them. The attendant influx of baristas, bicycle repairmen, and brie merchants alone would account for a notable progressive uptick.

Flipping even one small red state like Wyoming would move three electoral votes reliably into the blue column.*

---

*   At least one such movement already exists, albeit a right-leaning one. In 2001, the Free State Project was founded to encourage 20,000 libertarians to move to New Hampshire in order to transform that state. Some 6,000 have signed up over that twenty-year period.

As it happens, such demographic shifts are already underway organically, with Americans migrating from urban blue states—where the cost of living tends to be high—to less expensive red ones, a pattern exacerbated by the COVID-19 pandemic and its aftermath.[4] It is not at all clear that this movement of souls will have the effect of tilting the vote in those red states instead of chipping away at the Democratic advantage in the blue states that are losing residents.

A somewhat more prosaic approach, but perhaps a more practical one, is to move the margins in purple states. Texas (with a whopping thirty-eight electoral votes), Georgia (with sixteen), and Arizona (with eleven) are all formerly red states that have recently moved into the toss-up column, with the last two both sending a pair of Democratic senators apiece to Washington in successive elections. Lobbying, consciousness-raising, voter registration drives, and get-out-the-vote campaigns have made the difference. It is grinding, unglamorous work, but time and again it has shown results.

A permanent shift in one or more of these states would have a profound impact on presidential races. Obviously, states can go the other direction as well, the prime example being Florida, which flipped from being at the center of several tight presidential races— memorably, in 2000—to a reliable Republican bastion in 2016, 2020, and the 2022 midterms.[5]

MOBILIZE THE BASE

Making new states and flipping the color of existing ones are flashy proposals. A more mundane—but possibly more practical—idea is to shore up Democratic constituencies within existing boundaries and restore those that have been lost. I spoke about this topic with Jim Bernfield, a campaign strategist who has spent twenty-five years working to elect Democrats at all levels, from presidents, governors, and senators to mayors, judges, and members of Congress.

"I don't think the Party lost its traditional white, working-class voters due to neglect," he told me. "For forty-five years the Republicans did everything they could to separate the Democrats from white male voters, at the same time that urban Democratic political machines were dying and the economy and culture was changing. White male voters were relatively simple to co-opt by the GOP."[6] Max Brooks, author of *The Zombie Survival Guide* and *World War Z*, agrees. (Who better than an expert on the zombie apocalypse to talk about the Republican apocalypse?) "Whenever you take any group and you leave them in the wasteland, somebody will come get them," he told me. "That's just basic history. If the Czar is not addressing the needs of his people, the Bolsheviks will. The Taliban came to power because Afghanistan was an absolute post-apocalyptic wasteland when the Soviets left. Humans are innately afraid of the future—that's just how we're wired. We crave order and answers and we'll take a lie over silence any day."[7]

"If they want to, I believe the Democrats can win back white working-class men," Bernfield said, citing CHIPS, the Infrastructure Investment and Jobs Act, and the Inflation Reduction Act as steps in the right direction. "It's a long game, but providing struggling working-class Americans with real opportunity is what cemented the New Deal as foundational to American policy and politics for a generation."[8]

It would be nice to think that a powerful weapon against autocracy is actual policy that makes a difference in people's lives and bonds them to democracy, rather than driving them to dangerous and illusory alternatives. But it is a cruel reality that even major policy achievements by Democrats and substantive programs that help ordinary Americans often have little electoral impact. Economists report that "Bidenomics," as it has come to be known, actually helps those in red states more than those in blue ones, even as many of those red voters demonize its originator, and even as Republican politicians take credit for benefits that they voted against.[9] But Bernfield remains philosophical: "If people can't see that the government did something positive for them coming out of that, then we've lost the ability to impact politics by doing good work."[10]

The flipside of the perennial Democratic hand-wringing over the loss of its white voters is the risk of losing its Black ones by taking them for granted.

Black women in particular put Democrats in the White House for several administrations in a row.[11] But you can't ignore (or at least underserve) a segment of the population and then every four years turn up pleading that the country is in existential crisis and beg that segment to save it. "We have to say to the Democratic Party that you can't just count on our vote," as the longtime civil rights activist Zoharah Simmons told me.[12]

It would be foolish and arrogant to presume that Black voters will always pull the Democratic lever and can't be wooed into the GOP fold, as significant numbers of Latinx voters recently have. It would defy reason on almost every level, but the Republicans have long ago proven their uncanny ability to get people to vote against their own self-interest.

"You've got to give people something that they care about," said Bernfield. "If they're not turning out, it's because they feel like what you're offering them is bullshit. Don't ask the Black community to pull white folks out of the fire. Create a world where they matter."[13]

ENACT CAMPAIGN FINANCE REFORM

Money was poisoning American politics long before *Citizens United v. Federal Election Commission*, but that 2010 ruling by the US Supreme Court, decided 5-4 by the Republican majority, took matters to a new level.

In an instance of mind-blowing naivete by allegedly smart people, the justices ruled that unlimited political expenditures by corporations would not corrupt the political process or sway elected officials.[*] "The appearance of influence or access . . . will not cause the electorate to lose faith in our democracy," Anthony Kennedy wrote for the majority. "By definition, an independent expenditure is political speech presented to the electorate that is not coordinated with a candidate.'"[14] Unless that was an instance not of mind-blowing naivete at all, but of blood-boiling deceit.

Contrary to the confident assurances of Mr. Kennedy and his conservative colleagues, *Citizens United* instead opened the door to an unprecedented deluge of money in US politics and its corrupting

---

* Later that year, an appeals court expanded the decision to allow political action committees to accept unlimited contributions under the same conditions, giving birth to the concept of the super PAC, as well as hybrid PACs, which can function in either manner.

influence.[15] Along with *Shelby and Dobbs*, it may have been one of the worst and most damaging decisions ever handed down by the Court, joining the dubious ranks of *Plessy v. Ferguson, Dred Scott v. Sandford, Buck v. Bell, Korematsu v. United States*, and *DC v. Heller.*

Election-related spending from super PACs and other independent groups reached $4.5 billion over the decade that followed, a twelve-fold increase over the previous twenty years. Of that, dark money contributions reached $963 million, an eightfold increase.[16] As the nonpartisan research group Open Secrets reports, "Conservative groups, such as Karl Rove's Crossroads GPS and the Koch brothers-backed Americans for Prosperity, dominated the dark money game, accounting for 86 percent of outside spending from these groups."[17] And not surprisingly, as Open Secrets reports, "The candidate with more money wins more often than not."[18]

Both parties have long been beholden to wealthy and powerful private interests, but only the Republican Party has made a religion of it, fervently arguing that "corporations are people" and that "money is speech." But even free speech has limits. Just as one cannot shout "Fire!" in a crowded movie theater, nor engage in slander or hate speech that aims to incite violence, it would be similarly foolhardy to let a certain kind of political speech—the kind that devours all other speech—run rampant out of some misguided First Amendment absolutism. Yet *Citizens United* and similar decisions attach no restrictions whatsoever, such that those with great wealth can overwhelm all other voices.

To make matters worse, *Citizens United* does not even require those who are speaking with their wallets to identify themselves. As Open Secrets explains, "Although super PACs are required to disclose their donors, that information doesn't go beyond the name and address of a nonprofit or company, in many cases leaving the true source of money hidden."[19] Corporate structures are often opaque by their nature, so not only can wealthy individuals and corporations pour money into political campaigns and lobbying efforts on a scale that less well-resourced citizens and organizations cannot begin to match, but they can do so in utter secrecy.

Even if fully transparent campaign finance disclosures were mandated by law, the mere fact of massive spending to influence public opinion—and to buy the indebtedness of our elected officials—would remain a severe threat to participatory democracy. Four years after *Citizens*, in *McCutcheon v. FEC*, the Supreme Court lifted limits on how much an individual donor could give to candidates and parties, guilelessly ignoring the danger of bribery and quid pro quos. Chief Justice John Roberts actually argued that it was not the government's purview to "target the general gratitude a candidate may feel toward those who support him or his allies, or the political access such support may afford."[20]

That is not even naivete by any measure, but rather, its opposite: a bright green light for officially endorsed graft and corruption.

"I don't begrudge the wealthy their wealth," the economist Darrick Hamilton, a professor at the New School, told Justin Schein and me for our documentary *Death and Taxes*. "What is problematic is the political power that their wealth allows them to wield in an undemocratic way."[21]

Recently, Americans have been giving to political candidates in record numbers, with small donors becoming critical to many campaigns.[22] But a single rich donor can dwarf them all, whether it's George Soros and Mike Bloomberg for the Democrats or Richard Uihlein and the late Sheldon Adelson for the Republicans.[23] Bloomberg's giving jumped from less than $1 million pre-*Citizens United* to $163 million afterward. But Adelson and his wife, Miriam, make Mike look miserly, with donations totaling $306 million in that same decade. Open Secrets reports that "even among super PAC donors, a tiny minority accounts for most of the money. The top 1 percent of super PAC donors accounted for 96 percent of funding to these groups in 2018."[24]

And it's not about to stop. Since the firehose was turned on in 2010, no effort to crank it shut—such as the For the People Act, defeated by Republican filibusters—has come even close to succeeding. Meanwhile, the FEC has never penalized anyone for skirting the rules to support a specific candidate by means of an outside group that is not supposed to coordinate with a given campaign.[25] In August 2022, a new right-wing lobby group called the Marble Freedom Trust, organized by Leonard Leo, was the recipient of a record-breaking donation of $1.6 billion from an anonymous donor—by some accounts, the largest single donation of that kind in

American history.[26] In a ferocious irony, such a donation was possible—and legal—only because of *Citizens United*, which the Federalist Society itself worked so hard to engineer. As a result, Leo and the Federalists will now have even more power in our legal system, an ouroboros-like infinite loop of right-wing American political corruption.

Thus, we are led to a sentence that is in the running for understatement of the year: overturning *Citizens United* and putting in place common sense regulations on the role of money in American politics would be an enormous benefit to our democracy, from which a great many other improvements would naturally flow.

Public financing of elections, the system that many other countries employ, wouldn't solve all these problems, but it would obviate a great many of them. Nor would it be easy to implement—witness the public option for health care, or the animosity to funding public education—but it would be easier than some of the other proposals that have been put forward, including many in this chapter. Short of that, legislation to limit the damage of *Citizens United*, and to place common sense restrictions on unregulated spending in political campaigns, would do a world of good.

When it comes to making one's voice heard, the wealthy will almost always be louder than anyone else. But to allow the rich to use their money to influence the electoral system in the most extreme and obscene manner, and to buy the loyalty of the so-called public servants who arise out of it, is a recipe for democratic self-destruction.

FORCE FAIRNESS ON THE MEDIA, KIND OF

Like the flood of money into politics, the rise of hyperpartisan news is a blight on society, and its destructive effects are self-evident.

Beginning in 1949, the Fairness Doctrine required TV broadcasters to offer opposing views on a given issue deemed in the public interest, as the FCC recognized the power of this new medium to shape the national discourse. There was some subjectivity in play over what constituted "the public interest," but the rule nevertheless prevented television networks from becoming unconstrained propaganda machines for any particular political party or point of view.

Since the doctrine's abolition by the FCC in 1987, we have seen the rise of highly tribal broadcast networks, the chief example of course being Fox, founded in 1996 by Roger Ailes, who had been Richard Nixon's television guru in his successful 1968 presidential run and who was later a top advisor to Reagan and George H.W. Bush. Today, Fox—as it never ceases boasting—is the most watched news network in the country, and one that spreads lies as part of its everyday remit.

The restoration of the Fairness Doctrine would radically reshape the landscape of American broadcast journalism for the better. But of course, when it comes to the power to manipulate minds, today we also must contend with the Internet, a Charles Atlas that makes TV look like a ninety-eight-pound weakling brushing sand off its face. No Fairness Doctrine could possibly police the net, whose sheer scope allows us to wallow in the warm bath of partisan discourse without the pesky bother of opposing views. The rise of tech and social media therefore presents a new paradigm for which preexisting protocols do not yet exist.

Since 2016 we have been made painfully aware of how social media can be co-opted by those with ill intent and how incredibly specific it can be in targeting any given population—or individual—with relentless, granularly tailored propaganda. The role of Cambridge Analytica in the election of Trump and in Brexit are two prime examples: both incredibly sophisticated, military-style psychological operations on a massive scale, relying on data harvested from tens of millions of largely unwitting citizens. The human brain is simply not evolutionarily wired to withstand this onslaught, and it's doubtful any adaptation to withstand it is happening fast enough.

In her 2022 memoir, the Filipina journalist and Nobel Peace Prize winner Maria Ressa, who was viciously attacked by her country's own despotic president, offers a blistering critique of Facebook, which she calls "one of the gravest threats to democracies around the world."[27] Ressa's book is rightly called *How to Stand Up to a Dictator*, but the dictator isn't Duterte—it's Mark Zuckerberg.

"Tech sucked up our personal experiences and data, organized it with artificial intelligence, manipulated us with it, and created behavior at a scale that brought out the worst in humanity," Ressa writes. "We all let it happen."[28]

Like many, Ressa was initially very bullish on the revolutionary journalistic possibilities of new media. In fact, *Rappler*, the innovative, woman-owned and run online news site she founded, was closely partnered with Facebook itself, until she realized how this new technology could be weaponized by the worst possible actors, and done with Facebook's eager assent and facilitation.

"Before I worked on the January 6 Committee," Tim Heaphy told me, "I didn't appreciate how many people in this country get their information exclusively through social media platforms. People who read *The New York Times* and listen to NPR every day are in the minority. Most Americans are getting their news from links in their increasingly siloed social media ecosystems."[29]

"QAnon was largely fueled by these algorithms and these affinity groups," Heaphy said, "and there's very little content moderation from the platforms. They explicitly say, 'We don't stand behind the veracity of this.'"[30] But the refusal of social media companies to moderate dangerous and deceitful content goes beyond merely trying not to alienate any potential customers—Michael Jordan's principle that "Republicans buy sneakers too."[31] Their algorithms read their users' usage and actively promote provocative content, pumping out that information with terrifying precision, and tending to amplify the worst voices.

When Facebook first emerged, who could have predicted that this silly divertissement for gossiping with your friends and looking at funny cat videos would turn into a malevolent multinational behemoth, mining our brains like the machines in *The Matrix* and threatening global democracy itself? Only the same people who foresaw that a vulgar, stubby-fingered game show host, D-list celebrity wannabe, and walking *Spy* magazine punchline best known for leching after teenage beauty contestants would become a dictator-in-waiting with an army of violent followers who would disrupt the 224-year tradition of peaceful transfers of power. Indeed, the two worked hand in hand very well, a pair of jokes that turned into urgent, hair-on-fire dangers to humanity worldwide.[32]

"Facebook, and the politicians benefiting from it, know full well the harms they are unleashing on the public," Ressa writes. "They are, by design, dividing us and radicalizing us—because spreading anger and hatred is better for Facebook's business."[33]

Clearly, Internet platforms are not the neutral bulletin boards that the tech companies pretend. But by their very nature, neither are they perfectly analogous to traditional publishers and broadcast media, and there is little agreement on the kind of governmental regulations that would make the web a better place without destroying what is unique and socially beneficial or infringing on freedom of expression. Unlike conventional "legacy" media, the interactive nature of social media makes it not only a place where disinformation and propaganda can spread, but also one where violent extremists can recruit and organize. Accordingly, tech companies must dispense with their disingenuous, shoulder-shrugging abdication of responsibility for the content they allow on their platforms and cease serving as breeding grounds for hate speech, incitement to violence, and cyberattacks from hostile foreign actors. If Facebook, Twitter, TikTok, WhatsApp, and other social media behemoths will not police themselves, the US government must regulate them. Ironically, this is one of the few areas in which left and right find some common ground, even though each thinks the other is the beneficiary of Big Tech's bias.[34]

AND THERE'S MORE

There are other basic changes that would improve American politics, such as merely making election day a holiday.[35] So would changes to the primary system, which has only figured prominently in US presidential elections since 1968.[36] As Fareed Zakaria writes, unlike a general election, where candidates must appeal to the widest possible swath of the electorate and moderation is typically an asset, "primaries ensure that the candidates chosen are selected by slivers of the parties—around 20 percent of all eligible voters, often far more extreme in their views than run-of-the-mill registered Republicans or Democrats."[37] Thanks to gerrymandering, those candidates are also frequently in "safe seats," where the opposing party has virtually no chance of winning, and "the only threat to them is a primary candidate who is even more extreme."

That dynamic is particularly dangerous in states without open primaries, even though open primaries themselves invite mischief. A simple and elegant solution to both problems would be ranked choice voting, in which voters list candidates in order of preference, thereby minimizing the impact of extremist and spoiler candidates, reducing toxic campaigning, and delivering results more representative of the will of the electorate than a "first past the post" system. In 2022, for example, Alaska's first foray into ranked choice voting resulted in the Democratic candidate for governor beating both GOP opponents—including Sarah Palin—in a state that for its entire history had been as Republican as any in the Union.[38] Instituted nationwide, ranked choice elections might remake the face of American politics dramatically.

Eliminating the debt ceiling would also constitute a massive improvement to American governance. Once a routine rubber stamp authorizing the United States to pay its bills, the congressional vote to raise the debt limit has been seized upon by the GOP as a means of blackmailing Democratic presidents.[39] Get rid of it, either by legislation, or by invoking Section 4 of the Fourteenth Amendment, which states that "The validity of the public debt of the United States, authorized by law . . . shall not be questioned." Will Republicans throw a hissy fit and mount legal challenges to that effort? You bet. Let them. We have lawyers too.

Another area of focus is the simple matter of political engagement.

"You have to play the long game the same way the Republicans have," Max Brooks told me. "Since 1932 they have been training up generations of lawyers and politicians and—more importantly—staffers. We don't do what they do, which is sit in tiny little rooms with no windows and fluorescent lights and do their homework: on statehouses, on lower court judges, on the Fairness Doctrine, on obscure little tax codes that change everything, on all these things that have elevated the Republicans to power."[40]

A re-dedication to the grinding, unsung aspects of politics, beginning at the local level, is entirely up to us, and can have a significant impact. It is also something over which the forces of antidemocracy have no say.

So long as free elections remain in play, ballot initiatives—especially those proposed by groups of private citizens—are another effective exercise of pure, direct democracy that can outflank partisanship and the designs of the powerful but ill-willed. "In every state where elected Republicans have attempted to undermine democracy, it's ballot initiatives that have countered that," an individual active in Democratic politics told me on condition of anonymity. "That's the way that you get around these gerrymandered, partisan, and honestly, non-representative politics: you allow the citizens to vote on issues directly."[41]

There is no better example of the power of ballot initiatives than on abortion. In the wake of *Dobbs*, the citizens of numerous states voted to protect abortion access, or at the very least to turn back efforts to further limit or criminalize it, even in Republican strongholds like Kansas, Kentucky, Missouri, Montana, and Ohio. "You see it over and over again," that individual told me. "If you put something that is immensely popular on the ballot, it will pass, even in a deep red state."[42]

That Democratic operative pointed out that ballot initiatives have also worked for the expansion of Medicaid and for criminal justice reform, even in a place like Florida, one of only a handful of states where a felony conviction came with a lifetime forfeiture of the right to vote, even after time served. But in 2018 Florida voters overwhelmingly repealed that law. Since then, the Republican state legislature has instituted a de facto poll tax—a requirement for full financial restitution, which is difficult to calculate and even harder to fulfill—that keeps most former inmates permanently disenfranchised.[43] But such GOP countermeasures will always be with us. Ballot measures remain one of the purest ways that the citizenry can push back.

"Republicans can use ballot initiatives too, but the policies they want are not popular. You can't get a ballot initiative restricting abortion access to pass even in a red state like Ohio, but you can get one to *expand* abortion access. It's one more democratic tool they're trying to get rid of."[44]

CHAPTER 8

Broader-Based Efforts

The previous two chapters addressed formal actions related to the American electoral system and the institutions that surround it. Now let us turn to a handful of more amorphous areas where we can shore up democracy that do not involve the mechanisms of government, per se, but are no less crucial.

DISRUPT DOMESTIC TERRORISM

It would severely disrupt the autocratic project if one of its chief prongs—vigilante violence, or the threat thereof—were effectively suppressed. Tim Heaphy described for me two things that came out of the January 6 Committee's work that he believes are essential to do that. One, as we have already discussed, is the need for law enforcement to take a rigorous look at its own bias and begin to recognize that white people waving Confederate flags and carrying AR-15s and talking about revolution pose a lethal danger, not just Black people driving down the road with a broken taillight. The other is the question of proactive defense.

"We keep getting this wrong," Heaphy told me, "where we have intelligence in advance that specifically suggests violence, and lots of resources and bodies available, but we don't fully operationalize that intelligence into a plan that adequately protects people, or in the case of January 6, the Capitol."[1] Heaphy faults a lack of communication among law enforcement agencies, but also self-imposed restrictions on information-gathering. "The FBI will not take any action based on open-source intelligence unless that intelligence in and of itself rises to the level of—in the language of the Bureau—sufficiently specific and credible to open a preliminary investigation.

They don't go knock on the door and say, 'We see that you posted on Facebook that January 6 is 1776 with a picture of you and an AK-47.' They're not wrong to have concerns about infringing on free association, based on their awful history of spying on people in this country. It's just a question of where to draw the line with respect to taking action."[2]

The US military must also root out radicalism within its ranks. In December 2021, three retired Army generals—Paul Eaton, Antonio Taguba, and Steven Anderson—published an op-ed in *The Washington Post* noting the alarming number of veterans and even active-duty service members among the insurrectionists on January 6, as well as acting Defense Secretary Chris Miller's deliberate withholding of military protection of the Capitol ahead of that day. They also raised the specter of the armed forces taking sides in a future election.[3]

But catching extremists before they can carry out acts of violence is the last line of defense. A far better plan is to keep them from being radicalized in the first place. The campaign against autocracy, not only in the military but throughout the general populace, will ultimately be won in the information space, where it will be necessary to eradicate the appeal of right-wing radicalism to any significant swath of the public. In that sense, the door-kicking-and-handcuffing phase of law enforcement and intelligence operations is subordinate to the broader campaign to win hearts and minds, and to sway the American people toward a positive vision of democracy, rather than a dark and twisted perversion of it.

"In my view, the fundamental division in this country is no longer left versus right," Heaphy told me. "It's those who are invested in the social contract and those who reject it. That, to me, is the core conflict we face. These are people that don't believe in government, that don't believe in the media, that don't believe in science, that don't believe in institutions on which others rely. Trump didn't create that. He surfed that to power, and it isn't going anywhere. Even if he is put to rest politically, that same stuff will still be present."[4]

HOLD THE BASTARDS ACCOUNTABLE

There is disrupting political violence before it happens, and then there is punishing it after it has done so.

A social system cannot function if it doesn't hold criminals accountable for their crimes. We have done it with rank-and-file seditionists who beat police officers and stormed the Capitol and spread excrement in its halls—it is even more imperative to take on those who spurred them to those deeds, and who continue to urge them on to even worse. If there are no significant consequences for the leader of an attack on the US Capitol and an attempt to murder the vice president and sitting members of Congress, it will only embolden the perpetrators of those acts going forward and inspire others. No sane country would let a high-powered group of its citizens attempt a violent coup d'état—led by a deposed head of state no less—without consequences, unless that country was keen to have them do it again.

To the extent that they admit Trump did anything wrong at all, Republicans argue for giving him a pass on the grounds that America needs "unity," and that holding him accountable will somehow prevent us from "healing" and "moving on."

Andrew McCarthy, a former federal prosecutor turned contributing editor at the pro-Trump *National Review*, took this position, arguing that while "no one is above the law, even the president . . . neither do we prosecute every provable crime. Other considerations often apply, such as preserving domestic tranquility and institutional integrity."[5]

Appeals for "unity" usually come from the guilty in an attempt to escape repercussions for their misdeeds. Cries for Biden and the Democrats to heal the breach are also ironic coming from the party that plunged this country into some of the most bitterly contentious years in contemporary American history under the thumb of the most hateful, bigoted, and divisive president in modern times, who even now continues to insist that the Biden administration isn't legitimate, and is readying its hockey sticks and fire extinguishers (and guns) for the next attack on the federal government.

Even some Democrats and independents have been in favor of leniency, including calls for Biden to pardon Trump in the interest of this "national healing."[6] Michael Conway, counsel for the House Judiciary Committee during Watergate, argued that a pardon would free Biden from allegations of pursuing a partisan vendetta, unlike

Trump, who wanted to jail his political enemies, and was unable to do so only because they'd committed no crimes (the clever bastards).[7] But Republicans certainly never care about the bad optics of their actions, and leaving prosecutions to the DOJ, without White House interference—as Biden has done, notwithstanding Republican lies to the contrary—accomplishes the same thing while still allowing justice to be done. More to the point, Trump's fans would cheer a pardon as exoneration, and weakness by the Democrats, encouraging further wrongdoing in the future without fear of consequences.

Many conservatives, *National Review*'s McCarthy among them, ultimately dismiss all the evidence against Trump as much ado about nothing, since a significant part of the country is cool with what he did.[8] In other words, since 30 percent of Americans believe the Big Lie, and that Trump was justified in trying to have his own vice president murdered, and that he had the right to steal top secret war plans and show them to people at his golf club, wouldn't it be better just to let him get away with it?[9]

Obviously, there are genuine banana republic–style pitfalls for an administration that pursues legal action against its predecessor. But when we are dealing with an attempted coup, the greater danger is not pursuing that action. The anxious Mr. Conway writes that "American democracy cannot tolerate the prosecution of political opponents."[10] But it can and should when they've committed unconscionable crimes. What American democracy cannot tolerate is looking the other way when violent, sadistic, openly corrupt kleptocrats hijack it, and then sitting on our hands and hoping it doesn't happen again.

Other advanced democracies have rightly prosecuted corrupt former heads of state without their republics collapsing, including Silvio Berlusconi, the proto-Trump Italian prime minister who was convicted of tax fraud by an Italian court in 2013, or Nicolas Sarkozy, the former French president who was convicted in two separate corruption cases by French courts in 2021. Two of the harshest punishments were in South Korea, which in 2018 convicted and imprisoned two successive ex-presidents—Lee Myung-bak and Park Geun-hye—for various corruption charges, sentencing them to fifteen and twenty-five years, respectively, after having previously convicted two other former presidents. That is not necessarily a model the US wants to emulate, but it is further evidence that other countries do not consider this sort of thing taboo. Peru has a special prison *just* for ex-presidents, with three of them incarcerated there currently.[11]

We've been here before, of course. When Gerald Ford pardoned Richard Nixon in 1974, the reasons he gave had to do with healing the nation and sparing the country further trauma and damage. (Try that logic the next time you're on trial for bank robbery.) I humbly submit that far from allowing us to move on from our "long national nightmare," Ford's excusal of Nixon's crimes, even if well-intentioned—and it's not clear that it was—did grievous harm.* It told America that you were a sucker if you played by the rules; that if you were rich and powerful enough, the laws didn't apply to you; that there was one set for those folks and another for the rest of us. It was a giant "fuck you" to ordinary Americans who were expected to obey the rules and could bet their bottom dollar that Johnny Law would come after them if they didn't.

In fact, Ford missed a tremendous opportunity to *reinforce* the rule of law, as it would have been Nixon's own party punishing him, rather than the opposition. Instead, Richard Nixon walked off into a well-feathered retirement distinguished by expensive homes in San Clemente and Upper Saddle River, lucrative book deals, and banquets thrown in his honor by his reactionary admirers. He never once admitted his crimes.

It will be even worse if we let Trump slide on crimes that make Nixon look like a jaywalker.

If Nixon had been prosecuted and punished for his crimes, how might it have altered the trajectory of the post-Watergate GOP? We can never know. But we do know that just six years after Nixon departed the South Lawn in *Marine One*, an even more right-wing Republican won the presidency, ushering in a conservative counter-revolution that continues to this day. Absent prosecution, the GOP

---

* Decades later, it emerged that Ford also acted out of what he told Bob Woodward was his friendship with Nixon, saying, "I looked upon him as my personal friend, and I always treasured our relationship, and I had no hesitancy about granting the pardon . . . I didn't want to see my real friend have the stigma."

was able to portray Nixon—at worst—as an unfortunate aberration rather than its natural result. Since then, the Republican Party has carried on with its unabashed grift of the American people, and has even been rewarded for its efforts.

We can go back even further, if we wish, to the 1869 decision not to proceed with trials of Jefferson Davis, Robert E. Lee, and thirty-eight other leading secessionists for fear of public furor, and concerns that the defendants would not be found guilty in the Southern states where the trials were scheduled to take place.[12] This abdication created, as the Civil War historian Elizabeth R. Varon writes, "the myth that the southern cause had been so noble that even the conquering northern armies had been forced to recognize it."[13] It is little wonder that Trump's apologists are making the same Br'er Rabbit argument now about the risks of prosecuting a former head of state.

The New York Times quotes former US Representative Tom Perriello of Virginia, who was a special advisor for the war crimes tribunal in Sierra Leone, that countries that have suffered national trauma and "skip the accountability phase end up repeating 100 percent of the time—but the next time the crisis is worse. People who think that the way forward is to brush this under the rug seem to have missed the fact that there is a ticking time bomb under the rug."[14]

Despite Donald Trump's lifelong lucky streak, he must answer for his sins, and so must his accomplices and enablers. If not, distrust in our democracy will only rise, and contempt will fester, and belief in the American experiment—already on life support—will wither and die. That is especially true as we continue to struggle with a violent domestic insurgency of pro-Trump fanatics . . . and a political party that represents them and is currently debating whether it wants to return to being merely obstructionist reactionaries or prefers to be the openly seditious party of lizard people hunters carrying guns on the floor of Congress and searching for Jewish space lasers.[15]

But there is another kind of accountability, a more abstract and intangible one. Masha Gessen recounts the early years of post-Soviet Russia, under Boris Yeltsin, when the country deliberately avoided a reckoning with the crimes and trauma of the USSR in that same sort of misplaced interest of healing, as well as reluctance to deal with the practical implications such a reckoning would unleash.[16] The result was that within a decade a new autocrat came to power. "The goal of reckoning," Gessen writes, "is moral restoration."[17] South Africa's Truth and Reconciliation Commission is a natural example, albeit one that grappled with a far greater and longer lasting crime.

The Back Row Manifesto's Tom Hall made this same point in the immediate aftermath of Trump's departure from office. "After years of gaslighting and the demolition of belief in the ability of our institutions to stand up to their debasement at the hands of Trump, we need more than just the truth," he told me. "Without a fundamental agreement about the impacts of Trumpist criminality on the country, and on us as a people, the will and pretexts for justice become impossible. How will we ever tell the truth about the past and build a future if there is no priority given to really grappling with trauma, with using every avenue to tell the story of what happened truthfully? That is the narrative that can deliver justice."[18]

DON'T BE INTIMIDATED

Like all bullies and cowards, Trumpists are seeking to intimidate us with threats of retribution. Lindsey Graham told Fox News that prosecution of Trump would lead to "riots in the streets," hiding behind the defense that it was a mere prediction and not a threat.[19] But Trump himself has said similar things, repeatedly, and without any pretense that his words were anything but a trumpet blast summoning his supporters to obey.[20]

Even before the indictments against Trump came down, *The Washington Post*'s Hannah Knowles quoted an anonymous GOP strategist sharing his fears "that this country could erupt in civil war."[21] So we're going to have a civil war because some people believe the president can do whatever the hell he wants—like a dictator, or a king—while others think that he ought to, ya know, obey the law? That is indeed a stark difference of opinion. But it's especially rich that the very voices warning us about the risks of civil war belong to the same conservative community that is recklessly fanning the flames of that war.

For nigh on seven years now we've been told how we must walk on eggshells lest we anger the great MAGA horde. Are we really going to back off these investigations and the pursuit of righteous account-ability for the people who tried to overturn a free and fair election because we're afraid it will *make them mad?*

Perhaps the best repudiation of this impulse toward timidity came from *The New York Times*'s Michelle Goldberg, in a piece called "The Absurd Argument Against Making Trump Obey the Law," in which she pointed out the bitter fruit of our failure to bring Trump to justice for his various deeds thus far:

> No doubt, Trump's most inflamed fans might act out in horrifying ways; many are heavily armed and speak lustily about civil war. To let this dictate the workings of justice is to accept an insurrectionists' veto. The far right is constantly threatening violence if it doesn't get its way. Does anyone truly believe that giving in to its blackmail will make it less aggressive? If we don't want the presidency to license crime sprees, we should allow presidents to be indicted, not accept some dubious norm that ex-presidents shouldn't be.[22]

Goldberg concludes that "those in charge of enforcing our laws should remember that the caterwauling of the Trump camp is designed to intimidate them . . . The only relevant question is whether he committed a crime, not what crimes his devotees might commit if he's held to account."[23]

When Senate Republicans declined to convict Trump over the Insurrection in his second impeachment, some of them—including Mitch McConnell—suggested that he could and should still be held to account in criminal and civil courts. Joining in this cowardly buck-passing was Senator Marco Rubio of Florida, who insisted that seeking accountability for an attempted coup would be "incredibly divisive," and endorsed the idea of a legal remedy instead.[24] Yet when FBI agents searched Mar-a-Lago in August 2022 in search of stolen government documents (such a politely exe-cuted event does not deserve the term "raid"), it prompted histri-onics on the right, where it was variously likened to the tactics of the Gestapo, the KGB, and Third World banana republics. The Biden administration was called "insidious monsters that have wrenched [the Republic] from the American People's control."[25]

There were calls to abolish the FBI, who were compared to Nazi "brownshirts."[26] One Florida state representative and congressional candidate for Congress called for dismantling of the entire federal government and the arrest of any FBI agent who set foot in the Sunshine State.[27] Right-wing shock jock Mark Levin said, "This is the worst attack on this Republic in modern history, period" (which may have come as news to Admiral Yamamoto and Osama Bin Laden).[28] Rubio, who had joined McConnell in suggesting that the criminal justice system, rather than impeachment, was the best venue for accountability for Trump, was now outraged that it was happening.[29]

ADDRESS ECONOMIC, RACIAL, AND GENDER-BASED INJUSTICE

The radically widening economic inequality that has plagued America ever since the rise of Ronald Reagan poses a threat to democracy every bit as real as any jackbooted fascist takeover.

The United States has, from the beginning, defined itself in contrast to the aristocratic Old World nations of Europe from whence we sprung. That self-flattering image, and the Horatio Alger "bootstraps" myth of rugged individualism, has never been quite true; it is aspirational at best, but deeply woven into our collective psyche as part of the so-called "American Dream." But to dream you must be asleep.* In her book *Bootstrapped: Liberating Ourselves from the American Dream*, Alissa Quart notes that the very idea of "pulling oneself up by one's bootstraps" is a physical impossibility, a nineteenth-century joke that entered the lexicon and slowly turned inside out.[30] As a serious admonition to those who have very little, economically speaking, it's especially cruel and dishonest when preached by the powerful and privileged who had no need to pull themselves up at all.

---

* The United States ranks a humble twenty-seventh in social mobility out of eighty-two countries measured in a recent study by the World Economic Forum, well below most of Europe, Japan, and even countries like Estonia, Malta, and Singapore.

Meanwhile, the deleterious economic effects of centuries of racial injustice continue to play out. Breaking that dynamic would be a tectonic shift in favor a more equitable and progressive America, denying the plutocrats and autocrats one of the chief wedges they have historically used to set working people of all races against each other—precisely the scenario that terrifies the one percent.

Historically speaking, a dire gap in economic equality is one of the most significant factors contributing to political instability and the risk of both authoritarianism and popular revolution, or one leading to the other, in interchangeable order.[31] In America, the question of economic inequality is further colored by that false promise of social mobility, trickle-down tax policy, and fearmongering over "socialism," to name just a few factors, all juiced by relentless plutocratic propaganda. But even if all those issues are set aside, there remains the glaring and undeniable fact that the concentration of such wealth in the hands of a very few gives that few a wildly outsized voice in our democracy.

For our documentary *Death and Taxes*, Justin Schein and I spoke with Amy Hanauer, Executive Director of the Institute on Taxation and Economic Policy. "In one recent year," she told us, "three American billionaires had as much in assets as the bottom 50 percent of the population combined. The hyperwealthy have a much greater control over our politics, much greater access to elected officials, and much more ability to push for laws that advantage them. So it's not 'one person, one vote.' And it becomes this kind of cyclical thing that gets worse and worse because the more money people have, the more power they have politically, and the more power they have politically, the more they can grow their money."[32]

Obviously, many very wealthy people are quite happy to have a disproportionate voice in our governance, despite its unfairness, and latch onto various quasi-aristocratic rationalizations for why that should be so. But if only for their own self-interest, they would do well to remember that economic inequality and injustice create discontent, anger, and other conditions that lead to political instability and open the door to various unwelcome outcomes.

To be clear: economic inequality is far from the only factor facilitating the rise of autocratic movements, and its absence is not a guarantee against such an outcome. Many European countries with robust social welfare infrastructures have also suffered right-wing turns in recent years. But a yawning gap between rich and poor, and the rightful perception of unfairness and injustice, certainly feed unrest and radicalism of all kinds, including the ascent of "strongmen" and other demagogues who promise to redress those wrongs while participating in the pillage.

Oligarchy, therefore, is autocracy's handmaiden. If we fail to address this issue, not only will we make a mockery of our claim to any kind of classlessness or social mobility, but we will dramatically increase the chances of social unrest and seed the soil for authoritarianism.

TWILIGHT'S LAST GLEAMING

The preceding litany is but a small subset of the measures that are in order in this time of crisis: the broader to-do list, going far beyond politics, could not possibly be contained within this manuscript. But one very basic thing that we can do to defend democracy is to reclaim the Stars and Stripes.

Per Samuel Johnson, patriotism is famously the last refuge of a scoundrel—an aphorism that was never truer than in the case of Trump, perhaps the least public-service-minded dude ever, yet one who predictably screams the loudest about the red, white, and blue. Given Trump's original line of work as a (fake) developer, I am even fonder of George Jean Nathan's quip that patriotism is the arbitrary veneration of real estate above principle, even if Donald has never evinced any shred of the latter. (The irony of Trump-as-patriot is twinned with the irony of this thrice-divorced serial adulterer, professional liar, cheat, greedhead, and preening porn star raw-dogger as a paragon of Christian faith and virtue.)

But the conflating of patriotism with blind loyalty to nation is as old as time and a staple of reactionaryism. In the John Birch mentality, any criticism of the United States is by definition disloyal, if not openly treasonous. It's an absurd position, of course, and one with dark, McCarthyite (or, yes, even fascist) implications when taken to its logical extreme. It is a further step beyond even that to equate the United States with its president, Louis XIV–style.

When I was a boy growing up on and around Army posts, mostly across the South, my father always flew the American flag outside our home. He still does so, as do many of our countrymen. It was inconceivable to me then that this act would ever have anything but benign associations. But now when I drive through a neighborhood where US flags fly from many of the eaves—in Staten Island, for example, or Long Island, or south Jersey—I am confident that I will soon see Trump 2020 flags and MAKE AMERICA GREAT AGAIN signs as well. And that makes me nervous.

The right has taken the Stars and Stripes hostage, claiming it and other emblems of patriotism as theirs and theirs alone. It's disheartening, but also just plain wrong. The right fetishizes the shibboleths of patriotism—the flag, the military, the Pledge of Allegiance, the national anthem—and insists that forced respect for them is a precondition of devotion to country. There is no awareness of what those things are supposed to represent—freedom of belief, freedom of expression, freedom to dissent—and no more perfect example of that than the brouhaha over Colin Kaepernick and other NFL players kneeling during the national anthem in respectful protest over police violence. Here again we saw angry white people howling in outrage that a group of fellow Americans visibly wronged—enslaved, disenfranchised, segregated, discriminated against, targeted, beaten, and even killed in systemic fashion—had the temerity to mention it.

The right has long tried to assert this monopoly on patriotism, with its bellicose foreign policy and its ostentatious displays of flag-waving. That conservatives are the best stewards of national security has always been a canard, considering the disastrous foreign policy misadventures that they have led us into. Under Trump, the GOP made an even worse dog's breakfast of US interests abroad, from getting played by Kim Jong Un,[33] to the idiotic withdrawal from the JCPOA,[34] to the undermining of NATO,[35] to the appalling abandonment of the Kurds and resuscitation of ISIS,[36] to the general emboldening of dictators around the world,[37] to blackmailing Kyiv while its soldiers died for want of Javelin missiles[38]—all while baldly serving the overall objectives of Vladimir Putin and Russia.[39]

Someone should look into that.

Indeed, when we look at the contempt it has shown for the rule of law and the most fundamental principles of American democracy over the past three years, there is a strong argument that the modern Republican Party is the most profoundly antipatriotic organization this side of the Klaus Fuchs Appreciation Society. Internationally, it has become a willing arm of Kremlin policy—a head-spinning turn for a party that once had Russophobia as its lodestar. Domestically, it has been ceaseless in its efforts to reject the pluralistic, diverse idea of the Founders in favor of something those Founders explicitly opposed: an autocracy with a state-ordained religion. The modern GOP is not even as enlightened as a bunch of guys who literally owned other human beings.

So let's reclaim our ownership of that ideal. Love of country and the principles on which it was founded does not belong to Lindsey Graham, or Mitch McConnell, or Jim Jordan and Matt Gaetz and Marjorie Taylor Greene, or Stephen Miller and Steve Bannon, or Fox News and Rupert Murdoch, and it certainly does not belong to Donald J. Trump.

It belongs to *us*.

HERE BE DRAGONS

Everything we have discussed thus far ought to be under consideration in order to shore up our embattled democracy. It's true that most of the proposals outlined in these pages will not pass with the current congressional disposition. Maybe none. Some might also scoff that even these reforms are but Band-Aids on a fundamentally unsavable patient, and that a far more drastic reimagination of America is required. But there is also a plethora of small, simple things we as individual Americans can do, almost without breaking a sweat.

Vote while you can, not only in presidential and other federal elections, but in midterms and off-year races, and at the state and local levels as well. Attend community meetings and town halls. Give to worthwhile candidates and causes. Run for office yourself if you have the stomach for it, starting with the school board or town council. Make your public engagement and your politics known, even if it's just a sign in your window or a bumper sticker on your car. Stay up on current events from credible media sources. Support your local newspaper and other press outlets with subscriptions. Sample what the other side is saying, while keeping your antennae up for spin, omission, and disinformation. Apply the same vigilance even to press outlets you trust.

But even if we succeed in shoring up our democratic institutions, thermostatics tell us that a Republican administration will eventually take power. That will be a catastrophe, so long as the GOP remains opposed to true participatory democracy, which we have every reason to believe it will. Unless the Republican Party miraculously rededicates itself to the fundamental principles of fairness, equality, and justice on which this nation was (aspirationally) founded, we can count on it to dismantle any protections we do succeed in putting in place, turn our representative democracy into a charade, and establish itself in permanent power.

If that happens, we will need a whole new menu of countermeasures.

PART THREE

THE PATH OF MOST RESISTANCE

CHAPTER 9

Onto the Barricades

Autocrats want you to be discouraged. Instilling a sense of apathy and resignation is one of their favorite and most frequently reached for tricks, as they prefer a public that believes it has no power to improve its lot and can't change things. But we do and we can—and the ferocity of their gaslighting is evidence of that power and how much they fear it. Human history is thick with examples, even with regimes far more brutal than we have yet faced in the United States.

"Ordinary people are not powerless to challenge the political and economic élite who have such disproportionate authority over our lives," writes Professor Keeanga Yamahtta-Taylor of Northwestern University. "But our power is often located outside of the institutions of tradition and influence."[1] In fact, even in the best of circumstances, when American democracy is functioning reasonably well, change typically comes from forces outside the government putting pressure on it—which is to say, from the people. Should a truly repressive, retrograde right-wing government come to power, the onus will shift even more in that direction.

The categories of resistance we will discuss in this section of the book cut across the whole range of human activity: political, economic, informational, religious (and nonreligious), technological, artistic, scientific, sociological, and interpersonal, to name but a few. But we need not think of this resistance as some gargantuan political thing, intimidating in its size and scope. Maria Ressa has spoken of democracy dying the death of a thousand cuts, but autocracy can be brought down in the same way. Many of those thousand cuts are in the seemingly small, quotidian actions of ordinary citizens like you and me. Our starting point is the simplest of all, which is the very way we think about what we are doing.

THE LIMITS OF TYRANTS

The psychological preparation for the pro-democracy struggle requires full-time vigilance to the ways that autocracy demands our complicity.

In his slim but seminal 2017 book, *On Tyranny*, Timothy Snyder advises us: "Do not obey in advance. Most of the power of authoritarianism is freely given." This impulse to bend voluntarily to an oppressive regime is what Snyder calls "anticipatory obedience," and need not even take the form of active support.[2] It can be simple apathy, and a Niemöllerian indifference to the sound of marching boots and knocks on neighbors' doors, and to the even almost-inaudible sound of democratic norms falling one by one.

We are often regaled with Frederick Douglass's famous line from 1857, that "Power concedes nothing without a demand." But it's well worth considering the longer quote, and the context of that maxim:

> Power concedes nothing without a demand. It never did and it never will. Find out just what any people will quietly submit to and you have found out the exact measure of injustice and wrong which will be imposed upon them, and these will continue till they are resisted with either words or blows, or with both. The limits of tyrants are prescribed by the endurance of those whom they oppress.[3]

The first thing to understand, then, is that the source of all political power, even in the most repressive police state, is the consent of the people.

"Obedience is at the heart of political power," wrote the political scientist Gene Sharp in his three-volume magnum opus, *The Politics of Nonviolent Action* (1973), calling the submission of the citizenry "the most important single quality of any government, without which it would not exist."[4] The citizens of free countries give their obedience gladly, while those living under despotic regimes give it less so. But they give it nonetheless.

"To say that every government depends on consent of the people does not, of course, mean that the subjects of all rulers prefer the established order to any other which might be created," Sharp continued. "They may consent because they positively approve of it—but they may also consent because they are unwilling to pay the price for the refusal of consent . . .The degree of liberty or tyranny in any government is, it follows, in large degree a reflection of the relative determination of the subjects to be free and their willingness and ability to resist efforts to enslave them."[5]

In other words, repression only works when the people are cowed by it.

Admittedly, it sounds naïve. How can an unarmed citizenry under the heel of a tyranny that controls all the levers of power, including a monopoly on violence as exercised by the police and armed forces, possibly avoid submission?

In his own epic history of nonviolence, *The Unconquerable World* (2003), Jonathan Schell writes of the delusion "that the foundation of all state power is force," arguing that it is a confusion of police power with political power.[6] "Terror, even as it keeps its practitioners in office for a time, destroys the foundations of their power," Schell argues, contending that "each time the Soviet Union used its tanks to crush a rebellion in Eastern Europe, it was diminishing its power, not increasing it." Even Clausewitz, Schell writes, was of the opinion that "military victories were useless unless the population of vanquished army then obeyed the will of the victor"—a formulation that calls into question the very definition of victory itself.[7]

But let's not stop with Clausewitz, an admirable enough figure as far as Prussian generals go. Even Adolf Hitler, the very model of the most monstrous totalitarianism, declared that occupying a conquered nation was largely a psychological matter. "One cannot rule by force alone," he wrote in the midst of subjugating much of Europe in July 1943. "True, force is decisive, but it is equally important to have this psychological something which the animal trainer also needs to be master of his beast. They must be convinced that we are the victors."[8]

Sharp then asks a bold question: What happens if the people refuse to accept militarily successful invaders—or domestic oppressors—as their political masters? His conclusion is that "noncooperation and defiance by subjects, at least under certain conditions," has the power to thwart those rulers, and even destroy them.

"If this is true," Sharp asks, "then why have people not long since abolished oppression, tyranny, and exploitation?" The answer, primarily, is that "The subjects usually do not realize that they are the source of the ruler's power and that by joint action they could dissolve that power"—and tyrants have every reason to keep them from so doing.[9] As we have just observed, inculcating a sense of resignation, hopelessness, and despair in the citizenry is the ruler's greatest tool. Sharp goes on to cite the South African philosopher Errol E. Harris that, consequently, a public subjected to despotism "become[s] its accomplices at the same time as they become its victims. If sufficient people understood this and really knew what they were about and how to go about it, they could ensure that government would never be tyrannical."[10]

"A nation gets the government it deserves," Harris wrote.[11] That is not to blame the victim or to allege weakness, only to say that a despotic regime can only remain in power if the citizenry is unwilling to mobilize sufficiently against it (without underestimating how difficult that mobilization might be). That is bitter pill for any nation to swallow, but it can also be inverted. If it is only the complicity of the ruled that enables their oppression, that acquiescence can also be withdrawn. Therefore, it is within the power of the oppressed to be the means of their own salvation.

It is this understanding that is central to any American defiance of an autocratic right-wing regime that might arise under Donald Trump and/or the Republican Party. We are the majority, and power flows only with our consent, which we have the capacity to withdraw. The question then becomes: how do we do that?

THE VILLAGE'S VOICE

When faced with a repressive regime, the traditional first step in pushing back has been to announce one's unhappiness. A discontented populace that gets out into the streets can certainly make clear to the ruling powers that it is not cool with what's going on, but it is a step that a shocking number of global citizens cannot even muster. (Let us leave aside for now those who not only won't object to tyranny, but applaud it.)

Such public displays of defiance were sorely lacking during Trump's term. Yes, those four years began with the stirring, pink pussy-hatted spectacle of the Women's March in cities around the world. On the day after his inauguration, some five million people took to the streets in the US alone, the largest single-day protest in American history. But that march proved to be an outlier. A million-strong march cannot be spun up every week, and even if it could, would soon lose its power. But during Trump's administration there was no permanent blockade around Trump Tower at Columbus Circle on the order of Occupy Wall Street, for example, or of Fox News headquarters in midtown Manhattan. In May 2017, when Trump made his first visit back to Manhattan after being sworn in as president, I fully expected my fellow New Yorkers to surround his high-rise in protest and provoke a national spectacle by refusing to let him leave. Without resorting to violence, the sight of tens of thousands of New Yorkers peacefully preventing the Secret Service and NYPD from bringing him out, and then ending that standoff by calmly stepping aside to allow the President of the United States to return to Washington, would have been a blunt announcement about who holds the ultimate power in America.

Instead Trump came to New York, conducted his nauseating business, then departed again as if was just another Thursday. How different the ensuing four years might have been if he had been given a stark reminder that the head of state serves at the pleasure of the people. Certainly it would not have completely deterred him from pursuing his vile agenda, but it would have made clear that he wouldn't be able to do so without an uproar that risked rising into something a lot more threatening than mere picketing.

But even as they acknowledged the power of a few indelible protests—like Dr. King's 1963 March on Washington or the 1967 March on the Pentagon—a great many veterans of the civil rights, anti-war, and feminist movements with whom I spoke questioned the value of "the big march."

"Demonstrations by themselves won't get it," the veteran civil rights activist Zoharah Simmons told me. "You have to have organization. When somebody gets killed by the police or something bad happens, people rise up, they get mad, and they march, but that is not being galvanized into movement structures."[12]

The great-granddaughter of an enslaved woman, Simmons had been a member of the Student Nonviolent Coordinating Committee, a colleague of John Lewis, and one of only a handful of female project directors during the Mississippi Freedom Summer while barely in her twenties. In that role she supervised dozens of other activists (many of them white male volunteers from the North), faced down Klan violence, was beaten by the police, and thrown out of Lester Maddox's restaurant by Maddox himself during a sit-in and arrested for her trouble. She argues that while demonstrations express widespread discontent at moments of maximum public outrage, they are no substitute for disciplined, strategic, long-term activism.

"When you think of what we did in Mississippi," Simmons says, "we might have mass meetings almost every other night. I mean, these people were doing hard labor jobs. They would go home, wash up, put on their Sunday best, and come to the church for the meeting. And these were giant educational sessions. You had the singing and the preaching and all that, but underneath it was really political education about what the situation was, what we could do about it, what the laws were, and how to implement our plan."[13]

As a professor of religion at the University of Florida, Simmons now lives in a state that offers a preview of what a nationwide right-wing American autocracy would look like, with complete GOP control of the legislature, the governorship, and the state Supreme Court, and the Democratic Party marginalized to the point of impotence—circumstances that are enabling its governor to pursue one of the most aggressive far-right agendas in the entire nation, including teaching schoolchildren the historical fiction that slavery was actually an excellent jobs training program.[14]

"We have to build relationships," says Simmons. "In Mississippi, the people who we identified as leaders were people who everybody in the community already knew. I knocked on the door of Mrs. Eberta Spinks, and said, 'Are you interested in having a Freedom Summer project here?' And she said, 'I've been waiting on you all my life.'"[15]

Jon Else, professor emeritus at the Graduate School of Journalism at UC Berkeley and a MacArthur "Genius" Fellow, concurred. "If you're gonna talk about activism, you have to talk about why you're doing the activism. Are you doing it to make yourself feel good? Are you doing it to empower people who are oppressed? If so, to what end? Is the activism very, very specifically aimed at practical change?"[16]

Else was series producer and cinematographer for *Eyes on the Prize*, the landmark 1987 PBS series on the Civil Rights Movement by filmmaker Henry Hampton. He came to that project with visceral first-person experience, having been a young volunteer in Mississippi in 1964 and '65, registering voters as what he calls a "lowest level pavement pounder" in SNCC. He was also on the steps of the courthouse in Selma, Alabama, when the racist sheriff Jim Clark went berserk in front of the national press.

"With SNCC and SCLC in the golden age of the Civil Rights Movement," Else told me, "I had the good fortune of being around a bunch of extremely smart people like Bob Moses and Judy Richardson who were very, very clear about the change they wanted to effect, and very clear and frankly visionary about how to actually effect change."

In Else's view, the success of that movement stemmed from its ability to speak to policymakers in ways that moved them to action. "But whether or not the policymakers are listening really depends on who the policymakers are. During the Gulf War there were a million people—including my wife and me—out on the street in the largest demonstration in the history of San Francisco, a very liberal town. All over the country there were huge demonstrations like that. But as far as I could tell, they didn't do bit of good, either with that first Gulf War, or the second war in Iraq. I don't think the Bush administration gave a shit about all these people in the street. During the Trump administration, forget it."[17]

Marches, rallies, and demonstrations, then, while the most obvious and visible form of protest, must be undertaken with an understanding of their limited utility—necessary but not sufficient—employed to demonstrate the scope of the opposition forces, to pressure policymakers, and to bolster our own morale, but with modest hope of bringing about change all by themselves.

"I still think everything is local," the Rev. Dr. Norvel Goff told me. "It's one thing to march and to protest. But after you've done that, how do we go beyond the protests? One of the ways is to organize effectively. In my belief, you must have a diverse coalition of persons who believe in human worth and human dignity and the respect of all communities to come together to bring about positive change. We start organizing, house by house, block by block, community by community, to push back on a daily basis at all levels. Sometimes it's a very slow process, but you still must stick with it. Because change will come if you keep pressing forward."[18]

THE LONG ARM OF THE OUTLAW

If marching in the streets and carrying signs is often not nearly enough, the next step is active noncooperation—actions announcing not only that we're unhappy, but that we're not gonna take it.

"Civil disobedience isn't just demonstrations; it's breaking the law," the author and historian James Carroll reminded me. "And part of that is a disciplined and radical commitment to nonviolence."[19]

As a Roman Catholic priest in the 1960s and early '70s, Carroll was a member of the Catholic Left, an associate of the Berrigan brothers, and a longtime activist in the Civil Rights and anti-Vietnam War movements, including Reverend King's Poor People's Campaign. The acts of civil disobedience in which he participated got him knocked on the head and jailed repeatedly. That is the point of deliberately challenging the regime and daring it to assert its power. If it does not do so, an important victory has already been achieved. More often than not, however, the state reacts violently, exposing its moral illegitimacy and awakening low-information citizens and the disinterested middle to that fact. One thinks of white police officers in the segregationist South carting peaceful civil rights protestors out of soda fountains during sit-ins in the 1960s . . . of the firehoses and attack dogs of Southern sheriffs like Bull Connor . . . of the Rev. Martin Luther King clapped into handcuffs and thrown into jail . . . of police cracking John Lewis's skull as he and other civil rights activists marched across the Edmund Pettus Bridge in Selma, named for a US senator who was a Klansman. And that state violence operates hand in hand with the vigilante violence of domestic terrorists, like the men who abducted, tortured, and lynched Emmett Till in rural Mississippi, or who shot and killed Medgar Evers outside his own home in the town of Jackson, or the Klansmen who killed four little Black girls in the bombing of the Sixteenth Street Baptist Church in Birmingham.

Yet the Civil Rights Movement prevailed.

Carroll also reminds us that the most effective acts of civil disobedience are rarely spontaneous, but are usually part of consciously organized, meticulously planned campaigns. Conservative, white-centric historians and public figures have—quite successfully—attempted to turn Rosa Parks into nothing more than a nice old lady who had had enough one day and refused to give up her seat on the bus, but in truth, she was a longtime activist who took that action as part of a deliberate, calculated challenge to the segregationist government, as an element of the NAACP's boycott of city buses in Montgomery, Alabama. (She was only forty-two at the time.)[20] Her historic act of disobedience also came on the heels of earlier acts of defiance there and in other cities, like that of fifteen-year-old Claudette Colvin, also under the aegis of the NAACP, where Mrs. Parks was a senior member.[21]

In the current moment, we can take inspiration from the brave acts of other pro-democracy dissidents facing down foreign regimes far more brutal than the contemporary Republican threat in the USA. The whole world is watching the widespread protests in Iran following the 2022 murder of Mahsa Amini by the country's "morality police" for the crime of wearing her headscarf too loose. Carroll also cited to me events in Israel as an impressive model for any future American resistance. In reaction to Netanyahu's brazen attempts to gut the Israeli judicial system, we have seen roads blockaded, diplomats and civil servants resigning their posts, cabinet members publicly voicing their opposition (and getting fired for it), military officials rebuking the prime minister, and even reservists refusing to show up for duty, at least until the horrific Hamas attack of October 7, 2023. At one point, some 300,000 Israelis took to the streets in angry protest—per capita, the equivalent of ten million Americans—forcing Bibi to back off some of his demands, if only as a tactical withdrawal while he regrouped.[22]

But civil disobedience need not be limited to familiar forms like sit-ins and shutdowns. On its website, the nonprofit group Nonviolence International offers a menu of three hundred tactics, ranging from nonviolent land seizures to hitting autocrats in the face with a pie, mock trials and elections, postal bombardment (like the human hair animal rights activists mailed en masse to Harrod's in 2012), leafletting from the air, the overloading of the administrative system, the *Lysistrata* strategy, boat blockades, public art, the renouncing of honors, flash mobs, teach-ins, rent withholding, dissemination of fake money, and many more.[23] In *Small Acts of Resistance* (2010), Steve Crawshaw and John Jackson detail eighty historical examples of innovative defiance: Polish people ritually taking their television sets for a walk in baby strollers to protest state-run

TV news; Uruguayan soccer crowds mumbling the national anthem but for the line "may tyrants tremble!"; Iranian cab drivers who refused to pick up religious clerics; a walkout by vote counters in the Philippines who declined to falsify election numbers; packs of dogs sent into the streets of Yangon bearing photos of Than Shewe (the leader of Myanmar's military junta) and the subversive graphic designer who designed that country's new paper currency to resemble the forbidden image of dissident leader Aung San Suu Kyi, rather than that of her father.[24] The possibilities are nearly infinite.

Consider a second Trump administration which is met not only with protests in the streets, but by the widespread refusal among the public to cooperate with ICE in the execution of hateful immigration policy; by "deliberate inefficiency and selective noncooperation," as Sharp calls it, among police, prosecutors, and even judges;[25] by bureaucrats slow-walking their duties; by the bureaucracy itself overloaded with a deluge of pointless requests, filings, and paperwork (as American anti-war activists did with the Selective Service System during the Vietnam War);[26] by churchgoers leaving their houses of worship en masse if those organizations refuse to stand up against the administration (as American abolitionists did in the 1830s when their churches refused to denounce slavery);[27] by consumers declining to deposit money in banks, or withdrawing it from the same (a technique used in the 1905 Russian Revolution,[28] and in 1966 in protest of investment in apartheid South Africa against First National City Bank and Chase Manhattan); or by the even more extreme measure of businesses refusing to accept greenbacks at all and operating by barter or mutual aid instead.[29]

But active dissent does not require the participation of millions: it can begin, Chinese proverb–like, with a single step by a solitary individual. In June 1963, the Buddhist monk Thích Quảng Đức calmly set himself on fire in the middle of a busy Saigon intersection in protest of the Diệm regime in South Vietnam, an act of shocking force that galvanized the attention of the entire world.[30] Five months later, the Diệm regime fell in a US-backed coup. The Arab Spring was similarly kicked off by the self-immolation of a Tunisian street vendor named Mohamed Bouazizi who was at his wit's end over government corruption and the bribes he had been forced to pay.[31]

I am not advising anyone to follow Quảng Đức's or Bouazizi's examples; bold acts of individual courage do not require the use of gasoline. Malala Yousafzai—a mere teenager at the time—drew global attention (and won the Nobel Peace Prize) for her astonishingly brave activism against the repressive regime in Pakistan. Marina Ovsyannikova, a broadcast news editor for Russian state television, ran on camera during a newscast in 2022 and held up a sign protesting the war in Ukraine, capturing global attention. Greta Thunberg, now a global icon, began as a solitary fifteen-year-old student boycotting class and sitting outside her school with a handmade sign.

Such actions can stand out within broader campaigns as well. The indelible image of a lone pro-democracy protestor in Tiananmen Square calmly facing down a column of tanks in 1989 comes to mind, as does Rosa Parks's iconic stand. But let us not be under any illusions. The Chinese government responded to the protests in Tiananmen—the Gate of Heavenly Peace—with a bloody massacre that killed hundreds and has only clamped down even harder in the decades since. Malala was shot in the head at the age of fifteen by a Taliban gunman infuriated by her activism. Marina Ovsyannikova fled house arrest while awaiting trial and is now a fugitive wanted by the Russian authorities. The conflict in Vietnam spiraled for another dozen years after Quảng Đức's suicide and resulted in a communist dictatorship. The Arab Spring collapsed. Tehran has met the current protests by killing hundreds of demonstrators, jailing many more, and executing others. Amnesty International reported that "Iran's intelligence and security forces have been committing horrific acts of torture, including beatings, flogging, electric shocks, rape and other sexual violence against child protesters as young as 12."[32]

They aren't called "tyrants" because they play nice.

Ironically, when popular discontent truly threatens the regime, it can force concessions and reforms, but it can also cause the government to push back with even more draconian forms of oppression out of fear for its very life. That is ultimately a losing strategy for the regime, as Schell notes, a sign of insecurity and desperation; indeed, such provocations by the resistance aim in part to incite exactly that kind of backlash, turning public opinion against the autocracy and causing it to bring on its own downfall. But that does not make the blows of the truncheons or the sting of rubber bullets, or the blood spilled by real ones, any easier to take in the meantime. Such backlash can also carry on for years, even decades, before that aforementioned arc of history brings an oppressive regime down. In other words, this struggle demands tenacity, commitment, and patience, and almost inevitably requires confrontation that both inflicts and invites pain.*

But above all, it requires a ruthless mental self-discipline to overcome the foe's effort to make us give up. "Don't focus on the outcome," James Carroll told me. "Because if you start by doing that, you'll be too discouraged to keep going. Focus on the importance of standing for the principle, and the truth, that's at stake in the present moment."

NEW AND IMPROVED: THE WHEEL

Fortunately, in summoning a movement to oppose a right-wing regime in the United States, it is not necessary for us to reinvent the proverbial wheel. Models abound.

In Poland, a trade union born in a shipyard—illegal at first, in a country under the heel of an authoritarian regime far worse than anything we are contemplating in the US—grew into a broad antiauthoritarian movement that eventually forced free elections in which its leader was chosen as the country's president. In the Philippines, the flagrantly corrupt Marcos regime, which robbed the country blind during its twenty-one-year reign, instituted martial law, stole elections, and even murdered political opponents like Benigno Aquino, was finally brought down by the People Power movement led by Aquino's widow, Corazon. In South Africa, Nelson Mandela and the African National Congress led a largely peaceful decades-long campaign to end apartheid and eject the white minority government, a campaign that saw Mandela himself imprisoned for twenty-seven years. That imprisonment was a particular object lesson in the weak spots of autocracy, as Pretoria's ham-handed brutality turned Mandela into a global hero, shaming the regime and bringing international pressure onto it. (Putin may have made that exact mistake with Alexei Navalny).

---

*   To that end, Chris Hedges notes that some of the most successful activists are couples, because they come to the struggle as a pre-bonded duo who can support each other.

In a campaign that inspired the South African cause, Gandhi led perhaps the most famous movement of peaceful political resistance in history, the struggle for India's independence against the greatest superpower in the world at the time. The price was painfully high: over the course of that decades-long campaign, British forces brutalized, imprisoned, and even massacred untold numbers of unarmed Indians, sometimes firing into crowds and killing protestors in cold blood. Gandhi himself was imprisoned numerous times. But slowly the Crown was worn down.

Note the qualifier "decades-long." It bears repeating that these struggles are not for the faint of heart. Our autocratic foes depend on as much.

As Jonathan Schell observes, Gandhi was, if not the first, certainly the foremost to reject the notion that force was a requirement in the fight for human rights, and to conceive of a successful, sophisticated, and cohesive strategy of nonviolence in its place.[33] To Sharp's point about the consent of the governed, and Snyder's about anticipatory obedience, Gandhi declared as early as 1909 that only the cooperation of the Indian people allowed the British to establish the Raj, or to maintain it. "The English have not taken India," he wrote in *Hind Swaraj*, "we have given it to them."[34]

But amid Gandhi's contemporary Western image as a saintly figure of peaceful protest, we would do well to remember that he did not merely fold his hands and say "namaste": he advocated the flagrant violation of British law via what he called *satyagraha*, "direct action without violence." That effort was twinned with the "constructive program" to make a better country, a task that did not require waiting for de jure political power to be obtained. In fact, Gandhi considered that secondary to it.[35]

Few, either in the West or India itself, thought such a strategy could result in the eviction of the English occupiers, but it did.

And these are but a handful of prominent case studies. In recent decades, surely the most dramatic example of popular unrest leading to political change was the fall of the Berlin Wall on November 9, 1989, and the collapse of the USSR and the entire Soviet empire in August 1991. In neighboring Czechoslovakia, a peaceful movement of students and activists led to the Velvet Revolution that ended four decades of communist rule in favor of liberal democracy under the playwright/dissident Vaclav Havel. Similar bloodless revolutions took place in other former Warsaw Pact countries. Notably, Havel, following Gandhi's example, aimed his activism not at overthrowing the regime but at "immediate changes in daily life . . . an unshakable commitment to achieving modest, concrete goals on the local level," as Schell writes. These measures included financial aid to dissidents at odds with the authorities and the families of jailed workers; an underground press; and a clandestine university teaching uncensored material in private homes.[36] Schell writes that Havel, along with fellow activists like Gyorgy Konrad in Hungary and Adam Michnik in Poland, "lowered their field glasses from the remote heights of state power and turned their gazes to the life immediately around them . . . Their new rule of thumb was to act not *against* the government but *for* society—and then to defend the accomplishments."[37]

Admittedly, it was not civil disobedience that precipitated the collapse of the USSR or its Warsaw Pact client-states. Outright protest was limited in a fully totalitarian state; structural issues within the communist system played the more central role, aided by external pressures deliberately applied by well-resourced foreign antagonists over eight decades. But when the end came, the throngs of citizens who poured into the streets spoke to what had long been germinating beneath the soil.

The greater lesson for us may be how readily many of those former Soviet states slid back into autocracy. After the historic triumph of Solidarity in 1989, Poland fell into the grip of the hard right–wing Law and Justice Party (PiS), which came to power democratically with a slim majority in 2015. Liberal democracy lasted barely a decade in Russia between the fall of the USSR and the ascendance of Putin, who like the PiS, accomplished that task not by an overt coup d'état, but by maneuvering within his country's political system, choking off every mechanism of opposition one by one until the country's claim to democracy was but a farce. Both are cautionary tales that speak to how fragile young democracies are. (Old ones too. Seventy-six years after Gandhi led India to independence, that country is now under the heel of the autocratic Narendra Modi.)

The struggle for democracy, therefore, is not a single contest that is won, but an ongoing project that requires eternal maintenance. Just as despots are not forever, neither is freedom from them.

IS THIS AMERICA?

In this country, there is no better example of a successful pro-democracy struggle than the Civil Rights Movement, itself the heir to the abolitionist movement that predates even the founding of the US.

Shall we quibble with the word "successful"? Racism remains a pox on our country, and discrimination, bigotry, police brutality, economic injustice, and other longstanding ills continue to roil the nation. But that in no way minimizes the achievements of the Black liberation movement, which carries on even now into the continuing campaign against racism and poverty led by successors to Dr. King, like the Rev. William Barber II.

Malcolm Gladwell notes that the Civil Rights Movement was a highly disciplined, rigidly organized hierarchical endeavor with centralized control, distinguished by formal planning, training of volunteers, and reconnaissance of locations and targets, under the auspices of groups like the NAACP, SNCC, and SCLC.[38] In the same way that Rosa Parks's historic refusal to give up her seat was no impulsive act but a carefully planned and deliberate operation, the entire movement was similarly strategic, targeted with near-military precision at very specific objectives.*

Gladwell cites the spread of the sit-in movement from Greensboro, North Carolina, noting that it was anything but random. Rather, "It spread to those cities which had pre-existing 'movement centers'—a core of dedicated and trained activists ready to turn the 'fever' into action":

> The Montgomery bus boycott required the participation of tens of thousands of people who depended on public transit to get to and from work each day. It lasted a year. In order to persuade those people to stay true to the cause, the boycott's organizers tasked each local black church with maintaining morale, and put together a free alternative private carpool service, with forty-eight dispatchers and forty-two pickup stations . . . By the time King came to Birmingham, for the climactic showdown with Police Commissioner Eugene (Bull)

---

*   Indeed, in *Waging a Good War: A Military History of the Civil Rights Movement, 1954–1968*, the historian Thomas Ricks offers a survey of the US Civil Rights Movement through an explicitly martial lens.

Connor, he had a budget of a million dollars, and a hundred full-time staff members on the ground, divided into operational units. The operation itself was divided into steadily escalating phases, mapped out in advance. Support was maintained through consecutive mass meetings rotating from church to church around the city.[39]

And what those activists confronted was harrowing. "In the Mississippi Freedom Summer of 1964," Gladwell writes, "thirty-seven Black churches were set on fire and dozens of safe houses were bombed; volunteers were beaten, shot at, arrested, and trailed by pickup trucks full of armed men. A quarter of those in the program dropped out. Activism that challenges the status quo—that attacks deeply rooted problems—is not for the faint of heart."[40] As Jonathan Schell wrote, "A civil-rights protestor in the South of the democratic United States in the early 1960s was almost certainly in more danger of physical violence than an activist in totalitarian Eastern Europe in the 1970s or 1980s."[41]

But the harm's way into which those activists put themselves was very deliberate.

Jon Else told me: "With SNCC and SCLC, we were always aiming at the folks in power who could actually change the laws. Getting that mad dog sheriff to attack the demonstrators with dogs in Birmingham, or flushing the lynch mobs out of the back alleys in Mississippi—that was not designed for white folks in Alabama or Mississippi. It was designed for members of Congress.* Because we were operating at a time when Congress and the executive were actually fairly functional, and you could actually shame Republican lawmakers into seeing what a bald-faced injustice was going on right in their backyard and doing something about it. It was all about finding the most effective targets with power high up in Washington."[42]

To Else's point, it is the public nature of these actions that gives them much of their power—which is to say, they are not paramilitary

---

* Sharp reports that David Halberstam compared Bull Connor's appalling violence to the Diệm regime's crackdown on Buddhist protestors, in that both campaigns backfired, largely due to the appalling optics of the use of state power against unarmed, nonviolent protestors, even if one did not recognize the rightness of the protestors' cause, and the injustice of their attackers'.

acts aimed at taking ground, but informational ones aimed at galvanizing attention and changing minds, or what Sharp calls "political jiu-jitsu."[43] The media is therefore crucial, and not limited to a domestic audience. "The whole world is watching!" went the chant of protestors at the 1968 Democratic National Convention in Chicago as Mayor Daley's baby blue–helmeted riot police attacked them with nightsticks and tear gas. Likewise, during the Civil Rights Movement, Zoharah Simmons stressed the impact of televised violence in pressuring the federal government (the Southern state governments did not care), knowing as it did that the credibility of the United States as the self-styled leader of the Free World was on the line. "We only had three channels—ABC, NBC, and CBS—and it was all on the six o'clock news," she told me. "Everybody was watching."[44] Autocrats want to control the media for that very reason, but in the increasingly shrunken global community, it's almost impossible to keep large protests quiet when photos and videos inevitably leak out thanks to smartphones.

Condemnation from abroad, especially when it is broad-based and uniform, can harden an autocracy's resolve, if it feels further besieged and seeks to turn external criticism into an advantage by rallying the public with xenophobic appeals to faux patriotism and the specter of foreign enemies against whom it is the nation's only defender. But no country can truly go it alone when the weight of world opinion—and excommunication from the global economy—is arrayed against it. Pariah states are invariably ruinous and unsustainable. The role of international outrage in forcing an end to the apartheid regime in South Africa stands as a prime example.

"If there's one thing that I feel very certain about," Else told me, "it's that you have to figure out why you're doing any particular action. Organizing movements and actions will always have an effect for the people who are involved. It gives people a sense of agency, which they may otherwise be missing. But is it actually gonna change things? Does that matter to you? Is it gonna change things now? Is it gonna change things a year from now, or ten years from now?

"When we were in Mississippi in the summer of '64, trying to mount a challenge to the segregated all-white delegation to the Democratic Convention, Lyndon Johnson and Hubert Humphrey came up with a compromise that was unacceptable to the folks who'd risked their lives for this effort. But getting Fannie Lou Hamer on national television that summer saying, 'Is this America?' set the stage in many ways for the Voting Rights Act, which followed only a year later. So the victory is not always right in front of you."[45]

I asked Else what we can do in the current era, when Republican politicians are beyond that kind of shame.

"Call me old-fashioned, but we still have an electoral system in this country, with all its imperfections," he replied. "We still have a Congress that makes laws, we still have an executive that gets elected and appoints Supreme Court judges, and we still have a Senate that has to confirm them. So what I do is voter registration. I was dipped into that by my heel in Mississippi in the 1960s, and that's what I can do most effectively. I go out into the rural parts of California every election cycle, and I find some key congressional race, and I walk the precincts. I'm in the parking lot at Walmart with my clipboard registering voters. I'll register anybody, but that Walmart parking lot in Modesto is pretty much full of immigrant, first-time voters. And it's frustrating: you may spend a whole day and register three voters. But we actually flipped the district out there a couple cycles ago, where 55,000 people voted in the midterm election, and the Democratic candidate ousted the Republican by nine hundred votes, and he's now in his third term. As long as we have an electoral system, that's where I put most of my energies."[46]

That is exactly the point. Voting rights is the most important element in our democracy, and precisely why the neo-autocratic GOP is going after it. So long as the electoral system is functioning at all, it remains a pivotal front in this struggle.

The Civil Rights Movement is only the most prominent example of the power of the people in American life. The anti–Vietnam War movement, which galvanized millions of young people (and others) across the country, undeniably helped bring significant pressure to bear on successive administrations to end its war in Southeast Asia. Anti-war fervor helped drive LBJ out of the 1968 presidential race, and—in a bitter irony—helped Nixon take his place, only to continue the war for another five futile years at a cost of 21,000 additional American dead and hundreds of thousands of Vietnamese lives. But ultimately even he had to bend to public clamor, accelerated by the revelations of Ellsberg.

Two subsequent movements in the 1970s and '80s, both centered on college campuses, proved again the power of idealistic young people as a political force. The nuclear freeze movement played a substantive role in forcing the US to scale back the madness of the arms race and helped prompt landmark nonproliferation treaties in the Reagan era, while the anti-apartheid movement shamed universities and other organizations into divesting from financial interests in South Africa and helped spur the passage of the Comprehensive Anti-Apartheid Act of 1986, enacted over Reagan's veto by a Republican-controlled Senate.[47]

I'll repeat that. A *Republican*-controlled Senate.*

And these are not outliers. Throughout its history, American life has been shaped by determined dissident movements. The suffrage movement of the early twentieth century—which itself grew out of the abolitionist movement of the previous century—got women the vote, a struggle that continues with the ongoing fight for equal pay, the fight against workplace discrimination and harassment, the fight for reproductive justice, and in the struggle of #MeToo. The labor union movement put an end to the most exploitative working conditions of American industry in the nineteenth and early twentieth centuries, and—for a time—played a major role in remaking American life and reining in naked capitalism. The gay rights movement made astounding gains over a relatively brief period on behalf of a constituency that has been among the most reviled and persecuted in human history and remains so in large parts of the world.

The novelist Alix Kates Shulman, a leading figure in the Second Wave feminist movement and the coeditor of the recent anthology *Women's Liberation! Feminist Writings that Inspired a Revolution & Still Can*, listed some of the things she and her colleagues did in the 1960s and '70s.

---

* Indeed, the long, slow, but ultimately successful campaign to bring down the minoritarian white regime in South Africa represents a case study in all the various levers available to overthrow a tyranny, collectively used: domestic resistance led by a disciplined anti-government movement; mobilization of public opposition; widespread international protest (much of it student-led) that forced financial divestment; and, eventually, foreign condemnation and economic pressure preparatory to Pretoria's collapse not in a sudden revolution, but in a negotiated handover of power.

"We had demonstrations, like the 1968 Miss America protest. We disrupted legislative hearings. At a hearing on prostitution I stood up and read Emma Goldman; we were trying to make them arrest us. One of the earliest presentations I organized was at the annual meeting of the American Library Association and the Children's Book Council. We had a slideshow showing the outrageous sexism in popular children's books. We had speakouts on taboo subjects; the first one was the Redstockings Speakout on abortion, in the West Village in 1969. We established battered women's shelters, and made a push to get childcare in companies. In fact, we were so successful that it grew into an international movement and Congress passed an excellent childcare law, both houses, and Nixon vetoed it on the grounds that it was going to destroy the family.[48]

"At the time there was no mass awareness that the status quo for women was wrong," Shulman told me. "So what we needed to do was change the attitude of women—who are half the human race—toward our position in society and in the world. This meant meeting in person and speaking the truth about our experience. Soon all over the country, in a million living rooms and in church basements, this was going on. It was transformational."[49]

Shulman stressed that once a demographic is awakened in that way, it will no longer stand for injustice or the perpetuation of the status quo. "The thing about consciousness-raising is that it usually goes from zero to a hundred instantly, and frequently—certainly for me—it happened at the very first meeting. And it was a permanent change. I've never heard of somebody who is an 'ex-feminist.' Once you see the truth, you can't stop seeing it."[50]

You might say: But those movements—feminism, and the anti-nuclear movement, and even the Black liberation movement—were confined to specific policy goals, not the overthrow of an entire repressive regime. Fair enough. But the tactics and strategy are the very same ones that can be applied to even more sweeping political goals.

As in any negotiation, the more extreme positions make moderate ones more tolerable to the opposing party in any eventual settlement. Alexander Hamilton's proposal of a life term for the US president moved the Overton window at the Constitutional Convention when some of the delegates were nervous at the prospect of even a four-year term.[51] In the past forty-plus years, Earth First!, the Animal Liberation

Front, and other radical groups have chained themselves to trees, broken into industrial testing facilities to free lab animals, and engaged in other acts of civil disobedience. While those actions typically met with popular disapproval, over those same decades the causes of environmentalism and anti-animal cruelty have gone mainstream. Greenpeace largely destroyed the global whaling industry with confrontational tactics like high-speed waterborne assaults that pitted rubber Zodiacs against giant whaling ships, putting the lives of their own members in the way of high-pressure water cannons and even electric harpoons. (A splinter group, Sea Shepherd, is even more aggressive.)

Jon Else singles out the 1971 action in Media, Pennsylvania as another example, when ten anti-war and peace activists broke into an FBI office and stole nearly a thousand classified documents exposing the Bureau's vast, illegal surveillance of American citizens.[52] "At its gentlest, you would call it civil disobedience," Else told me, "and at its least gentle, you would call it a crime. But a conscious, *directed* political crime—and one that had a concrete effect."[53] The publication of those documents awakened the American public to the depths of Hoover's—and Nixon's—criminality. Coming just a few months before the Pentagon Papers, it surely also influenced the willingness of *The Washington Post* and *New York Times* to risk prosecution by publishing those stolen government documents.

Ten years later, Daniel and Phillip Berrigan and the other members of the Plowshares Eight broke into a General Electric plant in order to smash the nosecones of nuclear missiles and pour blood on company paperwork, making the White House and Pentagon more willing to deal with "moderate" antinuclear activists.[54] "That was the radical edge of the nuclear freeze movement," James Carroll told me, "and the radical edge is an essential part because it's what empowers the moderate, liberal part of the movement."[55]

"There are some very, very specifically targeted kinds of activism like the Media break-in that can blow open something like COINTELPRO," Else told me. "That was one that was perfectly conceived, and perfectly targeted, with a clear goal in mind. And it succeeded."[56]

Not all do, of course. Else related to me how he and other activists in the civil rights era had been inspired by the anti-fascist volunteers in the Spanish Civil War in Orwell's *Homage to Catalonia*. "What we missed was that the bad guys won. Franco won the war and ruled Spain for forty years, and Orwell got shot and his comrades were all killed or rotted in Spanish jails. It didn't end well.

"But it's liberating to discover at an early age what it is you are willing to die for with your activism—and *not* die for with your activism."[57]

WHITE PEOPLE PROBLEMS

All the struggles of various oppressed or besieged groups of our countrymen are but branches of a single struggle, and they are inextricably intertwined. "Intersectionality" is another of those terms that makes conservatives sneer, but they once sneered at the idea of integrated lunch counters too, and that women could be doctors, and that "redskin" was a slur.

The belated awareness of white people about political repression in the United States may be overdue, but it's welcome. If a determined pro-democracy movement truly arises in this country over the coming years, it cannot foolishly (or arrogantly) attempt to stand apart from existing human rights movements, such as Black Lives Matter, the feminist movement, or the movement to protect trans people, who are a special target of right-wing bigotry. On the contrary, any substantive anti-GOP resistance will have to be part of a cohesive, multipronged campaign that encompasses all of these fights.

But being an ally to those causes does not mean taking them over.

Echoing Else's emphasis on voter registration, Zoharah Simmons notes that one area where white volunteers can make an important difference is in get-out-the-vote efforts. "White activists need to go into the White community to organize and educate because Black folk can't even go into that community."[58]

Else concurs. "There are White folks in Modesto that may talk to me if I knock on their door and ask them to register to vote that would not talk to a young Black woman, even though that young Black woman may have lived in Modesto her whole life and I'm an outsider. And there are resources that white people can muster simply because of our privilege that Black folks may not be able to. In the '60s, the whole point of us going to Mississippi was to get arrested and shot and beat up in the full view of the national press."[59] In fact, the Freedom Summer was consciously devised by SNCC to convert passive allies—sympathetic white college students and politicians in the North—to active ones by means of an "invitation to enter" the movement.[60]

"We were the sons and daughters of bankers and businessmen and college professors and journalists," Else told me, "and the press was going to follow us—and sure enough, they did. And sure enough, when a couple of white guys got murdered in Mississippi, the national press that had ignored thousands of murders of young Black men there suddenly took note, and suddenly it was on the front page of *The Washington Post*, and suddenly Lyndon Johnson was calling up J. Edgar Hoover and saying, 'You better get your butt down there.' So I think we can do that."[61]

I put that same question to the Rev. Dr. Norvel Goff, asking his advice for the large number of white people who want to do the right thing but don't know what to do, or how to do it. He told me:

"Well, the first thing I would say is, many of *us* don't know what to do. And we won't know what to do until we come together and learn from one another in terms of what works, what doesn't work, how do you view this versus how I view it, and how can we come to some common ground."[62]

A NOTE ON FORCE

Careful readers—and even some careless ones—will likely note that throughout history a number of pro-democracy movements have transitioned from peaceful protest to armed struggle. Some of those movements we openly laud, whether it is the French Resistance fighting the Nazis, or our own uppity colonists revolting against Mad George III. But here we enter extremely fraught terrain.

I am not a pacifist. My grandfather was a sailor in World War I and my father was a career US Army infantry officer who, as a young company commander in Vietnam, was gravely wounded in one of the worst firefights of the war, the battle of the Ia Drang River Valley.[63] I myself was an infantry and intelligence officer in Germany during the Cold War and in Iraq during the 1991 Persian Gulf War.

So I do believe that there are political circumstances under which the use of force may be necessary (even if neither of those are good examples).

But the resort to violence is a deadly serious decision that opens the door to the worst kind of might-makes-right barbarism. If we can only institute democracy by physical force and not through a mandate of the people, what's to stop our foes from installing a repressive antidemocratic regime by the same method in an arms race divorced from moral power? This is not a matter of high-minded idealism but a recognition that violence is not a sustainable basis for power in the long run. Force is the bluntest of political tools, one that far too many laymen overestimate in its effectiveness and are therefore all too eager to employ. Given the attendant risks, and inevitable suffering, it ought to be the action of last resort.

Therefore, this book will not contemplate any violent efforts to resist a right-wing autocracy in the United States. Military action is appealing and romantic for a nation weaned on tales of our brave forefathers taking up arms against their colonial oppressors. We see that romanticism very much in play on the far right, with its self-flattering comparison to the Minutemen and other Revolutionary War figures. We certainly saw plenty of QAnon clowns, larping *Call of Duty* dipshits, and Walter Mitty *Soldier of Fortune* fantasists among the insurrectionists on January 6. But this adolescent urge to fancy themselves "heroes," and to kill people and break things, is a nauseating impulse for which we rightly revile and criticize right-wingers. Therefore, let us not emulate them.

In *The Unconquerable World*, Jonathan Schell writes that violence has "become dysfunctional as a political instrument."[64] Even in those anti-government campaigns that had military components, such as Ireland's or South Africa's, force was often not the deciding factor. The image of Bobby Sands starving himself to death in the Maze prison in Northern Ireland in 1981 did more for his cause than every bullet he ever fired or bomb he ever set off. We know his name today not because of any of those acts—indeed, probably in spite of them—but because of his final, nonviolent one, part of the famed "dirty protest," fought by IRA political prisoners using the most elemental tools imaginable, from nudity to feces-smeared prison walls, which was itself part of an Irish tradition of fasts and hunger strikes that goes back to its 1919-21 war of independence. The giant oil painting of Sands that hangs over the bar at the Ireland's 32 pub on Geary Street in San Francisco isn't there because of the bombing of the Balmoral Furniture Company in Dunmurry.

To understand this dynamic, it's important to understand how wars are won, and rarely is it by driving every last enemy rifleman, clerk, and cook into the sea. They are won by exerting sufficient pressure such that the other side no longer has the stomach to carry on, or else concludes that the cost of doing so is too high. That is a matter of perception, and of public will, and it applies whether the foe is foreign or domestic, and whether the conflict is violent or not.

The 1968 Tet Offensive marked the decisive turning point in the Vietnam War—the American War, as the Vietnamese called it, to distinguish it from previous campaigns against the French, Japanese, and French again. But that was not because the Viet Cong defeated the US military on the battlefield.* It was the turning point because afterward, the US government no longer had the will to carry on, having seen the determination of its opponent, and the price that would have to be paid to defeat him. It was the turning point because the American public had grown weary of the war and lost faith entirely when the enemy mounted such an audacious strike at the very moment our military and civilian leaders alike were assuring us that victory was at hand.[65]

Similarly, pro-democracy movements—even those that have an ancillary military wing—are typically won by the force of their moral argument and by a sustained campaign of nonviolent action that convinces the public to turn against the ruling regime. Conversely, the ruling autocracy doesn't win because it locks every dissident up, which is a practical impossibility against a truly determined resistance. It wins when it succeeds in making the resistance quit out of despair when its own struggle feels unwinnable.

In other words, all warfare is psychological warfare.

---

* In fact, the VC—the National Liberation Front, in their own parlance—wound up decimated in the counteroffensive, to the advantage of their brethren, the forces of North Vietnam, in the postwar landscape, by the Pentagon's own assessment.

The presumption that nonviolence is limited in its efficacy, and falls short against the most brutal forms of totalitarianism, is very common. But is it accurate? Undoubtedly so, when it comes to a toe to toe military battle against an invading army. But in strategic counterattack as an asymmetrical means of resistance, it may be as good if not better, precisely *because* of the enemy's military might.

Military conflict involves adversaries fighting with the same quiver of weapons, even if they are mismatched. A violent rebellion can therefore be quashed by superior force (usually). But the same suppressive methods are less effective against a nonviolent protest, as armed soldiers are ill-equipped to address those tactics except by brutality and massacre, which are often counterproductive.[66] The power of nonviolent action, then, is that it neutralizes the opponent's strengths, *particularly* an opponent who has an overwhelming advantage in terms of brute force.[67] A nonviolent struggle is therefore asymmetrical not only in terms of the relative physical might of the two sides, but in the means of that struggle as well.

Sharp writes:

> When violence is committed against people who are, and are seen to be, nonviolent, it is difficult for the opponent to claim "self-defense" for his use of extreme repression, or to argue that the severe repression was for the good of the society as a whole. Instead, the opponent is likely to appear to many people as a villain, and many will believe that the worst accusations against the opponent are being confirmed, and that they are witnessing "deepening injustice."[68]*

Sharp reminds us that nonviolent action is *action*, not passivity, pushing back against the derision that peaceful resistance is weak beer—again, a charge deceitfully deployed by its targets, with an

---

*   The same is true of vigilantes and terrorists who attack peaceful protestors. Sharp cites the white supremacist bombings in January 1957 during the Montgomery bus boycott, which caused several prominent segregationists to reverse course—not because they had changed their minds on race, but because the horror of what had been done in their name had, even for them, gone beyond the pale at last.

ulterior, deterrent-based motive.[69] "The maintenance of nonviolent discipline in the face of repression is not an act of moralistic naivete," he writes, but a "prerequisite for advantageous power changes."[70] Sharp also notes that critics are quick to jump on cases where nonviolent action has failed, and far less quick to record where violence has similarly fallen short. If nonviolent resistance is so ineffective, he asks, why is it met with such ruthless response by the state?[71] In point of fact, the extremity of that response is a testament to the power of nonviolence and the threat it poses to the established order.[*]

"The opponent prefers violence," Sharp writes, noting that even the Nazis generally sought provocations—real or fabricated—to lend legitimacy to their actions: the suspension of civil liberties justified by the Reichstag fire; the Anschluss, predicated on complaints about the plight of ethnic Germans in Austria; the seizure of the Sudetenland, premised on false claims of Germany's historical borders; even the invasion of Poland, excused on the basis of a fake seizure of a German radio station by Polish forces.[72] "Nazis wanted violence from their opponents," Sharp writes. "If it did not happen anyhow, the Nazis either falsely attributed violence to the opposition or provoked them to commit it."[73][**]

Former Nazi generals interviewed by the British military historian Sir Basil Liddell Hart reported that they were relieved when violent guerrilla actions began to displace peaceful protest in occupied countries such as Denmark, Norway, the Netherlands, and to a lesser extent in Belgium and France, as it allowed them to reach for the martial tools of brutal repression with which they were more comfortable.[74] "They were experts in violence," Hart writes, "and had been trained to deal with opponents who used that method. But other forms of resistance baffled them—and all the more in

---

[*] Even the American war for independence began as a nonviolent struggle, a strategy that Sharp believes would have led to victory more quickly than the armed conflict that ensued after Lexington and Concord.

[**] Here Sharp cites the successful opposition of Norwegian teachers to edicts from the Quisling regime, and Guatemalan resistance that forced the resignation of the strongman General Jorge Ubico in 1944. There are even a handful of examples of successful civil disobedience against the Nazis—chiefly, a week-long protest by hundreds of German women outside the Rosenstrasse community center in the heart of Berlin in the freezing cold winter of 1943.

proportion as the methods were subtle and concealed. It was a relief to them when resistance was violent, and when nonviolent forms were mixed with guerrilla action, thus making it easier to combine drastic repressive action against both at the same time."[75]

Armed force is most useful for defending the nation against foreign attack. It would be madness to allow a hostile invader to roll in unimpeded and conquer one's homeland, only to mount a campaign after the fact—nonviolent or otherwise—to evict him. But if armed defense fails and the country is conquered, or if it falls under the iron hand of a domestic tyranny, nonviolence may stand as good a chance as guerrilla warfare—or better—of overthrowing the oppressor.

In *Why Civil Resistance Works: The Strategic Logic of Nonviolent Conflict* (2010), the political scientists Erica Chenoweth and Maria Stephan surveyed 323 resistance movements over the 106 years from 1900–2006 and found that nonviolent movements had a success rate of 53 percent compared to only 26 percent for violent ones. Nonviolent movements also resulted in democratic outcomes more frequently. The authors' research caused them to formulate the "3.5% rule," which sets that number as the threshold of citizen participation necessary for a resistance movement to succeed. In their study, all the movements that met that standard were nonviolent.[76]

Three and a half percent of the adult US population is about nine million people, the same number of people who bought Matchbox 20's 1996 album *Yourself or Someone Like You*. That seems a highly achievable number for an anti-MAGA, pro-democracy campaign in America should a second Trump regime come to power. We're not talking about *Thriller* here.

Schell makes a similar argument that nonviolence can actually be more effective than the force of arms, citing the record of Gandhi, King, and Mandela, compared to the long-term outcomes and repercussions of various wars. "*Satyaghara* was not some pale sister of violence," he writes, "embraced for her virtue alone," but a strategy that offered practical advantages.[77] For that matter, "soft power" played a key role in the ascent of the Nazis themselves, who infamously took control of the German government via election, which is to say, by marshaling public support and undermining that of their opponents. Therefore, even as we contemplate how best to use the levers of nonviolent persuasion, we must be aware that the other side is using them as well.[78]

Yet even Schell stops short of absolute pacifism across the board, rejecting the idea that "one rule was applicable to all imaginable situations."[79] Arguing strictly on pragmatic terms, Saul Alinsky believed that a campaign of nonviolence made sense for the American Civil Rights Movement, given that segregationist whites in the former Confederacy were well-known for their quick resort to the most murderous violence, making an armed uprising by Black people a fraught proposition.[80] Instead, as we have noted, the image of white Southerners brutalizing peaceful Black protestors, including children, was the image of the Jim Crow system damning itself before the world.

Similarly, Alinsky notes that Gandhi was working with the tools he had at hand, aiming at the most vulnerable points of his English foe by the most effective means available. Had he other tools, he might have used them. In Alinsky's view, Gandhi's brand of nonviolent resistance "would never have had a chance against a totalitarian state such as that of the Nazis."[81] That may be, but a military challenge would have stood even less of a chance. It is the very brutality of a police state—and its overwhelming domestic monopoly on armed power—that makes violent insurgency so difficult.

It could be argued that a military component to a pro-democracy movement is a helpful factor in putting pressure on the regime, much like extreme acts of nonviolent civil disobedience such as the Berrigans'. But the opposite can also be true. Introducing violent elements into a previously nonviolent struggle can alienate the public and undermine the campaign, giving the autocracy justification for its own violence—per Hart's research—and its portrayal of the entire resistance movement as dangerous outlaws.[82] That is why agents provocateurs so often try to infiltrate pro-democracy movements and foment violence, a tactic used by the FBI and other US government agencies against the civil rights and anti-war movements of the 1960s. In 2020, the political scientist Omar Wasow published scholarship suggesting that left-wing and civil rights violence in 1968 actually drove a small but statistically significant portion of the white electorate into Nixon's camp in November of that year.[83] The fact that the violence was in response to far worse violence by the state and by right-wing vigilantes—such as the murders of Martin Luther King and Robert Kennedy, ongoing warfare in Vietnam, and the response to protests in the US—doesn't change Wasow's conclusion so much as drape it in cruel irony.

That temptation to violence can be strong, especially in cases where the oppressor's hand is so heavy. But it is usually self-defeating.

The Black Panther Party for Self-Defense—its original, full name is instructive—was formed in Oakland in 1966, a place and time when Black people were routinely being attacked and killed by the police. It was quite hard to argue against the notion of members of that community taking up arms to defend themselves. It's an ethos conservative white people, who tend to be very attached to the frontier ideal of self-reliance and protecting one's own, ought to be able to relate to. But they don't.

Instead, the Panthers' overt embrace of the Second Amendment was the exact thing that has allowed the American right to demonize it, even prompting the NRA of that time to take a hardline pro-gun control stance.[84] (You may have noticed it has since changed its tune.) To this day conservatives almost invariably cite the Panthers when trying to indict the Black liberation movement, even though none of the violence committed by the Panthers—mostly shootouts with police—ever came close to the violence committed against Black Americans over the course of US history from slavery to the Klan to thousands of lynchings during Reconstruction and Jim Crow to the FBI's wanton murder of Fred Hampton himself in 1968.

The Black Panthers certainly held a romantic grip on the American imagination, as evidenced by their enduring appeal in popular culture. But the Panthers probably did themselves and the movement more good with their free school breakfasts for children than they did with their shotguns and rifles.[85] It is even more true of the Weathermen, who committed far more acts of violence than the Panthers, and who are not remembered as great Americans by most, or even as well as their hero John Brown.[86]

You know who is? John Lewis.

CHAPTER 10

It's the Economy, Stupid

The flow of money is a chokepoint at which the mechanisms of power are most vulnerable, some examples of which we have already touched upon. Strikes, slowdowns, boycotts, and the like are forms of protest (and in some cases, civil disobedience) effective not only in raising public awareness, but as concrete, specifically targeted actions that prevent those mechanisms from operating as they normally would.

David Atkins notes that "democracy's defenders have an advantage" in that we "represent the majority of America and are also the main drivers of the country's culture and economy."[1] Democratic counties "produce more than 70 percent of America's GDP. US cities—overwhelmingly blue—are responsible for the vast majority of the country's cultural and economic output.[2] Blue states are overwhelmingly donors to the states that despise them and seek to disenfranchise them. The nation's most successful companies are typically located in ultra-liberal areas."[3]

We have seen how demographic trends—increasingly urban, politically progressive, young, and non-white—threaten the GOP and have motivated it to adopt antidemocratic tactics. Atkins believes that these same trends can also force Big Business, which still represents a formidable faction within the Republican Party, to recognize on which side its Wonder Bread is buttered. We know that this dynamic is real, and that this technique works, because of the way the Republican Party now regularly styles itself the victim of so-called "cancel culture" and howls about the behavior of allegedly "woke" corporations, from Disney to Starbucks, and even famously conservative companies like Cracker Barrel (condemned for a Facebook post celebrating Pride month).[4]

When they take away your vote, not everyone can put their body on the gears of the machine in protest or go to jail for their beliefs. But everyone can vote with their dollars.

HIT 'EM IN THE POCKETBOOK

If, as Republicans like to say, corporations are people, then they can be vulnerable to pressure just like old-fashioned, flesh-and-blood people. Grassroots boycotts of companies complicit in the Republican regime are a direct way to inflict pain at those organizations' most sensitive pressure point—their wallet. Corporations can be confronted with the full force of public disapproval and compelled to withdraw their support, as Toyota was when it was revealed that the company was one of the major donors to pro-insurrectionist politicians,[5] or when AT&T was shamed into dropping the far-right One America News from its platform (albeit not as fully as it claimed).[6] One of the great advantages of this tactic is that it requires no propagandizing, or argument, or appeal to the foe's better angels, if it has any. It is purely transactional, with the targeted companies made to feel the consequences of their collaboration.

As Levitsky and Ziblatt write, "Business leaders may not be natural allies of Democratic activists, but they have good reasons to oppose an unstable and rule-breaking administration. And they can be powerful partners. Think of recent boycott movements aimed at states that refused to honor Martin Luther King's birthday, continued to fly the Confederate flag, or violated gay or transgender rights."[7] Indeed, a 2011 study by Northwestern University's Kellogg School of Management found that a quarter of the 133 boycotts that it studied between 1990 and 2005 were successful in extracting at least some concessions from the targets.[8] Of course, as *The Atlantic*'s James Surowiecki notes, that means 75 percent were unsuccessful. But 1 in 4 remains a formidable record.[9]

Perhaps the most well-known example of an effective boycott in the US was the 1965–70 boycott of California grapes organized by the United Farm Workers and its antecedent and associated organizations under the leadership of Cesar Chavez. Apropos of that campaign, Saul Alinsky advises focusing boycotts on products that are not essential and can be readily foregone—grapes yes, bread no—and/ or targeting those boycotts at a single business, driving customers to their competitors, rather than an entire industry.[10]

Sometimes it is easy to identify a target, such as Goya, whose CEO was (and remains) a vocal supporter of Donald Trump, or Chick-fil-A, whose fundamentalist Christian owners have donated significant sums of money to anti-LGBTQ+ causes.[11] Other times it can be hard to disentangle the ownership, in the complex web of multinational global corporations. But even when the financial impact of a boycott is negligible, the symbolic impact can be significant in terms of consciousness-raising, putting these companies on notice that their behavior is neither invisible nor acceptable.[*]

It can work the other way as well, of course. In 2022 Target shamefully buckled under right-wing pressure and removed LGBTQ-themed products that it has long sold during Pride month.[12] After right-wingers fulminated over a Bud Light campaign that included a trans spokesperson, Anheuser-Busch suspended the marketing team, which resulted in progressives turning against the brand too.[13] Which speaks to the rock-and-a-hard-place position of companies trying to navigate partisan waters.[**]

The right often gripes that this sort of economic pressure is a kind of "censorship"—or even less generously, blackmail—even though they readily engage in it themselves.[14] The former accusation is empirically incorrect, the latter hypocritical. Only the state can censor, whether it's speech or economics. By contrast, when consumers make choices, for whatever reason, that is the very exercise of free speech on their part, and the market operating as it is intended to do, which is the very heart of capitalism.

---

*   Goya is instructive. Calls for a boycott actually caused its sale to rise, which researchers at Cornell attributed to brand loyalty and—apropos of Alinsky—"the difficulties of finding an adequate substitute." Its CEO, Robert Unanue, continued to support Trump, repeating the Big Lie as late as 2021.

**   Contra Goya, *The Atlantic's* James Surowiecki reports that the right's boycott of Bud Light had a significant effect on Anheuser-Busch's bottom line, in part because it was relatively painless on the part of the boycotters (there were plenty of other beers right-wingers could turn to), and because of the public, performative nature of beer consumption.

The ultimate testament to the power of this kind of economic starvation is that nation-states themselves routinely rely upon it. In almost every case of international outrage, the first step is a call for economic sanctions. That approach is invariably derided by some as timid; the deriders are often the same people who are keen to reach instead for bombs, which have an even worse track record of effecting lasting change. But properly applied, denial of commerce can have a powerful effect; the cause it serves is a separate matter. The US maintained an embargo on Cuba for decades, contributing to the grinding poverty and crippling opportunities for development in that country. We currently use sanctions on Iran to deter its nuclear ambitions, and on Russia over its grotesque war of aggression in Ukraine, to name just two. Yes, refusing to buy a can of Goya beans is not in the same league as cutting off the Nord Stream pipelines, but it is the same principle, and enough Americans refusing to patronize such companies will serve notice that they cannot bed down with the autocracy without facing punishment from the people.[15]

It can be complicated when the target isn't a single corporation, or a given industry, as in the grape boycott, but is instead one of the fifty states that is pursuing an antidemocratic agenda. Should we boycott Florida as a vacation destination? Or should we flock there and spend our dollars in solidarity with Disney in its battle against DeSantis?* The question speaks to the debate about whether boycotts and sanctions only hurt innocent people without applying appreciable pressure on the villains who are their true targets.

The dilemma was in play domestically in 2021, when Georgia enacted a series of restrictive new laws aimed at suppressing the vote under Republican Governor Brian Kemp, a notorious practitioner of that cause.** Major League Baseball pulled the 2021 All-Star Game

---

* Let's set aside for now the notion that one of the biggest entertainment conglomerates on Earth is somehow an oppressed victim in the struggle for human rights.

** As Georgia's secretary of state for eight years, Kemp instituted many of the measures that experts believed suppressed and skewed the vote there—measures that then benefited him when he ran for governor and won, as reported by *The New Yorker's* Jelani Cobb. In other words, the guy who won the election was the guy who had just been in charge of making the election rules.

from Atlanta, while numerous Hollywood and independent film productions announced that they would no longer shoot in the state, which had long been a popular location due to attractive tax incentives and an established infrastructure for film.

It is certainly true that ordinary working people suffer when out-of-state business turns away in protest. But at the same time, to carry on rewarding a Republican government even as it institutes loathsome policies is to grant the Brian Kemps of the world permission to act with impunity.[16] Punishing Georgia might well allow Kemp to rally his voters against these snotty outsiders, a proven strategy in the old South. But do we want Kemp to run for his next public office—US senator perhaps, or president—touting how he suppressed the Black vote to his white nationalist voters while simultaneously crowing that he brought booming economic times to his state to the mainstream?

"Whatever you think about American corporations," Jon Else says, "people listen to them. If you can coerce or shame them with boycotts and bad press, they can be very useful. During Trump's Muslim ban, Tim Cook of Apple was very publicly critical of it, fiercely so, and so was Hamdi Ulukaya, the founder of Chobani yogurt. Sergey Brin, the founder of Google, actually went up to the San Francisco airport and was part of a sit-in. Are there things wrong with Google and Apple? Of course. But we shouldn't dismiss those allies when they step forward."[17]

That, of course, is the very "wokeness" that conservatives decry. Their estimate of how many corporations are actually in this forward-thinking category is lavishly exaggerated, of course, and the extent to which a profit-driven business will ever put principle ahead of the bottom line is questionable. But fortunately for democracy, a stable, contented citizenry who feel agency in the political system, who have faith in institutions because those institutions treat them justly, and who are invested in the community, is a good state of affairs for everyone.

Consider the financial industry, a powerful constituency—far too powerful, some would say—and one with a proprietary interest in a stable, productive society. Unrest is bad for business. The evidence is in Wall Street's history of hedging its bets by contributing heavily to both political parties.[18] (A completely different problem, it's fair to say, as we have previously discussed.) The GOP's pro-business bent has traditionally made it the favorite of bankers and financiers, but that is already changing as the Trumpist version of the GOP has proven to be economically reckless, neither respecting conventional conservative positions on matters like trade policy nor acting as a reliable steward of American economic security.

Where once the Rockefeller wing of the Republican Party exploited the reactionary fanatics, or imagined it did, it is now inarguably the other way around. But there is surely a wedge to be found in the differing economic agendas of various Republican factions . . . or more correctly, the fact that one faction of the GOP has an economic agenda at all and the other doesn't. The alliance between plutocrats and religious zealots has been very effective for the American right, but it has always been an uneasy fit. "Religious fundamentalism across the board is anti-capitalist and anti-growth and at odds with what the economy wants," one anonymous expert told me, citing opposition to birth control, which wreaks havoc with family planning, keeps half the potential workforce at home raising babies, and creates single-income households, as an example.[19]

Purely for its own self-interest, and without any appeal to altruism, the mechanisms of capitalism can be mobilized to preserve the kind of democratic society in which it has historically thrived.[20] It can put money behind pro-democracy candidates, make its commitment to participatory democracy known, and cut off support to a Republican Party that can no longer be trusted to oversee it. Transactional and non-ideological as they are, pro-business elements can be made to turn on a right-wing regime that threatens their bottom line. We have it within our power to push them to do so.

STRIKES AND BALLS

Boycotts leverage the power of the consumer; slowdowns, stoppages, and strikes marshal the power of the producer to force the powers that be to the bargaining table, win concessions, and even topple them entirely. "Supply side" economics, it turns out, goes both ways.

Globally, there is perhaps no better example of this power than Solidarity in Poland, where the firing of its cofounder, Anna Walentynowicz, a welder and crane operator at the Gdańsk shipyard, triggered a strike in August 1980 that sparked the entire movement.

That movement went on to use the strike as its principal weapon in a decade-long campaign of patient, steadfast, and peaceful pressure that ultimately brought that regime to its knees.

A general strike represents a dramatic escalation from the ordinary kind, as well as the most blunt possible demonstration that political power ultimately resides with the people. Shutting down the entire economy and bringing American life to a halt would be a reminder that, ultimately, no regime, not even the most authoritarian, can rule without the consent of the governed, even when tyrants try to assert otherwise. The plebeians of Rome mounted what were essentially general strikes—probably the earliest example in recorded history—as early as 494 BCE.[21] Gandhi made use of the *hartal*, a temporary general strike, in the Indian independence struggle.[22] In more recent times, the events of May 1968 in France present the most prominent example of the tactic, stretching from the factories to the universities to the streets of Paris and other major cities.[23]

But the kind of complex campaign Solidarity carried out in Poland, let alone the broad-based discipline required for a general strike, cannot be accomplished without granular organizing, which traditionally has been provided by unions.

The contributions of labor unions cannot be overstated. Many of the workplace norms we take for granted in the United States—the eight-hour day and forty-hour week, the weekend, overtime, safe working conditions, pensions and benefits, an end to child labor—are the hard-won fruits of that movement. Which may be why the plutocracy has always hated and attacked them.

"Unions provided phenomenal benefits for regular people over the course of the twentieth century," says Amy Hanauer of the Institute on Taxation and Economic Policy.[24] "But after Reagan broke the PATCO strike and fired all the air traffic controllers, we saw incredible erosion in the ability to join a union. So today, even though most people would like the ability to do that, unionization levels are at an all-time low. And that's because of repressive tactics that are taken by many employers when somebody tries to join a union or when workers try to form one."*

---

* Reagan, ironically, remains the only US president ever to have been the head of a union, the Screen Actors Guild. PATCO had even endorsed him for the presidency. Look for the union label, indeed.

That systematic effort to destroy the union movement continues even now, representing a strategic, preemptive assault on a movement that can be mobilized to defend democracy.[25] As an institution, labor unions remain a mainstay of Democratic support, even as a significant chunk of their membership has defected to the GOP, particularly among the white working class. That phenomenon is itself headshaking, as people who have no common cause whatsoever with the plutocracy—quite the opposite, in fact—are seduced into voting against their own economic interests, often via a none-too-subtle appeal to racism.

"My dad always told this great story about being on the subway as a little boy in the '30s," Max Brooks, son of the comedian Mel Brooks, told me. "These two factory workers were sitting there, blue-collar guys, with their beat-up lunch pails and holes in their shoes, reading the newspaper and saying, 'Ah, these reds, we gotta get 'em!' And my dad, as a little boy, was like, 'Shouldn't you *be* a red?'"[26]

While in office from 2011 to 2019, Republican Governor Scott Walker of Wisconsin infamously made a crusade of destroying public unions. As a result, union membership in Wisconsin today is at an all-time low.[27] Nationwide, it is half what it was forty years ago.[28] The powerful right-wing lobbyist Grover Norquist cited Walker's efforts as a model, arguing that if it were "enacted in a dozen more states, the modern Democratic Party will cease to be a competitive power in American politics."[29]

But the GOP's hopes for Walker's program as a paradigm it could export—and the otherwise lifeless Walker himself as potential US president—lasted only until the people of Wisconsin unseated him in 2018 and drove him into the political wilderness from which he has yet to emerge. Turns out breaking unions and destroying the livelihood of working people like a mob of baseball bat–wielding scabs has limited popular appeal.

The defense of unions and the union movement is therefore a key aspect of the fight to defend democracy, and to preserve one of our strongest means to regain it should it slip out of our grasp.

Saul Alinsky championed another market-based technique, which he called "shareholder activism."[30]

In 1967, Rochester, New York was a company town virtually owned lock, stock, and barrel by Eastman Kodak, whose racially discriminatory practices were legion.[31] (Alinsky memorably called it "a huge southern plantation transplanted north."[32]) Working together with a Black civil rights organization called FIGHT—Freedom, Integration, God, Honor, Today—Alinsky recognized that the usual measures like a boycott would not work, as Kodak had a near monopoly on 35mm film, and asking the American people to stop taking photos was untenable. Instead, he hit on the idea of obtaining the proxies of sympathetic shareholders. What began as merely a way to obtain entrée to Kodak's annual meeting morphed into a more strategic effort to get Kodak stockholders from all over the country—including universities, churches, unions, nonprofit foundations, mutual funds, and even private individuals—to assign their proxies to Alinsky and FIGHT, enabling them to extract significant concessions and reforms from the company, a victory that few thought achievable. That was a wonkish and non-spectacular strategy that lacked the drama of a street confrontation, but it nonetheless brought Kodak to heel—and scared the hell out of other corporations that feared they would be the next target. It was also an approach that would later be employed in the campaign to force divestment of US investment in South Africa, particularly among colleges and universities.

Kodak was also the site of successful organizing by the Rev. Dr. Norvel Goff in the 1990s, while he was pastor of an AME church in Rochester. As head of the city chapter of the NAACP, Goff led a campaign that forced the company to pay millions in damages for racial and gender discrimination and to change its business practices. That in turn led to reforms at numerous other area businesses, including the city's gas and electric utility, Blue Cross, and Xerox. I asked him how he and his colleagues were able to effect such remarkable change.

"We had hundreds of individuals who came to the NAACP with complaints. We requested a meeting, brought facts, did the kinds of things that would foster an open line of communication. And when the management looked into it, they saw the light, and that it was in their best interest to try to eradicate these problems.

"For those who have goodwill, I think once you know better, you do better," Rev. Goff told me. "It's not the 'gotcha' moment of, 'You're racist, you discriminate, you hate Black people and Brown people and women.' No. I'm not trying to destroy you and neither of us is trying to destroy our community. We want to make it a better place for everybody—not just some, but everybody. And I think that that voice comes through."[33]

THE DEVIL IS IN THE DEMOGRAPHICS

A tax revolt is another time-honored means of active resistance against a tyrannical regime. Again we harken back to Gandhi, who made use of the technique, most notably in the Kheda district of western India in 1918, where he eventually forced the British to rescind a crippling tax increase it had tried to impose on the region's impoverished farmers, during a famine and cholera plague, no less. For that matter, a tax revolt was at the core of the very founding of the United States, as self-styled patriotic conservatives who would shriek at the alleged criminality of such tactics would do well to remember.

An American tax revolt would also pierce one of the right wing's most cherished myths. A hoary Republican talking point, dating back to Reagan, is that of "makers and takers," the notion that some Americans (hardworking, tax-paying, pale of pigmentation) contribute to the common good through the sweat of their collective brow, while others (shiftless, lazy, non-white) merely leech off the former.[34] It's a handy trope for reactionary politicians, not to mention a form of racist dog whistling to their white nationalist base. But like many of the GOP's stickiest talking points, it's at odds with the facts.

As we have noted, Democratic-leaning counties and states produce more than 70 percent of America's GDP.[35] Accordingly, they overwhelmingly send more money to Washington in the form of tax revenue than they get back, while it is deep red states, especially in the former Confederacy, that suck hardest on the federal teat. The economist Paul Krugman, whom Justin Schein and I also interviewed for *Death and Taxes*, reports that "in 2019 the federal government spent almost twice as much in Arkansas as it collected in taxes, de facto providing the average Arkansas resident with $5,500 in aid," even as the state's new governor, former Trump press secretary Sarah Huckabee Sanders, "pledged to get the 'bureaucratic tyrants' of Washington 'out of your wallets.'"[36]

The *Washington Post*'s David Montgomery quotes David Becker, executive director of the Center for Election Innovation & Research and coauthor with Major Garrett of *The Big Truth: Upholding Democracy in the Age of the Big Lie*, speculating about a second Trump term, and pondering how long before California asks, "'Why aren't we requiring the federal government to pay for its use of the naval bases in San Diego and Camp Pendleton and other places? . . . There are a lot of people who would say, 'Oh, that would never happen.' [But] what we've seen in the last two years we thought would never happen."[37]

For California, New York, Illinois, and others to refuse to fund a right-wing government that abuses and insults its constituents would be a sharp demonstration of progressive America's raw political power, giving the lie to the "makers and takers" canard, and possibly forcing substantive concessions, if not threatening the entire autocratic venture.

In an American autocracy, blue neighborhoods, cities, and even whole states can function as enclaves of democracy even as right-wing madness rages elsewhere. Ironically, we see the opposite happening in the most hard-line red states, which are increasingly turning themselves into fiefdoms of radical right-wing theocracy, like Texas, Tennessee, or DeSantis's self-styled "Free State of Florida." Blue state governments must be prepared to think of themselves as bastions of democracy in a sea of revanchism. In the parts of the United States where progressivism remains strong, where pro-democracy leaders remain in power, and where a large majority remain committed to genuine democracy, those states can codify rights and values that are under attack elsewhere and nationwide: on abortion, on gun control, on voting rights, on environmental protections. This balkanization is not the preferred scenario by any means, and is not sustainable in the long term. But it may prove a helpful and strategic—if temporary—approach in the short term.

Though few recognized it as such, we came surprisingly close to something like this during the COVID-19 pandemic, at a time when Trump was claiming the virus would magically disappear. I spoke to a prominent doctor, a familiar presence on TV in that period, who asked: "When Trump failed, what saved us? Governors." It was policymakers at the state level who not only put out scientifically correct information, but actively considered more radical measures.

"The Northeast was inches away from blocking itself off from the rest of the country. Cuomo was telling the administration, 'If you guys don't step up, we're just going to close our borders and trade amongst ourselves, because we at least are following the science.'"[38]

Purely as a temporary measure, an economic trading bloc of prosperous, Democratically controlled states—especially contiguous ones, like the Northeastern and mid-Atlantic states—would constitute a powerful bargaining lever and demonstration of defiance and of economic might. There is also something to be said for disabusing Americans of all political persuasions of the myth that white Republicans are subsidizing the rest of us, for letting red America know that we will not be taken advantage of, and for leveraging that power.

Admittedly, the threat of a plague made more tolerable otherwise extreme measures like blockades, restrictions on interstate travel, and border-like checkpoints for Americans crossing state lines. It would be a tragedy to see barricaded American cities, or neighborhoods within them, on the order of "Free Derry" in Northern Ireland. Violence would be almost inevitable, absent a tactical restraint that the incipient right-wing American autocracy shows few signs of possessing.

Needless to say, such a revolt, taken to its extreme, could put the very union at risk. But it is already at risk, and Republicans have shown no qualms about pushing it further in that direction, from brinksmanship over the debt ceiling to reckless talk of secession and "a national divorce," as Rep. Marjorie Taylor Greene of Georgia put it. In Texas, talk of secession from the United States is practically a cottage industry.[39]

Another oft-heard option should Trump win back the White House, usually floated half in jest, is that of leaving the country altogether. People talk of dual citizenship, of EU passports obtained on the strength of immigrant ancestors, of bank accounts in Portugal. It's understandable, and there may be times when such an exodus is highly advisable. No one begrudges a German Jew who fled the Third Reich: on the contrary, we look back on those who did not leave when they could as tragically foolhardy. But in America in the here and now, there's a strong argument for digging in and not giving up.

Expatriation is an option only available mostly to the privileged; the majority of Americans has no resort to that luxury. More to the point, forfeit is hard to respect when the struggle is still very much ongoing. In post-Saddam Iraq, those Iraqis who stuck around through the years of tyranny, voluntarily or not, had much more public credibility in trying to build a new regime than returning exiles, even when those exiles had fled for perfectly legitimate reasons, sometimes even to save their own lives.[40]

For those who have the resources to escape, the temptation is only human, but there is something to be said for staying put and sticking together. Are we really going to surrender this country to the right-wing horde and leave the poorest and most vulnerable of us to deal with it?

The hell we are.

CHAPTER 11

Mrs. Orwell's Lament

George Orwell's mother must have mixed feelings. What her son did so well, eight decades ago, was teach us how the control of information—indeed, of language itself—is central to authoritarianism. His is a household name, albeit already a nom de plume. But "Orwellian" is anything but a compliment, reducing Mrs. O's bragging rights around the mah-jongg table.

It is no surprise that an autocracy seeks to control the narrative that defines public intercourse. Think of euphemisms like "alternative facts," "family separation," "tort reform," and of course "pro-life," all of which we have foolishly allowed into routine discourse. (Going back even further we find "ethnic cleansing," "constructive engagement," and "re-location camp.") But this is a preemptive linguistic surrender that gives the right wing a significant and undeserved advantage. Time and again we let them dictate the very terms of the conversation—inaccurately—deriding earned benefits like Social Security as "entitlements," or the estate tax as "the death tax," or accepting the rebranding of "global warming" as the less threatening "climate change," with nary a polite throat-clearing by way of complaint. Ceding the very terms of the debate to the other side means having that debate on their turf. In fact, it often forfeits the match right from the start.

Ironically, one of the best examples of that dynamic is the term that represents information subversion itself: fake news.

"Fake news" describes fictions created for dissemination as propaganda. Bizarrely, the concept has its origins in the Russian avant garde, as described in *HyperNormalisation*, the 2016 film by the British documentarian Adam Curtis. The leaders of the early Soviet Union, and the highly aggressive intelligence services that ministered to them, quickly recognized the potential of such techniques and employed them to befuddle the people preparatory to the manipulation (or simple elimination) of the popular will. In the post-Soviet era, that tradition has enthusiastically been continued by Vladimir Putin, who, lest we forget, was a KGB lieutenant colonel. The Kremlin has proven to be expert at sowing doubt and confusion that exhausts one's ability to think critically, at clouding reality with a fog of disinformation, and at generating cynicism that causes the average citizen to simply give up.

Or, in the earthier terms of Steve Bannon, "flooding the zone with shit."[1]

There is an infuriating symmetry in the fact that the term "fake news" entered the Western lexicon on the lips of an American quisling who was its foremost beneficiary. As Masha Gessen explains, fake news refers mostly "to false stories proffered by the likes of Breitbart, Russian internet trolls, or Macedonian teenagers who made a killing off gullible Americans by posting made-up tales on social networks."[2] But Trump inverted the term to attack the legitimate press, a ploy perfectly matched to his own hideous nature, in which every accusation is a confession.

The kind of blind allegiance that demanded by an autocrat depends upon this willful obliteration of what we quaintly used to call "truth," eliminating the very basis for challenging his power. It commands the public to accept whatever the autocrat says even when they know it is not so, a literalization of Orwell's "final, most essential command" in *1984*, to reject the evidence of your own eyes and ears. When the de facto state-run television network feeds its tens of millions of viewers lies and they accept them uncritically, the very existence of empirical facts is under assault . . . just as it is when an American president himself tells those viewers that his inaugural crowd was the biggest ever, or that he can re-route a hurricane's path with a Sharpie, or that a pandemic will just magically disappear.

This obliteration of the truth was among the most poisonous of Trump's legacies. "Logic can be met with logic, while illogic cannot—it confuses those who think straight," wrote the psychoanalyst Joost A.M. Meerloo, as quoted by the journalist Chris Hedges in a Trump-era piece for *Truthdig*. "The Big Lie and monotonously repeated nonsense have more emotional appeal in a cold war than logic and reason. While the enemy is still searching for a reasonable counter-argument to the first lie, the totalitarians can assault him with another."[3] Meerloo—writing in the '50s—was speaking of generic Big Lies, like the Big Lie that the Holocaust had never happened, and even earlier and precedent to that, the Big Lie that Germany had been "stabbed in the back" at Versailles (the *Dolchstoßlegende*). But his description applies perfectly to the Republican Big Lie that the 2020 election was stolen, and to contemporary right-wing gaslighting in general.

Trump, of course, lies as readily as he breathes, and not just for the usual practical reasons. Very often the purpose of his lies is purely to demonstrate sheer power—over his followers, over those who hew to demonstrable reality, over reality itself—by flaunting his ability to defy even observable facts.[4]

More than seventy years ago, Hannah Arendt crystallized this dynamic in *The Origins of Totalitarianism*:

> The totalitarian mass leaders based their propaganda on the correct psychological assumption that . . . one could make people believe the most fantastic statements one day, and trust that if the next day they were given irrefutable proof of their falsehood, they would take refuge in cynicism; instead of deserting the leaders who had lied to them, they would protest that they had known all along that the statement was a lie and would admire the leaders for their superior tactical cleverness. The result . . . is not that the lie will now be accepted as truth and truth be defamed as a lie, but that the sense by which we take our bearings in the real world—and the category of truth versus falsehood is among the mental means to this end—is being destroyed.[5]

STOP THE PRESSES

Naturally, a political movement that insists that reality is whatever its maximum leader says it is will be hostile to a free press that stands irritatingly in the way of the autocratic endeavor. If the facts cannot be readily dismissed, the best and easiest solution is to attack the credibility of the messenger who announces them. Not for nothing do despots, Trump very much included, demonize journalists as "the enemy of the people."

Trump took that demonization to a neo-Stalinist extreme, but it was not a new tool in the Republican kit. During the previous administration, the American right waged a relentless war on the facts in its campaign to destroy Barack Obama at any cost, and by extension to undermine criticism of conservatism's own agenda: on tax policy, on the climate emergency, on foreign adventurism, and more. It succeeded all too well.[6] By 2016, a large chunk of the American electorate was accustomed to dismissing any inconvenient truths that did not jibe with its preexisting worldview. Confirmation bias became the guiding principle of news consumption.

While that instinct cut across ideology, it found especially fertile ground on the right, where contempt for the media, resentment toward "elites," and susceptibility to conspiracy theory are traditionally highest. And the more august the journalistic source—*The New York Times*, *The Washington Post*, NPR, CNN—the more urgent the need to discredit it. (The same impulse also applies to individuals, from Robert Mueller to Anthony Fauci to Jack Smith.) The fragmentation of journalism driven by the Internet and other new technology, and the concomitant capacity to spread stories virally regardless of whether they are true or not, has contributed mightily to this phenomenon.

That phenomenon is often characterized as "siloing," but Masha Gessen notes that the analogy is unfair and misleading, implying the existence of competing media ecosystems equally circumscribed by partisan ideology. But consumers of *The New York Times* and *Washington Post* are regularly exposed to opinions from columnists and op-ed contributors representing a wide range of ideological belief, many at odds with their own. Consumers of Breitbart and Fox News are not, and instead daily bathe in comforting propaganda that reinforces their existing biases.[7]

The Washington Post media columnist Margaret Sullivan (formerly the public editor of *The New York Times*) writes of her shock at being at the 2016 Republican National Convention in Cleveland and seeing T-shirts for sale emblazoned with the image of a noose and the words: *Rope. Tree. Journalist. Some assembly required.*[8] But such frothing hatred, both for individual reporters and journalism at large, became the right-wing norm in the Trump era. Almost more worrying were the more sophisticated and oblique attacks on the press.

As with elections, one of the distinguishing features of modern autocracies is the *illusion* of a free press, the better to appear "democratic" and fend off accusations of censorship. Instead of kicking down doors, arresting reporters, and shuttering news outlets, the modern autocracy simply marginalizes the *lügenpresse* to the point of uselessness. Putinist Russia, again, is the textbook example (though the Kremlin is not above simply murdering journalists as well).[9] In such a system, a few independent media outlets are allowed to operate, albeit under tremendous pressure, to give the impression of liberalism, while in fact the state severely restricts and controls the news. American media can look forward to further efforts in that direction should the Republican Party gain power.

The Fourth Estate prides itself on being the most formidable line of defense against tyranny—that "democracy dies in darkness," as *The Washington Post's* masthead has proclaimed since February 2017, at the beginning of the Trump era. We are in a time when it would be a vast public service for the press to prove it. But in order to do so, traditional media will have to abandon many of the norms that comprise its traditions and find new, aggressive, and sometimes uncomfortable ways to defend the capital "T" truth against a foe that has neither constraints nor morals.

In the 2016 presidential campaign, we saw that the American media had no idea how to deal with a demagogue like Trump. As an obscenely entitled and pathologically dishonest con man, he had spent a lifetime lying and cheating with abandon and impunity. When he turned to politics—largely to promote his brand, and by all accounts without any real thought of winning anything at all—the mainstream media seemed completely unprepared for how to treat him.[10] They were like medieval lancers facing a modern army wielding tanks and machine guns, incapable even of comprehending how to counter this new weaponry. The press treated Trump with the same rules and decorum to which it had subjected conventional politicians, laughably unaware that he intended to run roughshod over every protocol, norm, and nicety under the honor system that was American politics heretofore. He was a media terrorist who made a laughingstock of the informal guidelines intended to contain him, and indeed turned those norms into weapons that further devalued real journalism and fed his wrecking machine. By the time the press realized that it could not control him, and that they were unwittingly complicit in this atrocity, it was too late.

In fact, many in American journalism have yet to figure that out.

FOXES AND CHICKENS

It is an article of faith in the right wing—and even in much of ordinary, apolitical America—that the mainstream media favors the left. It is a claim that, Alice in Wonderland-like, is simultaneously completely true and completely false. As Stephen Colbert memorably quipped at the 2006 White House Correspondents' Dinner, "reality has a well-known liberal bias"—a joke that isn't a joke at all.[11] By reporting from a world rooted in empirical truth, the media is indeed biased . . . against the perfidy of right-wing "alternative facts" and "fake news," in the correct sense of the term. But conservatives never cease trying to get into the heads of reporters to cause them to self-censor, pulling their coverage rightward for fear of being criticized even when they are being perfectly accurate—a process Eric Alterman, professor of journalism at CUNY and formerly a columnist for *The Nation*, *Rolling Stone*, *The American Prospect*, and other outlets, calls "working the refs."[12]

Here is how that dynamic, and the conservative lie of the "liberal media" in general, works in practice.

The press reports the facts, which reflect the objective reality that progressives, centrists, and even reasonable conservatives accept and endorse. But more often than not, those facts are at odds with the bizarro world that right-wingers inhabit. When the press reports those damning facts, the right wing then screams, "See? The media is biased against us!" Consumers of right-wing media blithely accept that charge and come to believe that the MSM is unreliable. The right-wing powers-that-be are thus further freed to behave as they wish, without appreciable public accountability. A more perfect perpetual motion machine of faux outrage and manufactured impunity is hard to imagine.

So, yes, the MSM certainly is biased, and in precisely the way that it should be. It is the right wing's bias for falsehoods, conspiracy theory, and toxic horseshit that is the problem. I invite you to ask yourself whether the profoundly capitalist pillars of the mainstream media so hated by conservatives are indeed bastions of Marxism peopled with revolutionaries who want to tear down the system, given that they are themselves giant, profit-driven corporations, like *The New York Times*, or owned by even bigger media corporations, like NBC (which is a subsidiary of Comcast), or CNN (a subsidiary of Warner Bros. Discovery), or by billionaires like Jeff Bezos of Amazon, like *The Washington Post*. We can leave aside altogether the Murdoch-owned *Wall Street Journal*, part of a family empire that also includes Fox News, *The New York Post*, numerous British and Australian tabloids, and other right-wing media properties worldwide.

The fact of the matter is that the mainstream media tends to tilt not left but center-right. The proof of this crypto-conservatism—and often not so crypto—is in its reportage, which consistently reflects an undeniable starboard list, from advocacy of conservative-friendly economic policies to brazen cheerleading for the second Iraq War. (Alterman makes this precise argument in his book *What Liberal Media?* from way back in 2003.)

Yet the notion of "the liberal media" has been such a successful campaign of relentless brainwashing that even the allegedly liberal media itself lives in abject terror of it, consistently bending over backwards to prove otherwise. Witness the pitiful spectacle of Chris Licht, the chairman and CEO of CNN, who soon after taking the job in the fall of 2022 visited Republican leaders on Capitol Hill to assure them that his network would cover them fairly, a display of groveling self-abnegation that the conservative *Washington Free Beacon* gleefully called an "apology tour."[13] (Licht would soon go much further, of course, airing the appalling Trump town hall from New Hampshire in May 2023 that eventually led to his firing.)

Needless to say, that river only flows one way. As Media Matters' Matt Gertz writes, it's impossible to imagine the leading lights of the right-wing media worrying about angering the left or doing anything to appease them.[14] On the contrary: right-wing media is unabashed in serving as the propaganda arm of the GOP, and in targeted ways. "(If) MSNBC is the lefty mirror image of Fox News . . . it needs to pick up its game in the propaganda department," writes *The Washington Post*'s media critic Eric Wemple. "MSNBC has no analogue to Hannity, a guy with the message discipline of a coxswain."[15]

Fox happily swims in the sea of Kellyanne Conwayesque alternative facts, facts that are tailored to its needs at any given moment and subject to change without notice as those needs evolve. When confronted with this obvious bias, reactionaries will first deny it ("Fair and balanced!"), then grudgingly say Fox is no more biased than MSNBC, as if the two are coequal offenders. "The difference is that MSNBC doesn't lie," as Eric Alterman pointed out to me. "I'm not a fan of that kind of TV, but they don't put anything up there that they don't think is true. Whereas Fox lies—we know that. It's obvious to everyone."[16]

There is no need to dignify the "opinion" celebrities-cum-carnival barkers like Hannity or Carlson by pretending that they are real journalists. They themselves alternately embrace the label when it suits them and disavow it when it does not. The stepson of an heiress to the Swanson TV dinner fortune, Tucker Swanson McNear Carlson comes from a family that made its money feeding Americans garbage in front of their televisions, and he is carrying on that proud tradition.[17] But for the GOP, this arrangement is a twofer of incalculable proportions. First, Republicans have on their behalf a steady drumbeat of relentless propaganda pounding into the homes of millions of Americans night and day. Second, the inexplicable public treatment of that drummer as a legitimate journalistic organization on a par with CNN, MSNBC, or the broadcast networks itself devalues the whole idea of news, again to the right wing's advantage.

"Thanks, in part, to the willingness of most mainstream journalists to treat Fox News as just another news source," Alterman wrote back in 2016, "right-wing ideologues have shifted the political 'center' closer to the conservative fringe with every election."[18] The net result is that the GOP has an entire propaganda empire at its disposal—America's most watched news network, as it is fond of bragging—the center of an even larger right-wing mediasphere that includes the Sinclair behemoth, ubiquitous talk radio, local outlets, and social media. The Dems have nothing analogous. In that sense, the whole term "mainstream media" is dead wrong. As the academic Nicco Mele, formerly the director of Harvard's Shorenstein Center on Media, Politics and Public Policy, points out, as measured by sheer, indisputable numbers, the right's dominance of the press is so vast that it truly is the MSM.[19]

YOU DON'T NEED A WEATHER CHANNEL TO KNOW WHICH WAY THE WIND BLOWS

A few years ago, I got into an argument online with a conservative who was peddling some conspiracy theory or another.* When I sent her a Snopes link disproving her claims, she responded that she doesn't read Snopes because "I like to make up my own mind."

Yes, and I don't read weather reports because I like to decide for myself what the temperature is.

The only reason that conservative media outlets and right-wing politicians can pander like they do is because there is a base to pander to. These news consumers are almost beyond reasoning with because they have been conditioned to disregard any facts that clash with their worldview there on Earth 2. As apostate Republican and Never Trumper Ron Filipkowski says, "the traditional media is constitutionally incapable of being a counter to the alternative ecosystem the right wing has constructed. Our media is structured to report facts about the way the world functions in a liberal society, not act as a counterweight to an else-worlds propaganda machine."[20]

In our increasingly tribal culture, we are often told that it is valuable to get out of the proverbial bubble and expose ourselves to what the other side of the political divide is saying, if only in a "know your enemy" sort of way, or more generously, to open one's mind.**

---

* My own fault. I've since stopped windmill-tilting.

** One of the most famously apocryphal anecdotes in modern American politics is that of the late Pauline Kael, the much-esteemed film critic for *The New Yorker*, who, shocked by Nixon's landslide in '72, is said to have remarked that she didn't see how it was possible when everyone she knew had voted for McGovern. Kael never said any such thing—essays debunking the tale are practically a cottage industry in themselves—but the story has lived on because it is

It's an admirable impulse, but not very helpful in efforts to sway our reactionary countrymen. Cruelly, experts tell us that debunking disinformation and "fake news" only tends to spread it.[21] Both our brain chemistry and heuristics give lies an edge, as mere repetition of a falsehood, even to refute it, merely hardwires that misinformation into our neural circuitry.[22]

Recent scholarship suggests that mere exposure to fake news, even with one's guard up, can have damaging physiological effects on the brain. "One of the biggest barriers to correcting misinformation is the fact that hearing the truth doesn't delete a falsehood from our memory," according to the neuroscientist Richard Sima.[23] Brain imaging studies conducted by the cognitive psychologist Stephan Lewandowsky "found evidence that our brains store both the original piece of misinformation as well as its correction." Put another way, as Sima says, "the falsehood and its correction coexist and compete to be remembered." One study found that even a single exposure to a piece of "fake news" had a damaging effect.[24]

Still, some proven techniques do exist for countering fake news. One is the so-called "truth sandwich," as propagated by the influential UC Berkeley linguist George Lakoff: a recitation of the actual facts, followed by a refutation of the falsehood in question, followed by a restatement of the truth.[25] Sima also advocates a proactive, preemptive technique he calls "prebunking," which prepares the brain "to recognize misinformation before we encounter it," in much the same way as a vaccine protects your immune system.[26]

But any dip in the pond of right-wing media certainly makes it very easy to understand why and how people who bathe in those waters every day are as pinwheel-eyed and impossible to reason with as they are. Of course, *someone* has to keep an eye on what the right is saying: perhaps a few brave reconnaissance scouts, in HAZMAT suits, their biometrics monitored by doctors ready to rush them to decompression chambers, can reconnoiter what Fox are up to and periodically report back to the rest of us before entering a prolonged period of detox and re-education.

---

such a useful fable by which conservatives can disparage smarty-pants liberals (like people who write for *The New Yorker*, or read it) for dwelling in a bubble and being out of touch with Real America.

Going forward, the American media must first abandon its pre-Trump mentality that grants all politicians the presumption of goodwill, and reports their words and deeds uncritically, in the name of a foolish obeisance to the false god of Objectivity. Indeed, Maria Ressa objects even to the word objectivity, which, along with "impartiality" and "balance," she believes are "often hijacked by those with vested interests."

"When a journalist confronts the powerful," she writes, "it is easier and safer to write it in a 'balanced' way. But that's a coward's way out. A good journalist, for example, would not give equal time and space to known climate deniers and climate change scientists. Good journalists lean on the side of evidence, on incontrovertible facts."[27]

The second step is for American journalists to overcome their fear of name-calling by the bullies of the right and accept that they will be vilified no matter what they do, so they might as well do the right thing. That means being unafraid of false allegations of bias that, ironically, cause them to overcompensate in favor of the conservative side. Margaret Sullivan therefore writes that journalists must avoid "old-style performative neutrality," especially "when covering politicians who are essentially running against democracy."[28]

Take, for example, the press's aversion to the word "lie."

Well into the Trump's administration, journalists were still highly reluctant to use that word to describe what was issuing from the president's face hole. Editors often explain their position on the grounds that a lie is a deliberate falsehood, and because we cannot read minds, we can't know for certain whether the person saying it is in fact being deceitful, or is merely mistaken, or was themselves deceived. ("The logic eventually became strained," Sullivan writes, "given that Trump blithely repeated the same rank mistruths over and over.")[29]

But that is like saying that if someone balls up his fist, takes aim, and forcefully rams it into your nose, we can't know for sure if he intended to punch you or not. Not even if he has a lifelong history of nose-punching.

Alterman—author of not one but two books on presidential lying—has no patience for that position. "If it's a person's job to know that something is true or not, and they don't know it, I don't care what their intentions are," he told me. His preferred definition of "lie" fits the standard used in a court of law, where willful ignorance is no defense when an individual can reasonably be expected to know better.[30] A bank robber cannot shoot up a savings & loan and then claim in court that he didn't think anyone would get hurt.

In the future, we must put an end to this namby-pamby preference for fascist-friendly euphemism, if we want that future to include a functioning democracy. Sullivan correctly argues that framing and context are everything, that simply reporting what a candidate says is insufficient in this fraught new world of disinformation and demagoguery. She makes special mention of headlines and news alerts, which by their nature are brief and lack nuance, yet are often "as far as many news consumers get."* She further argues that proponents of the Big Lie do not deserve a media platform, and journalists should remind their audience that the individual in question is an election denier even when covering them in other contexts. She cites a public radio station in Harrisburg, Pennsylvania, WITF, that began running sidebars and taglines on all its stories when covering Republican members of the state legislature and the state's US congressional delegation who denied that Biden was the rightful president.[31]

Sullivan also counsels against traditional campaign coverage that risks normalizing an extremist candidate by reporting uncritically on speeches, rallies, and debates, and resorting to the usual "horserace" mentality—a point frequently made by the esteemed NYU journalism professor Jay Rosen as well.[32] This tougher stance also means rejecting restrictive rules that campaigns try to impose on journalists covering them. Sullivan cites the decision of the *Cleveland Plain Dealer* not to cover a 2022 midterm rally for Republican US Senate candidate J.D. Vance (with special guest Ron DeSantis) because of such rules, instead publishing white space.[33] Yet so far there is little sign that these adjustments are underway in the broader culture.

---

* Part of the problem, incredibly: *The New York Times's* executive editor Dean Baquet reported that, with newfound dominance of the digital edition, the senior leadership does not write or approve headlines for the paper edition, and may not even look at them until after they have gone to press. Such was the case with the headline "Trump Urges Unity Against Racism" after he failed to condemn the role of white supremacism in two mass shootings during the same weekend, one in El Paso, Texas, and another in Dayton, Ohio.

CLOUDS' ILLUSIONS I RECALL

Another crucial step for this new vision of American journalism is an end to bothsidesism.

In the twenty-three years since Paul Krugman's quip about a flat earth, the practice of giving "both sides" equal credence even when one side is plainly wrong has become toxic, particularly at a time when one of our two parties has embraced dangerous falsehoods as core beliefs. We should no more indulge the demand that those beliefs be treated with equivalent respect than we should teach creationism alongside evolution, or present Holocaust denial as a perfectly valid alternative belief, or suggest that horse dewormer and an FDA-approved vaccine are equally effective treatments for a lethal virus.

In June 2016, even before Trump nailed down the GOP nomination, Eric Alterman cited a *New York Times* story from March of that year detailing Trump's repeated incitements to violence among his supporters, to which the *Times* appended the qualifier that "Both sides are fueling this." Were they, though? When? And according to whom? *The Times* didn't bother to say.

"These pathologies have long been with us," Alterman wrote. "But they have reached a crisis point in recent years, as conservatives have grown ever more brazen in exploiting them, successfully shifting the boundaries of political discourse well beyond what the rest of us recognize as readily observable reality."[34]

Yet the American press insists on indulging in the trope of "on the other hand." ("To be sure" is another formulation that reporters like.) Even now on CNN and NPR, one can hear right-wing voices given a forum without significant pushback from the interviewers, presumably in the interest of "hearing all sides." Yes, sunshine is the best disinfectant, but it's not sunshine when Republicans are given an audience of millions and allowed to spew their lies unchallenged. Particularly when they already have their own network for that purpose.

Presciently, Alterman was even writing about the Fourth Estate's failures on the specific issue of voting rights back in 2016, citing a study by Media Matters that found "baseless complaints about voter fraud were given the 'he said/she said' treatment in the [*New*

York] *Times* in 60 percent of the relevant stories published in 2013 and 2015—a 10 percent increase over the previous two years."[35] Margaret Sullivan, the *Times*'s public editor at the time, herself raised the issue, prompting the Gray Lady's national editor Sam Sifton to argue, defensively, that "It's not our job to litigate it in the paper . . . We need to state what each side says."[36]

Even if what one side says is total horseshit, I guess.

Today the Republican attempt to put a chokehold on the electoral process is benefitting from that same "both sides" treatment. A glaring example: Reporting in January 2022 about the high number of Trump voters who believe Joe Biden was not legitimately elected president (69 percent, to be precise), *The Washington Post* felt compelled to add: "Republicans' rejection of Biden's victory is not novel. In a fall 2017 Post-UMD poll, 67 percent of Democrats and 69 percent of Hillary Clinton voters said Trump was not legitimately elected president."[37] What the *Post* didn't say is that Donald Trump eagerly fanned those flames to delegitimize his successor, while Hillary Clinton graciously—and admirably—did the opposite. That is a shameful sin of omission and a near-textbook case of "bothsidesism" and the dangers of faux objectivity in the mainstream media.

Writing in the very same *Washington Post*, Jennifer Rubin laid down a sharp indictment of this phenomenon, citing "the mainstream media's refusal to recognize that we no longer live in a political world in which two political parties engage within acceptable bounds of democracy."[38] Moreover, Rubin has specific, concrete proposals for what the media ought to be doing, and dire warnings about the cost of the failure to do so:

> Why isn't Senate Minority Leader Mitch McConnell (R-Ky.) quizzed as to how his party can take direction from a former president who plotted to overthrow the election? Why isn't every Trump-picked candidate quizzed as to whether they buy the "big lie" of a stolen election and asked to renounce violence? Will debate moderators confront Republican candidates with questions as to whether President Biden won the election and whether they would oppose state legislative efforts to overturn the will of their voters by submitting an alternative slate of presidential electors to the House in 2024?[39]

That is the kind of aggressive but fair reporting that will call autocracy to account and which is truly "objective."

In a subsequent 2021 piece for *The American Prospect*, Alterman described a concept called Fournierism, named for Ron Fournier, former Washington bureau chief for the Associated Press.[40] Writing for *The Atlantic* in 2016 about Mitch McConnell's unprecedented refusal even to meet with Merrick Garland, Fournier conceded that Republicans were in thrall to an angry base that brooked no compromise with Democrats, but then took off on a Baryshnikov-quality *grand jeté* to claim that "the GOP isn't the only party captive to its special interests. If the roles were reversed and a Republican sat in the Oval Office, I believe Democrats would block the lame duck's nominee."[41]

"Here you have the very essence of Fournierism," Alterman wrote. "If reality doesn't cooperate, you can always blame 'both sides' in some alternate universe."[42] Paradoxically, the more outrageous the Republican norm-breaking, the more the mainstream media feels compelled to find a both-sides analogue.

In 2016 Fournier was also a chief proponent of the both-candidates-are bad-fallacy. Like many, I grew weary of the mantra, heard from both right and left. (My standard retort: "Yes, but one is bad like acne, while the other one is bad like leprosy.") Alterman was similarly clear-eyed about the two choices and what was at stake, writing:

> (R)eporters and pundits covering the 2016 campaign will be doing the public a particularly grave disservice if they continue to draw from the "both sides" playbook in the months leading up to the November election. Now that Donald Trump has emerged as the presumptive Republican nominee for president, some simple facts about him and his campaign should be stated clearly and repeatedly, not obfuscated or explained away or leavened into click bait. Trump is a pathological liar and conspiracy theorist, a racist, misogynist, and demagogic bully with a phantasmagoric policy platform and dangerously authoritarian instincts. Hillary Clinton's flaws and failures are many, and they should not be discounted, either. But they are of an entirely different order. Love her or hate her, at least we don't have to wonder whether she believes in democracy. When it comes to sane and even semi-sensible policy proposals for America's future in the 2016 presidential election, there is only one side.[43]

We will be writing a similar epitaph about 2024 unless American journalism undergoes a significant change in how it does business.

BEWARE OF SHINY OBJECTS
OR, HOW NOT TO COVER A TYRANT

Ultimately, the problem is deeper than simply the media's cluelessness about how to cover Trump in a principled, credible way. The problem is that it doesn't want to.

Trump was and remains a phenomenon too tempting for the media to resist in a profit-driven competition for eyeballs and eardrums. One study estimated that during the 2016 GOP primaries alone Trump accrued roughly $2 billion in free coverage—what media experts call "earned media," a misnomer if ever there was one.[44] In that regard, even the debate over left/right bias is moot.*

"Did journalists create Trump?" a shellshocked Sullivan wrote way back on Election Night 2016. "Of course not—they don't have that kind of power. But they helped him tremendously."[45] Later that same night, she expanded that critique into what she termed a "call to action" for her fellow reporters as they prepared to cover now President Trump, cautioning against normalizing his behavior, and hoping that they would not resort to the lazy narrative that "I guess Americans just wanted change," when the truth was, what his followers really wanted was "to throw the entire government and its values onto the bonfire."[46]

In that hope, she would be bitterly disappointed over the four years to come, as press repeated and amplified and commented upon his every impulsive, all-caps, sent-from-the toilet-in-Mar-a-Lago post, dissecting each one like archaeologists poring over mystic runes.

In future, this temptation to play into the would-be autocrat's hands with non-stop coverage of his every provocation, much of it uncritical and voluntarily acceding to the tormentor's terms, must be resisted. But the early signs are not encouraging, from the breathless,

---

*   As *The Atlantic*'s George Packer reported, within a month of Trump leaving office, "*The Washington Post* lost a quarter of its unique visitors, and CNN lost 45 percent of its prime-time audience . . . When he returned as a presidential candidate and criminal defendant, cable-news-network ratings climbed again."

round-the-clock coverage of Trump's indictments, to CNN's appalling Trump town hall in May 2023. Prior to 2016, the press might have had the excuse of inexperience, having never faced a demagogue on this order before. But it no longer has any alibi for covering Trump like a normal candidate, or pretending that it doesn't know what he's going to do when the cameras come on, or what the potential damage to the country will be if we let him run amok.

In fact, the entire endeavor of election coverage has to be rethought. The media prefers its traditional paradigm of a horserace because it makes for exciting copy. How is this campaign ad doing? Did a recent gaffe alienate female voters? What is the impact of the latest jobs report on polling in the Midwest? But all that is in the dustbin of history, as it is woefully unsuited to a campaign in which one of the two candidates is a pathological liar and neofascist who has demonstrated all too well his ability to turn the media's own norms and protocols against it.

Regarding how to handle Trump's public statements going forward, *The Washington Post*'s Megan McArdle quipped that for non-journalists, the answer is easy: ignore them.

"Sure, I understand that you might be anxious about his vile provocations," she wrote in October 2022, "but your fretting about every stupid tweet isn't going to change anything. I promise that if Trump does something that you urgently need to know about—like getting elected president—we in the mainstream media will hasten to tell you about it."[47]

McArdle noted that, historically, the media's answer as to which of Trump's tweets were newsworthy "has been 'all of them,'" and "It is no exaggeration to say he climbed into the presidency on the shoulders of the hundreds of journalists who kept treating his pronouncements as matters of epic importance, even if it had been tapped out one-handed while schmoozing around Mar-a-Lago."[48]

> But in point of fact, it's no longer news that Trump likes to say terrible things on social media. It isn't news that he likes to threaten people, attack important civic institutions, tell baseless lies and rub elbows with bigots. No one in the country—in the world—can possibly be unaware of the kinds of things Trump likes to tweet or the revulsion this produces in establishment media.[49]

McArdle went on to propose that "(r)ather than leaping to condemn his every pronouncement, we should treat Trump's Twitter account the way we'd treat some random account with five followers and a penchant for rancid verbal attacks: as if it were generally beneath our notice." She acknowledged "that his outrages have real power, unlike the random nobody," but that is the very problem.[50] As with all fake news, repeating his lies and provocations—or even just reporting on them—only serves to further spread his filth and abet his demagoguery.

But there is a catch-22 here. Trump has long engaged in fiery, violence-promoting rhetoric that no previous American president had remotely approached. As he ramps up that rhetoric on the 2024 campaign trail—viciously attacking the judges and prosecutors in his various legal cases, arguing that shoplifters should be shot on sight, suggesting that General Mark Milley ought to be executed—we run the risk of becoming inured. There is no longer any debate about "taking him literally but not seriously," or vice versa. It is the great challenge of American political journalism in 2024 to report on this outrageous danger and raise the alarm, without slipping into being Trump's useful idiots. As Brian Klaas writes, "The man who, as president, incited a violent attack on the US Capitol in order to overturn an election is again openly fomenting political violence while explicitly endorsing authoritarian strategies should he return to power. That is *the* story of the 2024 election. Everything else is just window dressing."[51]

ALL THE NEWS THAT FITS

At the very dawn of the Trump presidency, Masha Gessen predicted the fate of the press under the new regime, suggesting that journalists would have to decide whether to "fall in line or forfeit access."[52] Her predictions largely proved correct, and may even look overly optimistic when the next Republican autocrat takes power, or the last one returns for an encore. It is not hard to imagine pretexts for marginalizing news outlets that are critical of the administration, revoking their broadcast licenses, deluging them with litigation and legal injunctions, hamstringing them with looser libel laws, or even shutting them down altogether. In Alabama, Ohio, and Kansas, local sheriffs have already arrested and charged small town journalists and newspaper publishers whose reporting has displeased them.[53]

For now, despite Fox, and the Trumpian attacks on the press, and the general hostility toward the media among conservatives, the Fourth Estate is actually quite robust in the United States. There are plenty of other nations where the situation is much more fraught—Russia, for example, where reporters regularly fall out of windows, get gunned down on the street, or find themselves suspiciously poisoned.

In the Philippines, *Rappler* was such a thorn in the side of the Duterte regime that in 2020 the government concocted to convict Maria Ressa of the dubious crime of "cyberlibel." After *Rappler* corrected a typo in a seven-year-old story linking a prominent Duterte supporter to judicial corruption and the drug trade, human trafficking, and murder, the government argued that that correction constituted republication, exposing Ressa to criminal liability for an article she published before the law against it was even passed.[54] Along with the other seven cases the Trump-aligned Duterte regime has pending against her, she faced up to one hundred years in prison.[55] But Duterte's attacks on *Rappler*, which he has also falsely accused of being funded by the CIA, succeeded mostly in making Ressa—already a Fulbright scholar and *Time* magazine Person of the Year—a global icon.[56] In 2021 she won the Nobel Peace Prize. She remains free today—and outspoken—while currently appealing her conviction in the cyberlibel case.

Both before and after those attacks, *Rappler* remains a model of how an honest, aggressive news organization can present a challenge to an autocracy, even an openly brutal one that seems otherwise unconcerned about its public image.

When I asked Eric Alterman about how the mainstream media could best push back should a full-blown right-wing autocracy come to power in the US, he rejected the very premise. "The question assumes that the mainstream media members *care* about preserving democracy," he told me. "They don't. They care about their businesses. So whatever I would want them to do, they won't . . . Speaking broadly, there are a lot of people who really care about doing their jobs the best they can, but they care mostly about what their colleagues think of them, and what their competitors think.

They don't want to offend their readers and they want to impress their colleagues. The stuff about democracy and human rights and the Earth surviving—that's all nice, all things being equal, they would be for that. But these other things come first. There are exceptions—people who are so talented, and who manage to stay true to their values and still be good journalists as defined in the mainstream media. But they're very rare and they don't usually last long."[57]

You might ask how we can lambaste the American media for being ineffectual, and in the next breath lament the state of democracy if it is wiped out. But that is the very point. The press retains the power to provide an invaluable, even irreplaceable service as part of our democracy. If it does not exercise that power now, it may lose it altogether. There are many many American journalists who are doing heroic work. But there are also many journalistic institutions that have abdicated their core responsibilities, like a SWAT team that won't confront a school shooter, standing idly by and letting the carnage carry on. In fact, they risk that shooter calmly striding up to them and confiscating their weapons, leaving them even more helpless, and no longer by choice.

CHAPTER 12

Information Wants to Be Free

One of the strongest journalistic weapons in the pro-democracy fight is the local press. But working against it is the growing consolidation of major media outlets by a handful of giant conglomerates and hedge funds for whom maximization of readers and viewers (which is to say, dollars) is the prime directive.[1] That militates against reportage that alienates anyone, or speaks truth to power, as the much-abused saying goes. There is also the minor matter of those interests sharing the ethos of the right wing in many cases, and benefiting from its policies.

"Local news is the oxygen of democracy, the most trusted source for the most essential information," says Nancy Gibbs, director of the Shorenstein Center on Media, Politics and Public Policy at Harvard, "and we've long known why dying newsrooms damage communities."[2] And yet the disturbing pattern of local newspapers shuttering has become routine. Since 2005 roughly 2,500 dailies and weeklies have closed, leaving fewer than 6,500 nationwide, a drop of almost 40 percent.[3] Two more disappear every week, and most communities that suffer that fate will not get a digital replacement, let alone a print one. Penelope Muse Abernathy, a visiting professor at Northwestern University and a leading expert on this worrying phenomenon, has mapped "dead zones"—some 200 American counties with no local paper, and another 1,600 with only one outlet. She also found a third of US newspapers that existed roughly two decades ago will be out of business by 2025.[4]

One possible remedy is that of publicly owned newspapers (and TV and radio stations and online news portals) that "decouple news from profit," as Sally Kohn, the communication strategist, founder, and CEO of the progressive think tank Movement Vision Lab, told me.[5] The concept has been tried in the past, only to be killed by for-profit commercial ventures. But as those for-profit newspapers themselves now go the way of the dinosaurs, there may be a window for publicly owned municipal newspapers to rise again, a "public option" in the journalism space. But in Congress, the Local Journalism Sustainability Act, which offers tax credits for local newspapers and small news nonprofits, has languished in the House since being introduced in 2020.[6]

The challenge is even greater in the non-urban parts of the country that are right-wing strongholds, with the remotest, poorest, least-wired areas hit the hardest. "Invariably," Abernathy states in a report for Northwestern University's Medill School of Journalism, "the economically struggling, traditionally underserved communities that need local journalism the most are the very places where it is most difficult to sustain either print or digital news organizations."[7] Among the consequences: a decline in voting, a rise in graft and corruption, and fertile ground for misinformation and disinformation. According to Margaret Sullivan, the report asserts that "Seventy million Americans now live in areas without enough local news to sustain grass-roots democracy."[8] Facebook groups, rife with rumors and lies, are a shitty replacement.

But it's even worse than that, since as Gibbs writes, "(t)he very places where local news is disappearing are often the same places that wield disproportionate political power." Recall the statistics cited earlier regarding the disproportionate voting power of the residents of South Dakota. Yet "about half of South Dakota's 66 counties have only a single weekly newspaper. Seven counties have no newspaper at all." In other words, "The citizens whose votes count the most might have the hardest time learning about the issues and candidates running in their communities—because there's no longer anyone reporting on them."[9] That suits the right wing just fine.*

What's even more disturbing is how the void is being filled.

---

*   Lightly peopled Democratic states like Vermont and Delaware have similarly outsized clout, but because they are geographically smaller, with more densely concentrated populations, and better access to high-speed Internet, they don't represent the same kind of news deserts. "Delaware's three small counties have 13 newspapers," Gibbs notes. "Vermont's 14 counties have 39."

The archconservative Sinclair Media Group is the largest owner of TV stations in the US, with 173 to its name, and a well-founded reputation for using them to push its far-right agenda. Sinclair makes a point of not advertising which stations it owns.[10] Fox-like, it also functions as an overt arm of the Republican Party while hiding behind the masquerade of legitimate news. Soon after the 2016 election, Jared Kushner bragged to a group of business executives in New York City about the deal the Trump campaign had struck for coverage by Sinclair.[11] After Trump's victory, Ajit Pai, the Trump-appointed head of the FCC, eliminated or relaxed restrictions that had previously limited the company's expansion. Sinclair also hired as its chief political analyst Boris Epshteyn, formerly a member of the Trump White House press office, who instituted "must-run" verbatim ten-minute political commentary segments promoting the messages Trump wanted heard.[12]

And it gets worse. The journalist Ryan Zickgraf coined the term "pink slime journalism" to describe websites that mimic the look and feel of local papers, but publish "partisan noise, produced by dark-money-funded propaganda factories." Zickgraf describes the *Mobile Courant*, the online news site covering his hometown in Alabama, that has no actual reporters or editors and instead simply publishes press releases from the office of Republican Senator Tommy Tuberville. More than 1,300 such sites already exist. A chief purveyor, Metric Media, claims to publish "over 5 million news articles every month," making it "the largest producer of local news in the United States," vastly outnumbering even Gannett, the largest newspaper chain in the US. Ironically, pink slime depends on the high regard that local news continues to sustain among the public, even as confidence in national news organizations continues to drop—in part because of right-wing attacks on it.[13]

THE SONG REMAINS GERMANE

If we cannot rely on the traditional journalistic challenge to autocracy—and we would be wise to assume that we cannot—it will fall to entities outside the mainstream to provide a proper prodemocratic counter narrative.

"Journalism as an institution has to be reinvented for the twenty-first century," Shoshana Zuboff, professor emerita at Harvard Business School, told Maria Ressa for her memoir *How to Stand Up to a Dictator*.[14] In the Philippines, Ressa and *Rappler* pioneered social media-based "citizen journalism," which relies on the contributions of private individuals capturing events on their cellphones. In the US, an organization called States Newsroom that is devoted to covering politics at the state level has opened small but vital news outlets in thirty-four states over the past several years. An even older model comes from the progressive journalist I.F. Stone, whose independently published newsletter ran from 1953–1971, concomitant with the heart of the Cold War and US involvement in Vietnam. Working totally outside the mainstream media infrastructure of his day, Stone did not depend on insider access of the kind that Alterman decries, freeing himself from the dance of favors that often compromises journalists working within "the system." A newsletter may seem neither new nor radical in terms of a twenty-first-century reimagination of journalism, but it worked. Brian Eno famously quipped that the first Velvet Underground album only sold 30,000 copies, but everyone who bought it started a band.[15] At its peak, *I. F. Stone's Weekly* had a readership of only 70,000, but every one of them seems to have become a journalist, written a book, or—years later—started a blog.[16]

The anti-Trump apostate conservative Ron Filipkowski writes that "It isn't the media's job to fight partisan battles and the media as it currently exists simply isn't configured to fight bad-faith, malicious propaganda and disinformation. But also, there are things that can be done by a partisan political group that traditional media cannot, will not, and should not do."[17] But Democrats have long been hapless at messaging: on the economy, on national security, on immigration, all areas where the public perennially sees the GOP as more trustworthy, even though it has been disastrous in all those areas. As Jennifer Rubin notes, Democrats seem "temperamentally unsuited to calling out their opponents as anti-democratic or un-American."[18] Only James Carville seems to be the exception.

We have to let go of that Marquess of Queensbury thinking.

Filipkowski argues that "Democrats should take the fight directly to the right on their own platforms," and bemoans the fact that the left has not already taken up this approach. "Either Democrats fail to recognize what is happening, don't understand it, or think that a handful of PACs and White House press conferences are sufficient to deal with it. Either way, they're wrong. The DNC's 'War Room' looks like a Victorian tea party compared to what Republicans do on a daily basis."[19]

Progressives are also at the disadvantage of arguing for nuanced policies, as opposed to simplistic, reptile brain ones. That would present enough of a challenge even if reactionaries weren't also willing and eager to lie their asses off on top of it. That is why there's no left-wing talk radio, at least not the commercially successful kind. The very nature of progressive dialogue—open, inquisitive, fact-based—is antithetical to the form, which thrives on pro wrestling–style mockery and rewards facile bumper sticker sloganeering.

"I believe that many of the people who have been turned by lies can be won back with irrefutable truth," Filipkowski writes, "but the truth has to be put right in front of them, meeting them where they are."[20]

I am less convinced than he that MAGA Nation will listen to reason, and a lie famously goes round the world while the truth is still lacing up its Nikes and making sure the bows are neat. But I do think it is essential to counter the relentless right-wing narrative. The price of failure will be enormous.

Perhaps the most important way in which *Citizens United* damaged US politics was in spurring the relentless torrent of political ads that now bombard the American people 24/7. Unless and until campaign finance reform is enacted, advertising will continue to be an arms race, where wealthy progressives can use their financial resources for the common good, and creative professionals working on behalf of democracy can have a profound effect.

Jim Bernfield, who has made political ads for thirty years, including producing Hillary Clinton's famous "3 a.m." spot in 2008, told me that after months of media coverage of a campaign, no thirty-second ad will change a voter's mind in and of itself. "At the presidential level, ads are icing, not cake. But what ads can do is work within the culture to shape the national conversation, the news, reporters' POVs, and the conventional wisdom."

When it comes to the content itself, Bernfield reiterates the sad truth that negative ads with simplistic, often inaccurate messages penetrate more readily than positive, nuanced ones, much the same way that fake news elbows out the real kind. "It's a lot harder to break into viewers' consciousnesses with a six-point plan than with a negative. A good negative goes straight to the amygdala."[21]

"Whether you're a brand or a politician, there are only two levers," Rob Schwartz, CEO of the mammoth advertising agency TBWA\Chiat\Day New York, told me. "A brand will either make you scared, like Volvo, with a safety message, or they'll empower you, like Nissan or Cadillac. But optimism is a hard sell. And whatever the message is, it's going to have to go viral, because there is no real mass media anymore. There isn't one campfire everybody is around, like when there were just three TV networks."[22]

In terms of political struggle, the information space is not limited to traditional media like newspapers and magazines, or film, TV, and radio, or even formal advertising, and never has been. Outside the battlements of the MSM, there are untold opportunities for making a statement and influencing the national conversation, particularly in our high-tech age. Start a blog, a vlog, or a podcast. (Don't you have one already?) For the retro-minded, start an old-fashioned mimeographed zine and hand it out at all-ages concerts. Scrawl graffiti on the walls of the corner store, the subway, or the town water tower. Display symbols of solidarity and resistance on your clothes and your bike or your car and your possessions, so long as you can do so without the cops or right-wing thugs kicking the shit out of you. Keep doing it even if they do kick the shit out of you.*

Do those things seem absurdly mild? Perhaps they are, individually. But collectively they can constitute a force to be reckoned with. Luckily, in this effort, technology is our ally.

---

* Sometimes even the oppressor's own symbols can be turned against him. Gene Sharp cites the French gentiles who insisted on wearing the yellow star during the Nazi occupation as another way of registering public unhappiness with the regime. Do note: most were arrested and imprisoned.

THE BLUEBIRD OF UNHAPPINESS

In the thirty-plus years since the Internet slipped the bounds of DARPA and took root in the general public, the democratization of media we were promised has not really materialized. In fact, it has largely gone in the other direction—hardly the first time that the utopian allure of a new technology failed to come through.

The Internet is often rightly derided as a place where users submerge themselves in a toxic bath of confirmation bias. Infamously, there are almost no standards of journalistic ethics in the Wild West of the cyberspace, where disinformation is rife, especially when backed by giant, deep-pocketed players with ill intent. But the Internet is also a place where one can slip free from the tyranny of geography and leap across space to connect with kindred spirits, share information, and more importantly, organize. It is therefore the front line of both the spread of disinformation and the fight against it.

The strongest testament to the power of the Internet is the lengths to which authoritarian governments go to suppress it, from China to India to Turkey to Iran. In the US, the Republican impulse to demonize "Big Tech" springs from that same well, even as—in a bitter irony—right-wingers themselves prodigiously use social media, creating an all-but-unpoliceable challenge for law enforcement and the Intelligence Community. During the Arab Spring of 2010, Twitter proved to be a useful tool for organizing protest and acts of defiance against various regimes, even if the broader movement ultimately failed. A decade later, *The New Yorker*'s Jelani Cobb has written about the power of social media in making the video of George Floyd's murder go viral—the open-casket shock of Emmett Till's disfigured corpse writ large by technology.[23]

This is the positive, democratic power of tech: a means to give voice to ordinary people and allow us to share information at speeds and across distances never before possible.

But Elon Musk's purchase of Twitter, and his management of it since, is a case study in how yet another egomaniacal right-wing billionaire can turn a social media platform into a safe haven and organizing space for the far right. As Cobb notes, that is precisely why his acquisition of Twitter was so worrying, attended as it was by a performative, fake claim of commitment to "free speech,'" followed by the quick reinstatement of right-wing trolls who had previously been booted (and even payola to keep them onboard),[24] and the stifling of progressive voices, including the labelling of NPR as "state-affili-ated media."[25] Meanwhile, Musk palled around at the Super Bowl with Rupert Murdoch, the kingpin of a media empire that is well beyond state-affiliated, unless it is more accurate to say that the Republican Party is Fox-affiliated, and a subsidiary at that.[26]

But is social media really the revolutionary tool for political activism that some claim?

In an influential 2010 piece for *The New Yorker* titled "Small Change," Malcolm Gladwell challenged the popular notion that "the traditional relationship between political authority and pop-ular will has been upended, making it easier for the powerless to collaborate, coordinate, and give voice to their concerns." That has certainly been the conventional wisdom. Gladwell cites the role of Twitter in anti-communist street protests in Moldova in 2009, and in protests later that same year in Iran, when the State Department actually asked Twitter to delay scheduled maintenance in order to keep a critical organizing tool available.[27] Mark Pfeifle, a former national security advisor in the Bush 43 administration, even called for Twitter to be nominated for the Nobel Peace Prize.[28]

But Gladwell contended that social media platforms like Twitter actually had little impact in Moldova and Iran, serving mainly to impress Western reporters looking in from the outside, figuratively and literally.

"The Western media certainly never tired of claiming that Iranians used Twitter to organize and coordinate their protests fol-lowing President Mahmoud Ahmadinejad's apparent theft of last June's elections," the Radio Free Europe/Radio Liberty correspond-ent Golnaz Esfandiari wrote in *Foreign Policy*. But Twitter's main role was only to spread word of what was going on to the wider world outside—a valuable service, but not the same as being an organiza-tional tool within the country.[29] (Twitter did not even support the use of Farsi.[30])

"Twitter's impact inside Iran is zero," Mehdi Yahyanejad, man-ager of the popular LA-based Farsi website Balatarin, told *The Washington Post*. In fact, the Iranian government itself reportedly used the platform to spread disinformation, false rumors, and even to help it identify, locate, and arrest key figures in the protests.[31]

Gladwell contrasts political activism via social media unfavorably with the 1960 lunch counter protests in North Carolina and with the Mississippi Freedom Summer of 1964. Social media, he writes, is excellent at getting people to do low-effort things, like signing petitions—the sort of thing that "doesn't involve financial or personal risk"—risk such as "spending a summer being chased by armed men in pickup trucks."[32]

That weakness of social media is a function of the casual, almost painless nature of the relationships formed there. By contrast, Gladwell reports that personal connection to others in a given movement is the best indicator of who will stay committed to the cause—what the Stanford sociologist Doug McAdam calls a "strong-tie" phenomenon. This pattern, Gladwell writes, holds true irrespective of ideology, from the Civil Rights Movement to the mujahadeen of Afghanistan to the pro-democracy movement in East Germany. By contrast, "the platforms of social media are built around weak ties. Twitter is a way of following (or being followed by) people you may never have met. Facebook is a tool for efficiently managing your acquaintances, for keeping up with the people you would not otherwise be able to stay in touch with. That's why you can have a thousand 'friends' on Facebook, as you never could in real life."[33]

"The world is totally different now because of technology," the feminist pioneer Alix Kates Shulman told me, to that point. "People don't get together—we do everything online. That's a huge difference from our movement, which was done in person: in-person presentations, in-person disruptions, in-person organizing. That was the main way that we changed the consciousness of the entire country."[34]

"In the '60s we were knocking on doors," Zoharah Simmons said. "I relish hearing from the young people about what they think, because this is a brave new world. But I still can't see how we can do it without some face-to-face. You know, on the Internet you can find any answer to anything you want on any issue. But people are so uninformed about what it means to be a citizen, and what our rights are." She laughed, "So in many ways, we're smarter than ever and dumber than ever."[35]

Gladwell faults the decentralized leadership structure of social media networks, arguing that they have trouble reaching consensus, thinking strategically, and setting goals. That contention bumps up against the egalitarian ethos of a movement like Occupy, with its bottom-up leadership structure and "people's mic" oratory. But admirable as Occupy was, it's not possible to say that it was anywhere near as successful as the Civil Rights Movement.

In short, the instruments of social media "are not a natural enemy of the status quo," Gladwell writes, noting its paradoxical nature. "It makes it easier for activists to express themselves, and harder for that expression to have any impact."[36]

As reported by Megan Garber in *The Atlantic*, the psychologist John Suler coined the term "online disinhibition effect," meaning "the tendency for people in digital spaces to act in ways they never would offline."[37] We are all familiar with it. The same impulse that makes us all tougher and more aggressive behind the steering wheels of our cars than in person makes the Internet the great bathroom wall of contemporary human discourse.

On that front, tech has also accelerated the resurgence of the white power movement, if only because the process of indoctrination can happen faster, as Peter Hutchison, director of *Healing from Hate: Battle for the Soul of a Nation* (2020)—a feature documentary that examines the root causes of such extremism—told me.[38] A subculture that was once limited to a shadowy underground, widely dispersed geographically, and forced to communicate largely via carefully whispered word of mouth, is now able to find and radicalize new recruits with speed and ease.

Jaron Lanier, the polymath tech guru and virtual reality pioneer, has argued convincingly why social media is destructive by its very nature, with its business model that depends on feeding humankind's worst impulses, and its powerful, sophisticated algorithms that the feeble human mind is not wired to withstand. Ironically, what Lanier is proposing (in books like *You Are Not a Gadget* and *Who Owns the Future*, but most pointedly in 2018's *Ten Arguments for Deleting Your Social Media Accounts Right Now*) is a form of civil disobedience against social media itself, a mass exodus from the industry leaders—Facebook, Twitter, Instagram, et al.—that would force them to provide a better product.[39]

Beyond consumer-grade social media, the full potential of tech as a new frontier in the political-military spectrum of conflict has yet to be exploited. We have already seen devastating cyberattacks launched by North Korea (on Sony Pictures), by Russia (on the US in December 2020, to name just one), and by the US itself (the Stuxnet attack on Iran), as well as by nongovernmental actors, such as the 2021 ransomware attack on the Colonial Pipeline that cut off gas and jet fuel to the southeastern US. Certainly the most famous group operating in this arena is the quasi-anarchist "hacktivist" collective Anonymous, which first made its name with cyberattacks on the Church of Scientology and went on to strike targets ranging from the US government to the Islamic State, child porn websites, the Westboro Baptist Church, and corporations including PayPal, Visa, and Sony.[40] Most recently, in response to the war in Ukraine, Anonymous and others have launched cyberattacks on the Russian state, disabling key Kremlin websites, leaking government data, and disrupting Moscow's war effort.[41] These attacks have also penetrated the wall of Kremlin censorship to speak directly to the Russian people, who otherwise rarely hear the unvarnished truth. The American hacker community could similarly disrupt a reactionary regime in America, using denial of service attacks, malware, ransomware, and other techniques, even as right-wing hackers could do the same to pro-democracy forces. Such is the double-edged nature of all powerful weapons.

In case you missed it, technology moves fast. The rise of AI, VR, deep fakes, and even newer tech of which we can't even conceive will likely present new and mind-boggling challenges before these words are even published. The potential for bad actors to abuse artificial intelligence is as vast as our understanding of AI is tiny. We are barely beginning to grasp its implications, but a good rule of thumb is that any new, groundbreaking technology will first be used for porn, and then for political repression.* If we are going to engage in cyberspace and other tech as part of a pro-democracy resistance—and we must, because it cannot be ignored—it will fall to us to find ways to use its vast potential to benefit all humanity.

---

* "The Porn Pioneers," *The Guardian*, September 29, 1999, https://www.theguardian.com/technology/1999/sep/30/onlinesupplement.

CHAPTER 13

Hey Teacher, Leave Them Kids Alone

Control of how we remember the past is seminal to the autocrat's ability to manufacture consent in the present. (Oceania is at war with Eurasia and has always been at war with Eurasia.) It is no coincidence, then, that all across the country, particularly in—you guessed it—the former Confederacy, efforts are underway to restrict the scope of what our children are taught, to ban books that offend conservative sensibilities, to limit what topics teachers may discuss and, in some cases, even the very words they are allowed to use or prohibited from using, under penalty of dismissal. One can hardly imagine a more chilling or un-American scenario.

The right wing would like to wall off any view of our past that breaks with its most cherished myths, or any vision of the United States as pluralistic society, or any urge for questioning of its own authority or challenges to its preferred narrative. Such legislation has been proposed in some thirty-five states and passed in many of them; if a Republican regime comes to power nationwide, we are sure to see that effort spread to every corner of the country, even those that strongly disagree.[1] The result will be not only the further entrenchment of the white nationalist myth, but also a benighted populace baptized in bullshit and untrained in thinking for itself and questioning what it is fed. *Nota bene*: that is what the right prefers.

Educators are therefore essential players in a pro-democracy pushback to that aspect of a looming autocracy.

GEORGE SANTAYANA, WHITE
COURTESY PHONE

There may be no better example of this dynamic in action than the angry reaction of right-wing politicians, pundits, and ordinary conservatives over Nikole Hannah-Jones's 1619 Project, which seeks to rectify the record and correctly establish the historical role of slavery in the founding and evolution of this country.[2] The same segment of the population that in the '50s and '60s didn't want little Black children to go to school alongside white ones—who were fine with using cops and attack dogs and firehoses and church bombings to stop that—now wants to prevent their grandchildren from learning that they did so.

That conservative defensiveness, however, is more than just a matter of juvenile opposition to the notion that America is not perfect: it is a last-ditch defense for a cornered class of people who are seeing their political power slipping away and trying to hang on to what has become minoritarian rule—the same existential panic that animates the radicalization of the modern GOP at large and undergirds its entire autocratic project. The removal of their foundational myth, and the comforting delusion that our forefathers were unimpeachably noble people who built this country through initiative and innovation and the sweat of their collective brow—that is to say, that they did not steal this land and murder its original inhabitants and grease its development with centuries of slave labor—is a key loss for the right, as it obliterates the faux moral legitimacy behind their continued domination of American life.

Opposition to the 1619 Project is often lumped together with "critical race theory," with the avowed purpose of using it as a cudgel to attack progressivism, and to gin up panic among white Americans over the darker pigmented hordes that allegedly seek to replace them. Among the pushback: the laughable 1776 Project, which aims to present an even more reactionary, whitewashed view of American history. Ironically, that very "politicization" of history is the same allegation the right slings at the 1619 Project. But of course, all history is political and cannot be divorced from those ramifications. The only question is which version of history has the weight of facts and evidence on its side.[3]

As the historian and author James Carroll told me, "I think it would be a terrible outcome if, ten years from now, there are half a dozen American states in which children effectively have been excused from Black History Month. That would reify this new way in which the Confederacy has come back to us."[4] But of course, the right wing does not intend for that excusal to be limited to just a half dozen states.

For some there is an objection to an honest accounting of US history, full stop. For others, the argument is that this material is somehow too "traumatizing" for children to learn—meaning white children, whom they believe are too sensitive to be told about their own history.[5] (These critics make the same argument about sexuality, particularly anything related to the trans community.) It is unclear at what age these critics think this ain't-no-Santa-Claus revelation ought to be dropped on white children, or why they believe there isn't an age-appropriate way to discuss basic human values and our collective story at every level. Not on their list of things that are traumatizing for children: an epidemic of mass murders in American schools by gunmen toting semiautomatic rifles like the AR-15 and its variants, a problem that plagues the United States alone among developed countries.[6] One would be forgiven for suspicion of their motives, or for detecting a desire to indoctrinate American children from their most formative years.

The right wing has also aggressively sought to take control of local school boards, already a contentious space due to the COVID-19 pandemic.[7] The vision of that historically anti-science, anti-intellectual, anti-knowledge segment of the American body politic seeking not only to protest medical measures taken to protect our children, but also to take propagandistic partisan control of what those children are taught in the academic realm, is deeply disturbing to say the least.

At the university level, the right is engaged in an attack on the tenure system, which itself originated as a means of protecting scholars from political interference and intimidation.[8] Tellingly, Professor Hannah-Jones—a MacArthur "Genius" Fellow and a Pulitzer Prize winner—has been a prominent victim of that campaign. When the University of North Carolina announced plans to offer her a chair in its journalism school, right-wing alumni mounted a pressure campaign on the school's board of trustees. Though the university was embarrassed when that campaign was made public and did eventually offer her the tenured position, the damage was done and she instead joined the faculty of Howard University.[9] Wouldn't you?

PRIVATE AGENDAS AND PUBLIC OPTIONS

The American right wing has always been hostile to public education—another giveaway that they are not trustworthy stewards of the national well-being.[10] People who would prefer that others remain ignorant are not exactly advertising their goodwill.

"I love the poorly educated," Trump quipped after winning the Nevada primary in 2016—maybe a stab at inclusivity, if one is inclined to be generous, but more likely just saying the quiet part out loud.[11] Since the days of Ronald Reagan the GOP has advocated abolishing the Department of Education entirely, and Trump did his best to do so from within via the appointment of Betsy DeVos, an overt opponent of public education, as his Secretary of Education. The push for charter schools paid for with tax dollars, and for school vouchers, are all part of a longstanding campaign to gut public education, which not coincidentally would hit economically struggling families and people of color disproportionately hard. More broadly speaking, it's part of a general antipathy to the communitarian spirit in favor of an every-man-for-himself society where the wealthy and privileged have an enormous advantage and the have-nots can pound sand.

That should come as no surprise, as public education does nothing to aid the autocratic effort, but only hinders it, by creating informed citizens with a grasp of history who can think for themselves and challenge orthodoxies. It's worth remembering that one of the things that first drove the conservative passion for alternatives to public schools—or "government schools" as those conservatives often call them—was a fervent desire to remove their children from a newly desegregated school system and to put them in private ones where de facto apartheid could be maintained.[12]

If free public education had not been part of American life since the mid nineteenth century and were a new proposal being put forth today by a Democratic administration, one can easily imagine the

GOP howling in opposition, crying "socialism!" and arguing that this idea was governmental overreach, just as it has done over the idea of free public health care, another thing many other advanced democracies provide as a matter of course.

The tragedy is that attacks on education are not only inherently cruel and immoral, but are self-destructive for our society on even the most practical level, even in matters that conservatives themselves claim to venerate. Shantel Palacio, an educational consultant, doctoral candidate in education policy at the University of New Hampshire, and formerly a senior staffer and strategic advisor in the New York City Department of Education, told me: "There's a school of thought that says, 'Hey, we *want* an uneducated population that's just going to be worker bees and do what we tell them.' But if we want to have a booming economy, then we need to have an educated population that can fuel it."[13] This is an argument that transcends partisanship and does not even require any goodwill on the part of the right wing—just a pragmatic recognition of its own economic self-interest.

Palacio also notes that the practical consequences of right-wing attacks on education go beyond a poorly educated workforce, as bad as that is, as the ill-conceived attempt to suppress intellectual inquiry tends to backfire as students advance. "What we see at the collegiate level is that undergraduates arrive—particularly white undergraduates—and for the first time learn about some of the things that have happened in American history, and are angry that no one taught them this before. 'Why didn't I know this? What is wrong with the education that I grew up with?' Suddenly they're in a position where they have to go into a world that is diverse, and multicultural, and travel to different countries for the first time, and there are so many things that they're not prepared for, and they're not happy about that."[14]

That is not a phenomenon that any right-wing autocracy can stop, short of turning every American college into a theocratic indoctrination mill like Hillsdale College, or Liberty University, or Patrick Henry College—which they would be quite happy to do. But Palacio believes that they are doomed to fail.

"Everyone has to decide if they want to look honestly at the history of our country or if they want to keep moving with their eyes closed."[15]

A fundamental part of any resistance to a new American autocracy must include a concerted effort to defend the educational process, to protect free and open academic inquiry, and to make sure that critical thinking, not right-wing indoctrination, is the lodestar of American education. That instruction in critical thinking is the very heart of education: training subsequent generations to question orthodoxies, to scrutinize sources and motives, to verify the reliability of the information that is presented to them, and to recognize and dismantle a false argument. Some students in America are taught these skills, but many are not, often reflecting the widening gap in the quality of education between the haves and the have-nots, exacerbated by the pandemic and by conservative elements that actively want to keep the population susceptible to their propaganda.

Teachers, students, and parents at all levels are the rank and file in this struggle, from grammar school to grad school. We must insist on honest curricula that promote rigorous intellectual inquiry unfettered by partisanship, and reckon with the truths of American history, good, bad, and ugly. Teachers' unions must stand against any political infringement on the educational process. Students must demand that their education not be circumscribed by ideological agendas. Parents must push back against that same circumscribing, and even against other parents who endorse it, to include running for seats on school boards. The "parents' rights" movement is dangerous enough when it is a genuine collective of right-wing parents trying to institute retrograde curricula: it's even worse when Astroturfed as a front for powerful, deep-pocketed right-wing lobbyists and the ideologues they serve. Let's press for parents' rights of our own, including the right to see our children—all children—properly educated and not sheltered from necessary truths, or fed a twisted vision of how we came to be the nation we are, or of the kind of nation we aspire to be.

Of course, those dictates can be embraced by people of all political stripes: the conflict turns on subjective definitions of terms like "ideological agendas," "indoctrination," and "political infringement." But here is where liberalism in its classical definition has the advantage. Progressives don't fear the truth and are confident about how our ideas will fare in a free and open exchange of ideas. We *want* to hold arguments up to scrutiny to be judged by empiricism and evidence, and by a society of educated citizens with open eyes and hearts and minds. Those who don't have already announced their bad faith and lost the debate.

We know that teachers can have some of the most profound influences on young minds. Imagine, then, a decentralized, underground network of such progressive teachers, deftly circumventing the system and inculcating true American values in the next generations of schoolchildren. In Florida, Black churches have already begun teaching what the Sunshine State's public schools will not—a model for what we may need to do on a much bigger scale.[16] A clandestine movement of valiant educators, cleverly working within and around a repressive academic system, might be the last line of defense for democracy, and the starting point for its resurrection in the next generation.

THE CASE FOR DECENCY

Critical thinking is not a mission that can be delegated or sloughed off to schools alone. Mothers, fathers, older siblings, and other family members have daily opportunities to drill that instinct into little heads and create inquisitive, open-minded, morally grounded adults who question authority, check facts, and display a healthy curiosity and skepticism about information that is presented to them as received wisdom.

"When I was growing up, my parents would watch the news all day long, 24/7," Shantel Palacio told me. "And some issue would come up and my mother would ask me, 'Do you believe in this particular policy?' If I said yes, she'd said, 'Why? What's good about it?' And I would explain why. And she would say, 'OK, and what's bad about it? What do conservatives think about it? What do liberals think about it?' I didn't know at the time, but she was teaching me how to think. 'What is the information that you're hearing? Can you back it up? Who is the policy forgetting?'"[17]

The much broader parental imperative is as seminal as it is simple: to raise decent human beings. That is as hard a task as any we care to name, but the ripple effects of success—or failure—are tsunami-like. The entire struggle against autocracy would be infinitely easier if we as a people were infused with an innate sense of fairness, kindness, and common decency, and if we raised our children to treat their fellow human beings—all of them—with dignity and respect.[18]

Empathy, love, and respect are all values that we can inculcate in the next generation, and they are not the exclusive province of any given political ideology, almost all of whom profess respect for those values, with varying degrees of evidence to back up their claims. Even taking politics out of the equation, that effort would have a profound and lasting impact on the health and well-being of the republic. Strike up a sarcastic chorus of "Kumbaya" if you wish, but if we want to preserve our democracy, an excellent starting point—a prerequisite, even—is to be decent human beings ourselves. That alone would go a long way toward making America great, again or otherwise.

CHAPTER 14

Do No Harm Is Not Enough

In contemporary America, a confluence of crises—the long struggle for affordable medical care, the COVID-19 pandemic, the ongoing epidemic of senseless gun violence, and the battle over bodily autonomy for half the species—have thrust public health to the front of the national dialogue. Therefore, even in the best-case scenario of continued Democratic control of the federal government, to say nothing of the worst-case of a Republican takeover, the US medical community will be forced to engage in several intensive fights, all of which speak directly to the fate of democracy.

THANKS, OBAMA

The US continues to be the lone advanced democracy that is somehow unable to provide decent health care for its citizens.[1] The reasons are manifold but are almost certainly connected to the pathological American fear of anything that could remotely be labeled "socialism," even when it makes a lot of sense. On that count, the Affordable Care Act was at once a startlingly mild reform of the system and a herculean achievement, a paradox that speaks to the dysfunction of American politics as a whole.

It's a perfect irony that Republicans thought the term "Obamacare" was going to be an insult when they coined it. Perhaps they did not think Americans would be glad to have something approaching affordable health care. But going on fourteen years since its passage, and amid relentless, irrational Republican efforts to undo it, the popularity of the plan speaks for itself, and Republicans have only themselves to blame that it's an honorific that will be permanently attached to the forty-fourth president's name.[2]

Ironically, the two parties' positions on health care have reversed since the 1990s, when it was the Republicans who were keen on solving the problem through private insurance, to include the individual mandate that would later turn into a right wing *bête noire*.[3] Famously, in some of its provisions the Affordable Care Act very much resembled "Romneycare," the plan Mitt Romney instituted in Massachusetts when he was its governor, but became the object of astonishing right-wing hatred as soon as it was proposed by Barack Obama. That reversal speaks to how politicized the topic has become, and how divorced from rational policymaking. It might also be viewed as yet another example of how the Republican Party successfully "moved the center," in Naomi Klein's phrase, so that a policy like the individual mandate that was once considered center-right is now somehow thought of as center-left, pushing a truly center-left plan, like a single-payer system, off the table entirely.[4]

A system that ties your health care to your place of employment could hardly be more consciously designed to yoke wage earners to their jobs, to reduce their bargaining power, and to keep most of the citizenry in permanently precarious thrall to their employers. Nothing inspires trembling obedience like a system where being laid off also means losing the ability to see your doctor or pay for medicine for your children.

"The fact that we haven't gotten rid of employer-based health insurance as a mandate is crazy," a physician involved in health care advocacy told me. "If the federal government came in and said, 'We're gonna provide a national health program that is available to anybody that wants it, and because of that, small businesses are no longer going to be required to provide health insurance for their employees,' I think that would be really popular with Republicans, purely on the numbers. But I think we've made the case very poorly about the value of public health care."[5]

Under the radar, the search for a publicly funded essential health plan is actually gravitating to something like a workable solution in the expansion of Medicaid, which forty states and DC have already done. "It's the only public-facing program that the federal government can expand," my doctor source told me, "but states have to do it themselves. Once it's implemented in all fifty states, you have the leverage for expanding the existing basic health program that you can then improve."[6] It would be a very American solution, and a testament to our screwed-up politics, if at last we somehow developed an affordable public option for health care in the most convoluted, Rube Goldberg way possible.

Amid that ongoing struggle, the COVID-19 pandemic represented a dramatic escalation in the confluence of public health and politics. The coronavirus seemed almost tailor-made to exploit all the GOP's worst sins and weaknesses: in particular, the conservative contempt for education and intellect—and science above all—which seemed designed with almost O. Henry-like perfection to render America uniquely vulnerable. The right wing's demonization of a vastly credentialed lifelong public servant like Dr. Anthony Fauci was a reprise of the attacks on Robert Mueller and Alexander Vindman before him, the degree of vitriol being in direct proportion to the stature of the foe. Likewise, the destruction of the administrative state that Steve Bannon promised with his dime store Leninism had been achieved, so that when a crisis of epic proportions arose that only the federal government could address, there was only a shell of that government left to respond.[7]

The pandemic showed like nothing before just how low Trump had brought the United States in less than four years. A world that once looked to the US for leadership in almost every area now gazed in shock upon America's overwhelmed hospitals and Depression-level lines of jobless workers and petulant citizenry refusing to take the simplest of precautions to fight the virus—incredibly, encouraged in that suicidal recklessness by their own leaders—even as smaller, far less well-equipped countries managed to stave off calamity.[8] A country that never ceased crowing over its shared sacrifice in World War II was now a country in which millions would not even wear a mask in the interest of the national good. Trump's ghastly failure to grapple with COVID-19 turned the United States into something it had never been before: an object of pity. It was the height of irony—or was it the depths?—that it was because of him that Americans were banned from entry to almost every country on earth. Trump had his wall after all . . . except that we were the ones confined within it.[9]

Today in America, attacks on expertise, on empiricism, on anything that conflicts with a preordained ideological or religious point of view have become the norm. Post-COVID, the right's anti-science mindset has even taken on long-proven childhood vaccines against diseases like measles, mumps, and rubella that were once routine. Anti-vax sentiment in America is not new. But what *is* new is that the pandemic energized that segment and allowed it to spread from the fringe to a larger segment of the population. But the funny thing about science is that a virus, or a cancer, or a forest fire, or a hurricane does not care what you think or how you vote.

OF HIPPOCRATES AND HYPOCRITES

The other arena where medicine and politics collide most dramatically is of course abortion.

It is no mystery why Republicans are so insistent on controlling the bodily autonomy of American women: it is baked into the premodern, patriarchal ideology under which women do not have full rights as human beings. That generally matters little to the plutocratic class, except as a vestige of the pre-feminist past, but it's essential to the Christian dominionists with whom those plutocrats are allied. The realist faction of the GOP knows that the party's stance on abortion is an electoral loser: Americans consistently support common sense abortion rights by a roughly 2 to 1 margin, which is a blowout by contemporary US standards.[10] In off-year elections in 2023, three staunchly red states all voted to protect abortion access, including a constitutional amendment guaranteeing it in Ohio, reelection of a Democratic governor in Kentucky over a Republican challenger who favored a near-total ban on the procedure, and a return to Democratic control of the state legislature in Virginia, where the Republican majority had tried to outlaw the procedure after fifteen weeks.[11]

And we see the practical impact of opposing that public will. Businesses are thinking twice about building facilities and setting up shop in states with draconian abortion laws.[12] Parents are reluctant to send their children—daughters and sons alike—to college in those states.[13] Health care providers are closing their doors and moving to more hospitable climes.[14] But still the Republican Party cannot extricate itself from the suicide pact it has made with the religious right.

It's instructive to note that these same people who adamantly claim to defend the lives of what they call the "unborn" also tend to oppose nutrition programs for hungry children, economic assistance to poor families, family leave, workplace support for single mothers like on-site daycare, and a whole range of other programs to help those children once they are in fact born. In that regard, the movement that likes to call itself "pro-life" is more correctly identified as "forced birth."

There are some acts which we forbid because they are incompatible with a functioning society: murder, robbery, and fraud, for example. But there are many other acts where there is no such consensus or imperative. Some Americans believe that drinking alcohol is an abomination and would never engage in such a practice. For nearly a decade in the 1920s we tried to enforce their beliefs on the entire nation, with dismal results. Similarly, members of the anti-abortion movement feel very strongly—to say the least—that a fertilized egg is a human being. But a vast majority of Americans feel otherwise.

We don't have to solve the philosophical debate about when life begins to determine how to deal with abortion on a purely legalistic level. Both pro-life and pro-choice Americans, to use their own preferred terms, ought to be equally in favor of a functioning democracy that allows for divergent opinions, even on highly contentious matters. Absent a consensus, in a pluralistic democracy the only workable solution is a compromise that allows for the free exercise of the beliefs of all. (And it is important to remember that *Roe* itself was a compromise.[15]) The old bumper sticker still obtains: "Don't believe in abortion? Don't have one."

But forced birth radicals are unwilling to tolerate a society in which other citizens are free to make their own health care decisions. In fact, because they believe abortion is so sinful, some of them are even willing to engage in ghastly acts of violence to prevent them. But in the end, their absolutist stance is self-sabotaging. The conviction that life begins at conception is but a small step from equal protections for other forms of "potential life," a position that would also outlaw in vitro fertilization, freezing of embryos, stem cell research, cord blood banking, and even contraception, presumably with vigilante violence to prevent those as well. The state of Alabama has already taken a dramatic step in that direction.[16]

In reality, then, it is not the permittance of safe, legal abortion that threatens our society, but homicidal domestic terrorism in opposition to it, including the intimidation of patients (some of them still minors), the bombings of abortion clinics, and the murder of doctors. For decades, that illegal campaign of terrorist violence has operated in parallel with an aggressive, well-funded political campaign to chip away at abortion rights, and to pack the courts with radically anti-abortion judges, with the ultimate goal of overturning *Roe*, full stop—a two-track pattern that is disturbingly similar to the broader white nationalist insurgency that bedevils us today.[17]

In response, the pro-choice movement organized along classic civil rights lines to defend the right of American women to control their own health care. But that movement lost the fight in 2022, thanks to the justices that Donald Trump of all people was able to put on the Supreme Court. Today the United States has more restrictive abortion laws than even heavily Catholic countries like Ireland[18] or France.[19]

But the forced birth movement is not stopping there. Not content with individual states making abortion illegal, sometimes without exceptions for rape, incest (which is rape by definition), or the life of the mother, those activists are attempting to institute a nationwide federal ban.[20] Not only are American women in places like Texas and Oklahoma unable to obtain an abortion, but anyone who assists them in seeking one is also subject to charges, whether it is a doctor, a family member who does no more than offer advice, or an Uber driver who transports the patient. Idaho has passed legislation that would enable it to bring criminal prosecutions against doctors *in other states* who provide abortion services to Idaho residents.[21] Cutting-edge technology is even being employed to surveil anyone even contemplating an abortion, including seizure of cellphone data from apps that track menstrual cycles.[22] Forced birth advocates are also working toward a legal reinterpretation of the 1873 Comstock Act that would make it impossible for doctors in blue states even to obtain the physical tools needed to conduct the procedure.[23]

But to truly achieve their goals at a time when more than half of all abortions in the US are medicinally induced, it is necessary to attack more than just surgical abortions.[24]

"Fundamentalists hate the abortion pill more than almost anything else," an ER doctor told me, "because it is safe, it is effective, and it is private, and they want abortion to be unsafe, they want it to be ineffective, and they want you to be shamed. So they are coming after the FDA authorization, which will undermine the entire biopharmaceutical industry."[25]

It is a measure of the GOP's ruthlessness, and its skill at gaming that legal system, that it went forum-shopping and found the most fanatically Atwoodian judge in all America—in north Texas—in order to make the abortion drug mifepristone illegal nationwide. Never before had an American judge reached into the system and overturned FDA approval of a drug—safely used by millions of American women for more than two decades—without even a whiff of scientific cause.[26] Though the Supreme Court has kept the drug available while an appeal is being adjudicated, the ultimate fate of mifepristone is surely barreling toward a final ruling.

Beyond abortion rights, the exploitation of this quirk of jurisprudence speaks to a far greater danger. What is to prevent fundamentalists from bringing cases in Amarillo, Texas on a whole range of contentious matters, allowing that lone federal judge to dictate national policy on Obamacare, on vaccines, on guns, school prayer, same-sex marriage, voting rights, or anything else?

Much more worrying even than an attack on a particular drug, forced birth advocates are looking for a way to codify their core belief that a fertilized egg is a human being, with all the same rights, from counting in the census to credit in the carpool lane.

"The Court would love to find for fetal personhood," my doctor source told me, "because abortion then becomes murder, and you can never, ever end a pregnancy under any conditions. The collateral damage of that legal concept cannot be overstated, but it doesn't seem like the Court really cares, because the only people that would be damaged by it are women, by mandating that the moment an egg is fertilized, it has equal rights to the person carrying it. That is how we lose abortion access in America."[27]

Only mandated appropriations by Congress can prevent that outcome and only public pressure can force such measures.

Prior to *Roe*, in the days of coat hangers and life-threatening back-alley abortions, a clandestine, community-based underground network existed to help American women obtain abortions. After

1973 it went dormant, and few of its old members ever imagined they would need to revive it.

"During the feminist movement, there was a group in Chicago and another in LA who learned how to do safe abortions," Alix Kates Shulman told me. "The LA group also taught self-abortion, which was illegal, with a technique called menstrual extraction. It was a little group, like all of our groups, a dozen people, but they went on a national tour and taught us how to find our cervix by using a speculum and a mirror and a flashlight. Few American women had ever seen the inside of their bodies before." Shulman recalled that the members of both groups were eventually arrested, in the case of the LA group, for practicing medicine without a license. (Of course, these days it is the Supreme Court that is doing that.) "In the end they were acquitted, but they were prepared to go to prison," Shulman said. "I'm prepared to go to prison, too," she laughed, defiantly. "I'm ninety now. Let them haul me off to prison!"[28]

Today, the advent of pharmaceutically induced abortion has changed the nature of the clandestine abortion network, making it somewhat easier to assist women via a robust underground railroad—with nurses at its center—that has emerged to smuggle abortifacients into the United States.[29] But the process remains fraught practically, legally, and medically. Like all such movements, it relies on funding from generous benefactors and friends—in cash, so it can't be tracked. The forced birth movement is also keen on the harshest possible punishment for its foes; in Texas, doctors can face ninety-nine years in prison for violating the abortion ban, which, broadly construed, could include overseeing the administration of a drug.[30] Thus, covert usage of mifepristone is usually undertaken without the requisite medical supervision, leading to increased risks to the health of the patient.[31]

Ironically, economics may provide a means to protect some form of abortion access, even within a right-wing regime. One doctor described for me the chaos that will ensue if the right wing can get FDA authorization for the removal of a safe and effective medication a quarter-century after the fact, on the most spurious grounds. If they succeed, lawyers for the pharma companies could bring cases against every manufacturer of every drug on the market and systemically remove all their competitors by stripping away their FDA authorizations. On the table, then, is the potential collapse of the entire pharmaceutical industry.[32]

"These religious ideologues are willing to dismantle the entire FDA authorization process to get rid of a pill that is safe, effective, and private—that's how much they want to control women. They obviously don't care about women, or about people's lives, but they also don't care what damage it does to the economy."[33]

Here again we see a possible wedge that can be driven between those religious fanatics and ordinary pro-business Republicans, and a way to mobilize the capitalist system—and the power of Big Pharma—that stands to lose hugely in this scenario. "Why do you think the Supreme Court stayed the decision and sent it back to the Fifth Circuit? It was because hundreds of pharmaceutical executives wrote an amicus brief describing that chaos. When it overturned *Roe*, the Court didn't really appreciate the damage of women's health care becoming so unpredictable, or of criminalizing doctors, or any of the other consequences we're seeing. And they don't really care about any of that. But I just don't think this Court is interested in dismantling systems that will make the economy collapse."

It is not heartwarming to think that only avarice can protect basic human rights. "It's not that I think they'll do the right thing, even by accident," says the doctor. "They will do the thing that will protect the economics, and that will be an outcome that is, by accident, beneficial to society."[34]

ALL POLICY IS HEALTH POLICY

As the far right seeks to impose its misogynistic, lethally anti-scientific agenda on the whole country, the medical community has a unique opportunity to stand up and resist. That resistance can range from simply providing fact-based medical information to counter the disinformation that floods the American conversation, to providing pro bono services and volunteer work to offset inequities in health care, to working to expand access to crucial prenatal and neonatal care and childhood nutrition, to leveraging the power of the profession to make lifesaving drugs more affordable and available, to mobilizing the entire medical community in opposition to any political movement that hurts the American people.

"One thing we did during the Trump administration was to start an organization to get physicians on television," a doctor involved in health care advocacy told me. "But we needed help, because we were also working our regular jobs as physicians. We need to have a bootcamp ready for physicians trying to get the message out. We also need the media to want to cover it, because bad actors are always going to find a platform. And that goes back to figuring out a way to bring truth back to media legislatively, and how to hold media accountable."[35]

Amy Thogmartin runs Centivox, a public health communication firm that trains health care practitioners in how to talk to the media and other audiences on behalf of progressive policies. "In our experience, it's about trust," she told me. "The distrust of institutional medicine and public health officials in certain communities creates fissures where misinformation and disinformation can seep in and take hold, and bad actors capitalize on that lack of trust.

"Doctors and nurses are the most trusted professions in America, so we need to have them more civically engaged and forward-facing, and target those communities that have the highest levels of distrust in public health information and institutions. In the Black community, the US public health system has heartily earned that distrust, historically. Poor white communities that are Republican strongholds have been another of our strategic priorities, and that's been a lot harder."[36]

Thogmartin notes that, historically, the AMA has discouraged American physicians from being politically active, though that has not stopped Republican politicians who are MDs, like Ronny Jackson or Ron and Rand Paul. Then again, the AMA's own history is grim, with its historical opposition to universal health care, long-time exclusion of Black doctors from its membership, and refusal to take a stand against segregated hospitals that created a dearth of Black physicians that persists to this day. (As of 2023, less than 6 percent of all American physicians are Black.[37]) Like many American institutions, the AMA has at least begun grappling with that history: it remains to be seen how far the reforms go, and if the association can become a positive force. But in any event, physicians cannot wait for that to happen, or for a bureaucracy to take the lead.

"The right uses the term 'activist' as a slur," my doctor source told me, "but if you look at like the doctors they trot out at hearings on abortion or guns, they teach their doctors how to be involved in legislative action, how to be voices in the community, how to talk to Congress. Democrats don't."[38] A prime example is the deceptively named American College of Pediatrics, a right-wing splinter group that has successfully lobbied to influence government policies on matters like conversion therapy for gay people, under the guise of being the umbrella organization for all US pediatricians, which it pointedly is not.[39] On the contrary: in 2012 the Southern Poverty Law Center designated it a hate group, which has not stopped mainstream Republican think tanks and lobbyists like the Heritage Foundation from actively supporting it.[40]

"All policy is health policy," Thogmartin told me. "Whether it's housing or taxation or national defense or climate, everything has health implications. So we need to start empowering physicians right now to be ground-level activists. We need them to understand the intersection of the clinical work they do and the policies around them, and be trusted voices to speak to the community on a local level."[41]

I asked Thogmartin if, in so doing, doctors and nurses risked compromising the very trust and credibility that their perceived neutrality has brought them. "That trust is already eroding right now," she replied, "But people still trust *their* doctor, and *their* nurse, one-on-one. Remaining above the fray is not an option when there is so much disinformation flooding the market. I would argue that health care providers have a moral and professional obligation to counter that. That does not mean explicitly choosing sides in a partisan political battle. But if they speak the scientific truth, the partisan impact will take care of itself."[42]

CHAPTER 15

In Gods We Trust

Across human history, organized religion has a lot to answer for. In our own current emergency, a number of American religious organizations are enthusiastically allied with the right wing, from Protestant fundamentalists to archconservative strains of both the Catholic Church and the American Jewish community. But people of faith and religious institutions also have a proud parallel tradition of social justice, and can be an equally powerful counterweight against the autocratic experiment.

Having sprung from the arrival of religious pilgrims fleeing persecution in the Old World (only to practice it in the New one), the United States remains a profoundly religious nation, where faith takes a far more prominent role in politics than in many advanced democracies. Witness the very different ways in which those partners in the second Iraq War, Tony Blair and George Bush, treated the evangelical Christianity that they shared. It may come as a surprise to many readers, both British and American, that Blair even *is* a born-again Christian.[1] On that count, the US is likely to have a gay president, and a female president, and a gay female president, before it has an openly atheist president.

Organized religious institutions and their members therefore can and must be instrumental to any broad-based anti-autocratic, pro-democracy resistance movement in this country. The moral high ground that such institutions occupy lends them credibility and gravitas, particularly with conservative Americans who might otherwise disparage protest movements. It is foolish to think that the autocracy can be shamed, but the image of ministers, priests, nuns, monks, imams, and rabbis leading peaceful public protest is not good optics for the ruling junta.

But the people we are calling upon to be part of this anti-fascist resistance are themselves also going to be locked in a struggle against elements within their own religious institutions who are aligned with those same neofascists.

ONWARD CHRISTIAN SOLDIERS

As we have seen, a twisted, reactionary version of religion is part and parcel of the American right from the very founding of this country, vastly accelerated in the Reagan era and continuing through Trump and into the present day, part of its adherents' exclusionary vision of this land as a white, Christian one, *e pluribus unum* be damned. They are keen to require mandatory school prayer; the posting of the Ten Commandments in school classrooms; instruction in the ahistorical belief in the supremacy of Christianity in American government; and a greater role for clergy in public life, particularly education. Christians, well-meaning and otherwise, who push for such intrusions of their faith into the public sphere may be genuinely unaware of the discomfort and alienation that creates for Americans of other faiths and for nonbelievers, in a country whose foundational documents explicitly promise both freedom *of* religion and *from it*. (Conveniently, they also ignore the actual religious beliefs of the Founders, many of whom were Deists, with a vision of God and Christianity quite unlike that of the modern American right.)[2] Well beyond mere discomfort, such policies reduce non-Christians to subordinate status, depriving them of their full constitutional rights as American citizens, and undermining the very core of democratic equality on which this country is ostensibly based.

One trick the right wing typically employs is a specious appeal to "religious liberty" that is much like the dishonest appeal to "color blindness" at the heart of Ibram X. Kendi's "second assassination" of Martin Luther King. While eager to deny others their constitutional rights—like the right to vote, or marry, or make one's own health care decisions—reactionaries often insist that their own rights are somehow being impinged upon by having to respect the beliefs of others.[3] They then turn that claim into an offensive weapon, arguing that they deserve a special waiver exempting them from compliance with the law on those spiritual grounds—or worse, that all Americans ought to be subject to their own beliefs.

You will be unsurprised to learn that this is but another disingenuous argument. One might very well claim, for instance, that being made to honor the basic personhood of Black people, or homosexuals, or women—like serving them in a restaurant, or hiring them for a job, or admitting them to a club—is a violation of one's religious beliefs: what the Center for Constitutional Rights calls "discrimination in the guise of liberty."[4] In fact, that was a longstanding claim of segregationists in the Jim Crow era, and a number of conservative Christians have petitioned for religious exemptions using a similar argument.[5] Taken to the extreme, one might just as easily argue that one's faith demands killing gay people, or Muslims, or nonbelievers. Would that too merit protection under the law on grounds of "religious liberty"?

Traditionally, the concept of religious liberty has been used to protect vulnerable believers and communities of faith against the tyranny of the majority, such as the right of Jehovah's Witnesses not to say the Pledge of Allegiance, or to be exempt from military service as conscientious objectors. That is because religious beliefs and practices tend to be noninvasive in nature—not unlike sexual acts between consenting adults. In other words, protecting them does not infringe on the rights or freedoms of anyone else, short of an absurd argument that one should not have to live in a country knowing that such things are practiced by others, even in private. But over the past few decades the formulation has been turned inside out, and with insidious intent. Now we see the concept deployed by the religious majority to enable it to practice bigotry, discrimination, and oppression of the less powerful under the guise of "victimhood"—a galling case of the powerful co-opting the arguments and techniques of the vulnerable and oppressed.

A prominent proponent of this ruse is the Alliance Defense Fund, a well-funded, homo- and transphobic right-wing Christian legal organization that counts Erin Hawley, wife of Missouri Senator Josh Hawley, among its top attorneys, and the DeVos and Prince families among its funders.[6] (The ADF also brought the mifepristone case in Texas.) In *303 Creative v. Elenis*, the ADF asked the Supreme Court to rule that a website designer could refuse to create a site for gay weddings.* There was no such real-world incident—the dilemma was purely hypothetical. Nevertheless, the Court complied. The First Amendment right against being compelled to express views that conflict with one's deeply held beliefs is already established; that is not the same as the right to refuse service as a business owner, for example, because your religious beliefs insist that homosexuality is an abomination. Yet Gorsuch—who wrote the majority opinion in *303 Creative*—gleefully conflated the latter with the former. As he is not stupid, one can only assume that he's merely dishonest.

Following that ruling, we can expect the cry of "religious liberty" to be invoked to excuse all manner of antidemocratic, bigoted, and discriminatory practices—a de facto means to oppress anyone who does not toe the autocratic line. It's no coincidence that the far right-dominated Supreme Court is not taking up cases of fundamentalist Muslims who want to opt out of the rules of American democracy or establish a parallel society under their own religious laws.

The hypocrisy and cognitive dissonance of those who, over more than two millennia, have turned the teachings of a poor, pacifist Jewish carpenter into an instrument of global oppression is truly gobsmacking. (At the most violent and appalling end of that perversion: the Ku Klux Klan, an ostentatiously quasi-religious organization whose defining emblem, tellingly, is a cross, and whose signature symbol of terror is a burning one.[7]) But historically, autocrats and their supporters have long understood the power of religion both to advance their own cause and as a threat to stop them. Therefore, they will make a concerted effort to drape their plans in the mufti of religious piety, and to discredit and denigrate progressive persons of faith, both laypeople and clergy, who stand up against them.

---

*   In *Masterpiece Cakeshop v. Colorado Civil Rights Commission* (2018), the Court had previously allowed a Colorado bakery to refuse to make a wedding cake for a gay couple, citing religious objections. But that case was decided, 7-2, on a process technicality regarding the civil rights commission's decision-making, punting the real issue for a few years.

WITH GOD ON THEIR SIDE

"Catholicism has long been associated with that temptation to use religion as a way of exercising power," James Carroll, among the most incisive American observers of the Catholic Church, told me, "which is why fascism has so often found a home in Catholic cultures. Spain, obviously, Italy and throughout Latin America. Even France."[8] But alongside that ugly history is a noble one of the progressive strain within the Church, one that remained true to the principles of the historic Jesus of Nazareth: humility, poverty, kindness, forgiveness, and service. It is also one in which Carroll himself—a former Roman Catholic priest—has long been a pillar.

Even as the fanatically right-wing Cardinal Spellman was spinning the lies of Vietnam as a Catholic country besieged by communist threat, the brave priests, nuns, and laypeople of the Catholic Left took a leading role in opposing US involvement there with acts of civil disobedience that repeatedly landed them in jail. But it is Spellman who today has his name on schools and parks and buildings all over New York City. Which means that progressive Catholics will remain on the outside of the Church establishment if they join in any future pro-democracy movement in the United States. "Right-wing Catholics are central to the white supremacist nationalist movement, the ones on the US Supreme Court most clearly," Carroll told me, noting that all six justices who comprise its right-wing supermajority are Catholic.* "It's no accident that the right-wing manipulators working behind the scenes for the last thirty years dipped into the well of Catholic reaction to bring up these figures and give intellectual substance to what's essentially an anti-intellectual, anti-historical, anti-pluralistic movement."[9]

Carroll contends that we are still in a centuries-old argument about the Enlightenment itself. "The Catholic Church didn't get over its condemnation of Galileo until about thirty years ago, when the Pope finally issued the statement saying he was right. The MAGA

---

*   As CNN reports, though Gorsuch has worshipped at Episcopalian churches since marrying into the Church of England, he was raised Catholic, attended a Jesuit prep school, did his graduate dissertation under the tutelage of a famous Catholic theologian, raised his own children in the Catholic tradition, and has never renounced his own Catholicism.

movement in the United States and its equivalents in other parts of the world is the climax of a movement that has been unfolding for three or four hundred years."[10]

But progressive Catholic priests, nuns, and laypeople can be in the vanguard of the pro-democracy cause, with preaching and lived examples that demonstrate why fascism is anti-Christian, and the exact opposite of what the faithful should aspire to, and by making local parishes centers of gravity for true Christian resistance in keeping with the teachings of the historic Jesus. That will mean continuing to defy Rome—on abortion, on birth control, and on women's rights. It will mean the risk of excommunication for some. (The US Conference of Catholic Bishops has already threatened to deny the sacrament of Communion to Joe Biden, only America's second Roman Catholic president.[11]) And it will mean calling out the corruption and intellectual dishonesty of Catholic conservatives on the US Supreme Court and elsewhere in the US government.

Jim Carroll and others have dedicated their lives to that sort of struggle for social justice, often at great personal sacrifice. The present crisis demands their services yet again.

But Rome is far from alone in its complicity with the autocratic project in America. The Reagan era may have marked the overt alliance of the GOP and the religious right, but its roots go back to the *Mayflower*, the Puritan strain, and the prosperity gospel that has informed American life from the start. "Protestant fundamentalism underwrote the savage Cold War years of the '50s, the Red Scare, and McCarthyism," Carroll says, "The phrase 'under God' was only introduced into the Pledge of Allegiance in 1954, during the height of the McCarthy era."

But Carroll also reminds us that the interchangeable use of "evangelical" and "fundamentalist" as synonyms is incorrect.

"The term has come to mean fundamentalist white supremacy, but in truth, not all evangelical Christianity is reactionary. Jimmy Carter was an evangelical. The Black Church is evangelical. In fact, evangelicalism has been a tremendous engine of liberation, not just in the United States, in the Black Church, but in alliance with liberation theology in Latin America, which is a battle that's not over. Fundamentalists, on the other hand, are people who read the scriptures uncritically, and if you read the scriptures literally, slavery can be justified, the hatred of Jews can be justified, the subjugation of women can be justified. That's why it's the perfect marriage for this fascist, ahistorical, anti-intellectual movement."[12]

In the United States, as Carroll notes, there is no greater example of the positive role of religious organizations in the human rights struggle than that of the Black Church in the Civil Rights Movement of the 1950s and '60s. Martin Luther King Jr.'s role as the leader of that movement cannot be separated from his Christian faith and his profession as a clergyman, and is a towering testament to how a religious institution can be the physical, moral, and strategic center of political resistance. In the present moment, there may be no more eloquent voice in America for the cause of peace, justice, and democracy than Rev. William Barber II, head of the contemporary Poor People's Campaign, a senior official in the NAACP, and a professor at the Yale Divinity School.

As we have noted, any broad-based secular resistance to a Republican autocracy will be inextricably intertwined with the cause of racial justice, both supporting and piggybacking off it, to the point where the two cannot really be separated. If race has always been at the burning center of the American crisis, then redressing those wrongs is an unavoidable prerequisite for staving off white nationalist tyranny on these shores, and working toward a truly just, truly equitable manifestation of the American promise.

RABBI WALKS INTO A BAR

Like abortion, guns, or school prayer, Israel is a Republican wedge issue, even as the Republican and Democratic commitments to the Jewish state are functionally identical.[13] Still, ever since the Reagan era, the GOP has wooed right-wing American Jews with its allegedly staunch support for Israel. A brief survey of fundamentalist Christian beliefs, however, reveals that this alliance has never had anything to do with respect for the Jewish faith, or with real affection for Jews, whom those Christians consider "unsaved" and doomed to eternal damnation: it only has to do with an interpretation of the Bible that requires the establishment of the state of Israel preparatory to the Second Coming of Christ, the Rapture, and the End Times.[14] But the

Republican Party has benefitted greatly from the votes of right-wing American Jews, and the campaign contributions of massive donors like Sheldon and Miriam Adelson, even as it has claimed that Jewish financiers like George Soros are the puppet masters of the left.[15] The Orthodox and Hasidic communities in particular have been ferocious strongholds of support for Trump.* This comes despite decades in which Jews were not welcome in Republican-dominated country clubs, when Nixon's appalling anti-Semitism was literally on tape, as was Trump's (one Jewish son-in-law does not a philosemite make), as Trump himself dined at Mar-a-Lago with the Holocaust denier Nick Fuentes, as Republicans continue to spread ancient anti-Semitic tropes, and Hitler-admiring right-wingers march through the streets of Charlottesville carrying tiki torches and chanting "Jews will not replace us!"[16]

One has to wonder what will become of these right-wing Jews if a Republican administration succeeds in establishing the theocratic regime it is openly promoting, one that defines the United States as an inherently Christian country.[17]

I asked Rabbi Michael Berenbaum, professor of Jewish Studies at the American Jewish University in Los Angeles, and Project Director for the creation of the US Holocaust Memorial Museum, how Judaism—like so many religions—can reckon with the conflict within between those who are on the side of social justice and those on the side of autocracy.

"Why is it that fundamentalists have this attraction to authoritarianism? We have to say it's because of the parts of the tradition they choose to emphasize." Berenbaum argues that most religions embody complex traditions whose texts can be read selectively to serve a desired political end, cherrypicked, and sometimes even invented out of whole cloth. "There is no direct teaching on abortion in all of

---

*   Days ahead of the 2020 election, *The Times of Israel* reported that 83 percent of Orthodox Jews in the US supported Trump versus only 13 percent for Biden, with 4 percent undecided. That number was up dramatically from 2016, when Orthodox support for Trump was at 54 percent. It is also an almost complete inversion of the American Jewish electorate at large, which a Pew survey in the same period reported to be 70–23 in Biden's favor. By statistical extension, that means non-Orthodox Jews voted for Biden in even greater numbers than that.

Protestantism, for example. There is the idea of charity toward the widow, the orphan, and the stranger, but nothing about abortion. Yet in the fundamentalist community, and in the Roman Catholic community, abortion has become the dominant issue."[18]

Berenbaum told me that the tradition of activism and commitment to social justice in Judaism is particularly acute because historically Jews have not had political power. "Democracy is a fundamental principle for the Jewish people because we've needed our rights protected in a variety of circumstances."[19] He also cited that tradition as part of the source of the great public protest by Israelis over Netanyahu's power grab there. On that count, there is another reason for GOP support for Israel: a feeling of kinship with an increasingly repressive, right-wing regime with its own faux-religious mandate.[20] Ironically, then, the Republican lie of its superior support for Israel is slowly becoming true, but not in a good way: only because the right-wing Netanyahu government, which it so admires, is taking that country away from its own democratic promise.

"Non-liberal religion is by its very nature authoritarian," Berenbaum says. "By contrast, liberal religion has been a source of commitment to democracy. To its enormous credit, Reform Judaism has emphasized social justice, and respect for human dignity, and human diversity, pluralism, and tolerance, almost to the exclusion of the divine. I'm a religious man, and I believe in those values. But as we've seen, that's not a given in all traditions."

"Jimmy Carter was the most religious president we ever had," Berenbaum pointed out. "He has lived a devoutly religious life. And yet the Christian right turned against him and took a much more secular man—Ronald Reagan—and made him a hero. Not to mention Trump, who's not only secular but an abomination."[21]

As Berenbaum notes, progressive, centrist, and even center-right American Jews must be at the forefront of pushing back against Trumpism, recognizing a flashing red warning sign that indicates grave risk to the Jewish community should the Republican autocracy take hold. That means not ceding the issue of "Israel" to the GOP and the right wing. It means prominently announcing Jewish support for progressive candidates and causes. It means arguing—civilly—with friends and family members when the subject comes up, and bringing it up in the first place, even if it's uncomfortable or provokes an argument. It also means standing with people of other faiths and secular communities when they are the victims of hate speech, hate crimes, discrimination, and oppression.

PASSION PLAY

The Founders of the United States were explicit in their separation of church and state for a very good reason, which is that the absolutism of religious faith is incompatible both with the compromise required for governance, and with the notion of a pluralistic, egalitarian society with freedom for all. "Once white supremacy is married to Christian piety, which makes it the will of God," as Carroll told me, "then all bets are off for democracy."[22]

It is of course ironic that some of the foreign enemies that right-wingers most despise, like radical Islamist fundamentalists, share a similarly theocratic agenda, distinguished only by the name and trappings of their god. One even senses in that right-wing enmity a certain envy.[23]

The attempt to merge authoritarian politics with a national religious identity is therefore an old and often successful tactic. "Tyrants have often embraced reactionary religion as an instrument of oppression and control," Carroll told me, citing the support of the Russian Orthodox Church for the war in Ukraine and its alliance with the Putin regime at large. "Putin is a cynic who hasn't got a religious bone in his body," Carroll notes, yet he has cannily married his autocratic project with a state-sponsored church in a classically fascistic way, in transparent appeal to the mythical idea of the 'Russian soul.'"[24] American neofascists are attempting the same trick.

But the role of religion and religious organizations in pushing back against autocracy is not limited to dramatic life-and-death actions like those of Dr. King, or even the lifelong activism of Carroll, Berenbaum, and Goff. Ordinary religious people and churches, mosques, and temples can do vast good for the cause of democracy by their quotidian actions, by making their voices heard in opposition to autocracy, by being moral centers of the community, and by simply refusing to be complicit. Their mere existence stands as a stark rebuke to their co-religionists who eagerly abet the proto-fascist cause and therefore bring shame on their faith. Even the "nonpolitical" everyday actions of kindness, love, and service to the suffering and less fortunate are highly political acts that by their very example strike blows against a movement that preaches hate, divisiveness, injustice, and cruelty.

I asked Rabbi Berenbaum what he thought individual members of his community—or any given religious community—could do.

"Most important, I think, is Micah 6:8: 'What is it that God demands of you, oh men? To do justly, and love mercy, and to walk humbly with thy God.'" He continued with a nod to Yeats: "I am what I call a passionate moderate. Why should extremism have all the passion? I think that the problem is that extremism has crowded out the center, and the center is without passion. So I'm very much in favor of a passionate center."[25]

CHAPTER 16

Fifth Column

In almost every industry there are opportunities to push back against the autocracy. Realtors, florists, sanitation workers, restauranteurs, shopkeepers . . . there is hardly an occupation that cannot in some way, large or small, register its defiance and contribute to the pro-democratic cause. It can be as simple as signage that signals political solidarity, services provided to the resistance movement, or participation in community efforts to stand against infringement of human rights. Everything that announces to the autocrats that the citizenry is not simply going to roll over and take it is a blow against the empire.

Some industries and professions, of course, offer more fertile ground for anti-autocratic activism than others. For the purposes of this survey, we will focus on four key and interrelated arenas: governance, law enforcement, the intelligence community, and the military.

RESISTANCE BY RED TAPE

We have touched briefly on what elected officials can do to stymie the autocracy from within. But bureaucrats, the permanent denizens of the governmental system, may be even more effective. Politicians come and go; civil servants are forever. Moreover, they often hold vast institutional knowledge, have far-reaching connections, and wield a kind of entrenched power within their fiefdoms, giving them significant power to undermine and sabotage antidemocratic Republican policies. And they can't easily be chucked out, even if Trump is trying to change the system so that he personally can fire them en masse.

The reputation of governmental bureaucracy as painfully hide-bound and inefficient is a tired cliché, but it didn't come out of thin air. Imagine if that sclerosis was weaponized by principled bureaucrats with the ability to thwart, deflect, and slow-walk every operational aspect of the autocracy, from the Bureau of Land Management to the Office of Management and Budget to the Department of Transportation to ICE, the FCC, FEC, SEC, and the entire alphabet soup of the US government.

Even during the Trump administration, elements of the bureaucracy continued to operate with some degree of independence—the DOJ's special counsel investigation of Russian interference in the 2016 election, and of Trump's willing acceptance of that help, being the prime example. Therefore, as we have noted, should Trump regain the presidency, he and his minions will undoubtedly clean house of anyone showing the slightest evidence of a spine and replace them with slavish MAGA ideologues. Indeed, they have openly announced their intention to do so. But even as a GOP autocracy is sure to try to capture every possible agency, it cannot suppress internal opposition completely, nor win a game of whack-a-mole with every progressive in office nationwide. City and state officials do not have to enforce every godawful federal policy, and can even buck them, as they have done with the sanctuary city movement, for example. The federal government has its means of retaliating, but so do the states—a rich irony for the party of states' rights.

That capacity for resistance is especially high in criminal justice and law enforcement, which are the front lines of the autocratic project. A great degree of subjectivity is baked into that realm by its very nature, from decisions made by rank-and-file police officers on the beat to prosecutorial and judicial discretion at the highest levels. The Border Patrol does not have to enforce inhumane immigration policies. Prosecutors do not have to pursue baseless, politically motivated cases. Judges, especially those with lifetime appointments, do not have to function as a cog in that machine and endorse neofascist edicts.

Sometimes even an individual member of the government can make an enormous difference. One immediately thinks of Elliott Richardson and William Ruckelshaus in the Saturday Night Massacre. In 2004, John Ashcroft, George W. Bush's attorney general, literally rose from the hospital bed where he was recovering from an illness to reject a plea from White House counsel Alberto Gonzales to reauthorize a secret government surveillance program, choosing instead to support acting AG James Comey (yes, that James Comey), after both men raced to his bedside in a bid to reach him first.[1] Ashcroft was an archconservative who had championed any number of loathsome policies. But he was also a man who, in the most dramatic moment of his political career, did the right thing.

Recent times have offered even more examples. During the tense months after the 2020 election, we saw state-level Republican officials like Brad Raffensperger and Gabriel Sterling of Georgia and Rusty Bowers of Arizona refuse to yield to Trump's pressure to overturn the results, despite being Trump voters themselves. If not for their courage, the US might have been plunged into a far worse—and potentially more violent—constitutional crisis.

Another hero in that story is retired federal judge J. Michael Luttig, a conservative icon long revered by Republicans, who spent fifteen years on the US Court of Appeals for the Fourth Circuit, "the most conservative judge on the most conservative court in America," as *The Washington Post* described him.[2] How Republican is he? So Republican that he is the man whose opinion—and stamp of approval—an agonizing Mike Pence sought while under pressure by Trump to block the certification of Joe Biden's victory. What Pence got instead was a ferocious rejection of the claim that a vice president had any such power. In the past, Luttig had often been mentioned as a potential Supreme Court nominee in his own right. But as former acting Solicitor General Neal Katyal quipped, "There's a good argument that Judge Luttig, by not being on the Supreme Court, did more for our democracy than most any sitting Supreme Court justice or past one."[3]

All these Republicans are shining exceptions to the shamefulness of the contemporary GOP. Theirs is the kind of courage that will be required by decent conservatives, putting country before party, if we want to save the democracy in which we all profess to believe.

THE SNOWDENS OF YESTERYEARS

When it comes to what can be done from inside the enemy camp, whistleblowers can also have a profound effect, as evidenced by how harshly they have traditionally been treated the world over.

Some of the great American whistleblowers include Ronald Ridenhour, the soldier who exposed the massacre at My Lai; Joseph Darby, the military police sergeant who exposed torture at Abu Ghraib; and the CIA whistleblower who anonymously raised the alarm about Trump's illegal pressure on Volodymyr Zelenskyy that led to his first impeachment. But the actions of perhaps the most famous whistleblower of recent times—former NSA computer intelligence consultant Edward Snowden—remain divisive. Snowden's exposure of illegal surveillance by the National Security Agency may have been a net good, but those who wish to portray him as a hero must contend with the ugly image of Snowden fleeing into the arms of Vladimir Putin, under whose protection he remains to this day. Snowden is now a naturalized Russian citizen. No word yet on when he's headed to the Ukrainian front.

A far more sterling example of a whistleblower, and one whose impact was titanic, would be Daniel Ellsberg, whose leaking of the Pentagon Papers to Neil Sheehan of *The New York Times* in 1971 prompted a hurricane of condemnation at the time. But Ellsberg—a former Marine Corps infantry officer and a RAND Corporation analyst who helped plan US strategy in Vietnam—did not come to the decision lightly, having previously tried unsuccessfully to slip that same information to anti-war senators like William Fulbright and George McGovern.[4] Ellsberg surrendered to the authorities to face the proverbial music—a funeral march—and was charged under the Espionage Act of 1917, among other statues. He faced 115 years in prison. (The case was eventually thrown out by a federal judge.)[5]

The consequences of Ellsberg's actions are almost impossible to overstate. The publication of the Pentagon Papers marked a turning point in US public opinion about the war, exposing perfidy and lies stretching over four presidential administrations, even as the Defense Department and White House were frantically assuring the American people that victory was within sight. The case also established a legal precedent protecting the right of the press to publish such material in the interest of the public good, even if attempts have been made to turn the decision against itself. The Nixon administration's furor led it to form its infamous "plumbers unit" to stop further leaks, beginning a pattern of break-ins and wiretaps that continued with the Democratic National Committee's headquarters in the Watergate hotel complex, a crime that ultimately brought down a US president. In that regard, then, Vietnam and Watergate are inextricably connected in a way that is often overlooked, with Ellsberg's actions the pivotal link.

In struggling against any future American autocracy, a single Ellsberg will be worth a thousand Snowdens.

DUTY, HONOR, COUNTRY

No informed person accepts the notion that the national security establishment is a bastion of liberal activism. The US Intelligence Community and military are famously peopled with conservative-leaning personnel, some leaning so hard that they are practically horizontal. But during the Trump years, his otherwise paranoid claim of a "deep state" was correct to the extent that career professionals in various Cabinet departments, federal agencies, and the armed forces were frequently the collective voice of reason, acting as a brake on Trumpian madness. As a former military officer, I take great, vicarious pride in that. It was the generals in some cases—not all—who were the cool, sober heads restraining out of control civilian leaders. It will likely be so again if a radical Republican regime takes power in the future.

During the Trump administration it was also reported that the CIA and other US intelligence agencies strategically withheld intelligence from the president for fear that he would turn it over to our enemies.[6] If that strikes you as a brow-raising violation of the chain of command, consider the fact that the IC had those concerns in the first place. Sadly, this course of action proved prudent, given Trump's demonstrated coziness with hostile foreign governments, not to mention the post-presidency revelations of his brazen theft of classified documents related to highly sensitive matters of national security and outrageous refusal to surrender them, and attendant deceit and obstruction.

It is understandably concerning to have one's spies working at cross purposes to the government that they ostensibly serve. Down that path lies obsidian darkness. But it may be a necessary evil when that government is itself on the side of evil. The men and women of our intelligence agencies are trained to employ subterfuge, sabotage, and the other dark tools of their trade in the interest of democracy. Under a future autocracy, the IC would inevitably be a high intensity space in which a struggle would unfold in secrecy between those intelligence officers who bow down to the autocrat and those who understand and respect the Constitution. The capitalized Deep State contains within it the potential to do exactly what its critics have alleged—but for democracy's sake.

The military is even more central to opposing the autocracy. Coup plotters don't routinely recruit generals because they like uniforms; the armed forces are an obvious fulcrum of political power, perhaps the ultimate one. A preemptive announcement by its senior leaders of their refusal to participate in war crimes or domestic oppression would be an enormous deterrent to further autocratic excesses. It might also help undermine the power of an autocracy if it did manage to come to power.

Despite the reputation of the armed forces as politically conservative, a great many US military professionals—especially senior officers and NCOs who have served this country for their entire careers—recognized that Trumpism was a dire threat to the democracy that inspired them in the first place.[7] Some are as vehemently opposed to Trump and his movement as any progressive you care to name. That is as it should be. No one should be more offended by Trump than the US military, whom he has consistently insulted throughout his long, draft-dodging life.[8] The current wave of right-wing radicalism represents a repudiation of everything that those of us who served this country in uniform joined up to protect and defend.

As with the other institutions of governance, Trump took a poisonous view of the military as his personal Praetorian Guard—"my generals," as he was wont to call them.[9] While in office he loved to co-opt the honor and iconography of the armed forces like the banana republic strongman he longed to be. Famously, he was most obsessed with having a May Day–style military parade in his honor, with tanks and missile launchers rolling down Pennsylvania Avenue while he stood in the reviewing stand like a Soviet premier. But this impulse went beyond pageantry. Trump's fascistic view of the military was manifested in the deployment of federal troops to the southern border to enforce an inhumane immigration policy, and the use of National Guard helicopters to disperse protestors from Lafayette Square ahead of a notorious photo op. He also entertained threats to invoke the Insurrection Act of 1807 and to use US troops to suppress BLM demonstrations, or even—as Michael Flynn advised—to enforce a declaration of martial law.[10] This was the same man who insulted American war dead as "losers and suckers,"[11] excoriated his senior generals as "dopes and babies,"[12] and recoiled at the presence of severely wounded veterans at White House events.[13]

A right-wing regime that orders the armed forces into action against its own citizens is a standard part of the autocratic nightmare. In that case, the subordination of the military to civilian control is weaponized *against* democracy. But the law of war is clear. US military members are not only permitted to disobey unlawful orders, like firing on unarmed fellow citizens engaged in peaceful protest, they are duty-bound to do so.

During the Trump administration we saw numerous defense officials, uniformed and not, strategically leveraging their influence to block the commander-in-chief's worst schemes. One such moment was the resignation of Secretary of State Jim Mattis, a retired Marine four-star general, and his subsequent scathing rebuke of his former boss in print. We saw even greater bravery—often at grave personal cost—from the likes of LTC Alexander Vindman, Ambassadors Bill Taylor and Marie Yovanovitch, Professor Fiona Hill of the National Security Council, and others. There was significant griping about the failure of some at the highest levels to do even more, about the belatedness of their resignations and public critiques, and the unearned cover they had provided Trump in the meantime. But matters might have gone much worse had a lesser man than Mark Milley been Chairman of the Joint Chiefs during Trump's final days, for example, from the election to January 6 to the moment the disgraced, twice-impeached, would-be despot departed the White House lawn aboard *Marine One*.[14]

That complaint speaks to whether, under a tyrannical regime, it is better for principled officials to refuse to be complicit and resign in protest—but risk replacement by nefarious actors—or to stay in place and try to prevent disaster. During the Trump years, a staffer using the pseudonym Anonymous published a scandalous piece in *The New York Times* titled, "I Am Part of the Resistance Inside the

Trump Administration," describing a group of government officials working to thwart Trump from within. (The author was later revealed to be Miles Taylor, chief of staff for the Department of Homeland Security, who went on to cofound the third party Forward.) For the right, it was precisely the sort of thing that fed panic about "the deep state." At the same time, numerous observers on the center and left questioned just how much good this internal "resistance" was doing, the implication being that some of these resisters were more interested in soothing their consciences while remaining in their positions than in truly acting as saboteurs.[15]

Another possibility is mass resignations. If a huge swath of the Department of Homeland Security, or State, or Defense, were to quit, the impact would be far greater than any single resignation, even of a Cabinet officer. True, it would offer the autocracy the opportunity to fill the entire department with loyalists, but it would also be a stark announcement of opposition to that autocracy that the American people—and the world—could not fail to note. It would also function as a de facto strike, albeit of limited duration, as the department could not be repopulated overnight.

Retired personnel have a freer hand in opposing the autocracy. During the Trump years, retired military officers like General Barry McCaffery, Admiral James Stavridis, Admiral William McRaven, General Michael Hayden, Major General Paul Eaton, and others lent force to the anti-authoritarian cause with their public dissent. (Prominent civilian retirees, such as former CIA Director John Brennan, did likewise.) On the right, there was the expected furor in response, the most reasonable version being that these military officers, retired or not, were violating sacrosanct protocol surrounding civilian control of the uniformed services.[16] But if a bunch of arch-conservative retired generals had stood up to lambast a Democratic president, you can be quite sure those officers would all be lauded as heroes by Fox Nation.

We previously noted *The Washington Post* op-ed of December 2021 by four retired generals warning of military collaboration with a future right-wing regime. In July 2022, seven retired four-star flag officers from four different branches of the armed services published a searing op-ed in *The New York Times* decrying Trump's actions (and inactions) in the coup of January 6 and his attempts to use the US military as part of it.[17] Was it "insubordination" or even "mutiny," as the hysterical right wing claimed? Hardly, especially when the fate of the nation hung in the balance.

But there are plenty of flag officers, both active and retired, who are fully onboard with a Trumpist vision of the USA, not to mention those on active duty who are fanatically pro-Trump but quiet about it. In May 2021, 124 retired generals and admirals calling themselves Flag Officers 4 America published an open letter in support of the Big Lie. (One of them was my division commander in the 82nd Airborne in the Persian Gulf War. Another was Dick Secord, the retired Air Force general who in 1989 pled guilty to lying to Congress over the $2 million he received as part of the Iran/Contra affair.)[18] Surely the highest-profile retired general in this camp, as we have observed, was Mike Flynn, who not only went all in for Trump, but eagerly donned the tinfoil beret of QAnon conspiracy theory.[19] Questioned in a video deposition for the House January 6 Committee, Flynn was asked if he believed the violence on January 6 was justified morally or legally, and if he believed in the peaceful transition of power in the United States. He took the Fifth Amendment each time. "It was a surreal moment," Barton Gellman wrote in *The Atlantic*. "Here was a retired three-star general and former national security adviser refusing to opine on the foundational requirement of a constitutional democracy."[20]

You can decide for yourself which group of retirees you find more convincing. But the mere fact that our generals are choosing sides is alarming.

A pair of political scientists—Jim Golby of the University of Texas and Peter Feaver of Duke—have argued that such openly political statements by former flag officers actually do little to sway public opinion and only hurt public faith in the credibility of our apolitical armed forces.[21] I don't take issue with their findings. But I think it is wildly off base to lump together an effort to defend the peaceful transfer of power and an effort aimed at just the opposite, or to present them as equivalent forms of political speech. When autocracy threatens the very life of the republic, senior members of the warrior caste have a responsibility to use their influence to try to stop it, whether that influence is great or minimal, even at the cost of a dip in the esteem in which the public holds the military—an esteem that was damaged in the first place by generals and admirals who are onboard with destroying democracy.[*]

Let us hope for more Milleys and fewer Flynns.

The willingness of the US military and Intelligence Community to remove themselves from active collaboration with a right-wing autocracy would be a massive blow to that regime. The Pentagon must correctly stand on the Constitution and the law of war and resist being used for the purpose. Individually and ex officio, US military leaders, from corporals in charge of five-man fire teams to the Chairman of the Joint Chiefs, should bluntly refuse to participate in violent suppression of free assembly and expression by the American people, or even to be used as props for partisan purposes or the furtherance of the autocratic project until it is clear that the US military will not abet the massacre of fellow Americans, or of democracy itself.

---

[*]   Trump's view of loyalty was very much the reverse. As Jeffrey Goldberg reported in *The Atlantic*, his final Secretary of Defense, Mark Esper, reported that Trump proposed recalling retired General Stan McChrystal and Admiral Bill McRaven to active duty so he could court-martial and imprison them for publicly criticizing him.

CHAPTER 17

Satire on a Saturday Night

Art is inherently political; even a long list of examples would be only a thimbleful of water out of a vast ocean. The books banned—and burned—by various authoritarian regimes would fill whole libraries. Theater is practically tailor-made for politically provocative work, in a straight line from *Coriolanus* to Brecht to Ariel Dorfman to Suzan Lori-Parks. Pop music, the lingua franca of youthful rebellion, has always had a subversive element that unnerves the powers that be, from R&B to rock 'n' roll to reggae and hip hop. Putin fears Pussy Riot enough to jail them, just as in an earlier generation, the leaders of totalitarian Czechoslovakia feared the Plastic People of the Universe, and the Soviets banned the Beatles.[1] That is fitting, as spirituals and the blues—born of suffering under slavery—are the wellspring of virtually all Western pop, including the R&B of the Jim Crow era ("race music," as it was often called), twinned with the folk music rising out of poor white and Black communities alike, that was the soundtrack to twentieth-century American progressivism.

"Art and music help people feel seen," Theo Kogan, lead singer of the all-female punk band Lunachicks, told me. "When fans see an artist on their side, making work that's speaking out for the marginalized, and for human rights, it's important. And I think Republicans fear that."[2]

Film, both narrative and documentary, can also have profound political impact, including that thing once known as "TV," and web content all the way down to TikTok videos meant to be viewed on a smartphone. While Hollywood's product is largely escapist, independent cinema has long been overtly political, nowhere more so than under truly repressive regimes like Iran, China, and Eastern Europe. French audiences rioted at screenings of *The Rules of the Game*, Jean

Renoir's deft 1939 satire of morally desiccated French society in the interwar period, foreshadowing the shameful collaborationism of the Vichy regime. Here in the US, *Citizen Kane* (1941) so incensed the fanatically right-wing media baron William Randolph Hearst that he is said to have pressured J. Edgar Hoover to destroy its wunderkind creator, kicking off the entire Red Scare–era witch hunt that soon engulfed the entire country in the madness of McCarthyism.[3]

Of course, those same reactionary forces can also marshal the power of cinema for their own ends: I refer you to *Birth of a Nation* (1915), which set the tropes of white supremacy in America, not to mention the entire oeuvre of Leni Riefenstahl.

We are now in an era that produces a lot more *Super Mario Brothers* than it does *Citizen Kanes*. Still, progressive-minded American filmmakers should recognize the potential they have to rattle political powerbrokers, even if the price of such celluloid activism might well be the same right-wing counterattack that left a broken Orson Welles doing voiceovers for frozen peas.

But there need not be a line between "artist" and "audience." Democracy is a call for creative expression by all, without arbitrary distinctions that sort us into creators and consumers. In punk, DIY is the rule. Graffiti is the very definition of art as rebellion, and literal lawbreaking, ranging from an angry scrawl to work that ought to be in museums and sometimes winds up there. There's never been a time in human history when the tools of art were more available and the means of delivering them to an audience were cheaper and more accessible.

Our battle cry then: Every citizen an artist, and every artist an activist.

WHAT CLOSES ON SATURDAY NIGHT

When we talk about the arts as an arena in the struggle against autocracy, one area that requires special attention is that of comedy, and satire in particular.

My wife, Ferne Pearlstein, and I spent two decades making our feature documentary *The Last Laugh* (2016), which explores whether there is any constructive place for comedy in approaching the Holocaust, and the relative power of satire or lack thereof.[4] For that film, Mel Brooks, whose very name is synonymous with comedy about Hitler and the Nazis, told us that he strongly believes in what he calls "revenge through ridicule."[5] He has certainly lived by that maxim, nowhere more so than in his scandalous debut feature *The Producers* (1968), which led to the hit Broadway musical some thirty years later. The esteemed comic actor Harry Shearer dissected its trajectory in our documentary, saying, "The whole essence of the joke of *The Producers* was, 'How could you possibly think that a musical about Hitler was acceptable?' That was the whole MacGuffin of the picture. By the time it gets to Broadway, a movie about a spectacular Broadway failure because it was in such bad taste becomes a Broadway hit because it's not in bad taste anymore."[6]

Echoing Brooks, the Israeli author and satirist Etgar Keret told us that "Humor is the weapon of the weak." His formulation is not an indictment of humor or those who use it, but rather, recognition that, for the downtrodden, ridiculing their oppressors is often the only means of counterattack available.[7]

It is no accident that groups that have traditionally suffered terrible oppression are often considered among the "funniest." (Then again, the English also have a wicked sense of humor, despite being mostly on the delivering end of imperialism.) For the underdog, humor functions as social commentary, a means of release, a coping mechanism, and—yes—a form of resistance. "Against the assault of laughter," Mark Twain famously said, "nothing can stand."[8] It is an appealing idea.

But in truth, satire has proven exceptionally poor at fighting tyranny. The legendary British comedian Peter Cook may have had the final word on the matter when he wryly observed how much the cabarets of Weimar Germany did to stop Hitler.[9]

Dictators historically are very resistant to comedic attacks. Hitler was famously dismissed by many as a joke when he first came to power, as was Mussolini, as was Trump for that matter, even if he is not quite in their despotic league. *The Last Laugh*'s main character, Auschwitz survivor Renee Firestone, recalled being a girl in Hungary in 1933 and fearfully asking her father about the new German chancellor and his anti-Semitic tirades. "My father told me, 'Don't listen to that comedian, don't you see he looks like Charlie Chaplin? He'll be out of power in no time.' Well, my father was wrong."[10]

Underestimating tyrants and treating them as mere clowns is but one risk. A greater one is believing that we can neuter them through ridicule when in fact we may be merely comforting ourselves with jokes that only like-minded people appreciate while the horror rolls merrily along. During World War II, ridicule of the Nazis, highbrow and low, was taken for granted as part of the war effort, from the enduring parody of Hitler in *The Great Dictator* (1940), to Warner Brothers, where the Nazis suffered terrible indignities at the hands of Bugs Bunny and his ilk. But even then, some argued that satire of the Nazis trivialized the threat. Ernst Lubitsch's *To Be or Not To Be* (1942), about a troupe of Polish actors outsmarting the Nazis, is considered a classic today, but at the time was widely panned for its humorous treatment of such a serious subject. Even Chaplin himself subsequently said that he would not have made *The Great Dictator*, one of the most admired films of all time, had he known of the atrocities of the Final Solution.[11] On that point, it's worth noting that Mel Brooks's professional lifetime of ridiculing Hitler is aimed at tearing down the legacy of the Nazis *after* the fact, aiming to forestall any future outbreaks of fascism. (Brooks himself was a US Army infantryman in Europe in World War II.)*

Indeed, in some cases satire can actually be counterproductive, venting in laughter the very outrage that might otherwise drive the people into the street—a dynamic that many autocrats understand all too well.

"Political humor usually thrives in dictatorships," Rudolph Herzog, the author of *Dead Funny: Humor in Hitler's Germany*, told us for *The Last Laugh*. "The more restrictive the regime is, the more people have the need to vent their frustrations and anger by way of humor and jokes." But Herzog explained that, contrary to the conventional assumption, the Nazis were surprisingly tolerant of jokes at the Führer's expense, especially in the early years of his reign, understanding that people engaged in laughter are not people engaged in an uprising.[12]

It's true that the Nazis did imprison a number of comedians and performers, some of whom had been active since the Weimar period,

---

* During Hitler's rise and prior to US entry into the war, US movie studios infamously shied away from critiques of the Third Reich, comic or otherwise, for fear of alienating the German market—a completely different, and cowardly, argument.

and as the tide turned against them in the war became less and less tolerant. But "[the humor] didn't translate into anti-Nazi protests," Herzog wrote in *Dead Funny*. "Those people who let off a bit of steam with a few jokes didn't take to the streets or otherwise challenge the Nazi leadership . . . 'Whispered jokes' were a surrogate for, not a manifestation of, social conscience and political courage."[13]

"So arguably it helped the regime in a kind of strange way," he told us. "We always wish that political humor somehow has a subversive effect, but if you really look at the facts, if you really analyze it, that's not the case."[14]

Seconding Herzog's point, Larry Charles, a legendary writer for *Seinfeld* and director of *Curb Your Enthusiasm* and the *Borat* movies, pointed out to us how the architecture of power is designed to accommodate and co-opt satire.

"The system knows that there are going to be protests about things, there are going to be complaints about things, there are going to be jokes about things. There's a certain amount of dissent built in, and it kind of perpetuates the very system that it's working against, because it gives the system space to exist. It's okay to say these things on TV, broadcast by the multinational media corporations that control them. They're letting you say it! If they really felt it was dangerous, then you wouldn't be able to say it."[15]

Jon Stewart was the darling of the progressive crowd during his original sixteen-year run on *The Daily Show*, roughly coinciding with the Bush and Obama eras. But did he and other progressive comedians have a real impact on the political climate during that period, or did they merely preach to the choir? Worse, was it possible—per Herzog and Charles— that the existence of that comedic release valve actually *hindered* real political engagement in the US? Of course, one can ridicule right-wingers and still organize against them. But when all we do is feel superior and compliment ourselves on how much smarter or better we are than our cretinous leaders, without doing anything else, who's laughing then?

ELBOWS OUT

With these caveats and limitations in mind, satire *can* be a powerful force in exposing the fatuousness of politicians, with actual real-world repercussions. In the late 1960s, *The Smothers Brothers Comedy Hour* was the top-rated show on CBS and regularly spoofed US involvement in Vietnam, which was then at its height. That was rare and bold on American television at the time, let alone on a prime-time comedy show, enough so to cause Lyndon Johnson to call CBS chairman Bill Paley to press him to get Tommy and Dickie under control.[16] But once he decided not to seek reelection, LBJ was savvy enough to relent, and actually wrote to the duo: "You have given the gift of laughter to our people. May we never grow so somber or self-important that we fail to appreciate the humor in our lives."[17] Even if he was being merely tactical, Johnson clearly recognized that showing his outrage in public would only make him look bad.

Richard Nixon was not so forward-thinking. After he took office in January 1969, CBS repeatedly warned the Smothers to back off. Tommy Smothers refused, and three months into the new administration, the network cancelled the show despite its high ratings.[18] (The show was replaced that summer by *Hee Haw*.)

It's equally clear that satire has utility in the present political climate. Chevy Chase's memorable impersonation of a bumbling Gerald Ford almost certainly helped doom Ford's presidential run in 1976. Similarly, in 2008, Tina Fey's withering portrayal of Sarah Palin cemented the public view of the neophyte Alaskan governor as a blithering idiot. The skewering of then private citizen Donald Trump by President Obama and host Seth Meyers at the 2011 White House Correspondents Dinner supposedly prompted Trump to seek revenge by running for office—in that case, an example of humor fomenting oppression, rather than combatting it, but still a testament to its power.[19]

The blowback from satire can get a lot worse than that. In 2005, the publication of a dozen political cartoons depicting the Prophet Muhammed in the Danish newspaper *Jyllands-Posten* set off a global firestorm that quickly escalated into street protests, riots, and even violent attacks on Danish citizens and Denmark's embassies in the Islamic world. Ten years later the controversy was still alive, and raw, when two heavily armed fanatics associated with the Yemen-based Al Qaeda in the Arabic Peninsula broke into the Paris offices of the French satirical newspaper *Charlie Hebdo* and murdered twelve people and injured several others.

But political cartoons have always had an outsized impact on politics: Thomas Nast skewered Boss Tweed, Garry Trudeau skewered

Nixon, and Jesse Duquette skewered Trump. Still, it remains shocking how "the funny pages" can stir such strong emotions and lead to
the most horrific violence. Clearly, one man's joke is another man's
incitement to murder, in case anyone is still unclear on the power—
and pitfalls—of humor.

In trying times such as these, the secret may be in keeping our
elbows sharp and aiming them where they count. Many comedians
like to see themselves as "equal opportunity offenders," gleefully dis-
respecting sacred cows of all political stripes. But like journalistic
bothsidesism, that ethos too often feeds the reactionary narrative by
normalizing right-wing politicians. Whether it's a professional comedian doing standup in front of the inevitable brick wall, or coworkers joking around the water cooler, we have to stay on guard against
comedy that serves only as a tonic or a distraction from dire threats,
rather than a weapon to attack them at the root. When we sit at home
and laugh at a late-night talk show host cracking toothless jokes about
Donald Trump's hair, or Marjorie Taylor Greene's dumbassery, what
we are *not* doing is organizing a formidable resistance. As Herzog
notes, the German people often told jokes about Goering being fat.
Such jokes were almost gentle—normalizing, in modern parlance—the
sort of jokes that would be made about any public figure. That kind
of comedy may have provided a brief thrill in mocking the Nazi
leadership, but it didn't really have any bite, let alone any broader
effect. What most Germans did not do was use humor to attack the
very legitimacy and horror of the Nazis.[20]

In other words, comedians can raise political consciousness, but
they cannot replace it. Satire and political humor are not an end
in themselves, or a substitute for direct action, only elements of a
broader and more robust campaign of dissent.

MERRY PRANKSTERS AND AGENTS PROVOCATEURS

Political satire need not be confined to the arts and entertainment.
Some of the best examples come from activists engaged in street
theater, culture jamming, and other methods used to galvanize attention, embarrass the government, and motivate change. By that definition, many acts of civil disobedience could be classified as "street

theater," though they generally are not thought of that way, except by their critics. But in a non-pejorative sense, such acts are theater in the best possible way.

The Yippies were masters of this approach, staging events laced with absurdist humor, like showering dollar bills onto the trading floor of the New York Stock Exchange in 1967, or running a pig for President of the United States the following year. ("If we can't have him in the White House, we can have him for breakfast," as they said.[21]) In his 1980 autobiography, *Soon to Be a Major Motion Picture*, Abbie Hoffman called the Stock Exchange stunt "the TV age version of driving the money changers from the temple," in which the shower of greenbacks drove the traders into a chaotic scramble. "A spark had been ignited," Hoffman wrote. "Not a drop of blood had been spilled, not a bone broken, but on that day, with that gesture, an image war had begun."[22]

But street theater need not be comic, and often is not. One of the most iconic images of the anti–Vietnam War movement was that of a flop-haired young protestor gently placing carnations in the bayoneted barrels of M14 rifles wielded by US Army MPs—in neckties and Class A uniforms, no less—during the 1967 March on the Pentagon.[23] That was no spontaneous act of a flower child, but a calculated piece of guerrilla theater carried out by a man named George Harris, who went on to become a founder of the avant-garde San Francisco theater troupe the Cockettes. (The photograph itself was nominated for a Pulitzer Prize.) Indeed, the queer community was a hotbed of street theater. In the post-60s era, the pinnacle of politically oriented street theater in the United States was ACT UP (AIDS Coalition to Unleash Power), which used dramatic "die-ins" and other demonstrations to raise public awareness about HIV and AIDS, and to shame the Reagan administration for its poor response. In terms of iconography, ACT UP's co-option of the Nazis' pink triangle—used to denote homosexuals in the concentration camps—was especially bold and unabashed. Its slogan SILENCE = DEATH is memorable to this day.[24]

ACT UP's protests have been inspirational to subsequent generations of activists. In one recent example, the photographer Nan Goldin—who had been involved in ACT UP in the '80s—led demonstrators who threw orange-colored plastic pill vials into the reflecting pool at the Metropolitan Museum of Art to protest its continued association with the Sackler family, the progenitors of the American opioid epidemic, and among the most prominent donors in the art world. Goldin's group eventually succeeded in making the Sackler family pariahs in that world, and getting its name removed from almost every major museum on the planet.[25] Other art-oriented provocateurs, such as the Guerrilla Girls, the Yes Men, and the Good Liars engage in similar political activism. Most recently, the group Birds Aren't Real has confounded the right wing with its straight-faced claim that there is no such thing as birds, only tiny surveillance drones operated by the CIA, effectively lampooning the absurdity of the conspiracy theories on which American reactionaryism thrives. BAR's never-break-character commitment to its conceit has made it impossible for its targets to find an effective retort.[26]

But like conventional protest and civil disobedience, street theater is most effective when it is part of a well-planned strategic endeavor with clearly identified goals.

"Lots of artists feel like they want do something in the world," Jacques Servin of the Yes Men told me. "They start out by going, 'Okay, I'm gonna make this cool project that's gonna raise awareness, and everybody will know about it, and then things will change.' And that's just not good enough."[27]

One of the Yes Men's favorite techniques—what they call "identity correction"—is to impersonate officials of various governments and corporations (including the WTO, McDonald's, and the US Department of Housing and Urban Development) and propose outrageous, almost Swiftian ideas, like a hamburger made from human feces and marketed to the Third World.[28] Perhaps their most famous action was on the twentieth anniversary of the 1984 Bhopal disaster, when Jacques Servin appeared on the BBC posing as a Dow Chemical spokesman and announced that the company was going to shutter its Union Carbide subsidiary and use the resulting $12 billion to pay restitution to the victims. The hoax set off panic at Dow, whose frantic denials in the press only further publicized it.[29]

"In a pseudo-democracy or whatever it is we're in, you have to think strategically," Servin told me. "You have to decide what the context is, and what tools you have at your disposal, and how they're going to have an effect on who and what you want to change. We don't always do that strictly," he laughed. "In fact, we have never done that strictly. And it's never been by ourselves—we've always been in cahoots with an activist organization."[30]

Echoing Peter Cook, the Yes Men write on their own (real) website, "Against a sociopathic president, satire is probably useless; it's better to become a poll worker, sign up for a phone bank, send some postcards to voters, or spread info about mail-in voting."[31] True enough, but also modest. People who aren't necessarily politically engaged may pay the kind of attention to provocateurs—especially if their actions are funny—that they wouldn't pay to ordinary, eat-your-vegetables kind of activists. And of course there's no reason that both can't happen at the same time. Faced with another Trump administration or a ghastly Republican regime in one form or another, conventional means of pushing back may be shut off. One of the few things left will be these guerrilla operations. They might as well make us laugh as the world burns.

"There is a cheerleading function to a lot of what we've done," Servin says. "Sometimes it ends up being about raising awareness and nothing else. You're not going to shame a corporation into doing the right thing unless millions of people find out. So it's mainly storytelling." He also notes that that storytelling ought to be carefully aimed at vulnerable spots in the oppressive regime. "You obviously can't change the dictator's mind, but you can help make the pillars of support for the dictator crumble. Go for the teachers, go for the police, go for the judges—the various things that the dictator needs in order to keep going."

But in an autocracy, where absurdity is already the norm, it can be hard to stay ahead of the satire curve. During the pandemic, the Yes Men, in conjunction with the Good Liars, created a fake Trump administration website called Doctors for Opening America, recruiting medical professionals to promote human sacrifice for the good of the country. "But it turned out there really *were* doctors who had been paid off to say, 'Yeah, a bit of death is okay, as long as we re-open America,'" Servin told me. "We tried to satirize it, but it was already real."[32]

The wellspring of much of modern guerrilla theater is France, which gave us the Letterists and Letterist International in the 1950s, and the Situationists of the late '50s and '60s, who were influential in the mass demonstrations that brought Paris to a standstill in May 1968. Here in America, the anonymous insurgents of San Francisco's Billboard Liberation Front have for many years sabotaged large scale outdoor advertising to send subversive, anti-corporate messages to Bay Area commuters.[33] The practice, known as *détournement*, hijacks existing material, particular logos and advertising, to deliver a message diametrically at odds with the original—often so perfectly rendered that it prompts a double take, as when a Burger King logo is altered to read Murder King. (In North America, the magazine *Adbusters* is surely the best known and most influential organ of the arts-based anti-consumerist movement.) Generally, détournement and other forms of culture jamming seek to expose the ubiquitous manipulation of our attention by corporate interests—the visual equivalent of noise pollution, bombarding us against our will everywhere we look.

But the line between art, entertainment, street theater, and civil disobedience can get blurry.

Sacha Baron Cohen is a professional actor and comedian, not a politician or an activist in the conventional sense. His work is distributed on some of the most powerful TV networks in the world, such as Channel Four and HBO, and in feature films distributed by giant motion picture studios like 20th Century, which are themselves owned by huge multinational corporate conglomerates—in that case, a literal part of the Murdoch empire. But when Cohen—in his Borat persona—gets a bar full of Arizona rednecks to sing gleefully along with what he claims is a popular Kazakh song called "Throw the Jew Down the Well," or convinces Republican congressmen to make PSAs promoting handguns for toddlers, or films Rudy Giuliani with his hand down his pants alongside an actress playing a fifteen-year-old girl, he is undeniably exposing the moral bankruptcy and general ghastliness of his targets, very much akin to what the Yes Men do.[34] Most impressively, with his straight-faced commitment to character, he frequently gets those targets to inflict the damage on themselves, dating back to his breakout character, the faux rude boy Ali G, and his straight-faced interviews of unsuspecting marks from Newt Gingrich to Pat Buchanan to Donald Trump. This is beyond mere comedy, and is certainly far beyond simple entertainment.

Similar pranksterism is practiced by the faux journalists of *The Daily Show* and *The Colbert Report*. Stephen Colbert astonishingly stayed in character as his bloviating O'Reillyesque right-wing pundit for nine years, even when testifying before Congress in 2010,[35] or hosting the 2012 White House Correspondents Dinner, to the sound of crickets in his unamused audience of Washington bigwigs.[36] When comedy goes beyond mere frivolity and successfully exposes the malfeasance, hypocrisy, and dangerousness of its targets, and damages their reputations and hinders their ability to continue their actions, it does a public service.

As Larry Charles told us for *The Last Laugh*, "Questioning dictators is pretty easy to do, especially in a so-called free society like we have. But questioning how free our society is, that to me is a much more controversial subject. People are not ready to really think about that too deeply, because it would spiral their lives into the chaos and disorder that is always beneath the surface of our world. When a comedian is talking to an audience that agrees with them, an audience that gets them and shares their sensibility—when you're talking to the converted—it can be funny, and provocative, and interesting, and thoughtful. But it's not really transgressing in any sort of true sense. When they throw me in jail for making *Borat*, then you'll know we've dealt with a taboo subject."[37]

CHAPTER 18

Take the Skinheads Bowling

We have previously discussed how blue states might work as a bloc to leverage their economic and demographic power against autocracy. But in the long term, what America needs is precisely the opposite of this separatism.

It is not news that our country has splintered into disparate subcultures that barely interact, consume news from the same sources, or—increasingly—can even be said to inhabit the same America. So long as that division persists—what Gene Sharp, as far back as 1973 in an unwitting foreshadowing of COVID-19, called "the social distance" between competing groups—all of the problems with which this book is concerned will persist, no matter what other measures we take.[1] Writing forty years after Sharp, Levitsky and Ziblatt concur, arguing that a broad prodemocratic coalition will be necessary to stop an American authoritarian movement, one that extends beyond merely the like-minded.

> Most effective coalitions are those that bring together groups with dissimilar—even opposing—views on many issues. They are built not among friends but among adversaries. This does not mean abandoning the causes that matter to us. It means temporarily overlooking disagreements in order to find common moral ground . . . A political movement that brings together—even if temporarily—Bernie Sanders supporters and businesspeople, evangelicals and secular feminists, and small-town Republicans and urban Black Lives Matter supporters, will open channels of communication across the vast chasm that has emerged between our country's two main partisan camps.[2]

Not an easy task, but a necessary one. Toward that end, a steep rise in empathy and an end to blind hypertribalism are prerequisites to any kind of healing in this country. So is remembering our shared Americanness. That does not mean condoning the sins of the last administration and its enablers, who even now still threaten the republic, nor meeting fascists and racists and misogynists halfway. But it does mean breaking the spell that those very forces are eager to exploit.

Most of us will never be engaged in Che Guevara-manqué, quasi-revolutionary actions. But any successful counter to the autocracy will hinge on the quotidian, low-key actions of tens of millions of us, day in and day out, potentially for years. Sharp notes the importance of maintaining personal connections, containing hatred, avoiding humiliating the other side, and working to gain trust and respect when possible.[3] Sometimes it can be as basic as a conversation with a friend or loved one with opposing views. In so doing, the key is to keep sanctimony at bay and see ourselves not as self-righteous saviors but as fellow human beings, flawed and vulnerable ourselves. For in the end, the struggle for democracy and human rights is likeliest to be won person by person, on the most fundamental human level.

BEFORE WE MAKE WAR, WE MAKE ENEMIES

By portraying its Democratic opponents as not just wrongheaded, misguided, or possessed of a different ideology, but as absolutely evil and an existential threat to the republic, the GOP deprives those opponents of the usual rights and protections of American citizenship, such that anything and everything is justifiable in opposing them. It is not a coincidence that the QAnon madness turns on allegations of Satan-worshipping, pedophilia, rape, and child sex trafficking, among the most terrible crimes imaginable. When a foe is that horrific, anything is justified. There is no sense of shame among Republicans when they engage in the exact behavior of which they accuse their opponents—whether it is using a private email server,[4] siphoning money out of charities,[5] or attacking the very law enforcement officers that they claim to revere[6]—because Republicans are "real Americans," and therefore entitled to do whatever they please, while Democrats, progressives, and all others are monsters by definition and everything they do is damnable, whether they really do it or not.

Robert Draper, author of *Weapons of Mass Delusion: When the Republican Party Lost Its Mind*, writes that the Trump supporters he encountered in his research frequently "could not conceive of Trump's adversaries possessing human attributes. Instead, they viewed Democrats, government bureaucrats, and members of the media like me as any combination of Communists, traitors, swamp creatures, and human scum."[7] Such is the power of propaganda, particularly on people who don't consume news from any other source.

That power is deeply alarming, making it all too easy to justify physical attacks against fellow Americans should political discourse deteriorate even further. We have already witnessed the ability of right-wing media to mobilize a violent uprising. It could get considerably worse. We see it in the people who believe that they are saving lives by bombing Planned Parenthood clinics, or a Big Lie adherent who feels justified in cracking eighty-two-year-old Paul Pelosi's skull with a hammer, or anti-Semites and racists who think they are serving their vengeful god by shooting up synagogues and Black churches.

Again, there is no equivalency on the left, except a false one. We may say that the right wing is an existential threat to the republic, but we do not say that its adherents are undeserving of constitutional protections, or so monstrous and irredeemable that we are entitled to violate the law in order to crush them. It is possible to adamantly oppose the views of the other side without stripping its members of their basic humanity. In fact, it is essential.

Nations at war, or in the midst of pogroms, invariably demonize the "enemy," the better to whip up popular fervor to justify the most ruthless acts of barbarism. After all, if these foes are subhuman, they are not deserving of mercy or compassion, and no holds are barred. That is why Hitler rhetorically reduced the Jews, the Slavs, the Roma, and others to the status of vermin; why the Ottoman Empire dehumanized the Armenian population before its genocide of that community from 1915 to 1917; why it is harder for an infantryman to kill an enemy soldier eye to eye with a bayonet than for a pilot to drop bombs on the anonymous, flyspeck population of a city from thirty thousand feet, let alone a drone operator working from an air-conditioned cubicle in Arizona, five thousand miles from the target.

In present-day Poland, the autocratic Law and Justice Party followed this same pattern, taking over the state broadcaster Telewizja Polska and turning it into a propaganda mill. (Imagine the BBC "taken over by the conspiracy website InfoWars" as Anne Applebaum, a dual citizen of the US and Poland, wrote.)[8] Its demonization of the regime's enemies was vicious enough that it inspired the assassination of the mayor of Gdańsk, who was stabbed to death during a charity concert. In Rwanda, hatemongering by RTLM (Radio Télévision Libre des Mille Collines, or Radio and Television of a Thousand Hills), a quasi-private entity subsidized in part by the Hutu-dominated government, played a significant role in inciting the ensuing genocide, characterizing Tutsis as "cockroaches" deserving of extermination.[9] The US considered jamming its broadcasts, but concluded that the cost—about $8,500 an hour—was too high.[10]

We are not yet at that Rwandan level in the United States. But the shift in the Republican portrayal of Democrats from the loyal opposition to traitors and ghouls and sexual predators is a waystation on that dangerous road.

How do we bring our fellow Americans out of that dangerous, autocracy-friendly mindset? Some cannot be reasoned with, nor swayed by presentation of facts, nor logic, nor appeals to morality, justice, or simple human decency. But a great many Americans who have allied themselves with this dangerous incarnation of the Republican Party—our friends, our parents, our siblings, our coworkers, our neighbors—can still be won back. I understand all too well that the very idea smacks of sanctimony, and that it is no more healthy for progressives to become so angry at the right wing that we let our own passion slip into something treacherous. If, God forbid, partisan rancor in the US ever reaches the stage of widespread political violence, an inability to remember the humanity in our fellow Americans will be a fast-burning accelerant to that fire. We are all susceptible to being swallowed by darkness, and it doesn't require any self-congratulation or misplaced sense of superiority simply to recognize when it has happened to our fellow Americans and the damage it is doing to us all.

(WHAT'S SO FUNNY 'BOUT) PEACE, LOVE, AND UNDERSTANDING?

Steven Hassan is an expert on cults who was once a member of the Reverend Sun Myung Moon's Unification Church. Like Chris Hedges, Hassan has characterized Trumpism as a literal cult, and written a book on the techniques of control he believes are in play.[11] Central to that effort is an empathetic, nonconfrontational approach that avoids judgment, argument, or allegations that the individual in question has been duped. Patience, compassion, and willingness to listen are helpful; insult and condescension are not, particularly since people in the grip of a cult have been conditioned to be wary of outsiders—even old friends—and to view *them* as brainwashed, not the other way around. Genuine curiosity can go a long way toward establishing (or reestablishing) rapport. A cohort of friends, family members, and other allies can also be helpful of course, so long as the person does not feel besieged or ganged up upon.

Hassan recommends putting the onus on that person—diplomatically—to make their case, rather than the converse. "Tell me more about why you believe the election was stolen. Because if all the information I'm seeing is wrong, I'd want to correct it. What is it that you've seen that has convinced you?"[12] Though we have learned during the Trump years that his supporters are largely impervious to facts, it's important to remember that, obviously, they themselves do not see it that way. In some cases, that verbalization can make the individual see the irrationality of what they have come to believe, and cause cracks to begin to appear in their belief system.

"All of us who have ever been in a cult know that every cult member has doubts," notes Janja Lalich, a professor emerita of sociology at California State University, Chico, who like Hassan, was formerly a member of a cult.[13] Lalich said that, during her years in the cult, she "had what she thought of as a little shelf in the back of her mind . . . where she stowed doubts, questions or concerns. 'At some point all of those things get too heavy and the shelf breaks and that's when they'll realize they need to get out,' Lalich says. 'Your job is to get them to put more things on their shelf.'"[14]

Disengaging the individual from media and propaganda that feeds a toxic worldview and encouraging them to consider legitimate sources of news and information instead, can be immensely valuable. If the person in question is an old friend, spending time together doing pleasurable shared activities over which you initially bonded—divorced from any political context—can remind them of the person they once were, as well as help fortify trust. And the more time they spend away from the cult and its other members the better.

"Most important," Hassan says, "remember that the person you knew and cared for before they were influenced by a cult still exists, and with consistent, respectful support they can gain the knowledge and strength to set themselves free."[15]

Again, I do realize that even speaking in terms of "deprogramming" can seem inherently self-righteous and therefore part of the problem. But even removing such terms from the equation, the basic principles of respect, openness, and civility are advisable in all personal engagement and political discourse.

"When I think about interpersonally interacting with people on the right, I'm not going to argue them out of their positions," Sally Kohn, founder and CEO of the progressive think tank Movement Vision Lab, told me. "No one in the history of forever has ever changed their mind by being yelled at. You have this whole group of people who find belonging in a side, but they could find belonging somewhere else. It's creating the possibility that you could be a part of a better, brighter, more inclusive, more just, more fair, more equitable future that's better for everyone. And I want you to feel like you belong in it, because I think you do. I think everyone does."[16]

That process begins with simply reacquainting ourselves with our fellow Americans, in a society that had become increasingly tribalized by political belief.

"Who do you hate?" asks Peter Hutchison, director of the documentary *Healing from Hate*, based on the book by the sociologist Michael Kimmel. "You hate people you're not exposed to. You can't 'other' someone who lives next door, who you work with, who you go to school with. You 'other' a race or a culture that you don't understand: the immigrants coming from Somalia or south of the border to take your job and destroy your way of life, or the Jews who are behind a global conspiracy to take over the planet. It's just really easy to hang your troubles and anxiety and your fears on people that you don't know or understand."[17]

By way of drying up that soil in which autocracy can take root, Yale's Timothy Snyder—like Hutchison—encourages Americans to get out of our comfort zones and mix with other people, especially those of differing views. But it's not just good advice; it's necessary for a healthy democracy.[18]

Hutchison cites Robert Putnam's 2000 book *Bowling Alone*, which recalls an America only "a generation ago, when we hadn't self-si-loed where we live, where we get our news, what we do for enter-tainment." Putnam writes of growing up in a time and place when his entire community would go bowling every Sunday. That simple communion amid crashing pins generated understanding and empa-thy through familiarity, even for people on the other side of the political aisle. "It's very rare anymore that people spend time with people who have a different set of beliefs than they do," Hutchison told me. "If we're not going to spend time doing things with people who don't share our precise viewpoint, of course we're never going to understand how they think or what they believe."[19]

And Putnam's book is now almost a quarter century old. That phenomenon has only worsened, badly, since then.

Admittedly, this call for connection, compassion, and understand-ing is precisely the opposite of what goes on in left-leaning media and among progressives at large when we rail against right-wingers. But let us not confuse these tasks.

Rebecca Solnit has written about what she calls a "hopelessly naïve version of centrism," centered around "the idea that if we're nicer to the other side there will be no other side, just one big happy family." Calling it an "inanity," she goes on to reject this "muddled cocktail" of moral relativism and touchy-feely concern for the valid-ity of everyone's feelings.

> The truth is not some compromise halfway between the truth and the lie, the fact and the delusion, the scientists and the propagan-dists. And the ethical is not halfway between white supremacists and human rights activists, rapists and feminists, synagogue massacrists and Jews, xenophobes and immigrants, delusional transphobes and trans people. Who the hell wants unity with Nazis until and unless they stop being Nazis?[20]

Solnit scorns the "idea that some people need to be flattered and buffered even when they are harming the people who are doing the flattering and the buffering, even when they are the minority, even when they're breaking the law or lost the election." She even goes to Paul Krugman's own iconic metaphor: "If half of us believe the earth is flat, we do not make peace by settling on it being halfway between round and flat. Those of us who know it's round will not recruit them through compromise."

> There are situations in which there is no common ground worth standing on, let alone hiking over to. If Nazis wanted to reach out and find common ground and understand us, they probably would not have had that tiki-torch parade full of white men bellowing "Jews will not replace us" and, also, they would not be Nazis . . . [Theirs] is a minority position but by granting it deference we give it, over and over, the power of a majority position.[21]

To that end, the empathy needed to reintegrate refugees from the MAGA movement is not an excusal of right-wing extremism, let alone of insurrection. We are not speaking of compromise with fascism, but of breaking its grip. "We all know that you do better bringing people out of delusion by being kind and inviting than by mocking them," Solnit writes, "but that's inviting them to come over, which is not the same thing as heading in their direction."[22] The extent of right-wing fanaticism in America cannot be denied, and we should not apologize for pointing it out. There can be no accommodation with it, no negotiating with terrorists foreign or domestic, no mollycoddling or namby-pamby attempts at appeasement.

Therefore, we must do both at once: oppose Trumpism without qualification, while peeling away persuadable Trump supporters and other right-wing adherents, one by one, to the extent that we can. The patient, empathetic approach is legitimate and advisable, especially when trying to have a civil discourse with friends, acquaintances, or even strangers in hopes of breaking the grip of reactionaryism. But let us not confuse that with the broader need to call out right-wing extremism when we see it and the necessity of working to defeat it as a broader threat, and to eliminate the conditions that allowed it to grow.

THE VALUE OF OIL STAINS

I spoke with the writer and radio journalist David Isay, another MacArthur "Genius" Grant recipient and founder of the oral history project StoryCorps. For the past several years, Isay has been focused on tribalism in America; his new project, One Small Step, seeks to bridge that gap by bringing Americans with wildly differing political views into one-on-one conversations, in the presence of a mediator, in hopes of finding some shared humanity. The key, Isay says, is that these conversations explicitly avoid politics. The goal is not for one participant to convince the other, or even to find common political ground: it is purely to learn to see people from "the other side" as genuine human beings worthy of respect and dignity.[23]

I asked him how that can be accomplished outside of the formal setting of One Small Step, without a mediator.

"I think it's just about actively seeking out people that you disagree with and building that muscle. When I first started One Small Step, I went on NPR to ask for volunteers, and I was on a plane when the responses started coming in. One was from somebody who called me a faggot and a snowflake and all this stuff. And I wrote him back from the plane and said, 'I'd like to do a One Small Step interview with you.' And he said, 'Yeah, and I'd love to take you to dinner.' Then I met the kid. He was like twenty-four or twenty-five years old, and the minute he looked me in the eye, I guarantee you, there was no way he was ever going to send an email like that again. The One Small Step conversation didn't even matter: it was shaking hands and looking each other in the eye, and he immediately apologized. So as much as you can get up close with people, the better."[24]

In addition to all its other benefits to society, the repercussions of One Small Step thus function as a kind of last-ditch fail-safe in the worst-case scenario of widespread political violence or even civil war in the US. "People are a lot more nuanced than you might believe," Isay told me. "So the trick is to get into the real world and meet people with diverse backgrounds and beliefs, and develop relationships with them, so that if push comes to shove, we'll have created enough of these little kind of strings of relationship that it can become kind of a rope that pulls in the other direction, away from the lies about who the other side is. I think it's much more difficult to move into something like violence when you see someone as a human being."[25]

Sally Kohn used that exact same word, *nuance*, noting how much of it is inherent in the human condition. "We allow for nuance in ourselves," she told me, "but often don't have the grace to see it in others."[26]

These efforts work best in the smallest possible circles: one-on-one, as in Isay's model, or in very small groups. "You can't hate up close," as Centivox's Amy Thogmartin told me. But she also expressed uncertainty about how to adapt her successful small group conversations—about public health, in her case—to a larger scale.[27] Perhaps it's impossible. But perhaps it's also unnecessary.

In counterinsurgency, there is a concept called the "oil spot theory," which focuses on working at very modest, local levels, often with tribal and village leaders, to win hearts and minds and pacify very small patches of territory one by one.[28] As each small area is won, they slowly accumulate in number, spreading out like an oil stain and linking up with others in surrounding areas, until larger swaths of territory—and, eventually, ideally, the entire country—is absorbed.[29] As a bonus, the harder lift of a top-down national reformation becomes moot, or at least secondary. It doesn't always work: often, in places like Iraq, it falls short for reasons having more to do with larger policy failures than any weakness of the tactic. But it's a model worth considering as we try to win back our brothers and sisters and defeat the autocratic movement that threatens us all.

It's important, after all, to remember that tens of millions of Americans *do* eagerly support Trump and the right-wing autocracy. They are a minority, but a large one. We can't condone their movement, but we do have to reckon with it, given that it represents not just a friendly difference of opinion but an actual threat to a peaceful society.

"[Thirty-four] percent of Americans said they did not trust the outcome of the 2020 election," Anne Applebaum wrote in a piece for *The Atlantic* shortly after the insurrection. "[Twenty-one] percent said that they either strongly support or somewhat support the storming of the Capitol building . . . and 32 percent were still telling pollsters that Biden was not the legitimate winner." The question she posed was: How do we as a nation go on together when such significant numbers feel that way?

The startling answer Applebaum proposes is: "Drop the argument and change the subject. That's the counterintuitive advice you will hear from people who have studied Northern Ireland before the 1998 peace deal, or Liberia, or South Africa, or Timor-Leste—countries where political opponents have seen each other as not just wrong, but evil; countries where people are genuinely frightened when the other side takes power."[30]

Applebaum argues for engaging in constructive activities that benefit all, and in the process forcing people to "work alongside people that they hate. That doesn't mean they will then get to like one another, just that they are less likely to kill one another on the following day."[31] It is very much the same concept as Isay's insistence on reacquainting ourselves with our fellow Americans in deliberately nonpolitical ways, or Sharp's suggestion of working together on community projects divorced from partisan politics.[32]

"In the years before and after the peace settlement in Northern Ireland," Applebaum writes, "many 'peacebuilding' projects did not try to make Catholics and Protestants hold civilized debates about politics, or talk about politics at all. Instead, they built community centers, put up Christmas lights, and organized job training for young people." Here in the US, for instance, she advocates reinvigorating AmeriCorps, "the national-service program, offering proper salaries to young people willing to serve as cleaners or aides at overburdened hospitals, food banks, and addiction clinics," and sending its participants into parts of the country politically different from their own. "This might not build eternal friendships, but seditionists and progressives who worked together at a vaccination center could conceivably be less likely to use pepper spray on each other at a demonstration afterward."

"Make the problem narrow, specific, even boring, not existential or exciting," Applebaum writes. "'Who won the 2020 election?' is, for these purposes, a bad topic. 'How do we fix the potholes in our roads?' is, in contrast, superb."[33]

America's seditionists, Applebaum writes, pose a "long-term social problem. True believers—especially those who are unemployed, underemployed, or so far down the conspiracy-theory rabbit hole that they can no longer cope with ordinary life—are part of an intense, deeply connected, and, to them, profoundly satisfying community. In order to be pried away from it, they will have to be offered some appealing alternative."

Yet Applebaum knows that this advice will not be greeted with universal warmth:

> Even as I write this, I can hear many readers of this article uttering a collective snort of annoyance. Quite a few, I imagine, feel that, having won the election, they don't want to pay for a bunch of happy-clappy vaccine volunteers, or new roads in rural America, or mental-health services and life counseling for the MAGA-infected— let *them* learn to live with *us*. I can well imagine that . . . many will resent every penny of public money, every ounce of political time, that is spent on the seditious minority.
>
> I know how they feel, because I often feel that way too. But then I remember: It won't work. We'll wake up the next morning, and they'll still be there.[34]

Applebaum, of course, was writing from the POV of a democratically controlled country dealing with a right-wing insurgency—which is to say, the present moment. We also have to contemplate the opposite. We can expect precious little reaching across the aisle, empathy, or attempts at comity from reactionaries if they are in charge. Therefore, this healing—in delicate but essential and unyielding tandem with accountability—has to take place now, in order to prevent that right-wing victory from occurring, after which no such empathy and understanding will be in the offing.

CHAPTER 19

Democracy for Beginners

Historians will have it easy when it comes to telling the story of the United States in the early twenty-first century. It will be one of two tales.

In one scenario, the US—the first country on Earth to establish a representative democracy—tragically committed a kind of political suicide, carelessly allowing the rise of a ruthless right-wing regime that used the very mechanisms of that democracy to destroy it. Terrible as that was, the autocrats succeeded only because too many Americans were not sufficiently bothered by the threat and could not rouse themselves to stop the small minority that were delighted by it; by the time a significant number awoke to the emergency they were in, it was too late. It was an especially bitter fate, given that the country had recently succeeded in removing that autocratic party from office, only to foolishly let it seize power again.

In the other scenario, that same country, born in outrageous contradiction, stained with the original sin of slavery and genocide, somehow managed to halt a homegrown autocratic threat, and in the process, fundamentally began remaking itself to be true to the democratic principles it pioneered.

Which of these tales will prevail remains to be seen. The good news is that it's within our power to determine the answer.

By design, this survey of pro-democracy measures has been, as the saying goes, a mile wide and an inch deep. To be exhaustive on the topic would require an encyclopedia-sized collection and decades to digest it. None of the measures we have discussed, whether executed by a quasi-functional republic fighting off a reactionary movement from within, or by the beleaguered citizens of a full-blown autocracy pushing back against their oppressors, are a guarantee of success. The commitment to democracy is a lifetime endeavor, with no days off, for which this book has been a mere pamphlet.

Autocracy in America is not new, and we can learn how to confront it from those who came before us, and who even now continue that struggle. Effective communication and control of the information space are paramount. In that effort, we must commune with our fellow Americans in the smallest possible groups, and work locally to improve life at the most direct level. Finally, we cannot lose faith by focusing on seemingly overwhelming long-term goals: focus on living the truth of the present, as James Carroll advises, moment by moment.

Ultimately, the final defense against autocracy is to destroy its appeal. A just and equitable society, where the rule of law is evenly applied irrespective of wealth, social status, race, ethnicity, place of origin, religious faith or lack thereof, sex, sexual orientation, political belief, or any other metric, will be infertile ground for autocracy and demagoguery to flourish. A society in which people feel they have agency, and a proper voice in their own governance, and a chance to make better lives for themselves and their children, is one in which con artist politicians will have only a paltry audience, and where alienation, anger, and divisiveness find no purchase.

But even in such ideal conditions, there will always be outliers, people who admire authoritarianism—so long as it benefits them—and are perfectly happy to oppress their fellow citizens, people who crave submission to a cretinous "strongman" and are ready to exchange freedom for security, or what they imagine security to be. We will never totally eradicate that mentality or its adherents, nor should we imagine that we can. What we should do instead is work to keep that cohort as small and powerless as possible.

I hesitate to suggest that the rise of Trump will lead to anything beneficial, even accidentally. Only a Pollyanna would cheerfully look for the proverbial silver lining here; it's probably mercury. But the wounds of Trump's reign have undeniably exposed sobering realities about who we are as a people, about the strengths and weaknesses of our institutions, and about our character as a nation. Those realities have not always been flattering. But they are invaluable.

Unless we act, the problems exposed by Trump's rise will still be with us decades from now. It is within our power to determine whether he goes down as the anomaly many of us would like to believe he is, or as the harbinger of a dark future for this country.

PLAY THE "MARSEILLAISE"

There is a feeling we feel every time we win any kind of victory over the tinhorn tyrant from Queens—the feeling in *Casablanca* when the patrons of Rick's Café Américain lift their voices in the "Marseillaise" and drown out a group of German soldiers singing the Nazi favorite, "Die Wacht am Rhein." That is the spirit in which we would be well advised to move forward as we contemplate an antidemocratic, theocratic, white nationalist regime trying to take power in the United States. We should not resign ourselves to the false belief that our foe is an unconquerable juggernaut: they are not, and we can beat them. It's worth remembering that this act of theatrical protest in *Casablanca* results in the Nazis angrily shutting the café down. But also, that the good guys ultimately win the war.

In the fall of 2023, the anti-Trump conservative Robert Kagan sparked something akin to mass hysteria in progressive and centrist circles with a piece in *The Washington Post* that called a Trump dictatorship a near-inevitability, including a grim, point-by-point litany of how efforts to stop it were likely to fail.[1] Kagan's goal almost certainly was to sound a wake-up call. But the ensuing depression among liberals risked becoming a self-fulfilling prophecy, to the point where numerous other pundits felt compelled to publish responses cautioning against defeatism—including Kagan himself.[2]

The right wing would like us to believe that their eventual triumph is a fait accompli, and that there is no point in resisting. But nothing could be further from the truth. "Authoritarians create a climate where they seem unstoppable," Ruth Ben-Ghiat told *The Washington Post*. "Creating an aura of destiny around the leader galvanizes his supporters by making his movement seem much stronger than it actually is. The manipulation of perception is everything."[3]

The fundamental paradox of America remains the same as it was when Tocqueville visited these shores in the nineteenth century.

The first nation on Earth to attempt to form a true representative democracy was also founded on twin crimes: the genocide of its original inhabitants and the abduction and servitude of enslaved people brought here by force to build that new nation. Can a country with that history shed the damage of its past and remake itself to be true to the values on which it was founded and continues to espouse? Can we make a second American Revolution, a slow and nonviolent one that acknowledges and repudiates that blood-soaked past and lives up to the lofty ambitions and ideals of our founders, flawed though they were? Are we going to face at last the sins of our past and the bitter paradox at the very core of our country's origin, and strive for the ideals we claim to revere, rather than ignore the ways we have fallen short, or flatter ourselves that we did not fall short at all? Are we going to care for the hungry, the poor, the ragged and the hopeless, the motherless children, the broken, the suffering and oppressed yearning to breathe free, the ones filled with righteous anger, the dreamers who came here seeking a new life in a place dedicated to freedom and democracy, or will we turn our backs and prove ourselves hypocrites? Are we going to be true to the notion of a nation founded on the equality of all people, or is the contradiction that those words were written by a slaveholder, however brilliant, too damning?

The fight against autocracy is a long one—eternal, in fact. For a majority of Americans, it has never been a threat great enough to occupy much of our bandwidth. For less fortunate others it is a familiar struggle, generations long. Shamefully belated though it is, it's time for those of us in the former category to recognize our common dilemma and band together. We must keep up our morale, and never let our determination flicker out, even if it occasionally flags. As Rev. Dr. Norvel Goff told me, "Without hope we are just lost. We've got to make sure that there's a brighter light. You can't curse the darkness—light a candle, and let your light shine, and before you know it, there will be other candles, and when all those lights come together, we'll bring about a brighter day."[4]

He smiled at his own eloquence. "You know what? I might use that in a sermon."

Ultimately, we are not just trying to stave off an autocracy, or resist it should it arise. We are trying to build a true democracy in a form that our country has never fully been able to mount, despite the best intentions of some, the opposition of others, and our collective delusion about how well we live up to the lofty principles which we claim to hold dear. It is impossible to achieve that goal if we are not clear-eyed about the past or the current state of play. The right-wing autocracy that now threatens the republic is gasping for air, recognizing that time and demographics are against it, and is making a final, panicked, ferocious attempt to hang on to power. If we can defeat it and fulfill the promise of the much-vaunted American experiment, we will earn the flattery we regularly dole out to ourselves, and all that poetry that makes our hearts swell. Naively or otherwise, I believe all that is within our capability as a people, even a people who so recently saw fit to elect as our leader Donald Trump.

It's in our hands.

Endnotes

Chapter 1: How to Tell When Your House Is On Fucking Fire

1   Jonathan Weisman and Reid J. Epstein, "GOP Declares Jan. 6 Attack 'Legitimate Political Discourse,'" *The New York Times*, February 4, 2022, https://www.nytimes.com/2022/02/04/us/politics/republicans-jan-6-cheney-censure.html#:~:text=WASHINGTON%20—%20The%20Republican%20Party%20on,the%20role%20of%20Donald%20J.

2   Jon Greenberg, "Most Republicans still falsely believe Trump's stolen election claims. Here are some reasons why," Poynter Institute, June 26, 2022, https://www.poynter.org/fact-checking/2022/70-percent-republicans-falsely-believe-stolen-election-trump/.

3   Adam Gabbatt, "Almost one in three of Republicans say violence may be necessary to 'save' US," *The Guardian*, November 1, 2021, https://www.theguardian.com/us-news/2021/nov/01/republicans-violence-save-us-poll.

4   David Atkins, "Saving Democracy Will Require Institutional and Civil Resistance at All Levels," *Washington Monthly*, December 4, 2021, https://washingtonmonthly.com/2021/12/04/saving-democracy-will-require-institutional-and-civil-resistance-at-all-levels/?fbclid=IwAR2lzT2N0j30Sa8Dnq19_hdqsQHcjwhSrQ7WtKsbtNAmTy-FTVnZxITiuNQ.

5   David Leonhardt, "Seven Surprises," *The New York Times*, February 6, 2023, https://www.nytimes.com/2023/02/06/briefing/chatgpt-ukraine-inflation-stories-2023.html.

6   Abe Asher, "Fox guest says 'MyPillow-ization' of GOP by 'cartoon characters' like Mike Lindell is hurting Republicans," *The Independent*, November 10, 2022, https://www.independent.co.uk/news/world/americas/us-politics/fox-news-mike-lindell-gop-b2222612.html.

7   "RNC Completes 'Autopsy' on 2012 Loss, Calls for Inclusion Not Policy Change," ABC News, March 18, 2013, https://abcnews.go.com/

Politics/OTUS/rnc-completes-autopsy-2012-loss-calls-inclusion-policy/story?id=18755809.

8   Interview with Tom Hall, November 9, 2022.

9   Barton Gellman, "Trump's Next Coup Has Already Begun," *The Atlantic*, December 6, 2021, https://www.theatlantic.com/magazine/archive/2022/01/january-6-insurrection-trump-coup-2024-election/620843/?utm_source=twitter&utm_campaign=the-atlantic&utm_medium=social&utm_term=2023-01-06T16%3A45%3A48&utm_content=edit-promo.

10   Atkins, "Saving Democracy."

11   Ibid.

12   Stef W. Kight, "Charted: GOP's state level dominance," *Axios*, August 8, 2022, https://www.axios.com/2022/08/09/party-control-state-legislature-republicans.

13   Atkins, "Saving Democracy."

14   Franco Ordoñez, "Trump allies craft plans to give him unprecedented power if he wins the White House," NPR, December 6, 2023, https://www.npr.org/2023/12/06/1217562544/trump-and-insiders-craft-plans-for-unprecedented-power.

15   Jelani Cobb, "The Enduring Power of Trumpism," *The New Yorker*, November 15, 2022, https://www.newyorker.com/news/daily-comment/the-enduring-power-of-trumpism.

16   Masha Gessen, *Surviving Autocracy* (New York: Riverhead Books, 2020), 171.

17   Cobb, "The Enduring Power of Trumpism."

18   Quint Forgey, "Barr bashes Trump but says he'd still vote for him in 2024," *Politico*, March 7, 2022, https://www.politico.com/news/2022/03/07/barr-trump-2024 00014597#:~:text=Barr%20pledged%20to%20vote%20for,leveled%20against%20the%20former%20president.

19   Paul LeBlanc, "McConnell says he'll 'absolutely' support Trump in 2024 if he's the GOP nominee," CNN, February 25, 2022, https://www.cnn.com/2021/02/25/politics/mitch-mcconnell-donald-trump-2024/index.html.

20   Chet Flippo, "Tom Wolfe: The Rolling Stone Interview," *Rolling Stone*, August 21, 1980, https://www.rollingstone.com/culture/culture-features/tom-wolfe-the-rolling-stone-interview-35552/4/.

21   Steven Levitsky and Daniel Ziblatt, *How Democracies Die* (New York: Penguin Random House, 2018), 167.

22   Jamelle Bouie, "The US Thinks 'It Can't Happen Here.' It Already Has," *The New York Times*, October 18, 2022, https://www.nytimes.com/2022/10/18/opinion/democracy-america-authoritarianism-midterms.html.

23   Flippo, "Tom Wolfe: The Rolling Stone Interview."

24   Gellman, "Trump's Next Coup Has Already Begun."

25 "Americans agree that the future of democracy is on the line in the 2024 election but disagree about who poses the biggest threat," *PBS News Hour*, December 15, 2023, https://www.pbs.org/ newshour/politics/americans-agree-that-the-future-of-democracy-is-on-the-line-in-the-2024-election-but-disagree-about-who-poses-the-biggest-threat.

26 Michelle Alexander, "We Are Not the Resistance," *The New York Times*, September 21, 2018, https://www.nytimes.com/2018/09/21/ opinion/sunday/resistance-kavanaugh-trump-protest.html.

27 Ibid.

28 Slavoj Žižek, "Resistance Is Surrender," *London Review of Books*, November 15, 2007, https://www.lrb.co.uk/the-paper/v29/n22/ slavoj-zizek/resistance-is-surrender.

29 Alexander, "We Are Not the Resistance."

30 Rebecca Solnit, "Why are US rightwingers so angry?" *The Guardian*, December 20, 2021, https://www.theguardian.com/commentisfree/ 2021/dec/20/rightwingers-us-social-change-coming.

31 Anne Applebaum, *Twilight of Democracy* (New York: Anchor Books, 2020), 22.

Chapter 2: The Plot Against America

1 "Party affiliation by state," Pew Research Center, retrieved June 23, 2023, https://www.pewresearch.org/religion/religious-landscape-study/compare/ party-affiliation/by/state/.

2 Brooke Berger, "Eisenhower and Nixon: Secrets of an Unlikely Pair," *US News and World Report*, February 15, 2013, https://www.usnews.com/opinion/ articles/2013/02/15/eisenhower-and-nixon-secrets-of-an-unlikely-pair.

3 Jeremy D. Mayer, "LBJ Fights the White Backlash: The Racial Politics of the 1964 Presidential Campaign," *Prologue Magazine*, National Archives, Spring 2001, vol. 33, no. 1, https://www.archives.gov/publications/prologue/2001/ spring/lbj-and-white-backlash-1.

4 Wallace Turner, "Reagan Remark a Campaign Issue," *The New York Times*, April 19, 1970, https://www.nytimes.com/1970/04/19/ archives/reagan-remark-a-campaign-issue-bloodbath-comment-fuels-oratory-in.html.

5 Interview with James Carroll, March 1, 2023.

6 Randall Balmer, "The Real Origins of the Religious Right," *Politico*, May 27, 2014, https://www.politico.com/magazine/story/ 2014/05/religious-right-real-origins-107133/.

7   Heather Cox Richardson, "The End of a Political Era: Movement
      Conservatism Gets Real," Bill Moyers.com, August 16, 2017,
      https://billmoyers.com/story/maga-movement-conservatism-era/.

8   McKay Coppins, "The Man Who Broke Politics," *The Atlantic*,
      October 17, 2018, https://www.theatlantic.com/magazine/archive/
      2018/11/newt-gingrich-says-youre-welcome/570832/.

9   Ibid.

10   Kim Phillips-Fein, "The Long Unraveling of the Republican Party,"
      The Atlantic, September 6, 2022, https://www.theatlantic.com/
      magazine/archive/2022/10/republican-party-extremist-history-
      hemmer-continetti-milbank-books/671248/.

11   Coppins, "The Man Who Broke Politics."

12   Ibid.

13   Ibid.

14   Paul Krugman, "Reckonings; Bait and Switch," *The New York Times*,
      November 1, 2000, https://www.nytimes.com/2000/11/01/opinion/
      reckonings-bait-and-switch.html?scp=13&sq=krugman%20shape%
      20planet%20bush&st=cse.

15   Jennifer Rubin, "The Media Has Given Republicans a Free Pass on
      Assaulting Democracy," *The Washington Post*, December 7, 2021,
      https://www.washingtonpost.com/opinions/2021/12/07/
      media-has-given-republicans-free-pass-assaulting-democracy/.

16   Colin Dwyer, "Donald Trump: 'I Could . . . Shoot Somebody, And
      I Wouldn't Lose Any Voters'," NPR, January 23, 2016, https://
      www.npr.org/sections/thetwo-way/2016/01/23/464129029/
      donald-trump-i-could-shoot-somebody-and-i-wouldnt-lose-
      any-voters.

17   Adam Serwer, "Birtherism of a Nation," *The Atlantic*, May 13, 2020,
      https://www.theatlantic.com/ideas/archive/2020/05/birtherism-
      and-trump/610978/.

18   Ta-Nehisi Coates, "The First White President," *The Atlantic*,
      October 15, 2017, https://www.theatlantic.com/magazine/archive/
      2017/10/the-first-white-president-ta-nehisi-coates/537909/.

19   Rebecca Solnit, "On Not Meeting Nazis Halfway," *Literary Hub*, November
      19, 2020, https://lithub.com/rebecca-solnit-on-not-meeting-nazis-halfway/.

20   Alex Shephard, "In Memoriam: The Trump Pivot," *The New Re-
      public*, October 23, 2020, https://newrepublic.com/article/159917/
      trump-biden-new-tone-debate.

21   Ross Douthat, "There Will Be No Trump Coup," *The New York Times*,
      October 10, 2020, https://www.nytimes.com/2020/10/10/opinion/sunday/
      trump-election-authoritarianism.html.

22 Eduardo Porter, "GOP Shift Moves Center Far to Right," *The New York Times*, September 5, 2012, https://www.nytimes.com/2012/09/05/business/the-gops-journey-from-the-liberal-days-of-nixon.html.

23 Newsweek Special Edition, "Would Reagan Pass a Republican Purity Test?" *Newsweek*, March 31, 2016, https://www.newsweek.com/ronald-reagan-republicans-gop-442360.

24 Leslie Thatcher, "An Interview With Mike Lofgren, Author of 'The Party Is Over,'" *Truthout*, August 3, 2012, https://truthout.org/articles/stone-cold-sober-an-interview-with-mike-lofgren-author-of-the-party-is-over/.

25 Jason Le Miere, "Is Trump Republican? Timeline of President's Shifting Political Views After He Sides with Democrats," *Newsweek*, September 7, 2017, https://www.newsweek.com/trump-republican-democrats-president-661340.

26 Oliver Laughland, "Donald Trump and the Central Park Five: the racially charged rise of a demagogue," *The Guardian*, February 17, 2016, https://www.theguardian.com/us-news/2016/feb/17/central-park-five-donald-trump-jogger-rape-case-new-york.

27 Caitlin Dickerson, "We Need to Take Away Children," *The Atlantic*, August 7, 2022, https://www.theatlantic.com/magazine/archive/2022/09/trump-administration-family-separation-policy-immigration/670604/.

28 Adam Serwer, "The Cruelty Is the Point," *The Atlantic*, October 3, 2018, https://www.theatlantic.com/ideas/archive/2018/10/the-cruelty-is-the-point/572104/.

29 Chris Hedges, "The Cult of Trump," *Truthdig*, October 29, 2018, https://www.truthdig.com/articles/the-cult-of-trump-2/.

30 Jonathan Chait, "How to Make a Semi-Fascist Party," *New York*, October 19, 2022, https://nymag.com/intelligencer/2022/10/how-to-make-a-semi-fascist-party.html?utm_source=Sailthru&utm_medium=email&utm_campaign=%26c.%20-%20October%2027%2C%202022&utm_term=Subscription%20List%20-%20Chait%20Etc.

31 Levitsky and Ziblatt, *How Democracies Die*, 26–31.

32 Ibid, 70.

33 Jennifer Rubin, "There are no moderate House Republicans," *The Washington Post*, January 11, 2023, https://www.washingtonpost.com/opinions/2023/01/11/house-republicans-no-moderates/.

34 Ibid.

35 Kagan, "Our Constitutional Crisis Is Already Here," *The Washington Post*, September 23, 2021, https://www.washingtonpost.com/opinions/2021/09/23/robert-kagan-constitutional-crisis/.

36   Ibid.

37   Alex Henderson, "Noam Chomsky slams the GOP's 'radical insurgency' and efforts to 'overthrow democracy'," *Alternet*, February 7, 2022, https://www.alternet.org/2022/02/noam-chomsky-slams-the-gops-radical-insurgency-and-efforts-to-overthrow-democracy.

Chapter 3: Alarm Will Sound

1   Masha Gessen, "Autocracy: Rules for Survival," *The New York Review of Books*, November 10, 2016, https://www.nybooks.com/online/2016/11/10/trump-election-autocracy-rules-for-survival/.

2   Ibid.

3   Masha Gessen, "One Year After Trump's Election, Revisiting 'Autocracy: Rules for Survival,'" *The New Yorker*, November 8, 2017, https://www.newyorker.com/news/our-columnists/one-year-after-trumps-election-revisiting-autocracy-rules-for-survival.

4   Patrick Healy and Jonathan Martin, "Donald Trump Won't Say if He'll Accept Result of Election," *The New York Times*, October 19, 2016, https://www.nytimes.com/2016/10/20/us/politics/presidential-debate.html.

5   Arlene Washington, "Donald Trump Uses Final Debate to Double-Down on Claim That Emmys Were 'Rigged,'" *The Hollywood Reporter*, October 19, 2016, https://www.hollywoodreporter.com/news/politics-news/donald-trump-final-debate-emmys-rigged-939984/.

6   Aaron Blake, "'What's the downside for humoring him?': A GOP official's unintentionally revealing quote about the Trump era," *The Washington Post*, November 10, 2020, https://www.washingtonpost.com/politics/2020/11/10/whats-downside-humoring-him-gop-officials-unintentionally-revealing-quote-about-trump-era/.

7   Jill Colvin and Steve Peoples, "Whose 'Big Lie'? Trump's Proclamation a New GOP Litmus Test," Associated Press, May 4, 2021, https://apnews.com/article/campaign-2016-election-2020-government-and-politics-3e0aaf0b8a5dfc825dc0ae1f3d30d4dc.

8   Michael Kruse, "The One Way History Shows Trump's Personality Cult Will End," *Politico*, April 16, 2022, https://www.politico.com/news/magazine/2022/04/16/history-shows-trump-personality-cult-end-00024941.

9   Maya Yin, "More Than 40% in US Do Not Believe Biden Legitimately Won Election—Poll," *The Guardian*, January 5, 2020,

https://www.theguardian.com/us-news/2022/jan/05/america-biden-election-2020-poll-victory.

10 Laura Jedeed, "The Cult of the January 6 Martyrs," *The New Republic*, March 6, 2023, https://newrepublic.com/article/170991/cpac-january-6-riot-prisoners.

11 Graig Graziosi, "Trump calls police officer who shot Ashli Babbitt a 'thug' during CNN town hall," *The Independent*, May 11, 2023, https://www.independent.co.uk/news/world/americas/us-politics/trump-ashli-babbitt-thug-cnn-town-hall-b2337214.html.

12 Ed Pilkington, "'January 6 never ended': alarm at Trump pardon pledge for Capitol insurrectionists," *The Guardian*, January 6, 2024, https://www.theguardian.com/us-news/2024/jan/06/trump-pardon-january-6-rioters-if-elected-president.

13 Jon Greenberg, "Most Republicans still falsely believe Trump's stolen election claims. Here are some reasons why," Poynter Institute, June 16, 2022, https://www.poynter.org/fact-checking/2022/70-percent-republicans-falsely-believe-stolen-election-trump/.

14 Eli Yokley, "Many Republicans Doubt Clinton Won Popular Vote," Morning Consult, July 26, 2017, https://morningconsult.com/2017/07/26/many-republicans-think-trump-won-2016-popular-vote-didnt/.

15 David Litt, "Claims of 'voter fraud' have a long history in America. And they are false," *The Guardian*, December 4, 2020, https://www.theguardian.com/commentisfree/2020/dec/04/trump-voter-fraud-america-false.

16 Ronald Brownstein, "The demographic makeup of the country's voters continues to shift. That creates headwinds for Republicans," CNN, May 16, 2023, https://www.cnn.com/2023/05/16/politics/demographic-changes-voters-fault-lines/index.html.

17 Timothy Snyder, *On Tyranny* (New York: Crown, 2017), 28.

18 Levitsky and Ziblatt, *How Democracies Die*, 12–13.

19 Brandon Tensley, "America's Long History of Black Voter Suppression," CNN, May 6, 2021, https://www.cnn.com/interactive/2021/05/politics/black-voting-rights-suppression-timeline/.

20 Levitsky and Ziblatt, *How Democracies Die*, 89–90.

21 "Voting and Voter Registration as a Share of the Voter Population, by Race/Ethnicity," Kaiser Family Foundation, November 2022, https://www.kff.org/other/state-indicator/voting-and-voter-registration-as-a-share-of-the-voter-population-by-raceethnicity/?currentTimeframe=0&sortModel=%7B%22colId%22:%22Location%22,%22sort%22:%22asc%22%7D.

22   Suevon Lee and Sarah Smith, "Everything You've Ever Wanted to Know About Voter ID Laws," *ProPublica*, March 9, 2016, https://www.propublica.org/article/everything-youve-ever-wanted-to-know-about-voter-id-laws.

23   "Debunking the Voter Fraud Myth," The Brennan Center for Justice, https://www.brennancenter.org/sites/default/files/analysis/Briefing_Memo_Debunking_Voter_Fraud_Myth.pdf.

24   Levitsky and Ziblatt, *How Democracies Die*, 184–185.

25   Olga Khazan, "Voter ID proponents point to laws in other countries," *The Washington Post*, July 12, 2012, https://www.washingtonpost.com/blogs/blog-post/post/voter-id-proponents-point-to-laws-in-other-countries/2012/07/12/gJQAVIGCfW_blog.html.

26   Keesha Gaskins and Sundeep Iyer, "The Challenge of Obtaining Voter Identification," The Brennan Center for Justice, July 18, 2012, https://www.brennancenter.org/our-work/research-reports/challenge-obtaining-voter-identification.

27   Levitsky and Ziblatt, *How Democracies Die*, 185.

28   Ibid., 184.

29   "Identification Requirements for Voting," VoteTexas.gov, https://www.votetexas.gov/mobile/id-faqs.htm.

30   Alison Durkee, "80% Of Americans Support Voter ID Rules—But Fewer Worried About Fraud, Poll Finds," *Forbes*, June 21, 2021, https://www.forbes.com/sites/alisondurkee/2021/06/21/80-of-americans-support-voter-id-rules-but-fewer-worried-about-fraud-poll-finds/?sh=5cda48101e0b.

31   Kevin Drum, "The Quick Way to End the Vote-Fraud Wars? A National ID Card," *Mother Jones*, July/August 2012, https://www.motherjones.com/politics/2012/07/national-id-card-voter-fraud-solution/.

32   Brentin Mock, "How the Right Is Building Its 'Poll Watcher' Network for November," *The Nation*, August 24, 2012, https://www.thenation.com/article/archive/how-right-building-its-poll-watcher-network-november/.

33   Lawrence Mower, "Police cameras show confusion, anger over DeSantis' voter fraud arrests," *The Tampa Bay Times*, October 18, 2022, https://www.tampabay.com/news/florida-politics/2022/10/18/body-camera-video-police-voter-fraud-desantis-arrests/.

34   Sam Levine, "'Death by a thousand cuts': Georgia's new voting restrictions threaten midterm election," *The Guardian*, October 5, 2022, https://www.theguardian.com/us-news/2022/oct/05/georgia-voter-suppression-registration-challenges.

35   Daniel Garisto, "Smartphone Data Show Voters in Black Neighborhoods Wait Longer," *Scientific American*, Octo-

ber 1, 2019, https://www.scientificamerican.com/article/
smartphone-data-show-voters-in-black-neighborhoods-wait-longer1/.

36   Alice Speri, "Voter Suppression Is the Real Election Scandal," *The Intercept*, October 27, 2016, https://theintercept.com/2016/10/27/
      voter-suppression-is-the-real-election-scandal/.

37   Paul Gronke and Paul Manson, "The State of Election Administration in
      2022," Democracy Fund, November 2, 2022, https://democracyfund.org/
      focus_area/voter-centric-election-administration/.

38   Sam Levine, "Two Georgia election workers cleared of wrong-
      doing in 2020 elections," *The Guardian*, June 23, 2023,
      https://www.theguardian.com/us-news/2023/jun/23/
      georgia-election-worker-cleared-trump-giuliani-vote-2020.

39   Michael Waldman, "The Great Resignation . . . of Election Officials,"
      Brennan Center for Justice, April 25, 2023, https://www.brennancenter.org/
      our-work/analysis-opinion/great-resignation-election-officials.

40   Michael Wines, "Freed by Court Ruling, Republicans Step Up Effort to
      Patrol Voting," *The New York Times*, May 18, 2020, https://www.nytimes.
      com/2020/05/18/us/Voting-republicans-trump.html.

41   Doug Bock Clark, "Close to 100,000 Voter Registrations Were
      Challenged in Georgia—Almost All by Just Six Right-Wing Activ-
      ists," *ProPublica*, July 13, 2023, https://www.propublica.org/article/
      right-wing-activists-georgia-voter-challenges.

42   "Joint Statement on Drop Box Watchers," Maricopa County, Arizona,
      October 22, 2022, https://content.govdelivery.com/accounts/AZMARIC/
      bulletins/333cdba.

43   Jeffrey Toobin, "The Legal Fight Awaiting Us After the Election," *The New Yorker*, September 21, 2020, https://www.newyorker.com/maga-
      zine/2020/09/28/the-legal-fight-awaiting-us-after-the-election.

44   Barton Gellman, "The Election That Could Break America," *The At-
      lantic*, September 23, 2020, https://www.theatlantic.com/magazine/ar-
      chive/2020/11/what-if-trump-refuses-concede/616424/.

45   Adam Serwer, "10 Dirty Ways to Swing an Election," *Mother Jones*, No-
      vember 1, 2012, https://www.motherjones.com/politics/2012/11/
      election-dirty-tricks/.

46   Tori Otten, "Republicans Are So Mad at the Huge Youth Turn-
      out They Want to Increase the Voting Age," *The New Repub-
      lic*, November 10, 2022, https://newrepublic.com/post/168732/
      republicans-mad-huge-youth-gen-z-turnout-want-increase-voting-age.

47   James Ridgeway, "The Mother of All Vote-Suppression Tactics?" *Mother
      Jones*, November 5, 2012, https://www.motherjones.com/politics/2012/07/
      felon-disenfranchisement-florida-vote-obama/.

48   Christina Maxouris, "More than 5 million people with felony con-
     victions can't vote in this year's election, advocacy group finds,"
     CNN, October 15, 2020, https://edition.cnn.com/2020/10/15/us/
     felony-convictions-voting-sentencing-project-study/index.html.

49   Ridgeway, "The Mother of All Vote-Suppression Tactics?"

50   Renee Harrison, "Think your vote doesn't count? Then why are
     people trying to suppress it?" *The Washington Post,* November 7, 2016,
     https://www.washingtonpost.com/posteverything/wp/2016/11/07/
     think-your-vote-doesnt-count-then-why-are-people-trying-to-
     suppress-it/.

51   Robert O'Harrow Jr. and Shawn Boburg, "A conservative activist's
     behind-the-scenes campaign to remake the nation's courts,"
     The Washington Post, May 21, 2019, https://www.washingtonpost.com/
     graphics/2019/investigations/leonard-leo-federalists-society-courts/
     ?utm_term=.1d2008ed2d75.

52   Jason Stanley (@jasonintrator), Twitter, September 5, 2022
     (since removed), https://www.publicnotice.co/p/aileen-cannon-
     special-master-trump-explained.

53   Daniel Victor, "McConnell Says Republicans Would Fill a Supreme
     Court Vacancy in 2020, Drawing Claims of Hypocrisy," *The New York
     Times,* May 29, 2019, https://www.nytimes.com/2019/05/29/us/
     politics/mitch-mcconnell-supreme-court.html.

54   Philip Bump, "A quarter of Republicans voted for Trump to get Supreme
     Court picks—and it paid off," *The Washington Post,* June 26, 2018, https://
     www.washingtonpost.com/news/politics/wp/2018/06/26/a-quarter-of-republ
     icans-voted-for-trump-to-get-supreme-court-picks-and-it-paid-off/.

55   Shira A. Scheindlin, "Trump's judges will call the shots for years
     to come. The judicial system is broken," *The Guardian,* October 25,
     2021, https://www.theguardian.com/commentisfree/2021/oct/25/
     trump-judges-supreme-court-justices-judiciary.

56   Beth Reinhard and Josh Dawsey, "Gov. Ron DeSantis used secre-
     tive panel to flip state Supreme Court," *The Washington Post,* June
     20, 2023, https://www.washingtonpost.com/politics/2023/06/20/
     gov-ron-desantis-used-secretive-panel-flip-state-supreme-court/.

57   Andrew Marantz, "A Supreme Court Case That Threatens the Mechanisms
     of Democracy," *The New Yorker,* December 11, 2022, https://www.newyo-
     rker.com/magazine/2022/12/19/a-supreme-court-case-that-threatens-the
     -mechanisms-of-democracy.

58   Naomi Klein, "The Supreme Court's Shock-and-Awe Judicial Coup,"
     The Intercept, June 30, 2022, https://theintercept.com/2022/06/30/
     supreme-court-climate-epa-coup/.

59   Colby Itkowitz and Isaac Stanley-Becker, "Democracy advocates raise
      alarm after Supreme Court takes election case," *The Washington Post*,
      July 1, 2022, https://www.washingtonpost.com/politics/2022/07/01/
      democracy-advocates-raise-alarm-after-supreme-court-takes-election-
      case/.

60   Hansi Lo Wang, "This conservative group helped push a disputed
      election theory," NPR, August 12, 2022, https://www.npr.org/2022/
      08/12/1111606448/supreme-court-independent-state-legislature-
      theory-honest-elections-project.

61   Klein, "The Supreme Court's Shock-and-Awe Judicial Coup."

Chapter 4: Oxygen and Cordite

1   Jennifer Rubin, "The truth about many in the GOP base: They pre-
     fer authoritarianism to democracy," *The Washington Post*, June 29,
     2021, https://www.washingtonpost.com/opinions/2021/06/29/
     truth-about-gop-they-prefer-authoritarianism-democracy/?fbclid=IwAR0t_
     B4Aw4m7M33PLJiPszC2KTWzxGAJVBAAohPFNraS9yHGq8uVGCJqz3A.

2   Jon Henley, "White and wealthy voters gave victory to Donald Trump, exit
     polls show," *The Guardian*, November 9, 2016, https://www.theguardian.
     com/us-news/2016/nov/09/white-voters-victory-donald-trump-exit-polls.

3   Olga Khazan, "People Voted for Trump Because They Were Anxious, Not
     Poor," *The Atlantic*, April 23, 2018, https://www.theatlantic.com/science/
     archive/2018/04/existential-anxiety-not-poverty-motivates-trump-support/
     558674/.

4   Mehdi Hasan, "Time to Kill the Zombie Argument: Another Study Shows
     Trump Won Because of Racial Anxieties—Not Economic Distress," *The
     Intercept*, September 18, 2018, https://theintercept.com/2018/09/18/2016-elec-
     tion-race-class-trump/.

5   Coates, "The First White President."

6   Abby Budiman, "Key findings about US immigrants," Pew Research Center,
     August 20, 2020, https://www.pewresearch.org/short-reads/2020/08/20/
     key-findings-about-u-s-immigrants/.

7   Trump, social media, right-wing news stir up antifa scares,"
     Associated Press, September 23, 2020, https://apnews.com/article/
     race-and-ethnicity-media-social-media-kentucky-racial-injustice-
     97624252a276dea5cfe2e79381df0248.

8   David Frum, "The Conservative Cult of Victimhood," *The Atlantic*, Jan-
     uary 11, 2021, https://www.theatlantic.com/ideas/archive/2021/01/
     conservatism-reaches-dead-end/617629/.

9   "Fatal police violence by race and state in the USA, 1980–2019: a network
      meta-regression," *The Lancet*, October 2, 2021, https://www.thelancet.com/
      journals/lancet/article/PIIS0140-6736(21)01609-3/fulltext#:~:text=Over%20
      this%20time%20period%2C%20the,·15%20%5B0·14–.

10   Publius Decius Mus (aka Michael Anton), "The Flight 93 Election," *The
      Claremont Review of Books*, September 5, 2016, https://claremontreviewof-
      books.com/digital/the-flight-93-election/.

11   Levitsky and Ziblatt, *How Democracies Die*, 92.

12   Saul Alinsky, *Rules for Radicals: A Pragmatic Primer for Realistic Radicals* (New
      York: Vintage Books, 1971), 44.

13   Ruth Ben-Ghiat (@ruthbenghiat), Twitter, March 18, 2023, https://twitter.
      com/ruthbenghiat/status/1637199533456097280.

14   Ibram X. Kendi, "The Second Assassination of Martin Luther King Jr.,"
      The Atlantic, October 14, 2021, https://www.theatlantic.com/ideas/ar-
      chive/2021/10/martin-luther-king-critical-race-theory/620367/.

15   *US Army Field Manual FM 7-98, Operations in a Low Intensity Conflict*, October
      19, 1992.

16   Tom Nichols, "The New Era of Political Violence Is Here," *The Atlantic*,
      August 15, 2022, https://www.theatlantic.com/newsletters/archive/2022/08/
      the-new-era-of-political-violence-is-here/671146/.

17   Geneva Sands, "White supremacists remain deadliest US ter-
      ror threat, Homeland Security report says," CNN, Octo-
      ber 6, 2020, https://www.cnn.com/2020/10/06/politics/
      white-supremacists-anarchists-dhs-homeland-threat-assessment/index.html.

18   Wayne Darsh, "Inside the Bible study massacre: A mom 'laid in her son's
      blood,'" CNN, December 17, 2015, https://www.cnn.com/2015/06/19/us/
      inside-charleston-bible-study-massacre/index.html.

19   Adam Withnall, "Charleston shooting: Five-year-old child who
      'played dead' among survivors in South Carolina," *The Independent*,
      June 18, 2015, https://www.independent.co.uk/news/world/
      americas/charleston-shooting-fiveyearold-child-who-played-dead-
      among-survivors-in-south-carolina-10327938.html.

20   Rebecca Carroll, "The Charleston shooter killed mostly black women.
      This wasn't about 'rape,'" *The Guardian*, June 18, 2015,
      https://www.theguardian.com/commentisfree/2015/jun/18/
      charleston-shooter-black-women-white-women-rape.

21   Fabiola Cineas, "A new report shows hate crimes on the rise—and it's prob-
      ably undercounting them," *Vox*, March 18, 2023, https://www.vox.com/
      policy/2023/3/18/23644339/hate-crimes-report-rise-in-hate-crimes.

22   Catie Edmondson and Mark Walker, "One Menacing Call After An-
      other: Threats Against Lawmakers Surge," *The New York Times*, Feb-

ruary 9, 2022, https://www.nytimes.com/2022/02/09/us/politics/
politician-death-threats.html.

23   Catie Edmondson, "Pelosi Attack Highlights Rising Fears of Political
Violence," *The New York Times*, October 28, 2022, https://www.nytimes.
com/2022/10/29/us/politics/paul-pelosi-political-violence.html.

24   Timothy Noah, "'We' Don't Have a Political Violence Problem. Republicans
Do.," *The New Republic*, November 1, 2022, https://newrepublic.com/arti-
cle/168391/political-violence-is-republicans-problem.

25   Sharon Zhang, "205 Republicans Vote Against Bill to Expand School Mental Health Services," *Truthout*, September 30, 2022, https://truthout.org/articl
es/205-republicans-vote-against-bill-to-expand-school-mental-health-services/.

26   David Leonhardt, "The Right's Violence Problem," *The New York
Times*, May 17, 2022, https://www.nytimes.com/2022/05/17/briefing/
right-wing-mass-shootings.html.

27   Mari Uyehara, "There Aren't Two Sides: Trump's Violent Rhetoric Is
What Got Us Here," *GQ*, October 25, 2018, https://www.gq.com/story/
trumps-violent-america.

28   Donnie O'Sullivan, "Republican congressman posts video depicting violence
against Ocasio-Cortez and Biden," CNN, November 9, 2021, https://www.
cnn.com/2021/11/09/politics/gosar-anime-video-violence-ocasio-cortez-bide
n/index.html.

29   Colby Itkowitz, "Guns are all over GOP ads and social media, prompting
some criticism," *The Washington Post*, March 31, 2022, https://www.washing-
tonpost.com/politics/2022/05/31/republicans-guns-ads-posts/.

30   Felicia Sonmez and David Weigel, "In campaign ad, GOP Senate
candidate shoots gun at actors playing Biden, Pelosi and Sen. Mark
Kelly," *The Washington Post*, February 10, 2022,
https://www.washingtonpost.com/politics/2022/02/10/campaign-
ad-senate-candidate-shoots-gun-actors-playing-biden-pelosi-sen-
mark-kelly-whose-wife-gabby-giffords-was-injured-arizona-rampage/.

31   Christina Wyman, "A Christmas card with guns? Lauren Boebert and
Thomas Massie start a new culture war," NBC News, December 10,
2021, https://www.nbcnews.com/think/opinion/christmas-card-
guns-lauren-boebert-thomas-massie-start-new-culture-ncna1285709.

32   Em Steck and Andrew Kaczynski, "Marjorie Taylor Greene indicated support for executing prominent Democrats in 2018 and 2019 before running
for Congress," CNN, January 26, 2021, https://www.cnn.com/2021/01/26/
politics/marjorie-taylor-greene-democrats-violence/index.html.

33   David Kurtz, "America Is In The Grip Of A Reign Of
White Supremacist Terror," *Talking Points Memo*, August 28,
2023, https://talkingpointsmemo.com/morning-memo/

america-is-in-the-grip-of-reign-of-white-supremacist-terror?utm_source=sub-stack&utm_medium=email&fbclid=IwAR2Coi83kWCg3j6eTPMk-taAK2RAu6C7nk6Wc4YGADNWQKTcNBZUvaIRL_o8.

34 Ben Hubbard, "The Franchising of Al Qaeda," *The New York Times,* https://www.nytimes.com/2014/01/26/sunday-review/the-franchising-of-al-qaeda.html.

35 Katie Worth, "Lone Wolf Attacks Are Becoming More Common—And More Deadly," *Frontline,* July 14, 2016, https://www.pbs.org/wgbh/frontline/article/lone-wolf-attacks-are-becoming-more-common-and-more-deadly/.

36 Interview with the Rev. Dr. Norvel Goff, May 19, 2023.

37 Norvel Goff, Jr. in *After Sherman,* directed by Jon-Sesrie Goff, 2023, https://divinity.yale.edu/news/norvel-goff-91-mdiv-heart-his-son-s-powerful-documentary-after-sherman.

38 KK Ottesen, "'They are preparing for war': An expert on civil wars discusses where political extremists are taking this country," The Washington Post Magazine, March 8, 2022.

39 Kathleen Belew, *Bring the War Home: The White Power Movement and Paramilitary America* (Cambridge: Harvard University Press, 2019).

40 Marshall Cohen, "1 in 10 defendants from US Capitol insurrection have military ties," CNN, May 28, 2021, https://www.cnn.com/2021/05/28/politics/capitol-insurrection-veterans/index.html.

41 Tom Dreisbach and Meg Anderson, "Nearly 1 In 5 Defendants In Capitol Riot Cases Served In The Military," NPR, January 21, 2021, https://www.npr.org/2021/01/21/958915267/nearly-one-in-five-defendants-in-capitol-riot-cases-served-in-the-military.

42 Barton Gellman, "What Happened to Michael Flynn?" *The Atlantic,* July 8, 2022, https://www.theatlantic.com/ideas/archive/2022/07/michael-flynn-conspiracy-theories-january-6-trump/661439/.

43 "Inside the 'constitutional sheriff' movement," NPR/*All Things Considered,* October 22, 2022, https://www.npr.org/2022/10/22/1130755532/inside-the-constitutional-sheriff-movement.

44 Tom Jackman, "Former FBI supervisor arrested in connection with Jan. 6 riot," *The Washington Post,* May 3, 2023, https://www.washingtonpost.com/dc-md-va/2023/05/03/ex-fbi-agent-arrested/.

45 Matt Zapotowski, "Rudy Giuliani is claiming to have insider FBI knowledge. Does he really?" *The Washington Post,* November 4, 2016, https://www.washingtonpost.com/news/post-nation/wp/2016/11/04/rudy-giuliani-is-claiming-to-have-insider-fbi-knowledge-does-he-really/.

46 Jaclyn Diaz, "A former high-level FBI agent faces charges for aiding a sanctioned Russian oligarch," NPR, January 23, 2023, https://www.npr.org/2023/01/23/1150797242/former-fbi-agent-charles-mcgonigal-russian-oligarch-oleg-deripaska.

47 Carol Leonnig, Devlin Barrett, Perry Stein, and Aaron C. Davis, "Showdown before the raid: FBI agents and prosecutors argued over Trump," *The Washington Post*, March 1, 2023, https://www.washingtonpost.com/national-security/2023/03/01/fbi-dispute-trump-mar-a-lago-raid/.

48 Interview with Tim Heaphy, May 10, 2023.

49 Betsy Woodruff Swan and Rachael Levy, "Violent online messages before Capitol riot went unshared by DHS, emails show," *Politico*, January 13, 2022, https://www.politico.com/news/2022/01/13/capitol-riot-online-messages-dhs-527027.

50 Michael Brown, "Tell Me How This Begins: Insurgency in the United States," *Homeland Security Affairs: The Journal of the NPS Center for Homeland Defense and Security*, March 2023, https://www.hsaj.org/articles/22129.

Chapter 5: Autocracy for Amateurs

1 Interview with Glen Woodbury, September 1, 2023.

2 Didi Kuo, "How the world has been 'made safe for autocracy,'" *The Washington Post*, April 22, 2022, https://www.washingtonpost.com/outlook/2022/04/22/why-world-has-been-made-safe-autocracy/.

3 Joshua Yaffa, "The Unimaginable Horror of a Friend's Arrest in Moscow," *The New Yorker*, March 31, 2023, https://www.newyorker.com/news/daily-comment/the-unimaginable-horror-of-a-friends-arrest-in-moscow.

4 Nathaniel Weixel, "Graham: Abortion 'not a states' rights issue,'" *The Hill*, September 20, 2022, https://thehill.com/policy/healthcare/3651788-graham-abortion-not-a-states-rights-issue/.

5 "With Roe dead, Republicans call for abortion bans in all states," *The Los Angeles Times*, June 24, 2022, https://www.latimes.com/politics/story/2022-06-24/supreme-court-abortion-decision-political-fallout.

6 David Pepper, *Laboratories of Autocracy* (St. Helena Press, 2021).

7 Interview with progressive activist, May 2023.

8 Jason Leopold, "For Obama, One Trump Term Wasn't a Big Worry but 'Eight Years Would Be a Problem,'" *Bloomberg*, September 30, 2022, https://www.bloomberg.com/news/articles/2022-09-30/obama-on-trump-1-presidential-term-is-okay-but-8-years-would-be-a-problem-l8t1lk89.

9   Jonathan V. Last, "Most aspiring dictators try to hide their intentions. Trump doesn't. And that's his secret sauce," *The Bulwark*, December 7, 2023, https://plus.thebulwark.com/p/most-aspiring-dictators-try-to-hide.

10   Lisa Rein, and Eric Yoder, "Trump issues sweeping order for tens of thousands of career federal employees to lose civil service protections," *The Washington Post*, October 22, 2020, https://www.washingtonpost.com/politics/trump-order-federal-civil-service/2020/10/22/c73783f0-1481-11eb-bc10-40b25382f1be_story.html.

11   Aaron Blake, "Trump's government full of temps," *The Washington Post*, February 21, 2000, https://www.washingtonpost.com/politics/2020/02/21/trump-has-had-an-acting-official-cabinet-level-job-1-out-every-9-days/.

12   Cristina Maza, "US Allies Probably Withhold Information From Donald Trump to Stop It From Leaking to Vladimir Putin, Intelligence Expert Says," *Newsweek*, February 4, 2019, https://www.newsweek.com/us-allies-donald-trump-intelligence-putin-1316601.

13   Jonathan Swan, Charlie Savage, and Maggie Haberman, "Trump and Allies Forge Plans to Increase Presidential Power in 2025," *The New York Times*, July 17, 2023, https://www.nytimes.com/2023/07/17/us/politics/trump-plans-2025.html#:~:text=Trump%20and%20his%20allies%20are,authority%20directly%20in%20his%20hands.

14   Paul Rosenzweig, "The 2024 Election Could Be the End of the Cases Against Donald Trump," *The Atlantic*, July 26, 2023, https://www.theatlantic.com/ideas/archive/2023/07/trump-2024-election-candidacy-criminal-appeal/674827/.

15   Michael Balsamo, "Trump blurs lines between personal lawyer, attorney general," Associated Press, September 29, 2019, https://apnews.com/article/donald-trump-ap-top-news-joe-biden-politics-impeachments-7d134da3dadd497e9af37c60278d68dc.

16   Ankush Khardori, "The Sequel Will Be Worse: Trump's former Justice Department officials fear a second term," *New York*, July 10, 2023, https://nymag.com/intelligencer/2023/07/trumps-ex-justice-department-officials-fear-a-second-term.html.

17   Chris Pandolfo, "John Bolton predicts Trump would withdraw from NATO in second term," Fox News, August 4, 2023, https://www.foxnews.com/politics/john-bolton-predicts-trump-withdraw-nato-second-term.

18   Edward Luce, "Putin holds a trump card in the 2024 US election," *The Financial Times*, May 15, 2023, https://www.ft.com/content/f44e81e6-3401-4e06-94e6-a24a952d6a40.

19   Kerry Picket, "Trump plans to abolish US Education Department if elected," *The Washington Times,* March 4, 2023, https://www.washingtontimes.com/news/2023/mar/4/trump-plans-abolish-us-education-department-if-ele/.

20   Brett Samuels, "Trump in DC speech calls for death penalty for convicted drug dealers," *The Hill,* July 26, 2022, https://thehill.com/homenews/campaign/3575157-trump-in-dc-speech-calls-for-death-penalty-for-convicted-drug-dealers/.

21   Brian Bennett, "Trump Calls for Moving Homeless to 'Tent Cities' in First DC Speech Since Leaving Office," *Time,* July 26, 2022, https://time.com/6200821/trump-homeless-tent-cities-2024/.

22   Greg Sargent, "Trump's awful threat to separate families should wake up Democrats," *The Washington Post,* May 12, 2023, https://www.washingtonpost.com/opinions/2023/05/12/trump-cnn-town-hall-family-separations-house-gop/.

23   Chas Danner, "Watch Trump Fondle an American Flag at CPAC," *New York,* February 29, 2020, https://nymag.com/intelligencer/2020/02/watch-trump-fondle-an-american-flag-at-cpac.html.

24   Robert Kagan, "This is how fascism comes to America," *The Washington Post,* May 17, 2016, https://www.washingtonpost.com/opinions/this-is-how-fascism-comes-to-america/2016/05/17/c4e32c58-1c47-11e6-8c7b-6931e66333e7_story.html.

25   Matt Ford, "It Matters That Joe Biden Used the F-Word," *The New Republic,* August 29, 2022, https://newrepublic.com/article/167563/biden-semi-fascism-maga-2022.

26   Andrew Mark Miller, "Trump blasts Biden's anti-MAGA speech: 'He's the enemy of the state'," Fox News, September 3, 2022, https://www.foxnews.com/politics/trump-blasts-bidens-anti-maga-speech-hes-enemy-state.

27   "Trump calls FBI search of Mar-a-Lago a 'travesty of justice,'" *Al Jazeera,* September 4, 2022, https://www.aljazeera.com/news/2022/9/4/trump-calls-fbi-search-of-mar-a-lago-as-travesty-of-justice.

28   Tom Nichols, "Trump Crosses a Crucial Line," *The Atlantic,* November 16, 2023, https://www.theatlantic.com/newsletters/archive/2023/11/trump-crosses-a-crucial-line/676031/?fbclid=IwAR3dQw30Qwj9CyRPgdwNpJ1ch-1ZDtK4dLQ3xgomSrIUhbpUr206yReipH8.

29   Jonathan Chait, "How to Make a Semi-Fascist Party," *New York,* October 12, 2022, https://nymag.com/intelligencer/2022/10/how-to-make-a-semi-fascist-party.html?utm_source=tw&utm_medium=s1&utm_campaign=nym.

30   Umberto Eco, "Ur-Fascism," *The New York Review of Books,* June 22, 1995, https://web.archive.org/web/20170131155837/http://www.nybooks.com/articles/1995/06/22/ur-fascism/.

31   Madeleine Albright, *Fascism: A Warning* (New York: Harper, 2018), 11.

32   David Frum, "There's a Word for What Trumpism Is Becoming," *The Atlantic*, July 13, 2021, https://www.theatlantic.com/ideas/archive/2021/07/theres-word-what-trumpism-becoming/619418/.

Chapter 6: Systemic Reforms (One)

1   Nicholas, Guyatt, "How liberals invented segregation: The real history of race, equality and our Founding Fathers," *Salon*, April 24, 2016, https://www.salon.com/2016/04/24/how_liberals_invented_segregation_the_real_history_of_race_equality_and_our_founding_fathers/.

2   "Republicans Use Filibuster to Block Voting Rights Bill," *The New York Times*, June 22, 2021, https://www.nytimes.com/live/2021/06/22/us/joe-biden-news.

3   "Republicans Block a Second Voting Rights Bill in the Senate," *The New York Times*, November 3, 2021, https://www.nytimes.com/2021/11/03/us/politics/senate-republicans-voting-rights-act.html.

4   "Joe Manchin and Kyrsten Sinema Literally High-Fived Over Their Refusal to End the Filibuster," *The New Republic*, January 17, 2023, https://newrepublic.com/post/170050/joe-manchin-kyrsten-sinema-high-fived-refusal-end-filibuster.

5   "Congress has a massive voting rights bill in its grasp. It must pass it, now," *The Guardian*, September 22, 2021, https://www.theguardian.com/commentisfree/2021/sep/22/congress-must-pass-voting-rights-bill.

6   Rep. Mike Simpson (R.-Ida.), "We Must Stop Democrats' Attempts to Take Over Federal Elections and Focus on Real Solutions," press release, May 9, 2022, https://simpson.house.gov/news/documentsingle.aspx?DocumentID=399497.

7   Kendall Karson and Meg Cunningham, "GOP warns HR 1 could be 'absolutely devastating for Republicans'," ABC News, March 20, 2021, https://abcnews.go.com/Politics/gop-warns-hr-absolutely-devastating-republicans/story?id=76555647.

8   "Free and Slave Populations by State (1790)," Teaching American History, https://teachingamericanhistory.org/resource/the-constitutional-convention-free-and-slave-populations-by-state-1790/.

9   "Population Estimate for 2022," StatsAmerica, Indiana University Kelley School of Business, https://www.statsamerica.org/sip/rank_list.aspx?rank_label=pop1.

10 Nancy Gibbs, "Newspapers are disappearing where democracy needs them most," *The Washington Post*, December 27, 2022, https://www.washingtonpost.com/opinions/2022/12/27/newspapers-disappearing-democracy-media/.

11 "Voters by Race By State," World Population Review, updated January 2023, https://worldpopulationreview.com/state-rankings/voters-by-race-by-state.

12 Alistair Dawber, "'Traitor' Liz Cheney feels the hatred as Republican schism widens," *The Times* (UK), February 19, 2022, https://www.thetimes.co.uk/article/traitor-liz-cheney-feels-the-hatred-as-republican-schism-widens-37mwl7qsk.

13 Nancy Benac, "Founding Fathers distrusted popular vote to pick a president," Associated Press, December 15, 2016, https://apnews.com/article/a80eba04186f4416a8c3d198d4023b31.

14 Levitsky and Ziblatt, *How Democracies Die*, 40.

15 Akhil Reed Amar, "The Troubling Reason the Electoral College Exists," *Time*, October 29, 2020, https://time.com/4558510/electoral-college-history-slavery/.

16 Jonathan V. Last, *The Bulwark*, July 9, 2022, https://plus.thebulwark.com/p/ranking-the-nightmares.

17 "National Popular Vote Interstate Compact," Ballotpedia, https://ballotpedia.org/National_Popular_Vote_Interstate_Compact.

18 "'Gerrymandering On Steroids': How Republicans Stacked The Nation's Statehouses," WBUR, July 19, 2016, https://www.wbur.org/hereandnow/2016/07/19/gerrymandering-republicans-redmap.

19 Ibid.

20 Elizabeth Kolbert, "Drawing the Line," *The New Yorker*, June 20, 2016, https://www.newyorker.com/magazine/2016/06/27/ratfcked-the-influence-of-redistricting.

21 David Daley, *Ratf**ked: The True Story Behind the Secret Plan to Steal America's Democracy* (New York: W.W. Norton, 2016), xvii.

22 Ari Berman, "The Courts Won't End Gerrymandering. Eric Holder Has a Plan to Fix It Without Them," *Mother Jones*, August 2019, https://www.motherjones.com/politics/2019/07/the-courts-wont-end-gerrymandering-eric-holder-has-a-plan-to-fix-it-without-them/.

23 Daley, *Ratf**ked*.

24 David Wasserman, "The six types of races that will decide control of the House in 2022," NBC News, September 21, 2022, https://www.nbcnews.com/politics/2022-election/six-types-races-will-decide-control-house-2022-rcna47412.

25 Michael Wines, "Maps in Four States Were Ruled Illegal Gerrymanders. They're Being Used Anyway," *The New York Times*, Au-

gust 8, 2022, https://www.nytimes.com/2022/08/08/us/elections/
gerrymandering-maps-elections-republicans.html.

26   Berman, "The Courts Won't End Gerrymandering."

27   Scott Bomboy, "Filibustering in the Modern Senate," National Constitution Center, December 9, 2022, https://constitutioncenter.org/blog/
filibustering-in-the-modern-senate.

28   Levitsky and Ziblatt, *How Democracies Die,* 135.

29   Burgess Everett and Seung Min Kim, "Judge not: GOP blocks dozens of
Obama court picks," *Politico,* July 6, 2015, https://www.politico.com/sto-
ry/2015/07/payback-gop-blocks-obama-judge-picks-judiciary-119743.

30   Alison Graves, "Did Senate Republicans filibuster Obama court
nominees more than all others combined?" PolitiFact, April 9, 2017,
https://www.politifact.com/factchecks/2017/apr/09/ben-cardin/
did-senate-republicans-filibuster-obama-court-nomi/.

31   Matthew Yglesias, "Mitch McConnell may be the greatest strategist
in contemporary politics," *Vox,* November 4, 2014, https://www.vox.
com/2014/11/4/7158293/mitch-mcconnell-strategist.

32   Jillian Reyfield, "Poll: Congress less popular than cockroaches, Nickelback,"
Salon, January 8, 2013, https://www.salon.com/2013/01/08/poll_congress_
less_popular_than_cockroaches_nickelback/.

33   C-SPAN, September 19, 2006, https://www.c-span.org/video/?194351-2/
senate-session.

34   Jane C. Timm, "McConnell went 'nuclear' to confirm Gorsuch.
But Democrats changed Senate filibuster rules first," NBC News,
June 28, 2018, https://www.nbcnews.com/politics/donald-trump/
mcconnell-went-nuclear-confirm-gorsuch-democrats-changed-senate-
filibuster-rules-n887271.

35   "About Filibusters and Cloture | Historical Overview," Senate.gov, https://
www.senate.gov/about/powers-procedures/filibusters-cloture/overview.htm.

36   Sarah A. Binder, "The History of the Filibuster," The Brookings
Institution, April 22, 2010, https://www.brookings.edu/articles/
the-history-of-the-filibuster/.

37   Louis Jacobson, "Fact-check: Have there been about 160 carve-outs
to the filibuster?" *The Austin American-Statesman,* December 11, 2021,
https://www.statesman.com/story/news/politics/politifact/2021/12/11/
fact-check-have-there-been-160-carve-outs-filibuster/6460696001/.

38   Elie Mystal, "The Senate Cannot Be Reformed—It Can Only Be Abolished,"
The Nation, November 12, 2021, https://www.thenation.com/article/politics/
abolish-us-senate/.

39   David Waldstreicher, "How the Constitution Was Indeed Pro-Slavery," *The Atlantic*, September 19, 2015, https://www.theatlantic.com/politics/archive/2015/09/how-the-constitution-was-indeed-pro-slavery/406288/.

40   Gerald Seib, "The Varied—and Global—Threats Confronting Democracy," *The Wall Street Journal*, November 21, 2017, https://www.wsj.com/articles/the-variedand-globalthreats-confronting-democracy-1511193763.

41   Eric W. Orts, "The Path to Give California 12 Senators, and Vermont Just One," *The Atlantic*, January 2, 2019, https://www.theatlantic.com/ideas/archive/2019/01/heres-how-fix-senate/579172/.

42   Mystal, "The Senate Cannot Be Reformed."

43   Ibid.

44   Danielle Allen, "The House was supposed to grow with population. It didn't. Let's fix that," *The Washington Post*, February 28, 2023, https://www.washingtonpost.com/opinions/2023/02/28/danielle-allen-democracy-reform-congress-house-expansion/.

45   Danielle Allen, "Just how big should the House be? Let's do the math," *The Washington Post*, March 28, 2023, https://www.washingtonpost.com/opinions/2023/03/28/danielle-allen-democracy-reform-house-representatives-districts/.

46   Danielle Allen, "Can the Capitol hold a much bigger House? Yes, here's how it would look," *The Washington Post*, May 2, 2023, https://www.washingtonpost.com/opinions/interactive/2023/capitol-house-representatives-expansion-design/?itid=ap_danielleallen&itid=lk_inline_manual_20.

47   Allen, "The House was supposed to grow."

48   Allen, "Just how big should the House be?"

49   Allen, "The House was supposed to grow."

50   Ephrat Livni, "Americans trust the Supreme Court more than other government branches," *Quartz*, October 26, 2019, https://qz.com/1735709/americans-trust-supreme-court-more-than-other-government-branches.

51   Jeffrey M. Jones, "Supreme Court Trust, Job Approval at Historical Lows," Gallup, September 29, 2022, https://news.gallup.com/poll/402044/supreme-court-trust-job-approval-historical-lows.aspx.

52   "Tracking the Trump criminal cases," *Politico*, June 13, 2023, https://www.politico.com/interactives/2023/trump-criminal-investigations-cases-tracker-list/.

53   Jack M. Balkin, "Why Liberals and Conservatives Flipped on Judicial Restraint: Judicial Review in the Cycles of Constitutional Time," *Texas Law Review*, December 2019, https://texaslawreview.org/why-liberals-and-conservatives-flipped-on-judicial-restraint-judicial-review-in-the-cycles-of-constitutional-time/.

54 "The Democrats' Plan To Pack The Supreme Court," Republican Policy Committee, April 22, 2021, https://www.Rpc.Senate.Gov/Policy-Papers/The-Democrats-Plan-To-Pack-The-Supreme-Court.

55 Tim Groseclose and Dennis Prager, "522 Justices? 2020 Could Set off a Supreme Court Packing Arms Race," *The National Interest*, October 17, 2020, https://nationalinterest.org/blog/2020-election/522-justices-2020-could-set-supreme-court-packing-arms-race-170.

56 Daniel Epps and William Ortman, "The Lottery Docket," *Michigan Law Review*, vol. 116, issue 5 (2018), https://repository.law.umich.edu/mlr/vol116/iss5/2/.

57 "Inside Pete Buttigieg's plan to overhaul the Supreme Court," NBC News, June 23, 2019, https://www.nbcnews.com/politics/2020-election/inside-pete-buttigieg-s-plan-overhaul-supreme-court-n1012491#:~:text=Under%20the%20plan%2C%20most%20justices,the%20district%2Dlevel%20trial%20courts.

58 Matt Ford, "It's Time to Abolish Supreme Court Confirmation Hearings," *The New Republic*, April 4, 2022, https://newrepublic.com/article/165982/abolish-supreme-court-confirmation-hearings.

59 Steven Levitsky and Daniel Ziblatt, "How American Democracy Fell So Far Behind," *The Atlantic*, September 5, 2023, https://www.theatlantic.com/ideas/archive/2023/09/american-constitution-norway/675199/.

60 Justin Elliott, Joshua Kaplan, and Alex Mierjeski, "Justice Samuel Alito Took Luxury Fishing Vacation With GOP Billionaire Who Later Had Cases Before the Court," *ProPublica*, June 20, 2023, https://www.propublica.org/article/samuel-alito-luxury-fishing-trip-paul-singer-scotus-supreme-court.

61 Joshua Kaplan, Justin Elliott, and Alex Mierjeski, "Clarence Thomas Had a Child in Private School. Harlan Crow Paid the Tuition," *ProPublica*, May 4, 2023, https://www.propublica.org/article/clarence-thomas-harlan-crow-private-school-tuition-scotus.

62 Nicholas Wu and Kyle Cheney, "Ginni Thomas tells Jan. 6 panel she still believes false election fraud claims, chair says," *Politico*, September 29, 2022, https://www.politico.com/news/2022/09/29/ginni-thomas-jan-6-panel-false-election-fraud-claims-00059627.

63 Maura Ewing, "The Search for Progressive Judges," *The Atlantic*, May 17, 2019, https://www.theatlantic.com/politics/archive/2019/05/progressive-prosecutors-judges/589222/.

64 Klein, "The Supreme Court's Shock-and-Awe Judicial Coup."

65 Steven Levitsky and Daniel Ziblatt, *Tyranny of the Minority: Why American Democracy Reached the Breaking Point* (New York: Crown, 2023).

66 Steven Levitsky and Daniel Ziblatt, "How American Democracy Fell So Far Behind," *The Atlantic*, September 5, 2023, https://www.theatlantic.com/ideas/archive/2023/09/american-constitution-norway/675199/.

67 Michelle Goldberg, "The Authors of 'How Democracies Die' Overestimated the Republicans," *The New York Times*, September 11, 2023, https://www.nytimes.com/2023/09/11/opinion/columnists/democracies-minority-rule.html.

Chapter 7: Systemic Reforms (Two)

1 "Distribution of Electoral Votes," National Archives, Jun 26, 2023, https://www.archives.gov/electoral-college/allocation.

2 "Wyoming: 2020 Census," US Census Bureau, https://www.census.gov/library/stories/state-by-state/wyoming-population-change-between-census-decade.html.

3 "Wyoming Election Results," *The New York Times*, November 3, 2020, https://www.nytimes.com/interactive/2020/11/03/us/elections/results-wyoming.html.

4 David Brooks, "Why People Are Fleeing Blue Cities for Red States," *The New York Times*, April 13, 2023, https://www.nytimes.com/2023/04/13/opinion/sun-belt-migration.html.

5 Max Greenwood, "How Florida became a conservative bastion," *The Hill*, May 15, 2023, https://thehill.com/homenews/campaign/3998391-how-florida-became-a-conservative-bastion/.

6 Interview with Jim Bernfield, April 21, 2023.

7 Interview with Max Brooks, April 17, 2023.

8 Interview with Jim Bernfield.

9 Timothy Noah, "You'll Be Very Surprised Who's Benefiting Most From Bidenomics," *The New Republic*, July 12, 2023, https://newrepublic.com/article/174252/bidenomics-benefits-red-states-more-blue-states.

10 Interview with Jim Bernfield.

11 Emily Swanson, "AP VoteCast: How Black women shape Democratic politics," Associated Press, August 3, 2020, https://apnews.com/article/barack-obama-race-and-ethnicity-politics-immigration-america-disrupted-e4081df9b4f0ccef9d4af734acf15165.

12 Interview with Zoharah Simmons, July 26, 2023.

13 Interview with Jim Bernfield.

14 Rep. Ted Deutch, "Supreme Court's Citizens United mistake just turned 10 years old. It's time to reverse it," NBC News, January 21, 2020, https://www.nbcnews.com/think/opinion/

supreme-court-s-citizens-united-mistake-just-turned-ten-years-ncna1119826.

15   "More money, less transparency: A decade under Citizens United," Open Secrets, https://www.opensecrets.org/news/reports/a-decade-under-citizens-united.

16   Ibid.

17   "Crossroads GPS Outside Spending," Open Secrets, https://www.opensecrets.org/outside-spending/detail?cmte=C90011719&cycle=2012.

18   "More money, less transparency."

19   Ibid.

20   Ibid.

21   Interview with Darrick Hamilton for *Death and Taxes*, directed by Justin Schein, November 29, 2022.

22   "Large Versus Small Individual Donations," Open Secrets, https://www.opensecrets.org/elections-overview/large-vs-small-donations.

23   "Who are the Biggest Donors?" Open Secrets, https://www.opensecrets.org/elections-overview/biggest-donors.

24   "More money, less transparency."

25   Dave Levinthal, "FEC lays bare internal conflicts and challenges in letters to Congress," The Center for Public Integrity, May 9, 2019, https://publicintegrity.org/politics/federal-election-commission-congress-fec-conflict/.

26   Kenneth P. Vogel and Shane Goldmacher, "An Unusual $1.6 Billion Donation Bolsters Conservatives," *The New York Times*, August 22, 2022, https://www.nytimes.com/2022/08/22/us/politics/republican-dark-money.html.

27   Maria Ressa, *How to Stand Up to a Dictator* (New York: Harper, 2022), 137.

28   Ressa, *How to Stand Up to a Dictator*, 142.

29   Interview with Tim Heaphy.

30   Ibid.

31   Jesse Washington, "We finally have answers about Michael Jordan and 'Republicans buy sneakers, too,'" *Andscape*, May 4, 2020, https://andscape.com/features/we-finally-have-answers-about-michael-jordan-and-republicans-buy-sneakers-too/.

32   Rachael Revesz, "Donald Trump boasted about meeting semi-naked teenagers in beauty pageants," *The Independent*, October 12, 2016, https://www.independent.co.uk/news/world/americas/donald-trump-former-miss-arizona-tasha-dixon-naked-undressed-backstage-howard-stern-a7357866.html.

33   Ressa, *How to Stand Up to a Dictator*, 142.

34   Katie Canales, "Social media was once a neutral battleground. Now, both Republicans and Democrats have demonized them to drive political agendas," *Business Insider*, October 27, 2021,

https://www.businessinsider.com/how-tech-social-media-platforms-were-politicized-content-moderation-2021-10.

35 William G. Gale and Darrell M. West, "Make Election Day a national holiday," The Brookings Institution, June 23, 2021, https://www.brookings.edu/articles/make-election-day-a-national-holiday/.

36 Richard Pildes, "Two myths about the unruly American primary system," *The Washington Post*, May 25, 2016, https://www.washingtonpost.com/news/monkey-cage/wp/2016/05/25/two-myths-about-the-unruly-american-primary-system/.

37 Fareed Zakaria, "America is now a tyranny of the minority," *The Washington Post*, October 27, 2022, https://www.washingtonpost.com/opinions/2022/10/27/america-primaries-driving-polarization-radicalization/.

38 Mike Catalini, "Explainer: How ranked choice voting works in Alaska," Associated Press, November 9, 2022, https://apnews.com/article/alaska-ranked-choice-voting-5ae6c163af2f8a70a8f90928267c4086.

39 Mark Weisbrot, "Debt Ceiling Has Become a Weapon Against Democracy in the United States," Center for Economic and Policy Research, June 1, 2023, https://cepr.net/the-debt-ceiling-fight-was-never-about-debt-it-was-about-republican-power/.

40 Interview with Max Brooks.

41 Interview with Democratic official, May 2023.

42 Interview with Democratic official.

43 Sam Levine, "Federal court rules Florida felons must pay off debts to state before voting," *The Guardian*, September 11, 2020, https://www.theguardian.com/us-news/2020/sep/11/florida-felons-vote-debts-ruling-election.

44 Interview with Democratic official.

Chapter 8: Broader-Based Efforts

1 Interview with Tim Heaphy.

2 Ibid.

3 Paul D. Eaton, Antonio M. Taguba, and Steven M. Anderson, "3 retired generals: The military must prepare now for a 2024 insurrection," *The Washington Post*, December 17, 2021, https://www.washingtonpost.com/opinions/2021/12/17/eaton-taguba-anderson-generals-military/.

4 Interview with Tim Heaphy.

5 Andrew McCarthy, "Prosecuting Trump will ruin our nation — and might not hold him accountable," *The Hill*, June 27, 2022, https://thehill.com/opinion/white-house/3537622-prosecuting-trump-will-ruin-our-nation-and-might-not-hold-him-accountable/.

6   Chip Muir, "Nine reasons Biden should pardon Trump," *The Hill*, June
      18, 2023, https://thehill.com/opinion/criminal-justice/4049903-nine-
      reasons-biden-should-pardon-trump/.

7   Michael Conway, "Why Biden should pardon Trump — and we
      Democrats should want him to," NBC News, November 17, 2020,
      https://www.nbcnews.com/think/opinion/why-biden-should-
      pardon-trump-we-democrats-should-want-him-ncna1247986.

8   Andrew C. McCarthy, "Prosecuting Trump could do
      more harm than good," *The Washington Post*, July 1, 2022,
      https://www.washingtonpost.com/opinions/2022/07/01/
      hutchinson-testimony-changes-calculus-on-indicting-trump/.

9   Ben Kamisar, "Almost a third of Americans still believe the 2020
      election result was fraudulent," NBC News, June 20, 2023,
      https://www.nbcnews.com/meet-the-press/meetthepressblog/
      almost-third-americans-still-believe-2020-election-result-was-
      fraudule-rcna90145.

10   Conway, "Why Biden should pardon Trump."

11   John Otis, "All the prison's presidents: Peru's special jail for ex-leaders is all
      full up," NPR, July 9, 2023, https://www.npr.org/2023/07/08/1186508281/
      peru-prison-ex-presidents#:~:text=LIMA%2C%20Peru%20—%20So%20
      many%20former,on%20the%20outskirts%20of%20Lima.

12   Heather Cox Richardson, "Letters from an American," June 13, 2023,
      https://heathercoxrichardson.substack.com/p/june-13-2023?utm_source=sub-
      stack&utm_medium=email&utm_content=share.

13   Ibid.

14   Reid J. Epstein and Lisa Lerer, "Democrats Are Determined to
      Pressure Biden to Investigate Trump," *The New York Times*, Janu-
      ary 9, 2021, https://www.nytimes.com/2021/01/09/us/politics/
      democrats-trump-crimes-prosecute.html.

15   Annie Grayer, "Capitol Police investigating after congressman dis-
      covered carrying a gun when attempting to go on the House floor,"
      CNN, January 22, 2021, https://www.cnn.com/2021/01/22/politics/
      congressman-gun-capitol/index.html.

16   Gessen, *Surviving Autocracy*, xvi.

17   Ibid., xix.

18   Interview with Tom Hall, "Back and Forth with The Back Row Man-
      ifesto," *The King's Necktie*, January 26, 2021, https://thekingsnecktie.
      com/2021/01/26/back-and-forth-with-the-back-row-manifesto/.

19   Philip Bump, "Trumpworld walks a line between predicting violence and
      threatening it," *The Washington Post*, August 29, 2022, https://www.washing-
      tonpost.com/politics/2022/08/29/trump-graham-violence/.

20 Rose Horowitch, "Trump warns of 'potential death and destruction' if he's charged in hush money probe," NBC News, March 24, 2023, https://www.nbcnews.com/politics/donald-trump/trump-warns-potential-death-destruction-charged-hush-money-probe-rcna76500.

21 Hannah Knowles, "GOP reacts to Trump search with threats and comparisons to 'Gestapo,'" *The Washington Post*, August 9, 2022, https://www.washingtonpost.com/politics/2022/08/09/trump-search-gop-reaction/.

22 Michelle Goldberg, "The Absurd Argument Against Making Trump Obey the Law," *The New York Times*, August 11, 2022, https://www.nytimes.com/2022/08/11/opinion/trump-fbi-raid.html.

23 Ibid.

24 Andrew Desiderio, "Senate Republicans uniting behind impeachment defense," *Politico*, January 21, 2021, https://www.politico.com/news/2021/01/21/senate-republicans-uniting-impeachment-defense-461217.

25 Knowles, "GOP reacts to Trump search with threats and comparisons to 'Gestapo.'"

26 Harold Maass, "The FBI's Mar-a-Lago raid: Who's wrong and who's right?" *The Week*, August 12, 2022, https://theweek.com/feature/opinion/1015868/the-gops-anger-over-the-fbi-raid-of-trumps-house.

27 Dan Ladden-Hall, "Florida Lawmaker Calls for FBI Agents to Be 'Arrested Upon Sight' After Trump Raid," *The Daily Beast*, August 9, 2022, https://www.thedailybeast.com/anthony-sabatini-florida-lawmaker-calls-for-fbi-agents-to-be-arrested-upon-sight-after-trump-raid.

28 Michael Luciano, "Mark Levin Declares FBI Raid on Mar-a-Lago 'The Worst Attack on This Republic in Modern History,'" *Mediaite*, August 8, 2022, https://www.mediaite.com/tv/mark-levin-declares-fbi-raid-on-mar-a-lago-the-worst-attack-on-this-republic-in-modern-history/.

29 Noah Berlatsky, "The FBI raid on Mar-a-Lago is the best thing that ever happened to the Republican Party," *The Independent*, August 9, 2022, https://www.independent.co.uk/voices/fbi-raid-mar-a-lago-republican-party-best-b2141808.html.

30 Alyssa Quart, *Bootstrapped: Liberating Ourselves from the American Dream* (New York: Harper Collins, 2023).

31 Gudrun Østby, "Inequality and political conflict," World Social Science Report 2016, UNESCO, 2016, https://en.unesco.org/inclusivepolicylab/sites/default/files/analytics/document/2019/4/wssr_2016_chap_25.pdf.

32 Interview with Amy Hanauer for *Death and Taxes*, directed by Justin Schein, March 31, 2023.

33   Josh Rogin, "Trump got played by Kim Jong Un—again," *The Washington Post*, February 28, 2019, https://www.washingtonpost.com/opinions/global-opinions/trump-got-played-by-kim-jong-un–again/2019/02/28/784a3228-3b8f-11e9-a2cd-307b06d0257b_story.html.

34   Samuel M. Hickey, "A worthless withdrawal: Two years since President Trump abandoned the JCPOA," Center for Arms Control and Non-Proliferation, May 11, 2020, https://armscontrolcenter.org/a-worthless-withdrawal-two-years-since-president-trump-abandoned-the-jcpoa/.

35   Eric Lutz, "Trump Privately Discussed Destroying NATO Alliance," *Vanity Fair*, January 15, 2019, https://www.vanityfair.com/news/2019/01/trump-privately-discussed-destroying-nato-alliance.

36   Luke Denne and Charlotte Gardiner, "Former US officials criticize Trump's decision to 'abandon' Kurds," NBC News, November 17, 2019, https://www.nbcnews.com/news/world/former-u-s-officials-criticize-trump-s-decision-abandon-kurds-n1084156.

37   Chrissy Stroop, "Republicans still have 'tremendous affection for dictators,'" *Open Democracy*, March 22, 2023, https://www.opendemocracy.net/en/5050/republicans-desantis-admiration-putin-orban-bolsanoro-ukraine/.

38   "Trump impeachment: The short, medium and long story," *BBC News*, February 5, 2020, https://www.bbc.com/news/world-us-canada-49800181.

39   Craig Unger, "How Republicans Spent Decades Cozying Up to Putin's Kremlin," *The New Republic*, March 18, 2022, https://newrepublic.com/article/165782/republicans-putin-history-relationship-manafort.

Chapter 9: Onto the Barricades

1   Keeanga Yamahtta Taylor, "The Case for Ending the Supreme Court as We Know It," *The New Yorker*, September 25, 2020, https://www.newyorker.com/news/our-columnists/the-case-for-ending-the-supreme-court-as-we-know-it.

2   Snyder, *On Tyranny*, 17.

3   Remarks on the twenty-third anniversary of the emancipation of West India, August 4, 1857; Social History for Every Classroom, American Social History Project, https://shec.ashp.cuny.edu/items/show/1245.

4   Gene Sharp, *The Politics of Nonviolent Action* (Boston: Porter Sargent Publishers, 1973), 16.

5   Ibid., 29.

6   Jonathan Schell, *The Unconquerable World: Power, Nonviolence, and the Will of the People* (New York: Holt Paperbacks, 2004), 241.

7   Ibid., 220–222.

8   Adolf Hitler, quoted in Sharp, *The Politics of Nonviolent Action*, 43.

9   Sharp, *The Politics of Nonviolent Action*, 44.

10   Ibid., 47 (quoting Errol E. Harris, "Political Power," *Ethics*, vol. XLVIII, no. 1, October 1957, 10).

11   Ibid., 30.

12   Interview with Zoharah Simmons.

13   Ibid.

14   Kevin Sullivan and Lori Rozsa, "DeSantis doubles down on claim that some Blacks benefited from slavery," *The Washington Post*, July 22, 2023, https://www.washingtonpost.com/politics/2023/07/22/desantis-slavery-curriculum/.

15   Interview with Zoharah Simmons.

16   Interview with Jon Else, March 29, 2023.

17   Ibid.

18   Interview with Norvel Goff.

19   Interview with James Carroll.

20   "Parks, Rosa," Stanford University, The Martin Luther King Jr. Research and Education Institute, https://kinginstitute.stanford.edu/encyclopedia/parks-rosa.

21   Taylor-Dior Rumble, "Claudette Colvin: The 15-year-old who came before Rosa Parks," *BBC News*, March 10, 2018, https://www.bbc.com/news/stories-43171799.

22   "Anti-overhaul protesters call to turn up heat as over 300,000 estimated at rallies," *The Times of Israel*, March 11, 2023, https://www.timesofisrael.com/anti-overhaul-protesters-call-to-turn-up-heat-as-over-300000-estimated-at-rallies/.

23   "Tactics," Nonviolence International, https://www.tactics.nonviolenceinternational.net/tactics.

24   Steve Crawshaw and John Jackson, *Small Acts of Resistance* (New York: Union Square Press, 2010).

25   Sharp, *The Politics of Nonviolent Action,* 330.

26   Ibid., 416–417.

27   Ibid., 199.

28   Ibid., 237.

29   Ibid., 244.

30   James M. Lindsay, "TWE Remembers: Thich Quang Duc's Self-Immolation," *Council on Foreign Relations*, June 11, 2012, https://www.cfr.org/blog/twe-remembers-thich-quang-ducs-self-immolation#:~:text=That%20was%20not%20the%20case,backed%20president%20of%20South%20Vietnam.

31 Robin Wright, "How the Arab Spring Became the Arab Cataclysm," *The New Yorker*, December 15, 2015, https://www.newyorker.com/news/news-desk/arab-spring-became-arab-cataclysm.

32 "Iran: Child detainees subjected to flogging, electric shocks and sexual violence in brutal protest crackdown," Amnesty International, March 16, 2023, https://www.amnesty.org/en/latest/news/2023/03/iran-child-detainees-subjected-to-flogging-electric-shocks-and-sexual-violence-in-brutal-protest-crackdown/?fbclid=IwAR0n6BZlFtXQrj UzirI3IUiH3Nlx5HVSaooBAnh9duNdTAp9oBQAXyGXyG4.

33 Schell, *The Unconquerable World*, 119.

34 Ibid., 127.

35 Ibid., 139.

36 Ibid., 195.

37 Ibid., 193–194.

38 Malcolm Gladwell, "Small Change," *The New Yorker*, September 27, 2010, https://www.newyorker.com/magazine/2010/10/04/small-change-malcolm-gladwell.

39 Ibid.

40 Ibid.

41 Schell, *The Unconquerable World*, 243.

42 Interview with Jon Else.

43 Sharp, *The Politics of Nonviolent Action*, 112–113.

44 Interview with Zoharah Simmons.

45 Interview with Jon Else.

46 Ibid.

47 Steven V. Roberts, "Senate, 78 to 21, Overrides Reagan's Veto and Imposes Sanctions on South Africa," *The New York Times*, https://www.nytimes.com/1986/10/03/politics/senate-78-to-21-overrides-reagans-veto-and-imposes-sanctions-on.html.

48 Interview with Alix Kates Shulman, May 9, 2023.

49 Ibid.

50 Ibid.

51 Madeline Clarke, "Alexander Hamilton's Vision of an American Monarchy," *Compass*, December 11, 2020, https://compassjournal.org/https-alexander-hamiltons-vision-of-an-american-monarchy/.

52 Tom Jackman, "The FBI break-in that exposed J. Edgar Hoover's misdeeds to be honored with historical marker," *The Washington Post*, September 1, 2021, https://www.washingtonpost.com/history/2021/09/01/fbi-burglary-hoover-cointelpro/.

53 Interview with Jon Else.

54 "A break-in at a King of Prussia missile plant," *UPI*, April 3, 1981, https://www.upi.com/Archives/1981/04/03/A-break-in-at-a-King-of-Prussia-miss ile-plant/3667355122000/.

55 Interview with James Carroll.

56 Interview with Jon Else.

57 Ibid.

58 Interview with Zoharah Simmons.

59 Interview with Jon Else.

60 Ivan Marovic, *The Path of Most Resistance: A Step-by-Step Guide to Planning Nonviolent Campaigns* (Washington, DC: International Center on Nonviolent Conflict, 2018), 49.

61 Interview with Jon Else.

62 Interview with Norvel Goff.

63 Lieutenant General (Ret.) Harold G. Moore and Joseph L. Galloway, *We Were Soldiers Once . . . and Young: Ia Drang—The Battle That Changed the War in Vietnam* (New York: Random House, 1992).

64 Schell, *The Unconquerable World*, 7.

65 Colonel (Ret.) Harry Summers, *On Strategy: A Critical Analysis of the Vietnam War* (New York: Presidio Press, 1982).

66 Sharp, *The Politics of Nonviolent Action*, 546.

67 Ibid., 453.

68 Ibid., 681.

69 Ibid., 64.

70 Ibid., 70–74.

71 Ibid., 545.

72 Ibid., 586–589.

73 Ibid., 588.

74 Ibid., 586.

75 Sir Basil Liddell Hart, "Lessons from Resistance Movements—Guerilla and Nonviolent," *Civilian Resistance as a National Defense*, ed. Adam Roberts, (Baltimore, MD: Penguin, 1969), p205, and *Defence of the West: Some Riddles of War and Peace*, (London: Cassell, 1950), p53-57.

76 Erica Chenoweth and Maria Stephan, *Why Civil Resistance Works: The Strategic Logic of Nonviolent Conflict* (New York: Columbia University Press, 2010).

77 Schell, *The Unconquerable World*, 131.

78 Ibid., 184.

79 Ibid., 9.

80 Alinsky, *Rules for Radicals*, 44.

81 Ibid., 38–41.

82 Sharp, *The Politics of Nonviolent Action*, 597.

83   Omar Wasow, "Agenda Seeding: How 1960s Black Protests Moved
     Elites, Public Opinion and Voting," Cambridge University Press,
     May 21, 2020, https://www.cambridge.org/core/journals/american-
     political-science-review/article/agenda-seeding-how-1960s-black-
     protests-moved-elites-public-opinion-and-voting/136610C8C040C3
     D92F041BB2EFC3034C.

84   Thaddeus Morgan, "The NRA Supported Gun Control When the Black
     Panthers Had the Weapons," History.com, August 31, 2018, https://www.
     history.com/news/black-panthers-gun-control-nra-support-mulford-act.

85   Ruth Gebreyesus, "'One of the biggest, baddest things we did':
     Black Panthers' free breakfasts, 50 years on," *The Guardian*, Octo-
     ber 18, 2019, https://www.theguardian.com/us-news/2019/oct/17/
     black-panther-party-oakland-free-breakfast-50th-anniversary.

86   Mark Rudd, "I Was Part of the Weather Underground. Violence Is Not
     the Answer," *The New York Times*, March 5, 2020, https://www.nytimes.
     com/2020/03/05/opinion/weathermen-greenwich-village-explosion.html.

Chapter 10: It's the Economy, Stupid

1   Atkins, "Saving Democracy Will Require Institutional and Civil Resistance
    at All Levels."

2   Mark Muro, Eli Byerly-Duke, Yang You, and Robert Maxim,
    "Biden-voting counties equal 70% of America's economy. What does
    this mean for the nation's political-economic divide?" The Brookings
    Institution, November 10, 2020, https://www.brookings.edu/blog/
    the-avenue/2020/11/09/biden-voting-counties-equal-70-of-
    americas-economy-what-does-this-mean-for-the-nations-political-
    economic-divide/.

3   "2023's Most and Least Federally Dependent States," Wal-
    letHub, March 15, 2023, https://wallethub.com/edu/
    states-most-least-dependent-on-the-federal-government/2700.

4   Greg Sargent, "Inside the GOP playbook: Attack 'woke' corpo-
    rations, protect their low tax rates," *The Washington Post*, April 14,
    2021, https://www.washingtonpost.com/opinions/2021/04/14/
    republicans-woke-corporations-taxes/.

5   Johanna Chisholm, "Toyota attacked by anti-Trump group after re-
    suming donations to Republicans who contested 2020 election cer-
    tifying the 2020 election results," *The Independent*, April 17, 2022,
    https://www.independent.co.uk/news/world/americas/us-politics/
    toyota-lincoln-project-ad-campaign-b2066649.html.

6   "AT&T, One America News to keep ad deal even after DirecTV drops network," Reuters, March 14, 2022, https://www.reuters.com/business/media-telecom/att-one-america-news-keep-ad-deal-even-after-directv-drops-network-2022-03-14/.

7   Levitsky and Ziblatt, *How Democracies Die*, 219.

8   "Boycotts and the bottom line," Kellogg School of Management, Northwestern University, https://www.kellogg.northwestern.edu/news_articles/2011/boycotts.aspx.

9   James Surowiecki, "The Bitter Truth About the Bud Light Boycott," *The Atlantic*, June 19, 2023, https://www.theatlantic.com/ideas/archive/2023/06/bud-light-boycott-consumer-effect/674446/.

10   Alinsky, *Rules for Radicals*, 159.

11   Justin Kirkland, "Chick-fil-a's Owner Is Newly Connected to Anti-Equality Act Donations," *Esquire*, June 3, 2021, https://www.esquire.com/food-drink/restaurants/a36622217/chick-fil-a-owner-donations-against-equality-act/.

12   Helen Reid, "Target Pride backlash exposes 'rainbow capitalism' problem, designer says," Reuters, May 31, 2023, https://www.reuters.com/business/retail-consumer/target-pride-backlash-exposes-rainbow-capitalism-problem-designer-says-2023-05-31/.

13   John Casey, "Boycott Budweiser for Validating Trans Hate," *The Advocate*, April 17, 2023, https://www.advocate.com/voices/budweiser-boycott-dylan-mulvaney.

14   Adam Serwer, "Boycott Bans Are an Assault on Free Speech," *The Atlantic*, March 9, 2023, https://www.theatlantic.com/ideas/archive/2023/03/supreme-court-arkansas-anti-israel-boycotts/673310/.

15   Martin Pengelly, "Goya Foods CEO repeats Trump's election lies, prompting calls for boycott," *The Guardian*, March 1, 2021, https://www.theguardian.com/us-news/2021/mar/01/goya-ceo-robert-unanue-cpac-donald-trump-boycott.

16   Eric Lach, "Brian Kemp Is the Martin Shkreli of Voter Suppression," *The New Yorker*, November 5, 2018, https://www.newyorker.com/news/current/brian-kemp-is-the-martin-shkreli-of-voter-suppression.

17   Interview with Jon Else.

18   Landon Thomas Jr. "Hedging Their (Political) Bets," *The New York Times*, October 3, 2007, https://www.nytimes.com/2007/10/03/business/03donate.html.

19   Interview with Democratic official, May 2023.

20   Jeffrey Sonnenfeld and Mark Penn, "How Big Business Fell Out of Love with the GOP," *Time*, March 9, 2023, https://time.com/6261170/big-business-fell-out-love-with-gop/.

21   Sharp, *The Politics of Nonviolent Action*, 75–76.

22   Ibid., 277–278.

23   Alissa J. Rubin, "May 1968: A Month of Revolution Pushed France Into the Modern World," *The New York Times*, May 5, 2018, https://www.nytimes.com/2018/05/05/world/europe/france-may-1968-revolution.html.

24   Interview with Amy Hanauer.

25   Paul Waldman, "Just How Much Do Republicans Hate Unions?" *The American Prospect*, February 13, 2014, https://prospect.org/power/just-much-republicans-hate-unions/.

26   Interview with Max Brooks.

27   "Union Membership Hits All-Time Low," The MacIver Institute, January 31, 2022, https://www.maciverinstitute.com/about-us/.

28   Niv Ellis, "Union membership falls to record low of 10.3 percent," *The Hill*, January 22, 2020, https://thehill.com/policy/finance/479400-union-membership-falls-to-record-low-of-103-percent.

29   Ari Berman, "How Wisconsin Became the GOP's Laboratory for Dismantling Democracy," *Mother Jones*, October 25, 2022, https://www.motherjones.com/politics/2022/10/wisconsin-2022-midterms-gerrymandering-redistricting-evers-michels/.

30   Alinsky, *Rules for Radicals*, 165–183.

31   "Saul Alinsky," Influence Watch, https://www.influencewatch.org/person/saul-alinsky/.

32   Alinsky, *Rules for Radicals*, 137.

33   Interview with Norvel Goff.

34   George Will, "Paul Ryan rethinks the 'makers' and 'takers' idea," *The Washington Post*, August 29, 2014, https://www.washingtonpost.com/opinions/george-f-will-paul-ryan-rethinks-the-makers-and-takers-idea/2014/08/29/62d02090-2ee4-11e4-9b98-848790384093_story.html.

35   Muro, Byerly-Duke, Yang, and Maxim, "Biden-voting counties equal 70% of America's economy."

36   Paul Krugman, "Can Anything Be Done to Assuage Rural Rage?" *The New York Times*, January 26, 2023, https://www.nytimes.com/2023/01/26/opinion/rural-voters-economy.html.

37   David Montgomery, "What Will Happen to America if Trump Wins Again? Experts Helped Us Game It Out," *The Washington Post*, October 10, 2022, https://www.washingtonpost.com/magazine/2022/10/10/country-after-second-trump-term/.

38   Interview with physician, May 16, 2023.

39   Al Weaver, "Greene stirs up political storm with 'national divorce' com-
      ments," *The Hill*, February 2, 2023, https://thehill.com/homenews/house/38
      70038-greene-stirs-up-political-storm-with-national-divorce-comments/.
40   Ariel I. Ahram, "Returning Exiles to Iraqi Politics," Columbia University,
      Middle East Review of International Affairs, vol. 9, no. 1, March 2005, https://
      ciaotest.cc.columbia.edu/olj/meria/meria_mar05/meria05_aha01.pdf.

Chapter 11: Mrs. Orwell's Lament

1   Brian Stelter, "This infamous Steve Bannon quote is key to understanding
     America's crazy politics," CNN, November 11, 2021, https://www.cnn.
     com/2021/11/16/media/steve-bannon-reliable-sources/index.html.
2   Gessen, *Surviving Autocracy*.
3   A.M. Meerloo, *The Rape of the Mind: The Psychology of Thought Control, Menticide,
     and Brainwashing* (1956), 70, https://ia904508.us.archive.org/21/items/
     joost-meerloo-rape-of-the-mind/%20Joost%20Meerloo_Rape%20of%20
     the%20mind.pdf.
4   Glenn Kessler, Salvador Rizzo, and Meg Kelly, "Trump's false or mis-
     leading claims total 30,573 over 4 years," *The Washington Post*, January
     24, 2021, https://www.washingtonpost.com/politics/2021/01/24/
     trumps-false-or-misleading-claims-total-30573-over-four-years/.
5   Hannah Arendt, *The Origins of Totalitarianism* (New York: Schocken Books,
     1951).
6   Terry Gross (interview with Dana Millbank), "How the Republican
     Party came to embrace conspiracy theories and denialism," NPR/
     Fresh Air, August 9, 2021, https://www.npr.org/2022/08/09/
     1116281152/how-the-republican-party-came-to-embrace-conspiracy-
     theories-and-denialism.
7   Gessen, *Surviving Autocracy*, 113.
8   Margaret Sullivan, "A call to action for journalists cover-
     ing President Trump," *The Washington Post*, November 9, 2016,
     https://www.washingtonpost.com/lifestyle/style/a-call-to-act
     ion-for-journalists-in-covering-president-trump/2016/11/09/
     a87d4946-a63e-11e6-8042-f4d111c862d1_story.html?itid=lk_inline_man-
     ual_22.
9   "Russia is Europe's most dangerous country for journalists,
     Reporters Without Borders says," *EuroNews*, December 30, 2022,
     https://www.euronews.com/2022/12/30/russia-is-europes-most-
     dangerous-country-for-journalists-reporters-without-borders-says.

10 Christianna Silva, "Trump Was Horrified When He Won the White House and Melania Cried, Book Claims," *Newsweek*, January 3, 2018, https://www.newsweek.com/mike-pence-donald-jr-and-melania-never-thought-trump-would-become-president-769701.

11 "Stephen Colbert's Blistering Performance Mocking Bush and the Press Goes Ignored by the Media," *Democracy Now!*, May 3, 2006, https://www.democracynow.org/2006/5/3/stephen_colberts_blistering_performance_mocking_bush.

12 Eric Alterman, "How False Equivalence Is Distorting the 2016 Election Coverage," *The Nation*, June 2, 2016, https://www.thenation.com/article/archive/how-false-equivalence-is-distorting-the-2016-election-coverage/.

13 Eliana Johnson, "CNN Chief's Republican Apology Tour," *Washington Free Beacon*, August 1, 2022, https://freebeacon.com/media/chris-lichts-republican-apology-tour/.

14 Matt Gertz, "Mainstream outlets let the right set the terms of the Pennsylvania debate," *Media Matters*, October 26, 2022, https://www.mediamatters.org/fox-news/mainstream-outlets-let-right-set-terms-pennsylvania-debate.

15 Eric Wemple, "No, MSNBC is not the Fox News of the left," *The Washington Post*, November 7, 2022, https://www.washingtonpost.com/opinions/2022/11/07/oz-fetterman-fox-news-burns/.

16 Interview with Eric Alterman, March 22, 2023.

17 Aaron Short, "The Tucker Carlson origin story," *Business Insider*, May 5, 2022, https://www.businessinsider.com/the-tucker-carlson-origin-story-2022-5.

18 Alterman, "How False Equivalence Is Distorting the 2016 Election Coverage."

19 Nicco Mele, "It's Not Inevitable," *Substack*, January 9, 2022, https://nicco.substack.com/p/its-not-inevitable.

20 Ron Filipkowski, "How Democrats Can Win the Information War," *The Bulwark*, January 11, 2022, https://www.thebulwark.com/how-democrats-can-win-the-information-war/.

21 Valentina Vellani, Sarah Zheng, Dilay Ercelik, and Tali Sharot, "The illusory truth effect leads to the spread of misinformation," *Cognition*, vol. 236, July 2023, https://www.sciencedirect.com/science/article/pii/S0010027723000550.

22 Richard Sima, "Why do our brains believe lies?" *The Washington Post*, November 3, 2022, https://www.washingtonpost.com/wellness/2022/11/03/misinformation-brain-beliefs/.

23 Sima, "Why do our brains believe lies?"

24 Gordon Pennycook, Tyrone D. Cannon, and David G. Rand, "Prior exposure increases perceived accuracy of fake news," National Library of

Medicine, The National Center for Biotechnology Information, National institutes of Health, September 24, 2018, https://www.ncbi.nlm.nih.gov/pmc/
articles/PMC6279465/.

25   Marcia Apperson, "Consider Using a 'Truth Sandwich' to Counter Misinformation," PBS Standards, April 22, 2020, https://www.pbs.org/standards/
blogs/standards-articles/what-is-a-truth-sandwich/.

26   Sima, "Why do our brains believe lies?"

27   Ressa, *How to Stand Up to a Dictator*, 72.

28   Margaret Sullivan, "If Trump Runs Again, Do Not Cover Him the
Same Way: A Journalist's Manifesto," *The Washington Post*, October
12, 2022, https://www.washingtonpost.com/magazine/2022/10/12/
margaret-sullivan-how-media-should-cover-trump-next-campaign/.

29   Ibid.

30   Interview with Eric Alterman.

31   Sullivan, "If Trump Runs Again."

32   Eric Johnson, "NYU's Jay Rosen says 2020's political journalism will
be even worse than 2016's," *Vox*, January 24, 2019,
https://www.vox.com/2019/1/24/18195097/jay-rosen-trump-
politics-media-horse-race-recode-podcast-2020-predictions.

33   Sullivan, "If Trump Runs Again."

34   Alterman, "How False Equivalence Is Distorting the 2016 Election Coverage."

35   Ibid.

36   Margaret Sullivan, "He Said, She Said, and the Truth," *The New York Times*,
September 15, 2012, https://www.nytimes.com/2012/09/16/public-editor/
16pubed.html.

37   Dan Balz, Scott Clement, and Emily Guskin, "Republicans and Democrats
divided over Jan. 6 insurrection and Trump's culpability, Post-UMD poll
finds," *The Washington Post*, January 1, 2022, https://www.washingtonpost.
com/politics/2022/01/01/post-poll-january-6/.

38   Jennifer Rubin, "The media has given Republicans a free pass
on assaulting democracy," *The Washington Post*, December 7,
2021, https://www.washingtonpost.com/opinions/2021/12/07/
media-has-given-republicans-free-pass-assaulting-democracy/.

39   Ibid.

40   Eric Alterman, "Altercation: The Sins of the Mainstream Media," *The
American Prospect*, December 23, 2021, https://prospect.org/politics/
altercation-sins-of-the-mainstream-media/?fbclid=IwAR1ARb2DxbwdX-
6sSHYmppCoIU4FJrywilbL33O9eF0LIF59ZtL_tFSyQYns.

41   Ron Fournier, "Behind the Supreme Court Stalemate," *The Atlantic*, February 16, 2016, https://www.theatlantic.com/politics/archive/2016/02/the-supreme-court-stalemate/463026/.

42   Alterman, "How False Equivalence Is Distorting the 2016 Election Coverage."

43   Ibid.

44   Nicholas Confessore and Karen Yourish, "$2 Billion Worth of Free Media for Donald Trump," *The New York Times*, March 15, 2016, https://www.nytimes.com/2016/03/16/upshot/measuring-donald-trumps-mammoth-advantage-in-free-media.html.

45   Margaret Sullivan, "The media didn't want to believe Trump could win. So they looked the other way," *The Washington Post*, November 9, 2016, https://www.washingtonpost.com/lifestyle/style/the-media-didnt-want-to-believe-trump-could-win-so-they-looked-the-other-way/2016/11/09/d2ea1436-a623-11e6-8042-f4d111c862d1_story.html.

46   Sullivan, "A call to action for journalists covering President Trump."

47   Megan McArdle, "What journalists should do if Trump returns to Twitter," *The Washington Post*, October 28, 2022, https://www.washingtonpost.com/opinions/2022/10/28/elon-musk-trump-twitter-return/.

48   Ibid.

49   Ibid.

50   Ibid.

51   Brian Klaas, "The Case for Amplifying Trump's Insanity," *The Garden of Forking Paths*, October 1, 2023, https://www.forkingpaths.co/p/the-case-for-amplifying-trumps-insanity.

52   Gessen, "Autocracy: Rules for Survival."

53   Paul Farhi, "In Alabama, another small-town paper hit in 'open season' on free press," *The Washington Post*, November 27, 2023, https://www.washingtonpost.com/style/media/2023/11/27/atmore-news-arrests-alabama/.

54   Ressa, *How to Stand Up to a Dictator*, 238–242.

55   "Facing possible jail time totalling 100 years, journalist Maria Ressa says she won't stop fighting for justice," Canadian Broadcasting Corporation, June 18, 2020, https://www.cbc.ca/radio/thecurrent/the-current-for-june-18-2020-1.5616058/facing-possible-jail-time-totalling-100-years-journalist-maria-ressa-says-she-won-t-stop-fighting-for-justice-1.5617289.

56   Paterno R. Esmaquel Ii, "Duterte falsely claims CIA funds Rappler," *Rappler*, October 12, 2017, https://www.rappler.com/nation/185098-duterte-false-claim-cia-funds-rappler-american-ownership/.

57   Interview with Eric Alterman.

Chapter 12: Information Wants to Be Free

1   Sunny Kim, "How hedge funds took over America's struggling newspaper industry," CNBC, June 11, 2021, https://www.cnbc.com/2021/06/11/how-hedge-funds-took-over-americas-struggling-newspaper-industry-.html.

2   Nancy Gibbs, "Newspapers are disappearing where democracy needs them most," *The Washington Post*, December 27, 2022, https://www.washingtonpost.com/opinions/2022/12/27/newspapers-disappearing-democracy-media/.

3   Margaret Sullivan, "Every week, two more newspapers close—and 'news deserts' grow larger," *The Washington Post*, June 29, 2022, https://www.washingtonpost.com/media/2022/06/29/news-deserts-newspapers-democracy/.

4   Penny Abernathy, "The State Of Local News: The 2022 Report," Local News Initiative, Northwestern University, June 29, 2022, https://localnewsinitiative.northwestern.edu/research/state-of-local-news/report/.

5   Interview with Sally Kohn, June 28, 2023.

6   "Local Journalism Sustainability Act," News/Media Alliance, https://www.newsmediaalliance.org/advocacy/advocacy/local-journalism-sustainability-act/.

7   Abernathy, "The State Of Local News: The 2022 Report."

8   Sullivan, "Every week, two more newspapers close."

9   Gibbs, "Newspapers are disappearing where democracy needs them most."

10 Lucia Graves, "This is Sinclair, 'the most dangerous US company you've never heard of'," *The Guardian*, August 17, 2017, https://www.theguardian.com/media/2017/aug/17/sinclair-news-media-fox-trump-white-house-circa-breitbart-news.

11 Josh Dawsey and Hadas Gold, "Kushner: We struck deal with Sinclair for straighter coverage," *Politico*, December 16, 2016, https://www.politico.com/story/2016/12/trump-campaign-sinclair-broadcasting-jared-kushner-232764.

12 Cecilia Kang, Eric Lipton, and Sydney Ember, "How a Conservative TV Giant Is Ridding Itself of Regulation," *The New York Times*, August 4, 2017, https://www.nytimes.com/2017/08/14/us/politics/how-a-conservative-tv-giant-is-ridding-itself-of-regulation.html?_r=0.

13 Ryan Zickgraf, "How 'pink slime' journalism exploits our faith in local news," *The Washington Post*, August 15, 2022, https://www.washingtonpost.com/outlook/2022/08/12/pink-slime-jounrnalism-local-news/.

14 Ressa, *How to Stand Up to a Dictator*, 249.

15 Kristine McKenna, "Lots of Aura, No Air Play," *The Los Angeles Times*, May 23, 1982 (see also "Everyone Who Bought One of Those 30,000 Copies Started a Band," Quote Investigator, March 1, 2016, https://quoteinvestigator.com/2016/03/01/velvet/#f+13138+1+1.

16   "I. F. Stone's Weekly," Spartacus Educational, https://web.archive.
      org/web/20080316092317/http:/www.spartacus.schoolnet.co.uk/USAs-
      toneW.htm.

17   Filipkowski, "How Democrats Can Win the Information War."

18   Rubin, "The Media Has Given Republicans a Free Pass on Assaulting De-
      mocracy."

19   Filipkowski, "How Democrats Can Win the Information War."

20   Ibid.

21   Interview with Jim Bernfield.

22   Interview with Rob Schwartz, July 21, 2023.

23   Jelani Cobb, "Why I Quit Elon Musk's Twitter," *The New Yorker*, No-
      vember 27, 2022, https://www.newyorker.com/news/daily-comment/
      why-i-quit-elon-musks-twitter.

24   Taylor Lorenz, "Far-right Twitter influencers first on Elon Musk's moneti-
      zation scheme," *The Washington Post*, July 14, 2023, https://www.washington-
      post.com/technology/2023/07/13/twitter-creators-payments-right-wing/.

25   Tristan Rove, "Twitter just designated NPR as 'state-affiliated media'—and
      Elon Musk approved Twitter's policy rewrite to intentionally change
      its status," *Fortune*, April 5, 2023, https://fortune.com/2023/04/05/
      elon-musk-twitter-npr-state-affiliated-nyt-verification/.

26   Oliver O'Connell, "'That can't be good': Elon Musk and Rupert Mur-
      doch spark reaction by sitting together at Super Bowl," *The Independent*,
      February 13, 2023, https://www.independent.co.uk/news/world/americas/
      elon-musk-rupert-murdoch-super-bowl-b2280971.html.

27   Gladwell, "Small Change."

28   Mark Pfeifle, "A Nobel Peace Prize for Twitter?" *The Christian Science
      Monitor*, July 6, 2009, https://www.csmonitor.com/Commentary/Opin-
      ion/2009/0706/p09s02-coop.html.

29   Golnaz Esfandiari, "The Twitter Devolution," *Foreign Policy*, June 8, 2010,
      https://foreignpolicy.com/2010/06/08/the-twitter-devolution/.

30   Mike Musgrove, "Twitter Is a Player In Iran's Drama," *The Washington Post*,
      June 17, 2009, https://www.washingtonpost.com/wp-dyn/content/arti-
      cle/2009/06/16/AR2009061603391.html.

31   Ibid.

32   Gladwell, "Small Change."

33   Ibid.

34   Interview with Alix Kates Shulman.

35   Interview with Zoharah Simmons.

36   Gladwell, "Small Change."

37   Megan Garber, "We've Lost the Plot," *The Atlantic*, January 30, 2023, https://www.theatlantic.com/magazine/archive/2023/03/tv-politics-entertainment-metaverse/672773/.

38   Interview with Peter Hutchison, "Healing from Hate: A Conversation with Peter Hutchison," *The King's Necktie*, February 22, 2021, https://thekingsnecktie.com/2021/02/22/healing-from-hate-a-conversation-with-peter-hutchison/.

39   Mark O'Connell, "The Deliberate Awfulness of Social Media," *The New Yorker*, September 19, 2018, https://www.newyorker.com/books/under-review/the-deliberate-awfulness-of-social-media.

40   Ryan Singel, "War Breaks Out Between Hackers and Scientology," *Wired*, January 23, 2008, https://www.wired.com/2008/01/anonymous-attac/.

41   Joseph Menn, "Hacking Russia was off-limits. The Ukraine war made it a free-for-all," *The Washington Post*, May 1, 2022, https://www.washingtonpost.com/technology/2022/05/01/russia-cyber-attacks-hacking/.

Chapter 13: Hey Teacher, Leave Them Kids Alone

1   Terry Gross, "From slavery to socialism, new legislation restricts what teachers can discuss," NPR/*Fresh Air*, February 3, 2022, https://www.npr.org/2022/02/03/1077878538/legislation-restricts-what-teachers-can-discuss.

2   Adam Serwer, "The Fight Over the 1619 Project Is Not About the Facts," *The Atlantic*, December 23, 2019, https://www.theatlantic.com/ideas/archive/2019/12/historians-clash-1619-project/604093/.

3   Derrick Clifton, "How the Trump administration's '1776 Report' warps the history of racism and slavery," NBC News, January 20, 2021, https://www.nbcnews.com/news/nbcblk/how-trump-administration-s-1776-report-warps-history-racism-slavery-n1254926.

4   Interview with James Carroll.

5   Ja'han Jones, "Oklahoma uses racist education law to punish schools for offending white people," MSNBC, August 1, 2022, https://www.msnbc.com/the-reidout/reidout-blog/oklahoma-hb-1775-critical-race-theory-rcna40916

6   Adam Lankford, "Public Mass Shooters and Firearms: A Cross-National Study of 171 Countries," National Library of Medicine, The National Center for Biotechnology Information, National institutes of Health, 2016, https://pubmed.ncbi.nlm.nih.gov/26822013.

7   Stephanie Hughes, "Conservative groups are spending big on school board races," Marketplace, Nov 7, 2022, https://www.marketplace.org/2022/11/07/conservative-groups-are-spending-big-on-school-board-races/..

8   Heather Hollingsworth, "Conservatives take aim at tenure for university professors," Associated Press, January 8, 2023, https://apnews.com/article/politics-colleges-and-universities-florida-state-government-texas-education-4f0fe0c5c18ed227fabae3744e8ff51d.

9   Katie Robertson, "Nikole Hannah-Jones Denied Tenure at University of North Carolina," *The New York Times*, May 19, 2021, https://www.nytimes.com/2021/05/19/business/media/nikole-hannah-jones-unc.html.

10   Brynn Tannehill, "The Republican Plan To Devastate Public Education in America," *The New Republic*, August 11, 2022, https://newrepublic.com/article/167375/republican-plan-devastate-public-education-america.

11   Melissa Fares and Gina Cherelus, "Trump loves 'the poorly educated' . . . and social media clamors," Reuters, February 24, 2016, https://www.reuters.com/article/us-usa-election-trump-socialmedia/trump-loves-the-poorly-educated-and-social-media-clamors-id USKCN0VX26B.

12   Tannehill, "The Republican Plan To Devastate Public Education in America."

13   Interview with Shantel Palacio, April 6, 2023.

14   Ibid.

15   Ibid.

16   Brittany Shammas, "After Florida restricts Black history, churches step up to teach it," *The Washington Post*, September 24, 2023, https://www.washingtonpost.com/nation/2023/09/24/florida-black-history-churches-teaching/.

17   Interview with Shantel Palacio.

18   E.J. Dionne Jr., "Why we should all be liberal: The power of an adjective," *The Washington Post*, March 12, 2023, https://www.washingtonpost.com/opinions/2023/03/12/liberal-adjective-michael-walzer-struggle-decent-politics/.

Chapter 14: Do No Harm Is Not Enough

1   "How Does the Us Healthcare System Compare to Other Countries?" Peter G. Peterson Foundation, July 12, 2023, https://www.pgpf.org/blog/2023/07/how-does-the-us-healthcare-system-compare-to-other-countries.

2   "US opinion on the ACA April 2010-March 2023," Statista, April 20, 2023, https://www.statista.com/statistics/246901/opinion-on-the-health-reform-law-in-the-united-states/.

3   Michael Cooper, "Conservatives Sowed Idea of Health Care Mandate, Only to Spurn It Later," *The New York Times*, February 14,

2012, https://www.nytimes.com/2012/02/15/health/policy/
health-care-mandate-was-first-backed-by-conservatives.html.

4   Jessica Taylor, "Mitt Romney Finally Takes Credit For Obamacare,"
NPR, October 23, 2015, https://www.npr.org/sections/itsallpoli-
tics/2015/10/23/451200436/mitt-romney-finally-takes-credit-for-obamacare.

5   Interview with physician, May 16, 2023.

6   Ibid.

7   Philip Rucker and Robert Costa, "Bannon vows a daily fight for
'deconstruction of the administrative state,'" *The Washington Post*,
February 23, 2017, https://www.washingtonpost.com/politics/top-
wh-strategist-vows-a-daily-fight-for-deconstruction-of-the-
administrative-state/2017/02/23/03f6b8da-f9ea-11e6-bf01-
d47f8cf9b643_story.html.

8   Benjamin Mueller and Eleanor Lutz, "US Has Far Higher Covid Death
Rate Than Other Wealthy Countries," *The New York Times*, February
1, 2022, https://www.nytimes.com/interactive/2022/02/01/science/
covid-deaths-united-states.html.

9   Erika Lee, "Americans are the dangerous, disease-carrying foreigners now,"
The Washington Post, July 8, 2020, https://www.washingtonpost.com/out-
look/2020/07/08/covid-travel-bans-americans/.

10   Scott Clement, William Bishop, and Robert Barnes, "Americans
broadly support Supreme Court upholding Roe v. Wade and oppose
Texas abortion law, Post-ABC poll finds," *The Washington Post*, November 16, 2021, https://www.washingtonpost.com/politics/2021/11/16/
post-abc-poll-abortion-supreme-court/.

11   Hannah Knowles and Caroline Kitchener, "Abortion rights advocates win
major victories in Ohio, Kentucky, Virginia," *The Washington Post*, November 7, 2023, https://www.washingtonpost.com/politics/2023/11/07/
abortion-ohio-kentucky-virginia-elecitons/.

12   Alexander Burns, "States With Abortion Bans Risk Losing Their Economic Edge," *The New York Times*, July 11, 2022, https://www.nytimes.
com/2022/07/11/us/politics/abortion-ban-states-businesses.html.

13   Philip Elliott, "Abortion Access Is Affecting Where College Students
Decide to Study," *Time*, April 20, 2023, https://time.com/6273561/
abortion-ban-colleges-red-states/.

14   Julie Rovner, "Abortion bans drive off doctors and close clinics, putting other health care at risk," NPR, May 23, 2023, https://
www.npr.org/sections/health-shots/2023/05/23/1177542605/
abortion-bans-drive-off-doctors-and-put-other-health-care-at-risk.

15   "*Roe v. Wade* was a compromise," *The Christian Century*, July 27, 2022, https://
www.christiancentury.org/article/editors/roe-v-wade-was-compromise.

16   Carter Sherman, "States push 'fetal personhood' bills despite outrage at Alabama IVF ruling. " *The Guardian*, March 24, 2024, https://www.theguardian.com/society/2024/mar/20/states-fetal-personhood-bill

17   Jennifer L. Holland, "Abolishing Abortion: The History of the Pro-Life Movement in America," *The American Historian*, Organization of American Historians, November 2016, https://www.oah.org/tah/november-3/abolishing-abortion-the-history-of-the-pro-life-movement-in-america/.

18   Niamh Kennedy and Emily Blumenthal, "Five years after Ireland's historic abortion referendum, access to care is still 'patchy,'" CNN, May 25, 2023, https://www.cnn.com/2023/05/25/europe/ireland-abortion-referendum-5-years-intl-cmd/index.html.

19   "France enshrines abortion as a constitutional right in historic vote," France 24, April 3, 2024, https://www.france24.com/en/europe/20240304-france-to-enshrine-abortion-rights-in-country-s-constitution.

20   Darragh Roche, "GOP Push for Nationwide Abortion Ban," *Newsweek*, July 15, 2022, https://www.newsweek.com/gop-push-nationwide-abortion-ban-3-weeks-after-calling-it-state-issue-republicans-1724909.

21   Aria Bendix, "Idaho becomes one of the most extreme anti-abortion states with law restricting travel for abortions," NBC News, April 6, 2023, https://www.nbcnews.com/health/womens-health/idaho-most-extreme-anti-abortion-state-law-restricts-travel-rcna78225.

22   Jennifer Korn and Clare Duffy, "Search histories, location data, text messages: How personal data could be used to enforce anti-abortion laws," CNN, June 24, 2022, https://www.cnn.com/2022/06/24/tech/abortion-laws-data-privacy/index.html#:~:text=Various%20online%20behaviors%20could%20become,civil%20rights%20attorney%20and%20tech.

23   Elaine Godfrey, "A Plan to Outlaw Abortion Everywhere," *The Atlantic*, December 6, 2023, https://www.theatlantic.com/magazine/archive/2024/01/anti-abortion-movement-trump-reelection-roe-dobbs/676132/.

24   Rachel K. Jones, Elizabeth Nash, Lauren Cross, Jesse Philbin, and Marielle Kirstein, "Medication Abortion Now Accounts for More Than Half of All US Abortions," Guttmacher Institute, February 24, 2022, https://www.guttmacher.org/article/2022/02/medication-abortion-now-accounts-more-half-all-us-abortions.

25   Interview with ER doctor, May 16, 2023.

26   Mariana Lenharo, "Abortion-pill ruling threatens FDA's authority, say drug firms," *Nature*, April 11, 2023, https://www.nature.com/articles/d41586-023-01044-7#author-0.

27   Interview with ER doctor.

28 Interview with Alix Kates Shulman.

29 Stephanie Taladrid, "The Post-Roe Abortion Underground," *The New Yorker*, October 17, 2022, https://www.newyorker.com/magazine/2022/10/17/the-post-roe-abortion-underground.

30 Kirk McDaniel, "Texas trigger ban on abortion goes into effect," *Courthouse News Service*, August 25, 2022, https://www.courthousenews.com/texas-trigger-ban-on-abortion-goes-into-effect/.

31 Taladrid, "The Post-Roe Abortion Underground."

32 Interview with physician.

33 Ibid

34 Ibid.

35 Ibid.

36 Interview with Amy Thogmartin, May 23, 2023.

37 Jacqueline Howard, "Only 5.7% of US doctors are Black, and experts warn the shortage harms public health," CNN, February 212, 2023, https://www.cnn.com/2023/02/21/health/black-doctors-shortage-us/index.html#:~:text=Only%20about%205.7%25%20of%20physicians,is%20Black%20or%20African%20American.

38 Interview with physician.

39 Lauren Weber, Caitlin Gilbert, and Taylor Lorenz, "Documents show how conservative doctors influenced abortion, trans rights," *The Washington Post*, June 15, 2023, https://www.washingtonpost.com/health/2023/06/15/abortion-transgender-christian-doctors/.

40 Ibid.

41 Interview with Amy Thogmartin.

42 Ibid.

Chapter 15: In Gods We Trust

1 Peter Oborne, "The special relationship between Blair and God," *The Spectator*, April 5, 2003, https://www.spectator.co.uk/article/the-special-relationship-between-blair-and-god/.

2 "The Founding Fathers' Religious Wisdom," Center for American Progress, January 8, 2008, https://www.americanprogress.org/article/the-founding-fathers-religious-wisdom/#:~:text=Many%20of%20the%20founding%20fathers,solving%20social%20and%20political%20problems.

3 Katherine Stewart, "'Religious Liberty' Used to Uphold Conservative Religious Privileges," American Bar Association, July 5, 2022, https://www.americanbar.org/groups/crsj/publications/human_rights_mag-

azine_home/intersection-of-lgbtq-rights-and-religious-freedom/
religious-liberty-used-to-uphold-conservative-religious-privileges/.

4   "Discrimination in the Guise of Liberty: Legal Analysis of Trump's Draft
     Executive Order on 'Religious Freedom,'" Center for Constitutional Rights,
     February 8, 2017, https://ccrjustice.org/religious-discrimination.

5   Tisa Wenger, "Discriminating in the name of religion?
     Segregationists and slaveholders did it, too," *The Washington Post*,
     December 5, 2017, https://www.washingtonpost.com/news/made-
     by-history/wp/2017/12/05/discriminating-in-the-name-of-religion-
     segregationists-and-slaveholders-did-it-too/.

6   David D. Kirkpatrick, "The Next Targets for the Group That Overturned
     Roe," *The New Yorker*, October 2, 2023, https://www.newyorker.com/maga-
     zine/2023/10/09/alliance-defending-freedoms-legal-crusade.

7   Dianne Post and Robert J. McWhirter, "Understanding Christian
     Nationalism: Is the Constitution in Trouble?" *Ms.* magazine,
     September 21, 2021, https://msmagazine.com/2021/09/21/
     christian-nationalism-constitution-jan-6-white-supremacy-
     insurrection/.

8   Interview with James Carroll.

9   Ibid.

10   Ibid.

11   Sherwood, "Biden threatened with communion ban
     over position on abortion," *The Guardian*, June 19, 2021,
     https://www.theguardian.com/world/2021/jun/19/
     biden-threatened-with-communion-ban-over-position-on-abortion.

12   Interview with James Carroll.

13   Eric Alterman, *We Are Not One* (New York: Basic Books, 2022).

14   Philip Bump, "Half of evangelicals support Israel because they believe it is
     important for fulfilling end-times prophecy,"
     The Washington Post, May 14, 2018, https://www.washingtonpost.com/
     news/politics/wp/2018/05/14/half-of-evangelicals-support-israel-
     because-they-believe-it-is-important-for-fulfilling-end-times-
     prophecy/.

15   Jacob Magid, "Orthodox Jews back Trump by massive margin, poll finds,"
     The Times of Israel, October 15, 2020, https://www.timesofisrael.com/
     orthodox-jews-back-trump-by-massive-margin-poll-finds/.

16   "Trump's long history of trafficking in antisemitic tropes," *The Wash-
     ington Post*, October 17, 2022, https://www.washingtonpost.com/poli-
     tics/2022/10/17/trump-history-antisemitic-tropes/.

17   Dr. Robert Jeffress, "America Is a Christian Nation," First Baptist Dallas,
     https://firstdallas.org/america-is-a-christian-nation/.

18   Interview with Michael Berenbaum, April 3, 2023.

19   Ibid.

20   Zack Beauchamp, "How Republicans fell in love with Israel," *Vox*, November 11, 2015, https://www.vox.com/2015/11/11/9708018/republicans-israel.

21   Interview with Michael Berenbaum.

22   Interview with James Carroll.

23   Michelle Goldberg, "The Right-Wingers Who Admire the Taliban," *The New York Times*, August 27, 2021, https://www.nytimes.com/2021/08/27/opinion/alt-right-taliban.html.

24   Interview with James Carroll.

25   Interview with Michael Berenbaum.

Chapter 16: Fifth Column

1   "The hospital room showdown," *Salon*, May 15, 2007, https://www.salon.com/2007/05/15/comey_testimony/.

2   Manuel Roig-Franzia, "A conservative judge helped stop Trump on Jan. 6. He wants to finish the job," *The Washington Post*, January 31, 2023, https://www.washingtonpost.com/lifestyle/2023/01/31/michael-luttig-judge-jan-6-trump-pence/.

3   Ibid.

4   Erick Trickey, "Daniel Ellsberg leaked his Vietnam secrets to senators first. They balked," *The Washington Post*, June 23, 2023, https://www.washingtonpost.com/history/2023/06/23/daniel-ellsberg-leaking-pentagon-papers-vietnam-war/.

5   Sanford J. Ungar, "The Pentagon Papers Trial," *The Atlantic*, August 1973, https://www.theatlantic.com/magazine/archive/1973/08/the-pentagon-papers-trial/663786/.

6   Shane Harris and Carol E. Lee, "Spies Keep Intelligence From Donald Trump on Leak Concerns," *The Wall Street Journal*, February 16, 2017, https://www.wsj.com/articles/spies-keep-intelligence-from-donald-trump-1487209351.

7   Mark Bowden, "Top Military Officers Unload On Trump," *The Atlantic*, November 15, 2019, https://www.theatlantic.com/magazine/archive/2019/11/military-officers-trump/598360/.

8   Lincoln Anthony Blades, "Donald Trump's Military Cowardice Goes Beyond His 5 Draft Deferrals," *Teen Vogue*, August 3, 2017, https://www.teenvogue.com/story/donald-trump-dodged-the-draft-5-times.

9   Susan B. Glasser and Peter Baker, "Inside the War Between Trump and His Generals," *The New Yorker*, August 8, 2022, https://www.newyorker.com/magazine/2022/08/15/inside-the-war-between-trump-and-his-generals.

10   Justin Vallejo, "Michael Flynn calls for Trump to suspend the
     constitution and declare martial law to re-run election,"
     The Independent, December 3, 2020, https://www.independent.co.uk/
     news/world/americas/us-election-2020/michael-flynn-suspend-
     constitution-martial-law-trump-reelection-b1765467.html.
11   Jeffrey Goldberg, "Trump: Americans Who Died in War Are 'Losers' and
     'Suckers,'" *The Atlantic,* September 3, 2020, https://www.theatlantic.com/pol-
     itics/archive/2020/09/trump-americans-who-died-at-war-are-losers-and-sucker
     s/615997/.
12   Carol Leonnig and Philip Rucker, "'You're a bunch of dopes and
     babies': Inside Trump's stunning tirade against generals," *The
     Washington Post,* January 17, 2020, https://www.washingtonpost.com/
     politics/youre-a-bunch-of-dopes-and-babies-inside-trumps-stunning-
     tirade-against-generals/2020/01/16/d6dbb8a6-387e-11ea-bb7b-
     265f4554af6d_story.html.
13   Jeffrey Goldberg, "The Patriot," *The Atlantic,* September 21,
     2023, https://www.theatlantic.com/magazine/archive/2023/11/
     general-mark-milley-trump-coup/675375/.
14   Glasser and Baker, "Inside the War Between Trump and His Generals."
15   Alex Shephard, "Don't Let Miles Taylor Get Away With Being a Fraud," *The
     New Republic,* October 28, 2020, https://newrepublic.com/article/159988/
     dont-let-miles-taylor-get-away-fraud.
16   Jim Golby, "America's Politicized Military Is a Recipe for Disaster,"
     Foreign Policy, June 18, 2020, https://foreignpolicy.com/2020/06/18/
     us-military-politics-trump-election-campaign/.
17   Steve Abbot, Peter Chiarelli, John Jumper, James Loy, John Nathman, Wil-
     liam Owens and Johnnie Wilson, "We Are Retired Generals and Admirals.
     Trump's Actions on Jan. 6 Were a Dereliction of Duty," *The New York
     Times,* July 21, 2022, https://www.nytimes.com/2022/07/21/opinion/
     january-6-trump-military.html.
18   "Open Letter from Retired Generals and Admirals," Flag Officers 4 America,
     https://img1.wsimg.com/blobby/go/fb7c7bd8-097d-4e2f-8f12-3442d151b57
     d/downloads/2021%20Open%20Letter%20from%20Retired%20Gener-
     als%20and%20Adm.pdf?ver=1620643005025.
19   Victoria Bekiempis, "Michael Flynn appears to have called Qa-
     non 'total nonsense' despite his links," *The Guardian,* November
     29, 2021, https://www.theguardian.com/us-news/2021/nov/29/
     michael-flynn-trump-ally-qanon-cia-left.
20   Gellman, "What Happened to Michael Flynn."
21   Jim Golby and Peter Feaver, "Former military leaders criticized the
     election and the administration. That hurts the military's reputation,"

The Washington Post, May 15, 2021, https://www.washingtonpost.com/
politics/2021/05/15/former-military-leaders-criticized-election-
administration-that-hurts-militarys-reputation/.

Chapter 17: Satire on a Saturday Night

1   Mark Beaumont, "The Plastic People of the Universe: How the
    violent suppression of a rock band led to revolution in
    Czechoslovakia," *The Independent,* March 14, 2021,
    https://www.independent.co.uk/arts-entertainment/music/features/
    plastic-people-of-the-universe-czechoslovakia-revolution-
    b1816340.html.
2   Interview with Theo Kogan (via email), August 2, 2023.
3   "William Randolph Hearst's Campaign to Suppress Citizen Kane," *American
    Experience,* April 30, 2021, https://www.pbs.org/wgbh/americanexperience/
    features/kane-william-randolph-hearst-campaign-suppress-citizen-kane/.
4   *The Last Laugh,* directed by Ferne Pearlstein, Tangerine Entertainment, PBS/
    Independent Lens, 2016.
5   Interview with Mel Brooks for *The Last Laugh,* September 24, 2013.
6   Interview with Harry Shearer for *The Last Laugh,* October 19, 2011.
7   Interview with Etgar Keret for *The Last Laugh,* April 24, 2012.
8   Timothy Egan, "We Need to Keep Laughing," *The New York Times,*
    January 4, 2019, https://www.nytimes.com/2019/01/04/opinion/
    trump-humor-political-satire.html.
9   John Bird, "Obituary: Peter Cook," *The Independent,* January 10, 1995, https://
    www.independent.co.uk/news/people/obituary-peter-cook-1567341.html.
10 Renee Firestone, in *The Last Laugh,* directed by Ferne Pearlstein, 2016.
11 Nicholas Barber, "The Great Dictator: The film that dared to laugh at
    Hitler," *BBC News,* February 5, 2021, https://www.bbc.com/culture/article/2
    0210204-the-great-dictator-the-film-that-dared-to-laugh-at-hitler.
12 Interview with Rudolph Herzog for *The Last Laugh,* April 30, 2013.
13 Rudolph Herzog, *Dead Funny: Humor in Hitler's Germany* (New York: Melville
    House, 2011), 3.
14 Interview with Rudolph Herzog.
15 Interview with Larry Charles for *The Last Laugh,* May 1, 2013.
16 Ronald G. Shafer, "The president was furious over a comedy skit.
    And it wasn't Trump fuming about SNL," *The Washington Post,*
    March 18, 2019, https://www.washingtonpost.com/history/
    2019/03/18/president-was-furious-over-comedy-skit-it-wasnt-
    trump-fuming-about-snl/.

17 "Letter from President Lyndon Johnson to Tommy and Dickie Smothers," Wish I'd Said That, https://wist.info/johnson-lyndon/36369/.

18 Marc Freeman, "'The Smothers Brothers Comedy Hour' at 50: The Rise and Fall of a Groundbreaking Variety Show," *The Hollywood Reporter*, November 25, 2017, https://www.hollywoodreporter.com/tv/tv-news/smothers-brothers-comedy-hour-oral-history-1060153/.

19 Amy B. Wang, "Trump was mocked at the 2011 White House correspondents' dinner. He insists it's not why he ran," *The Washington Post*, February 26, 2017, https://www.washingtonpost.com/news/arts-and-entertainment/wp/2017/02/26/did-the-2011-white-house-correspondents-dinner-spur-trump-to-run-for-president/.

20 Interview with Rudolph Herzog.

21 "Chicago cops squelch piggy nominations," *The Montreal Gazette*, August 23, 1968, https://news.google.com/newspapers?id=1IY1AAAAIBAJ&sjid=1Z-8FAAAAIBAJ&pg=4960,4621941&dq=pigasus+yippies&hl=en.

22 Abbie Hoffman, *Soon to Be a Major Motion Picture* (New York: Perigee Books, 1980), 106.

23 Steven Rutledge, "#Resist: The Drag Story Behind 'Flower Power,' the Iconic Photograph from 1967," *World of Wonder*, March 4, 2022, https://worldofwonder.net/resist-the-drag-story-behind-flower-power-the-iconic-photograph-from-1967/.

24 Michael Specter, "How ACT UP Changed America," *The New Yorker*, June 7, 2021, https://www.newyorker.com/magazine/2021/06/14/how-act-up-changed-america.

25 *All the Beauty and All the Bloodshed*, directed by Laura Poitras, Participant/HBO/Neon, 2022.

26 Taylor Lorenz, "Birds Aren't Real, or Are They? Inside a Gen Z Conspiracy Theory," *The New York Times*, December 9, 2021, https://www.nytimes.com/2021/12/09/technology/birds-arent-real-gen-z-misinformation.html.

27 Interview with Jacques Servin, May 11, 2023.

28 "Let Them Eat Hamburger/How McDonald's began to recycle their food," The Yes Men, https://theyesmen.org/project/hamburger/behindthecurtain.

29 Blake Gopnik, "The Yes Men: Revenge of the Pranksters," *The New York Times*, February 17, 2022, https://www.nytimes.com/2022/02/17/arts/design/yes-men-collective-carriage-trade-gallery.html.

30 Interview with Jacques Servin.

31 "Doctors for Opening America/Satire vs. Trump's human sacrifice," The Yes Men, https://theyesmen.org/project/doctorsforopeningamerica/behindthecurtain.

32 Interview with Jacques Servin.

33   Bruce Sterling, "Thirty Years of the Billboard Liberation Front," *Wired*, March 23, 2008, https://www.wired.com/2008/03/thirty-years-of/.

34   Naomi Alderman, "It's shockingly funny but Borat's rant about Jews also tells us some uncomfortable truths about ourselves," *The Guardian*, August 13, 2006, https://www.theguardian.com/commentisfree/2006/aug/14/film.comment; see also *Da Ali G Show*, season 3, episode 3, "Peace," 2004, https://www.youtube.com/watch?v=Vb3IMTJjzfo.

35   Nicole Allan, "Stephen Colbert Testifies in Congress, in Character," *The Atlantic*, September 24, 2010, https://www.theatlantic.com/politics/archive/2010/09/stephen-colbert-testifies-in-congress-in-character/63507/.

36   Jacques Steinberg, "After Press Dinner, the Blogosphere Is Alive With the Sound of Colbert Chatter," *The New York Times*, May 3, 2006, https://www.nytimes.com/2006/05/03/arts/03colb.html.

37   Interview with Larry Charles.

Chapter 18: Take the Skinheads Bowling

1   Sharp, *The Politics of Nonviolent Action*, 711.

2   Levitsky and Ziblatt, *How Democracies Die*, 218–220.

3   Sharp, *The Politics of Nonviolent Action*, 729.

4   Philip Bump, "But their emails: Seven members of Trump's team have used unofficial communication tools," *The Washington Post*, March 21, 2019, https://www.washingtonpost.com/politics/2019/03/21/their-emails-seven-members-trumps-team-have-used-unofficial-communications-tools/.

5   Dan Alexander, "How Donald Trump Shifted Kids-Cancer Charity Money Into His Business," *Forbes*, June 6, 2017, https://www.forbes.com/sites/danalexander/2017/06/06/how-donald-trump-shifted-kids-cancer-charity-money-into-his-business/?sh=3babb1b36b4a.

6   Alanna Durkin Richer, "Fierce Capitol attacks on police in newly released videos," Associated Press, June 19, 2021, https://apnews.com/article/donald-trump-joe-biden-capitol-siege-police-health-6b5a6c9d2069bf1325f684532d006013.

7   Robert Draper, "A Political Party Unhinged From Truth," *The Atlantic*, October 28, 2022, https://www.theatlantic.com/ideas/archive/2022/10/weapons-of-mass-delusion-book-excerpt-republican-party-trump/671907/.

8   Applebaum, *Twilight of Democracy*, 35.

9   Meredith Shepard, "Trump's 'Radio Machete,'" *Public Books*, July 23, 2019, https://www.publicbooks.org/trumps-radio-machete/.

10 Crawshaw and Jackson, *Small Acts of Resistance*, 191.

11 Steven Hassan, *The Cult of Trump: A Leading Cult Expert Explains How the President Uses Mind Control* (New York: Simon & Schuster, 2019).

12 Joe Hagan, "'So Many Great, Educated, Functional People Were Brainwashed': Can Trump's Cult of Followers Be Deprogrammed?" *Vanity Fair*, January 21, 2021, https://www.vanityfair.com/news/2021/01/can-trumps-cult-of-followers-be-deprogrammed.

13 Christopher Maag, "The 'Cult of Trump' can be healed. It will take years of work and empathy, not shouting," North Jersey.com, January 12, 2021, https://www.northjersey.com/story/news/columnists/christopher-maag/2021/01/12/cult-trump-can-fixed-but-takes-empathy-time-and-work/6613397002/.

14 Malia Wollan, "How to Get Someone Out of a Cult," *The New York Times*, September 26, 2018, https://www.nytimes.com/2018/09/26/magazine/how-to-get-someone-out-of-a-cult.html.

15 Steven Hassan, "I was a member of a cult. Here's how to bring QAnon believers back to reality," CNN, February 4, 2021, https://www.cnn.com/2021/02/04/perspectives/qanon-cult-truth/index.html.

16 Interview with Sally Kohn.

17 Interview with Peter Hutchison.

18 Snyder, *On Tyranny*, 83.

19 Interview with Peter Hutchison.

20 Rebecca Solnit, "On Not Meeting Nazis Halfway," *Literary Hub*, November 19, 2020, https://lithub.com/rebecca-solnit-on-not-meeting-nazis-halfway/.

21 Ibid.

22 Ibid.

23 Emily Bobrow, "StoryCorps Founder Dave Isay Believes in the Power of Conversation," *The Wall Street Journal*, March 10, 2023, https://www.wsj.com/articles/storycorps-founder-dave-isay-believes-in-the-power-of-conversation-b615aaef.

24 Interview with Dave Isay, January 17, 2023.

25 Ibid.

26 Interview with Sally Kohn.

27 Interview with Amy Thogmartin.

28 Bing West, "The 'Oil Spot' Theory of Counterinsurgency," *Slate*, September 26, 2005, https://slate.com/news-and-politics/2005/09/the-oil-spot-theory-of-counterinsurgency.html.

29 John Nagl, *Learning to Eat Soup with a Knife: Counterinsurgency Lessons from Malaya and Vietnam* (Chicago: University of Chicago Press, 2005).

30   Anne Applebaum, "Coexistence Is the Only Option," *The Atlantic*, January 20, 2021, https://www.theatlantic.com/ideas/archive/2021/01/seditionists-need-path-back-society/617746/.

31   Ibid.

32   Sharp, *The Politics of Nonviolent Action*, 727–728.

33   Applebaum, "Coexistence Is the Only Option."

34   Ibid.

Chapter 19: Democracy for Beginners

1   Robert Kagan, "A Trump dictatorship is increasingly inevitable. We should stop pretending," *The Washington Post*, November 30, 2023, https://www.washingtonpost.com/opinions/2023/11/30/trump-dictator-2024-election-robert-kagan/.

2   Robert Kagan, "The Trump dictatorship: How to stop it," *The Washington Post*, December 7, 2023, https://www.washingtonpost.com/opinions/2023/12/07/robert-kagan-trump-dictatorship-how-to-stop/.

3   Greg Sargent, "Enough with all the fatalism about a Trump dictatorship," *The Washington Post*, December 5, 2023, https://www.washingtonpost.com/opinions/2023/12/05/donald-trump-authoritarian-rule-second-term-maga/.

4   Interview with Norvel Goff.

ROBERT EDWARDS was previously an infantry and intelligence officer in the US Army, serving in Germany during the Cold War and in Iraq in the Persian Gulf War. A winner of the Nicholl Fellowship from the Academy of Motion Picture Arts and Sciences, he has written numerous screenplays for all the major studios, directed the feature films *Land of the Blind* starring Ralph Fiennes, Donald Sutherland, and Tom Hollander, and *When I Live My Life Over Again* (aka *One More Time*) starring Christopher Walken and Amber Heard, and produced the feature documentaries *Sumo East and West* and *The Last Laugh* with his wife Ferne Pearlstein, and *Death and Taxes* with Justin Schein. He has a BA in history from Lafayette College and an MA in communication from Stanford, and writes The King's Necktie, a blog about politics and culture.

Printed in the USA
CPSIA information can be obtained
at www.ICGtesting.com
JSHW021600010824
67338JS00009B/3

9 781682 196021